THE PRACTICE OF
HOSPITALITY MANAGEMENT

THE PRACTICE OF HOSPITALITY MANAGEMENT

Edited by   A. Pizam, Ph.D.
R. C. Lewis, Ph.D.
P. Manning, Ph.D.

Department of Hotel, Restaurant,
and Travel Administration
University of Massachusetts

AVI PUBLISHING COMPANY, INC.
Westport, Connecticut

©Copyright 1982 by
THE AVI PUBLISHING COMPANY, INC.
Westport, Connecticut

Library of Congress Cataloging in Publication Data
Main entry under title:

The Practice of hospitality management.

    Bibliography: p.
    Includes index.
    1. Hotel management.   2. Motel management.   3. Food
service management.   I. Pizam, Abraham.   II. Lewis,
R. C. (Robert C.)   III. Manning, P.
TX911.3.M27P725   647'.94'068   82-1675
ISBN 0-87055-401-8   AACR2

Printed in the United States of America

Contents

List of Contributors

James Abbey, Ph.D., College of Hotel Administration, University of Nevada, Las Vegas, Nevada

Robert G. Averill, Executive Director, Distinguished Inns and Historic Hotels Division, Robert F. Warner, Inc., New York, New York

Walter W. Ashcraft, Director, Division of Human Resources, National Restaurant Association, Washington, D.C.

Stephen P. Barba, President, The Balsams Grand Resort Hotel, Dixville Notch, New Hampshire

Thomas J. Beggs, MBA, School of Business, University of Southern California, Los Angeles, California

Carl J. Bellas, Management Science, Virginia Polytechnic Institute and State University, Blacksburg, Virginia

Hrayr Berberoglu, Hospitality and Tourism Management, Ryerson Polytechnic Institute, Toronto, Ontario, Canada

Uel Blank, Agricultural Economics Department, University of Minnesota, Minneapolis, Minnesota

Ernest P. Boger, Senior Lecturer—Marketing, Hotel Management Degree Program, University of the West Indies, Nassau, Bahamas

Richard W. Brown, Director, National Accounts, Villa Banfi, Long Island

Jon Canas, President, Dunfey Hotels Corporation, Hampton, New Hampshire

John D. Correll, President, Pizzuti's, Inc., Canton, Michigan

Alex F. De Noble, CPA, Small Business Management, Virginia Polytechnic Institute and State University, Blacksburg, Virginia

Don C. Dodson, Ph.D., Business Administration, Appalachian State University, Boone, North Carolina

David C. Dorf, CHSE, Director of Education, HSMA International, New York, New York

James F. Downey, Associate, Laventhol and Horvath, Boston, Massachusetts

James E. Durbin, President, Marriott Hotels, Washington, D.C.

Lynn Dykstra, President, National Culinary Apprenticeship Program, San Francisco, California

Sig S. Front, Senior Vice President and Director of Marketing, Sheraton Corporation, Boston, Massachusetts

Frank M. Go, Lecturer, Hospitality and Tourism Management, Ryerson Polytechnic Institute, Toronto, Ontario, Canada.

James M. Grahm, Executive Director, Personal Achievement Institute, Detroit, Michigan

Eric Green, National Partner, Management Advisory Services, Pannell, Kerr Forster, New York, New York

Bunny Grossinger, Grossinger's Hotel, Grossinger, New York

Wayne C. Guyette, Ph.D., Hotel, Restaurant, and Tourism Administration, University of New Orleans, New Orleans, Louisiana

Chester G. Hall, Ph.D., National Institute for the Foodservice Industry, Chicago, Illinois

Alan Hopper, Partner, Pannell Kerr Forstner, London, England

Jafar Jafari, Department of Habitational Resources, University of Wisconsin—Stout, Wisconsin

Atid Kaplan, Ph.D., Hotel and Restaurant Management, University of Denver, Denver, Colorado

Mahmood A. Khan, Ph.D., R.D., Foods and Nutrition, University of Illinois—Urbana, Illinois

Lothar A. Kreck, Ph.D., Hotel and Restaurant Administration, Washington State University—Pullman, Washington

Saul F. Leonard, CPA, Laventhol and Horvath, Los Angeles, California

Michael A. Leven, Executive Vice President, Americana Hotels, Chicago, Illinois

Robert C. Lewis, Ph.D., Hotel, Restaurant, and Travel Administration, University of Massachusetts, Amherst, Massachusetts.

Nita Lloyd, CHSE, Director, Corporate Sales, Hilton Hotels Corporation, Atlanta, Georgia and President, HSMA International, New York, New York

Leland L. Nicholls, Ph.D., Habitational Resources, University of Wisconsin—Stout, Wisconsin

Jack D. Ninemeier, School of Hotel, Restaurant, and Tourism Administration, University of New Orleans, New Orleans, Louisiana

George S. Odiorne, Ph.D., Business Administration, University of Massachusetts, Amherst, Massachusetts

James O'Keefe, Manager, Laventhol and Horvath, Boston, Massachusetts

Michael D. Olsen, Ph.D., Human Nutrition and Foods, Virginia Polytechnic Institute and State University, Blacksburg, Virginia

James S. Overstreet, Ph.D., Business Administration, Appalachian State University, Boone, North Carolina

Abraham Pizam, Ph.D., Hotel, Restaurant, and Travel Administration, University of Massachusetts, Amherst, Massachusetts

Stephen M. Race, Arthur D. Little, Inc., San Francisco, California

Arie Reichel, Ph.D., Management and Organizational Behavior, Graduate School of Business Administration, New York University, New York, New York

Robert D. Reid, Food Service and Lodging Management Program, Virginia Polytechnic Institute and State University, Blacksburg, Virginia

Leo M. Renaghen, Ph.D., Food Service and Housing Administration, Pennsylvania State University, University Park, Pennsylvania

Mel Sandler, Hotel Administration, University of New Hampshire, Durham, New Hampshire

Hershel B. Sarbin, Executive Vice President, The Ziff Corporation, New York, New York

Paul C. Sheeline, Chairman of the Board, Inter-Continental Hotels Corporation, New York, New York

Robert L. Sirkis, Arthur D. Little, Inc., Cambridge, Massachusetts

G. Kent Stearns, School of Hotel, Restaurant, and Tourism Administration, University of New Orleans, New Orleans, Louisiana

Joseph Varga, Director of Research, Robinsons Inc., Orlando, Florida

Peter Walsh, Partner, Pannell Kerr Forster, Calgary, Alberta, Canada

Albert L. Wrisley, Ph.D., Hotel, Restaurant and Travel Administration, University of Massachusetts, Amherst, Massachusetts

Peter C. Yesawich, Executive Vice President, Robinsons Inc., Orlando, Florida

Preface

The title of this book, *The Practice of Hospitality Management*, contains the rationale for its publication. In the relatively short period of thirty years since hospitality management was first introduced as a professional field, its practice developed and changed in both evolutionary and revolutionary ways. Providing an appropriate product and service to guests is no longer the major preoccupation of today's industry leaders. Contemporary knowledgeable hospitality management recognizes that proper applications of managerial techniques and practices in such areas as marketing, finance, information systems and the like are essential if a hospitality enterprise is to operate successfully. Today's successful hospitality manager must be versed in conceptual and technical tools drawn from disciplines such as psychology, engineering, operations research and mathematics as well as the nuts and bolts of everyday operations.

This book reflects the application of these varying tools and techniques in the managerial thoughts, practices, and philosophies espoused by many of today's industry leaders.

Articles appearing in this collection were presented at *The World Hospitality Congress: Hospitality Management—State of the Art and Future Prospects* that was held March 9–12, 1981 in Boston, Mass. This Congress was organized by the Department of Hotel, Restaurant and Travel Administration of the University of Massachusetts, Amherst and brought together for the first time leading executives, educators and scholars, world-wide, to discuss and exchange ideas related to present-day and future managerial thinking in the hospitality industry. The articles represent the thinking of those in the forefront of planning for the industry's future in what promise to be turbulent times.

The impact of inflation, technological advances, the handling of human and property resources, the need to reach the consumer, and strategic planning were the major elements that dominated the Congress and which are represented in this book. If there is one major theme that runs throughout these elements it is the theme of change. This theme of change and how it affects and will continue to affect planning, marketing, resource development, property building and restoration, consumer behavior, organizational design, financial management and other areas of management concern are apparent in the readings throughout the book.

It is anticipated that this book will serve as a valuable resource and reference for practitioners and educators alike. Practitioners will find in it current managerial methods and thinking that guide the industry today and will guide it toward the years ahead in confronting the problems of decision making under conditions of uncertainty. Educators will find the book to be both a basic primer and a rendering of advanced techniques that they can offer to students for the purpose of understanding the hospitality industry today and the prospects they will face tomorrow as future managers.

We wish to thank all the authors and/or presenters, as well as the many Congress participants who made the first World Hospitality Congress a success and who, directly or indirectly, made possible the publication of this book.

Abraham Pizam
Robert C. Lewis
Peter Manning

Acknowledgments

We would like to thank the individuals and organizations who have made available the photographs cited in the following list.

Stephen P. Barba   *p. 164*
Uel Blank   *p. 10*
Ernest P. Boger   *p. 412*
Budget Rent a Car Company   *p. 2*
Center for Continuing Education, Appalachian State University, Boone, NC   *p. 284*
Convention Photographers, Minneapolis, MN   *p. 264*
De Rosa's Restaurant, Westport, CT   *p. 104*
Dunfey Hotels Corp.   *pp. 30, 48*
©Frank M. Go   *pp. 101, 172, 340, 406*
Eric F. Green   *pp. 114, 132*
Chester G. Hall   *p. 238*
Hyatt Regency—Minneapolis   *pp. 144, 152, 188, 254, 340, 390, 459*
Hyatt Regency—O'Hare   *p. 340*
Inter-Continental Hotels   *pp. 120, 328, 376, 466*
Las Vegas News Bureau,   *p. 225*
Laventhol & Horwath, Philadelphia, PA   *p. 84*
MAI Basic Four Information Systems Division   *pp. 104, 440*
Marriott Hotels   *pp. 76, 94, 202, 272, 340, 354, 366, 454, 484, 497*
Miami Beach Visitors and Convention Authority   *p. 2*
New York Convention and Visitors Bureau   *p. 2*
The New York Hilton *Frontispiece,   p. 2*
Leland L. Nicholls   *p. 306*

Related AVI Books

Part I

The Economic Contribution of the
Hospitality Industry

The Economic Importance of the Hospitality Industry

John J. Casson

Recently, the news media have accorded far more attention than usual to the hospitality industry. The fast food chains have received considerable notice due to their changing business strategies. More elaborate dining establishments are also being granted increased recognition, reflecting the public's burgeoning interest in food. The rapid expansion of the less glamorous institutional caterers is receiving belated mention. The spurt in construction of luxury hotels has been the subject of a flood of news stories. Even the renovations and expansions of older hotels, especially those with landmark status, are being extensively publicized.

This increased attention certainly is a welcome development from the perspective of the hospitality industry. However, the newspaper columns, magazine articles, and television and radio coverage have neglected one important point: the economic importance of the hospitality industry. This is the topic of this chapter.

It is easy to understand why the significance of this sector of the economy is slighted. For example:

The hospitality industry does not represent an easily recognizable business sector. It is a loosely connected assemblage of two industry groups, the lodging and the food service industries.

The majority of the two industries are composed of a multitude of very small businesses. It has been estimated that they total close to one million. In Massachusetts alone there are more than a thousand lodging places.

Because of its fragmented composition, the hospitality industry has not been effective in publicizing its importance and in achieving its legislative and regulatory needs.

Little quantitative information is available about the industry. Lodging and food service establishments are key components of the service sector. From the perspective of government statistical programs, this is akin to the areas marked as uncharted and unexplored on ancient maps.

Economic illiteracy creates a final problem. The service sector is viewed by many as being less important than manufacturing, agriculture and other goods-producing industries.

One indication of the economic importance of the hospitality industry can be found in the magnitude of the revenues of its two principal component industries. In 1979, sales of eating and drinking places totaled $75.1 billion dollars. Receipts of the lodging industry amounted to $23.5 billion.

The fact that the hospitality industry is the source of livelihood for a very large segment of the population of the United States is perhaps the best evidence of its economic significance. Establishments classified as "eating and drinking places" provided jobs for 4.1 million or 4.3 percent of the 96.9 million people employed in 1979.

The importance of the restaurant industry as an employer also can be appreciated by comparisons with other sectors of the economy. The number of workers in eating and drinking places exceeded those in agriculture, was two-thirds higher than the combined number on federal and state government payrolls and more than three times greater than employment in the automobile industry.

The sector of the economy termed "hotels and other lodging places" serves as the source of livelihood for a smaller but, nonetheless, significant proportion of the labor force. In 1979, the lodging industry provided jobs for 1.1 million people, which represented 1.1 percent of total employment for the year. This was more than twice as many as were employed in newspaper publishing and printing and even exceeded the number of people on the payrolls of iron and steel mills.

Taken together, the restaurant and lodging industries provided employment for 5.2 million people in 1979, which represented 5.4 percent of the working population of the United States. This exceeded the total combined number of people employed in wholesale trade and communications.

The economic significance of the hospitality industry is also illustrated by the number of employees in associated occupations. There are, for example, more waiters and waitresses than kindergarten and elementary school teachers, twice as many cooks and chefs as lawyers, more bartenders than mail carriers, more hotel managers and assistants than dentists and as many bellhops, bell captains and hotel housekeepers and assistants as officers and sailors in the nation's Merchant Marine.   The contribution of the hospitality industry to employment is enhanced by the composition of its workforce. Restaurateurs and hoteliers contribute substantially to federal, state and local government efforts to provide jobs for the economically disadvantaged. In 1979, for example, workers classified as "black and other" filled 166,300 or 23.1% of the jobs in hotels and motels, far more than their 11.3% average for all industries. In the same year, 2.5 million or 60.7% of the workers in eating and drinking places were women, well above the national average of 41.7%. Teenagers account for a very large proportion of employees in restaurants, especially during peak travel periods. For many of these young people jobs in the hospitality industry are highly significant; they furnish their first experience in the workforce.

The regional importance of employment in the hospitality industry is substantial, although it can vary considerably from one state and urban area to another. In 1978, for example, hotel and amusement places accounted for 16.4% of total employment in Las Vegas and 28.7% for the entire state of Nevada. While hotels and lodging places provided only 0.5 percent of Connecticut's total employment, they accounted for 2.5 percent in Florida. Eating and drinking places furnished 3.6 percent of total employment in the District of Columbia and only 1.2 percent in Dallas-Fort Worth.

The economic contribution of the hospitality industry is enhanced by the geographic distribution of the jobs that it provides. A large number of employers are located in major cities that are visited by domestic vacationers, business travelers and foreign tourists. The overall unemployment and minority group jobless rates in the majority of these urban areas are well in excess of the national average. A significant proportion of food service and lodging establishment employees in these cities are members of minority groups.

The economic benefits derived from the hospitality industry are not confined to metropolitan areas. Many vacation destinations in the United States are located in coastal, mountain and other regions where employment opportunities are extremely limited. In such areas establishments catering to vacationers and conventioneers are frequently the principal source of employment.

INDIRECT BENEFICIARIES

The hospitality industry also impacts the economy through the personal consumption expenditures and savings of its workforce. Employees and proprietors of eating and drinking places and of hotels and other lodging places are directly responsible for furnishing a significant proportion of consumer purchasing power. In 1979, labor and proprietor's income from both industry groups totaled over $38 billion, which represented 2.6 percent of the total personal income for the nation. Retail establishments such as supermarkets, department stores and automobile dealers as well as financial institutions, including banks and insurance companies, benefit from the expenditures of this group.

The hospitality industry serves as a market for many other sectors of the economy. Hotels and motels, for example, account for a substantial share of the sales of the carpeting and furniture industries. Resorts and convention centers generate significant construction. Restaurants are a major source of demand for china and kitchen equipment.

The viability of the business organizations that comprise the hospitality industry is closely linked with a multitude of other industries. These include travel agencies, car rental companies, taxicab fleets, tour operators, retailers, theaters and charge card issuers. In addition, revenues of airlines, railroads, bus lines, convention and exposition centers and trade show operators correlate closely with the fortunes of restaurants and lodging establishments.

FISCAL CONTRIBUTION

Any substantial advance in the volume of business of restaurants, hotels and motels can provide a two-fold financial benefit to states and municipalities through its impact on their revenues and expenditures. Sales and gross receipts taxes are obtained from the outlays of vacation and business travelers within their borders. In 1979, for example, Colorado received $38.9 million from eating and drinking places and $9.7 million from lodging places through such levies. Together they accounted for $48.6 million or 6.6 percent of the state's sales and gross receipts taxes. Illinois received $173.9 million in revenue from eating and drinking places and $24.4 million in receipts from hotels and other lodging places in 1979. In combination, they furnished 5.6 percent of the state's revenue from total sales and gross receipts taxes. New Hampshire obtained 19.5% of such revenues from room occupancy and meal taxes during the same period.

Expenditures for meals and lodging also make substantial indirect contributions to the revenues of those states and municipalities that tax the incomes of business organizations and individuals. In addition, the hospitality industry furnishes a substantial portion of state and local real estate tax payments and various license fees.

The outlays of state and local governments also are affected by changes in the revenues of the hospitality industry. Any significant increases in the volume of business of lodging and food service establishments result in a rise in employment. This can reduce the numbers of people receiving unemployment compensation and welfare payments. Many of those employed by the hospitality industry, because of their specialized expertise or lack of skills, find it difficult to obtain employment in other industries. Thus, state and local government expenditures for job training programs and transfer payments can be reduced because of additions to the workforces of restaurateurs and hoteliers.

ECONOMIC DEVELOPMENT

The hospitality industry is making an important contribution to the development and preservation of many of the nation's natural, historic and cultural resources. Renovation and redevelopment projects are helping stem urban decay by revitalizing the downtown areas of a growing number of cities, towns and villages. Many of these projects are economically viable only because of their ability to attract vacationers and business travelers. Boston's Quincy Market and San Francisco's Ghirardelli Square are examples of undertakings where restaurants provide major contributions to the success of such projects. Lodging facilities are pivotal elements in the viability of other urban redevelopment efforts, such as Detroit's Renaissance Center and the proposed rehabilitation of Times Square in New York City.

EXPORT ENHANCEMENT

The hospitality industry also benefits the economy through its role in contributing favorably to the balance of international payments of the United States. Foreign visitor spending in the U.S. has been growing almost twice as fast as overall economic activity. In 1980, according to estimates of the United States Travel Service, the number of foreign arrivals in the U.S. totaled approximately 22.1 million, representing an annual advance of 11%. It is expected that U.S. international travel receipts from these visitors will amount to about $12.0 billion, a year-to-year gain of 20%. This equates to about four percent of total U.S. exports of goods and services for the year. According to the USTS, the number of foreign visitors to the U.S. in 1981 will, for the first time, exceed the total number of U.S. citizens traveling abroad. The USTS estimates that in the years ahead, "The rate of increase in U.S. international travel receipts will continue to be higher than the growth rate of U.S. travel payments abroad."

Expenditures of foreign visitors are especially important to the economies of several sections of the United States. In 1978, for example, the Far West and Hawaii were by far the largest regional beneficiaries of foreign visitor spending, according to estimates of the U.S. Travel Data Center. This is true whether measured in terms of employment, business receipts, payroll volume or tax revenues. However, since the United Kingdom has replaced Japan as the largest overseas source of foreign visitors, the level, geographic distribution and economic impact of visitors from abroad probably has shifted appreciably during the two subsequent years.

For some states the impact of foreign visitor spending can be substantial. In the first quarter of 1979, for example, expenditures of overseas visitors in Florida totaled $148.1 million, according to a state study. It was found that, on average, each of these travelers spent $70 per day and remained in Florida for 20 days. Restaurant meals and lodging accounted for a very large share of these expenditures.

The tax receipts derived directly from the outlays of foreign travelers can be considerable. The Arizona Office of Tourism estimated that during the twelve month period ending March 1978, Mexican visitors paid state and local sales and gasoline taxes totaling $8.7 million.

FUTURE GROWTH

What of the hospitality industry's future?

Excessive inflation, including rapidly rising energy costs, will continue to act as a restraint on the growth of revenues and add to the operating costs of restaurants, hotels and motels. According to the latest forecast of the Office of Corporate Strategic Planning at American Express Company, there will be increases of 9.9% in restaurant prices and 13.2% in lodging rates in 1981. Nonetheless, the long-term growth prospects for these industries and for their contribution to the nation's economic well-being remain quite bright. There are several reasons for expecting that their activity and their role in the nation's economic system will continue to expand.

One is that a growing number of people view vacations and weekend trips away from home as a necessity rather than a luxury of life. Some of the other reasons for anticipating the continued growth of travel and tourism in the United States were pointed out in a recent Department of Commerce report. "The turbulent generation of the 1960s, now entering the 35—44 age group, is more likely to travel and seek overnight accommodations than the average U.S. resident, and the number within this age bracket is expected to increase 70% by the year 2000, compared with an estimated 15% increase for the population as a whole. Other characteristics that may influence lifestyles and travel habits relate to smaller families with fewer child responsibilities, later marriages, higher divorce rates and more leisure time. Moreover, the spreading use of the four-day work-week and of 'flexitime' should increase the revenue of hotels, motels, and restaurants, and recreational facilities in the near future."

In addition, as the report pointed out, "the population has shifted to new age groups with greater spending power. People over 50 now constitute more than 27% of the U.S. population, and this group is expected to increase another 30% by the year 2000. Single-person households now make up one-third of all U.S. households, and they are increasing seven times faster than married ones." Both demographic groups have high propensities to take overnight trips and dine away from home.

The number of foreign visitors to the United States will continue to expand in the years ahead, the result of several developments. These include increasing affluence abroad, the depressed position of the dollar in foreign exchange markets, mounting recognition that the U.S. represents an international travel bargain and growing interest in the unique attractions of the United States. Therefore, foreign visitor expenditures for food and lodging will continue to make an increasingly important contribution to the U.S. balance of international payments in the years ahead.

The hospitality industry's greatest benefit to the nation's economic well-being in the future will result from the employment opportunities that it will provide for unskilled and skilled workers. Expansion and replacement requirements will, for example, create an average of 86,000 annual openings for cooks and chefs between now and 1990, according to projections of the Bureau of Labor Statistics. The annual numbers of vacancies are expected to average 37,000 for dining room attendants and dishwashers, 70,000 for waiters and waitresses and 8,900 for hotel managers and assistants.

The hospitality industry should be proud of its economic contributions and importance. Unfortunately, both are well kept secrets. It is in the interest of restaurateurs and hoteliers to draw attention to their significant role in the nation's economic system. Until they do so, the hospitality industry runs the risk of bearing a disproportionately large burden of regulatory and legislative measures adversely affecting business organizations. It also is likely to derive less benefit than it deserves from government actions advantageous to the private sector.

ACKNOWLEDGMENTS

The author wishes to thank Susan LaVoie for the research assistance that she provided while serving in the Office of Corporate Strategic Planning of American Express Company as a student intern from the Department of Hotel, Restaurant and Travel Administration, University of Massachusetts.

2

Interrelationship of the Food Service Industry with the Community

Uel Blank

This paper examines systematically the dynamic interrelationships between food services and the community of which they are a part. The primary focus is the commercial restaurant component. In the macro dimension — where food service patterns are examined against the overall U.S. economic and social fabric — they will be seen not only to reflect, but also to magnify, the vicissitudes of national moods. At the local level this analysis highlights their function as an essential component of the modern community.

Such analysis is necessary because, unfortunately, food services, in common with the entire range of hospitality services, continue to suffer from misunderstanding. Much of the society views them as not "essential" or at best their role is drastically underestimated. Part of this attitude is an extension of 19th century thought that places value primarily on tangible production and views services as "producing nothing". Further there is a lingering Calvinistic guilt that pleasure production is sinful and should not be indulged.

In actuality, those who are engaged in food service, from manager to bus boy/girl, can take pride in the industry of which they are a part. The modern economy and current life styles could not exist without it. Further, it appears destined to play an even more prominent role in the future.

Community developer/leaders have an obligation to understand and help others understand the productive output of food services to living quality, tourism and other industries. In producing its output, food service is a major factor in retail sales, employment and the development of secondary supplier industries. Thus, like most other economic ac-

TABLE 2.1. THE RELATIONSHIP OF PURCHASED MEALS TO DISPOSABLE PERSONAL INCOMES IN THE UNITED STATES: A HALF-CENTURY PATTERN 1930–1977

Year	Purchased Food and Beverage ($ Billion)	Disposable Personal Income ($ Billion)	Purchased Food as Percentage of Disposable Personal Income	Income Elasticity (YE) of Demand for Purchased Food and Beverage Period	YE
1930	2.78	74.5	3.7	1930–1935	0.27
1935	2.61	58.5	4.5	1935–1940	1.54
1940	3.89	75.7	5.1	1940–1945	1.09
1945	9.50	105	6.3	1945–1950	0.49
1950	11.1	207	5.4	1950–1955	0.79
1955	13.8	274	5.0	1955–1960	0.88
1960	17.2	352	4.9	1960–1965	0.92
1965	22.7	473	4.8	1965–1970	0.88
1970	31.5	669	4.7	1970–1975	1.01
1975	50.2	1063	4.7	1973–1977	1.22
1977	62.8	1273	4.9		

Source: Historical Statistics of the United States, Series G416-469.

tivities, it directly and indirectly generates jobs, profits, rents and tax base for the community.

FOOD SERVICES AND THE U.S. ECONOMY

The last half-century of food service development in the U.S. shows a dynamic interaction not only with the economy, but with technology and with evolving life style patterns — the way we live, work and play. Food services in some dimensions even exaggerate variations in these overall trends.

Table 2.1 gives a half century perspective by comparing purchases of food away from home with disposable income. Throughout the period the proportion of disposable income spent for food away from home averaged about five percent. But it varied — growing rapidly in the 1930's and early 40's, then declining until about 1970 and increasing at an increasing rate through the 1970's.

In Table 2.1 the two right hand columns give the income elasticity of demand (YE) for purchased food and beverages. YE expresses the relative change in food purchased away from home compared to relative changes in disposable income. A YE=1 means that relative changes in food purchased exactly match percentage changes in income. When YE is positive and larger than 1, purchases of meals away from home are growing as a proportion of disposable income. When YE is smaller than 1 the proportion is declining.

What was taking place to cause these changes in emphasis upon purchases of food away from home? The key factors can be outlined as follows:

Despite the depression of the 1930's many of the consumer trends established in the post World War I 1920's decade resumed after 1933. This especially included growth in use of automobiles, expansion of the highway system and hence increased travel away from home. The repeal of prohibition added a further impetus during the mid-1930's. Travel greatly accelerated in the early 1940's as the nation prepared for and engaged in World War II. Hence relative growth in food consumed away from home.

Another set of factors became dominant in the 1945 to 1970 era. Perhaps the most important was the great expansion in the birth rate requiring attention to care and nurture of families. Concurrently with and closely related was a boom in education at all levels. It was also mandatory that the nation catch up in housing which had seen only limited growth for a decade and a half. In addition, medicine received a disproportionate share of expenditures. These big ticket family consumption items partly displaced expenditures for food

TABLE 2.2.   GROWTH OF THE U.S. FOOD SERVICE, 1967–1977

| | Year | | Change |
	1967	1977	%
Food and beverage sales (millions)	$23,843	$63,276	+165
All retail sales (millions)	$310,200	$723,100	+133
Food and beverage employment (thousands)[1]	2,379	4,059	+71
Employed civilian work force (thousands)	74,400	90,500	+22
Places of refreshment			
sales (million)	$3,418	$19,527	+472
employment (thousands)[1]	296	1,157	+219

Source: U.S. Census of Business.
[1] Employment derived from paid employees in census week plus proprietors of unincorporated establishments.

and beverage away from home. The latter grew, but at a slower rate than disposable incomes.

Now, in the last decade, expenditures for away-from-home food and beverage have resumed their relative growth pattern. This resulted from still another set of factors. The baby boom grew up. There is now a relatively large number of teenagers and young adults in the population—with spending power and a strong propensity to spend for immediate consumption. Reinforcing this is the steady growth of married women in the work force—meaning that a high proportion of households have two wage earners—and no-one at home to prepare meals. Matching demand growth has been the supply response. Part of it is technological in that attractively-consumable food items can be widely available both in terms of time and geography. Another aspect of demand growth is in the expansion of specialized outlets, partly reflected by "places of refreshment" which are discussed below. Thus it is probable that Say's Law[1] was operating along with direct growth in demand variables to produce relative expansion in food consumed away from home.

U.S. Census of Business data for the 1967 to 1977 decade shows the dramatic relative growth in sales of U.S. eating and drinking places, Table 2.2. In this period U.S. retail sales more than doubled (in current dollars), growing by 133%. But sales of eating and drinking places outpaced even this — they grew by 165%.

Food away from home has a large component of personal service. For this reason employment measures show food services' contribution to be even greater than sales alone would indicate. The employed civilian work force grew by 22% in this 10 year period; eating and drinking employment

[1]Say's Law postulates: Supply creates its own demand. This is the basic principle of supply-side economics.

expanded by 71%.

Shifts within the food service types reveal another dimension of industry dynamics. In the same 10-year 1967-1977 period noted above, both sales and employment of places of refreshment grew at almost three times the corresponding rate for sales and employment of all eating and drinking places. Growth was a whopping 472% for sales and 219% for employment. Places of refreshment are limited menu places corresponding roughly to convenience food services. Their growth further documents adaptation to changes in demand — rapid growth in new away-from-home food consumers, including teenagers, young adults and upwardly mobile socio-economic population segments; plus rapid general expansion in the sales of modest level ticket items.

Perhaps the most exciting and useful aspect of this look at interrelations with the macro society comes from a look into the future. Let's take a simultaneous look at several "drivers of demand" for food service in the 1980's. One of these is the general economy. Most economists predict that the nagging problems of the 1970's will have lessened by the latter half of the 1980's. They are optimistic for this period. A healthy growing economy in the 1980's is not certain but it is a good bet. National demographics greatly improve its likelihood. Between 1977 and 1987 the number of Americans in their most productive years, the 35 to 49 age range, will have increased by almost one third, 31%, Table 2.3. Couple this with the fact that numbers of teenagers will be down in absolute terms by 17%, and the prediction that nearly 60% of married women will be in the work place, Table 2.4.

What do we have? A population with a high proportion in their most productive years, an increasing proportion of families with two wage earners, and smaller families, hence relatively low numbers of younger dependents (which also means less street crime, and relatively less spent for schooling). Such a population will be productive, they will have a high per capita disposable income — these factors will almost certainly have a salutary effect on the economy. They will also cause a high propensity to

TABLE 2.3.   U.S. POPULATION AGE GROUP PROJECTIONS, 1977–1987

	Numbers		
	1977	1987	Change
	millions	millions	%
Age group (years)			
under 13 (children)	44	49	up 11
13–19 (teens)	29	24	down 17
20–34 (young adults)	53	60	up 13
35–49 (middle age, younger)	35	46	up 31
50–64 (middle age, older)	32	32	down 1
65 and over (aged)	23	28	up 19

Source: U.S. Bureau of Census.

TABLE 2.4.   MARRIED WOMEN IN THE LABOR FORCE WITH HUSBAND PRESENT

Year	Percentage of all married women
1950	23.8
1960	30.5
1970	40.8
1978	47.6

Source: Statistical Abstract of the United States.

eat out—especially when we again note that there will be no one at home with inclination to prepare food.

This does not guarantee that every food service will grow. But it does say that the market opportunity will be there in abundance!

A COMMUNITY-FOOD SERVICE INDUSTRY MODEL

Interrelationships with the local community show specifics of the way in which food services deliver their output to the society and in so doing also contribute local employment, profits and tax base.

A special Minnesota survey is used here to show the food service impact since Census of Business data have been found subject to substantial underestimation (Blank and Olson 1981). Our survey found sales to be 30% larger than those reported by the Census of Business. Minnesota is a good state to use for illustration since its industry is approximately that of an average state; one-fiftieth the scale of the U.S.A.

The $1.5 billion of 1976 commercial restaurant sales estimated for Minnesota was 11.6% of the state's retail sales (estimated from Sales and Use taxes). These operations are a factor in employment for 276,000 full-time and part-time workers. This amounts to about one-sixth of the Minnesota labor force.

A model of the full dimensions of food service-community inter-relationships is shown in Fig. 2.1. This industry's product is sold through "forward linkages" to consuming units. In order to produce its output it must have "backward linkages" to the community through which it purchases the varied inputs needed for it to function.

Forward Linkages

Forward linkages are the specialized outputs of food services. These are sales of food and beverage products, services and ambience or, more broadly, life experiences. They are the reason for existence of the industry. Clientele are of many different types. Most sales are made directly to final consumers but it will be especially noted that an important function of the industry's output is in support of other industry.

In order to fully understand the function of these sales in the community they are noted as having several components:

Tourism. — consists of sales to tourists — defined here as all nonresidents who do not regularly commute to the given community to work. When making sales to tourists the food service industry operates like an exporting industry; that is it generates new dollars that help to expand the local economy. Studies in the Minneapolis-St. Paul metropolitan area (Blank and Petkovich 1979) estimate tourists spend $225 million there for food services. This is estimated at almost exactly 50% of total Minnesota food services sales to tourists. Thus tourism accounts for 30% of the food service industry sales. Tourism sales vary from community to community. In communities with relatively small numbers of out-of-the-area travelers it will be low. In northern Minnesota communities, attracting a large number of recreators because of its high quality natural waters and woodlands, food service sales to tourists may run over half the total. A 1970 study in the area near and including International Falls, found 54% of food service industry sales to tourists (Blank 1971). These travelers may have come into the community for a variety of reasons or combinations of reasons. Note some special interrelationships between tourists' travel purposes and the community's food service industry:

Those in the community for purposes of recreation/entertainment, conventions/conferences and as a stopover on the way to another destination may have been influenced in their travel decisions by the character of the community's food service industry. The food-away from-home experience may be a significant part of the amenity package sought. The food service offering may expand their expenditures in the given community by a factor of several times, e.g., will those driving in to a major sports event eat a meal in the community before and after the event or will they do it on the road or at home?

Those in the community to visit friends and relatives have been found to be a factor in food service sales. Their image of the food service amenities and that of the local residents whom they visit will affect their expenditures while in the community. Most tourism bureaus and food services ignore this component of travel; they do so to their own disadvantage since it is the largest single reason for travel away from home, accounting for 32% of all person-trips over 100 miles from home in 1977 (U.S. Dept. of Commerce, 1977). A study found that 10% of restaurant meals in an area receiving a substantial volume of outdoor recreation tourists involved "visits with friends and relatives" (Blank 1971). In Minneapolis-St. Paul it was estimated that tourists who were visiting friends bought seven percent of the total sales of food service (Blank and Petkovich

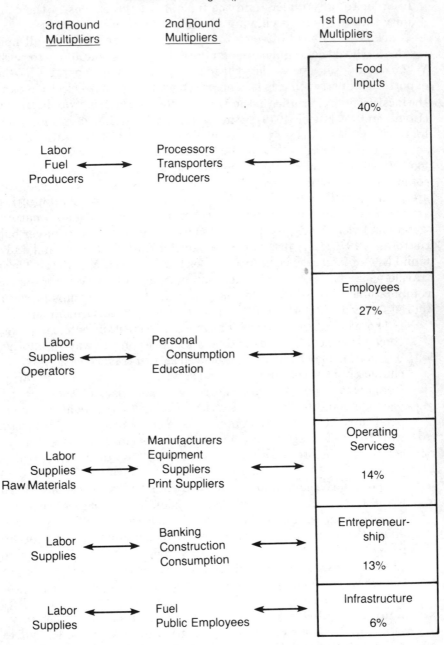

FIG. 2.1.   THE COMMERCIAL RESTAURANT INDUSTRY OF MINNESOTA

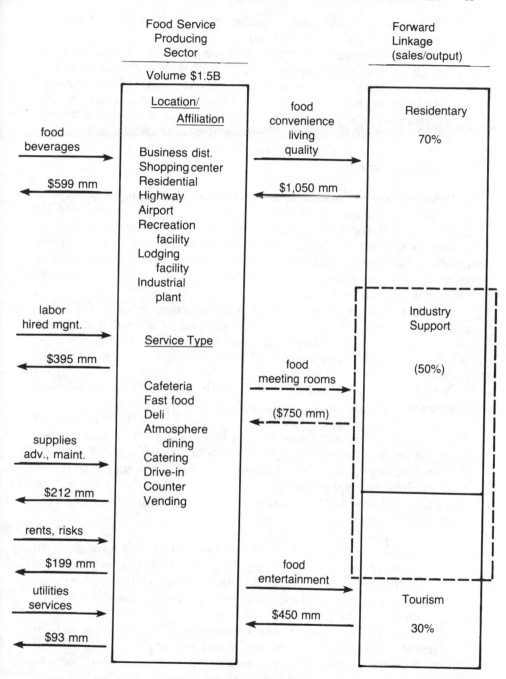

1979), note that this ignores purchases by their hosts in restaurants because they had guests in town.

Those traveling for gainful employment and for personal business might at first glance appear "stuck" with whatever food service is locally available. But many of these travelers have a high degree of control over their intinerary — how long they will be in one locality, where they stay ovenight and where they are at mealtime. Hence food and beverage sales to this group of travelers may also be highly flexible depending upon the appeal of the community's hospitality service offering.

Residentiary.—consists of sales to local residents. For all Minnesota food services this accounts for 70% of sales. These residents are of four different types that are usually complexly interrelated in reality — eating away from home : a) for purposes of convenience; b) under conditions of necessity; c) for business or institutional purposes; and d) to improve living quality by extending the range of life experiences, social contacts and entertainment.

Industry Support.—is a special role performed by food and other hospitality services since, in order to function, nearly all modern economic activity requires travel by some of its participants. Hospitality services provide the means for sustenance while these individuals are away from home.

This function overlaps both the residentiary and tourism segments of the forward linkage. In Minneapolis-St. Paul it was estimated that 67% of tourists' food purchases were also "industry support"; in outstate Minnesota this proportion was only one half this high. Thus in the entire state the tourism forward linkage consists one-half of industry support. A conservative estimate of the residentiary forward linkage is that it also is approximately one-half industry support (Blank and Olson 1981). In summary, industry support makes up at least 50% of all sales or $750 million in Minnesota annually.

Interrelated subparts include:

Business Travelers— modern business, social and governmental instituions require travel for management, sales, and technical consultation purposes. These people must have the means for living away from home. This aspect of industry support is also a part of community tourism.

Meeting/Conferencing—the functioning of nearly all aspects of private and public and of profit and non-profit systems in our society require face-to-face group communication. Food services frequently provide the physical setting. Note that this may be either a "residentiary" or a "tourism" forward linkage or some of both depending upon whether or not the conference participants are community residents or have traveled a distance and are therefore tourists.

Worker Convenience—going home for meals during work hours is impractical for most employed persons. Food services provide convenience and save time and travel.

The Food Service Producing Sector

In Minnesota the commercial food producing sector is estimated at $1.5 billion sales in 1976. This is over 11% of all retail sales in the state. It offers a widely varied range of food service, operating throughout Minnesota in metropolitan, rural and other types of settings and serving an equally varied clientele. Figure 2.2 illustrates some of this variety. It is not discussed further since the purpose here is to describe interrelationships rather than details of the food sector itself.

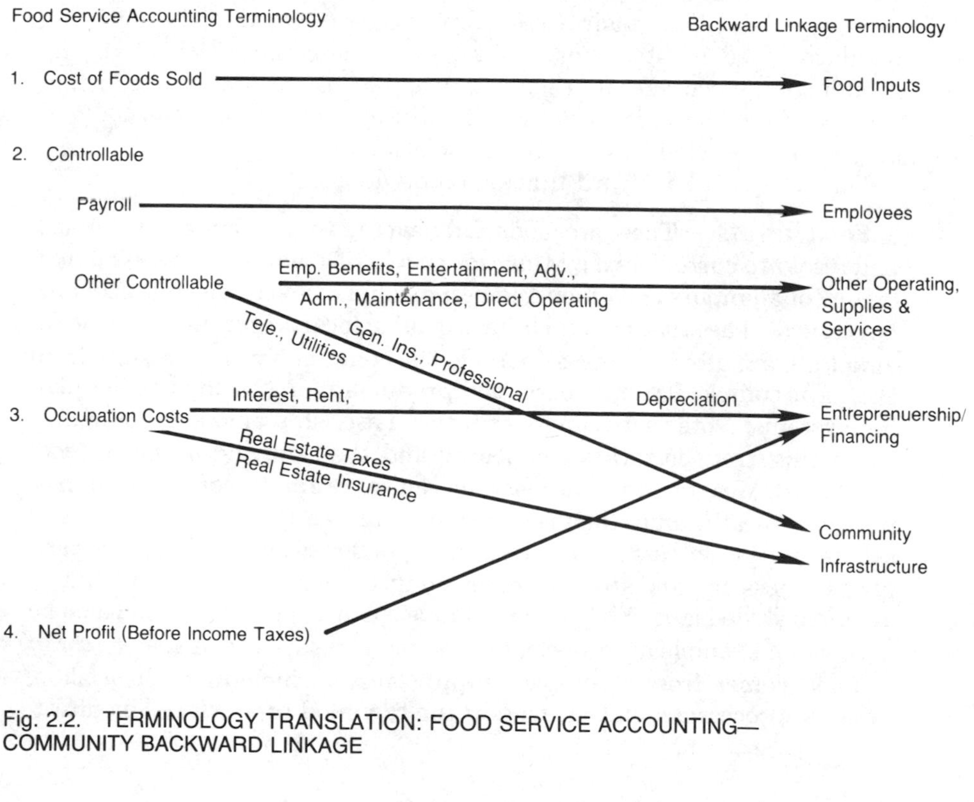

Food Service Accounting Terminology   Backward Linkage Terminology

1. Cost of Foods Sold ————————————————————————▸ Food Inputs

2. Controllable

        Payroll ————————————————————————————▸ Employees

        Other Controllable   Emp. Benefits, Entertainment, Adv.,
                              Adm., Maintenance, Direct Operating ————▸ Other Operating,
                                                                         Supplies &
                          Tele., Utilities   Gen. Ins., Professional   Services

                          Interest, Rent,   Depreciation
3. Occupation Costs ———————————————————————————▸ Entreprenuership/
                          Real Estate Taxes   Financing
                          Real Estate Insurance

                                                            ▸ Community
                                                            ▸ Infrastructure

4. Net Profit (Before Income Taxes)

Fig. 2.2.   TERMINOLOGY TRANSLATION: FOOD SERVICE ACCOUNTING—COMMUNITY BACKWARD LINKAGE

Backward Linkages

Backward linkages are all the things the food industry buys. They are the inputs provided by the community that make possible the industry's output to society. Significantly, it is through these purchases that the food service industry makes its economic contribution of jobs, profits, rents and tax base to the community.

Depending upon the size and complexity of the community in which a given firm operates, it may be necessary for parts of these purchases to be imported into the community. But the industry's nature is such that a high proportion of inputs is usually of local origin even in small communities. It is estimated that, in Minnesota, 60 to 75% of the first round of production inputs (backward linkages) are supplied from within the local county. For most retailing and processing firms the proportion of locally-produced inputs is much lower. It is important to note that the higher the proportion of locally supplied inputs, the greater the economic benefit to the local economy.

Terminology that has relevance to the community has been substituted for traditional food service accounting terminology in describing the backward linkages. Inputs have been renamed in Figure 2.1, and regroupings have been made, for example "Cost of Goods Sold" has been renamed "food inputs". Figure 2.2 shows the composition of the regroupings. Percentages for each new group have been determined using findings from the 1976 Minnesota Food Service Industry Survey and data of the National Restaurant Association (1979).

The groups of backward linkages include:

Food Inputs. — These are foods and beverage items that are processed and resold to customers. In Minnesota their 1976 value was $566 million or 40% of all inputs (31% food and non-alcoholic beverages; 9% alcoholic beverages). These items could be nearly all of local origin. Actually most, if not all, are often purchases outside the community. This results from the great complexity of modern food producing, processing and supplying systems. Note that there is an interrelationship among labor skills, processing/transportation technology and the type and origin of food purchased. Meat provides the most convenient example: some restaurants purchase meat in bulk (halves, quarters, etc.) and break it down themselves. It is in contrast to the purchase of portioned cuts. It transfers part of the processing and storage operation into the restaurant itself, but it requires skilled labor. Other staple foods, such as potatoes, could also be used as an example of processing in-house versus elsewhere.

Food comes from a complex supply system including wholesalers, brokers, processors, and ultimately the raw food producers. The direct suppliers may include a combination of the following types plus others:

Wholesale grocers
Fruit and vegetable vendors
Meat suppliers
Poultry products handlers
Fish and shellfish handlers
Frozen food and specialty foods
Dairy products
Bakery products
Alcoholic beverages
Other beverages - non-alcoholic, non-dairy

Employees.—include hired labor only and compare directly with "payroll" as a part of controllable expenses. The 1976 Minnesota food service industry payroll was $395 million or 27% of all inputs. In terms of full-time job equivalents employment is estimated at 90,000. In terms of individual people a total of 276,000 Minnesotans work full or part-time in the industry. This is 16% of the total work force.

The pattern of labor inputs varies greatly. On the one hand the purchaser of a small restaurant in effect "buys a job" for himself and his family plus a place for investing savings. Owners manage 70.5% of Minnesota food services, and unpaid family labor is included in the above figure of 276,000. On the other hand, capital, management and labor may be sharply differentiated in the case of a restaurant chain. All labor, including management, may be hired. In any event, most labor is supplied by the local community.

Other Operating Supplies and Services.—include a wide range of items needed to operate including advertising, maintenance, entertainment, administration, operating supplies and employee benefits. The group compares to "Other Controllable Costs" with the exception that utilities, etc., have been transferred to the Community Infrastructure Group. These items amounted to $211 million or 14% in 1976 in Minnesota. Their sources include local lumberyards, equipment services, and newspapers/printing as well as many suppliers at a distance.

Entrepreneurship/Financing.—this group includes the investment, ownership, risk and financing function. It totaled $199 million or 13% of all 1976 Minnesota inputs. It includes profits, return to owner-managers, return to unpaid family labor, and all interest and rents whether actually paid or imputed. In the case of a resident owned and managed operation this input may be fully supplied by the local community.

Community Infrastructure.—these are facilities and services that are necessary for the community to operate, and that are available to serve all citizens and businesses. In 1976, $93 million was paid for infrastructure services in Minnesota or 6% of all inputs. They include utilities, telephone, insurance (usually created by a grouping of firms to spread risk) and general community services. Some, such as utilities, gas, electricity, insurance and telephone may be private and paid for in proportion to use. Others such as roads, streets, street lighting, parks, police protection and fire protection may be supported through public taxation. Note that these may not all be locally supplied — examples are electricity and telephone in smaller communities. Note also that in some cases tax moneys are used to upgrade community aesthetics and living quality — through park development beautificatioin programs, and may also contribute to programs of tourism promotion.

Not shown here is the Minnesota sales tax which was $60 million and would have increased the infrastructure component to $153 million.

An extensive set of additional considerations further define the food service industry-community relationship. Most elaborate the linkages discussed above. Among the more important are the following.

Multipliers

When money is spent for food service it has a greater economic impact than simply one dollar for each dollar spent. Twenty-seven cents of each sales dollar goes into payroll. The employees respend their income using it for all the things needed to live, such as groceries and rent. The grocer in turn must pay his own employees as well as his own rent and buy his supply of groceries at wholesale. This chain continues at great length. One part of the employee multiplier chain is the educational system. In Minnesota 52% of food service managers reported having either a college degree or special training in the food service.

All other parts of the backward linkage, in turn, have their own backward linkages. "Food Inputs" was noted as the major input. Its supply extends backward through wholesalers, processors, transporters to the ultimate farm producers and further backward to the implement, fertilizer, etc. suppliers of those producers. United States restaurants require the output from one-fourth to one-third of U.S. agriculture.

The immediate supplier of the food service firm is called the "first round multiplier." Purchases from the supplier's supplier make up the "second round multipliers" and so on through third and subsequent "rounds". This multiplier commonly falls in the range of 2 to 3. It has been calculated for the U.S. food service at 2.3 (Maki 1981). This means that for each dollar spent by consumers for food away from home another

$1.30 of added economic activity is generated. This figure of 2.3 compares with a multiplier of 1.4 for all the "retail sector, except food services." In other words a restaurant purchase means much more in economic terms to the community than a department store purchase.

Where Do Diners Come From?

Food service customers are available from two primary sources:

The community must function sufficiently well as a place to live and/or as a supplier of income that it sustains a resident population having demand for food away from home. The better the local community functions, the greater the demand in numbers and types of meals away from home, hence the greater the opportunities for food service firms.

Travelers who are attracted to the community and need food services. Fig. 2.3 illustrates the great multiplicity of factors that may operate in a complex community to generate tourists. While most food services depend upon the community to attract travelers, a synergistic effect may sometimes be operating where food services become a major part of the attraction influence in their own right.

Resources and the Food Service Industry

It appears easy for most people to understand the relationship between local resources and many economic activities. Example: good soil and agriculture; power generation and aluminum production; high technology

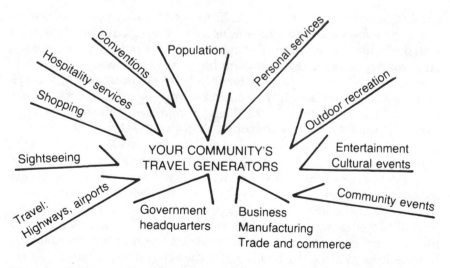

FIG. 2.3. COMMUNITY TRAVEL ATTRACTORS

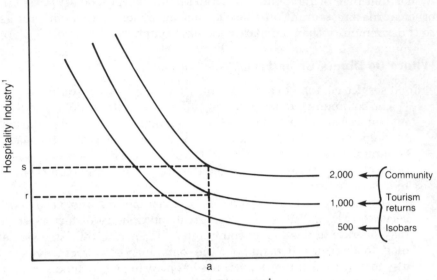
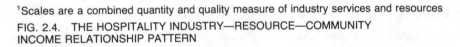

[1]Scales are a combined quantity and quality measure of industry services and resources

FIG. 2.4. THE HOSPITALITY INDUSTRY—RESOURCE—COMMUNITY INCOME RELATIONSHIP PATTERN

and computers. It appears difficult, however, for many people to connect community resources and economic activity generated through tourism with the hospitality industry of which food services are a significant part. Most tourist sales are made through hospitality services.

Figure 2.4 illustrates the relationship between a community's hospitality industry, its potential tourist attracting resources and its tourism income. The curved lines in the diagram represent return to the community in tourist income each having the value as labeled. They may be thought of as lines on a contour map with income levels rising above the plane of the paper. Note that with a level of attractions resources "a," only 1000 in community tourism income is attained with a hospitality industry development at the level of "r." But with the same level of resources, 2000 in income can be generated for the community with a level of "s" in hospitality services. As indicated in the diagram, community tourism can expand by either expansion in numbers or quality of hospitality services or by additions to the attractions resource.

A brief explanation of how the system works may be in order. Consider the case of a community with a major sports event or art gallery. Visitors may come because of either attraction. How much money they spend may depend upon food, and other hospitality, services available in the community. Will they eat at home, at some stopover on the way, or in the target community? In the same manner, a community with an excellent lake will realize little economic return from it unless it has rooms, meals and related hospitality-recreational service to sell.

Direct spatial resource requirements provide another and different type of insight. The building space in all Minnesota food services total only 570 acres. Even with parking lots not over 10,000 acres of space would be directly required. This intensive use of land to produce $686 million in value added from the $1500 million of food service sales compares with the extensive land use of Minnesota farm production. There 1800 times as much space, 18 million acres of harvested land, is required to produce only a little over 4 times the value added: $2.9 billion of value added on $5.5 billion total sales (Maki 1981).

The Food Service Industry — Nursemaid to the Labor Force

At any given time an estimated 11% of the teenage Minnesota population is employed in the food service industry. The industry plays a role in the early work experience of at least 25 to 30% of all teenagers. This proportion may even increase in the years ahead as relative numbers of teenagers decrease (absolute numbers of teenagers in the U.S. population are estimated to fall by 17% between 1977 and 1987).

The food service industry is thus a major factor in youth employment. It is also a major factor in helping to shape job attitudes on the part of the labor force. This is an important qualitative addition to the role of the food service industry as an overall contributor to jobs.

THE CHALLENGES POSED

This look at interrelationships of food services with the macro community at the national level and with the local community leaves challenges. These will be simply stated.

There appears to be potential for real growth in food service sales; what strategy is needed for each firm to realize its share of this potential?

Numbers of teenagers in our society will actually decrease in the decade of the 1980's. This has implications for markets; it probably will mandate even greater adjustments in labor management since teenagers have been an important pool of food service manpower.

What is the best strategy for an intensified public campaign so that investors and other public leaders fully understand the potential contribution of food services to the modern community: 1) to community industry and living quality; and 2) in the production of local jobs, profits, rents and tax base?

Can the entrepreneurship/financing input be upgraded? Much has already been said about management training. What about financing? Can creative means for food service financing such as through industrial revenue bonds be developed and used?

Part II

Strategic Planning

3

Strategic Corporate Planning

Jon Canas

The subject of this paper is "Strategic Corporate Planning"; in other words, the subject is "Planning" with two qualifiers, one being "strategic," the other one "corporate." First, let's deal with the planning.

Planning, per se, is what I call a motherhood and apple pie subject. It is a wonderful subject like talking about supporting the local charity; the more you talk about it the more everyone agrees. The problem occurs at the time of performance when the questions become:

—Why should I give?
—To whom should I give?
—How much should I give?

When talking about strategic corporate planning, the questions are:

—What is the purpose?
—Who should do it?
—How should it be done?

I would like to try to deal with all three questions in the hope that the answers to the first one will help shed some light on the other two. Then, because I am a practitioner, I will share some of the elements of the Dunfey Planning process to illustrate some of my points.

THE PURPOSE OF STRATEGIC PLANNING

A company works within an environment made up of factors of forces acting upon that company in either favorable or unfavorable, but always changing, ways. Those forces originating outside the company are, by definition, outside its control. Some of these external factors are:

— Industry Changes (Channels of Distribution)
— National & International Political Events
— Government Regulations
— Demographic Changes
— Life Style and Customer Trend Shifts
— Competitive Activity
— Parent Company Attitude, Objectives and Goals

Within a company there are internal factors, human and material resources, available to management to create a set of forces which will act with, or react to, the external environment. Some of those factors are:

— Condition of Products and Services
— Financial Resources
— Marketing Strength Through the Channels of Distribution
— Relationship with Customers
— Relationship with Existing and Potential Owners
— Relationship with Employees
— Management Skills and Will
— Corporate Fabric
— Management Tools and Methods
— Corporate Objectives and Strategies

The analogy between a company within its external environment and a ship at sea is striking. The captain of a ship can do nothing to modify the sea and wind conditions but will adjust the ship heading, sails trim, or engine speed (internal factors) to compensate for the changes in external cargo and ship. Pursuing the analogy, we shed some light on who does the planning and broadly speaking, how to do it. Indeed, it is the ship's captain who sets the ship's direction and speed at any given time, keeping in mind the specific purpose he has in going from Point A to Point B within a given time frame and an acceptable level of risk.

The primary responsibility of top management is to perform that captain's role, namely:

1. To determine Point B, i.e., the ultimate corporate objective which

we refer to as a *Mission.*

2. To be aware of the *External Factors* at work and anticipate (when and where possible) their effects upon the environment and the company.
3. To know the *Internal Factors* available to the organization and set them in motion to insure the best possible results towards the Mission within an acceptable level of risk.
4. Be ready to *Adapt to Changes* or lack of desired results; always keeping in mind the ultimate purpose.

To paraphrase Kenneth Andrews, Professor at the Harvard Business School, in his book, *The Concept of Corporate Strategy:*

The Planning Process begins with the assumption that every organization, every sub-unit in an organization, every group and individual should be guided by an evolving set of goals which permits movement in a chosen direction and prevents drifting.

In addition Andrews tells us:

Conscious attention to corporate strategy will be wasted if it does not *elevate the quality of corporate purpose and achievement.*

WHO SHOULD DO IT

Since the primary purpose of planning is to set a direction for the organization and its major components, that activity must rest with the top management of each planning unit. They are often referred to as Strategic Business Units.

Andrews tells us:

A Chief Executive's role is to be the architect of the organization's purpose

Some additional paraphrases from Andrews comment further on the role of the Chief Executive Officer:

Probably the most nearly unique skill to general management as opposed to the management of function or technical specialties, is the intellectual capacity to conceptualize corporate purpose and dramatic skill to invest it with some degree of magnetism.

The most difficult role of the Chief Executive of any organization is the one in which he serves as the custodian of the corporate objectives.

HOW IT SHOULD BE DONE

Corporations and individual hotels are used to the process of yearly budgeting which reflects short term financial planning. Since most United States corporations are in the habit of making decisions on a short term financial basis, most corporations confuse planning with budgeting. In most instance, the financial plan is based on a trendlining activity and as the result most companies create a box for themselves.

By definition, trendlining maintains current trends or status quo. It is the opposite of planning for change. Trendlining is, in fact, helpful to show what will happen if you don't change; it is interesting to note:

1. Trendlining good past results is wishful thinking based on the past and has no common measure with the future;
2. Trendlining bad past results may turn the box into a coffin!

Planning is a creative mental activity whereby one attempts to structure a brighter future given internal and external conditions, but basing the reasoning not exclusively on the past such as in trendlining, but basing it in fact on the future.

Andrews adds:

The execution of the process at a highly professional level will depend upon the depth and durability of the Chief Executive personal values, standards of quality, and clarity of character.

I have talked about planning in general but what makes planning "strategic planning" is the degree to which it shows a selection of a course of action against other alternatives. It is not trendlining. It is an expression of will on the part of the Chief Executive Officer and the Chief Operating Officer. Strategic planning not only leads the organization to a choice among alternative courses of action, it also shows the interplay and relevant impact of external factors. It also outlines the game plan in the use of internal factors, or resources of the organization, to improve its competitive standing.

CORPORATE PLANNING

Finally, let me address the issue of "corporate" planning. I will tell you some of the thinking which took us years to integrate into my own organization. It is wonderful to have a sophisticated planning process and great plans that delight the Chief Executive Officer and the Chief

Operating Officer, but the trick is to convey to the rest of the organization the expression of will and the game plan I've talked about. This can only be achieved by a structured, progressive and logical process that involves all management personnel of each hotel with their corporate counterparts and supervisors. Each hotel's strategic plan must fit with, and become a part of, the corporate strategic plan. In addition, each hotel plan must be broken down by department and by time frame. Finally, results must be regularly measured against expectations (not necessarily financial budget) within activities and strategies, evaluated and updated. This ongoing process is monitored by the unit management team and by corporate management. Such an approach requires and helps maintain the concept of shared responsibility between line and staff management. This is why a good planning process must be underlined by a commonly shared business philosphy and management approach. At Dunfey hotels we have created a "Dunfey Management approach" which is a formalized document dealing with major concepts at the root of our corporate fabric.

The following is a broad outline of the "Dunfey Planning Process":

A. *Overview*
   1. Dunfey Hotels is a company with a philosophy and a purpose which are outlined in the Dunfey Management Approach.
   a. The Principle of the business trilogy:
   Recognize the needs of Customers, Owners, employees and integrate!
   b. The expression of the Corporate Mission
   2. The Dunfey Planning Process outlines a practical way to integrate the realities of each market place (demand, our product, competition) with the "needs" of the business triology.
B. *Components*
   1. The Corporate Five Year Plan
   a. Corporate Mission
   b. Functional Objections & Strategies with proper allocation of resources
   2. Each unit has (in addition to the financial budget)
   a. Yearly Plan:
   Mission
   Yearly Objectives & Strategies
   Goals
   b. Quadrimester Plan:
   KRA
   Action Step
   Benchmarks
   3. A Corporate process to evaluate, modify, and approve.

CONCLUSION

Strategic corporate planning is an exercise in creative thinking that requires the skills to conceptualize. It is a discipline that requires a structure, a process and an organization not for theoretical purposes, but to practically express top management's will in the selection of alternative courses of action to improve the competitive standing of the organization. The final criterion of proper strategic corporate planning is whether the organization has achieved a commonality of purpose.

4

Strategic Planning for the Food Service Industry

Robert L. Sirkis and *Stephen M. Race*

There are as many definitions of strategic planning as there are consulting firms. When we talk about strategic planning at Arthur D. Little we mean an orderly process for determining the directions and management of a business or corporation. Strategic planning is concerned with the allocation of skills and resources based upon some anticipated future. Most corporations of any size are made up of a number of businesses. Strategic planning is basically done at two levels: the corporation and the business unit. This paper will focus on business unit strategic planning.

PRINCIPLES OF STRATEGIC PLANNING

There are five central principles to business unit planning:
1. Strategy centers within a corporation can be identified.
2. Planning is a data base activity.
3. Business is not random.
4. There are a limited number of strategies that a business can choose from.
5. Business is more condition than ambition-driven.

Strategy Centers Can Be Identified

The first principle of strategic planning is that within any corporation strategy centers can be identified. The terms strategy center and business unit are used interchangeably. A strategy center is a business area with an external market-place for goods or services and one which can independently determine objectives and execute strategies. The key point here is that in order to be a strategy center, you must be selling to an outside marketplace. For example, consider Sambo's, a coffee shop chain that operates a food distribution system. The distribution system services only that chain's needs and does not distribute food or products to other businesses. The distribution system would not, then, be a strategy center. Rather, this food distribution network would be part of the restaurant strategy center and we could develop plans for the distribution company as part of the restaurant chain's plans. If the distribution system had sufficient sales to outside firms, it would need to develop its own plans.

In determining the strategy centers within the corporation a number of tests can be applied. Competitors, prices, customers, quality or style, and substitutability are clues used to determine if businesses are separate business units or are part of one strategy center. When areas within corporations tend to be different on these clues, there generally are a number of different businesses.

Probably the best test in defining natural strategy centers is one of divestment or liquidation. That is, can the business, if divested from the corporation, stand alone and do the products that make the business have synergy?

Planning Is a Data-Based Activity

The second principle of strategic planning is that planning is a data-based activity. By data-based we mean based on fact. Information needs to be gathered on several levels. At the macro level planners need to look at the trends in the political, social, demographic, and economic arena. For example, much has been written about the maturation of the United States. In the next decade the number of 18-24 year olds (the group that traditionally has been the target customer for and the prime employee of major segments of the fast-food industry) will decline by over four million people. This trend will have a major impact on the fast-food industry in the coming years.

At the second level, we try to gather information about the industry and the market. By the industry we mean the firms competed against and by the market we mean the people who buy. Finally, we collect information about the strategy center itself. Here, we look for such things as how is this business doing relative to its competitors, what is the cost structure of the business, what are the financial trends for this business over the past few years.

The result of this analysis is a data bank about the industry and the trends that are likely to impact it in the future. As a result of this data collection we examine the macro changes likely to impact the strategy center, review industry trends, analyze competitors, develop the history of the business unit, investigate product profitability, and identify some major issues that will be facing both the planning unit and the industry over the planning horizon. The time frame is generally back five to ten years and forward approximately five years. Looking backwards and removing inflation's impact often gives surprising insight into a company's real performance.

Business Is Not Random

After identifying the strategy centers and collecting information, the third principle of planning is that business is not random. This is fundamental to planning because if business is merely a random event there is no need to plan. There are, however, discernible and predictable patterns of competition and performance. There are reasons why some businesses are successful and other competitors are failures. Success or failure can, to a large extent, be determined by analyzing the maturity of the industry in which we compete and our competitive position. According to the product life cycle hypothesis, products start out with low sales, build rapidly, and then fall off. Industries go through a similar life cycle. The maturation process can be characterized by four phases: embryonic, growth, mature, and aging. A number of factors provide clues in determining the maturity of a given industry: such clues as sales growth rate and growth potential; the breadth of the product line; number of competitors; share stability; share distribution; technology; and other relevant factors. Industries generally start out embryonic, pass through growth and maturity, and eventually are characterized as aging. These four phases are generally of unequal duration; and industry may be embryonic for a long period of time, pass quickly through growth, experience a protracted mature stage, and age very rapidly if replaced by new technology. This entire maturation process can take many decades or simply a few years, depending upon the industry.

These industry maturity clues can be applied to a variety of United States industries to develop the chart of examples shown in Figure 4.1. Home computers or genetic engineering are good examples of embryonic industries. They are as yet unproven, but the potential is enormous. Word processing equipment and home video products are good representatives of growth. They are witnessing a tremendous sales explosion and product innovation. Steel and tires represent mature industries. They are very cyclical and are driven by the general business environment. The fast food industry recently passed from the growth stage to the mature stage. Ship building and rail car manufacturing are examples of aging industries. Sales are decreasing as these industries are replaced by substitute products. As shown in Figure 4.1 certain industries move backwards and forwards. Industries can go through rapid changes in their maturity or reverse the maturation process due to one of four reasons: (1) a legislative change as demonstrated by the deregulation of air passenger service; (2) a supply interruption such as the oil embargo that moved coal mining back from aging into mature; (3) a social or attitudinal change, such as that caused by the incident at Three Mile Island which moved the nuclear control rod industry from a mid-growth to a mid-aging industry virtually overnight; and (4) a technological change or breakthrough demonstrated by the application of LED-LCD digital technology applied to wristwatches in the mid to late 1970's.

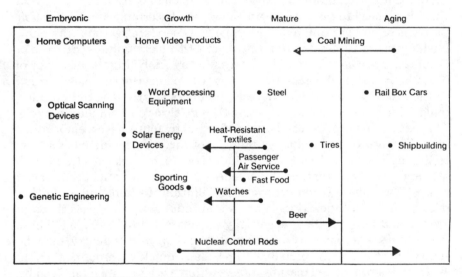

FIG. 4.1.   EXAMPLES OF INDUSTRY MATURITY

The important point is that there is no good or bad industry maturity position. A particular stage of maturity becomes bad only if the expectations or the strategies adopted by a business in that industry are inappropriate for that stage of maturity.

The second factor to look at to determine a business's strategic condition is its competitive position. Competitive position is a summary of the strategy center's strengths and weaknesses relative to those of its competitors and the bases of competition. While many planning models suggest that market share is the sole measure of competitive position other factors are also important. With our clients we develop a list of the things that need to be done in order to succeed in that industry. These key success variables are called the bases of competition. Typically, we find three or four key driving forces. While market share is important, there are other bases of competition. For example, in the national fast-food hamburger chain segment, a primary basis of competition is penetration—the competitor with the most units and largest market share at the local, regional, or national level can generate the greatest awareness and trial. Great penetration generally provides greater buying power and an increased ability to finance projects and functions. However, a second, very important basis of competition is the chain's concept. It needs to be broadly appealing and clearly communicated. Many regional and national chains will face increasing difficulties in the future. Even though they may have good market shares in their heritage markets, their concepts are not clearly defined. A "me too" concept will not work in the future. The same need for unit penetration and a clear concept is equally important in the hospitality industry.

The competitive position for all the relevant competitors in the industry can be observed by examining the operations and marketing know-how of individual competitors, the management system and the managers, and any special factors that may give one competitor a unique advantage. This competitive information can then be summarized by grading each competitor as better, the same as, or weaker than us on each basis of competition. These grades are summarized and each competitor and ourselves are placed on a continuum of competitive positions divided into five categories: dominant, strong, favorable, tenable, and weak.

After determining the industry maturity and the relevant competitive position of each competitor within the industry, competitors are arrayed on a matrix like that shown in Figure 4.2. Each box within the matrix has normative or generally applicable strategies associated with it. For example, a strong competitor in a growth industry will have markedly different strategies than a weak competitor in the same industry. Similarly, a strong competitor in a growth industry will have different strategies than a strong competitor in an aging industry. Consequently, the analysis of the business unit in terms of its strategic condition — its industry maturity and competitive position — has implications for strategy determination.

The matrix in Figure 4.2 represents the fast food industry. Some of these companies have been surprised when careful analysis of industry data indicated that the industry had reached the mature phase. By analyzing their performance on the basis of competition it could be suggested that McDonald's is in a strong position, Burger King and Wendy's are in favorable positions, and the larger regional and local

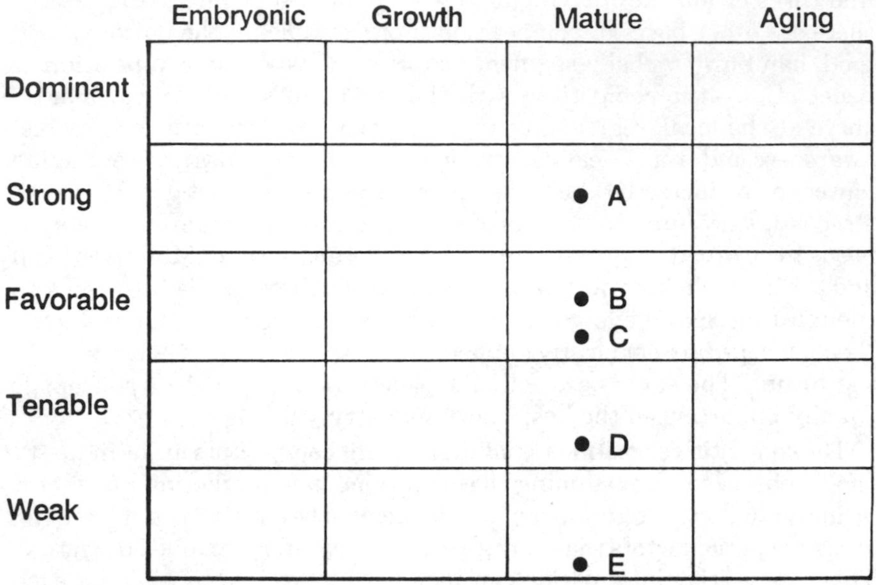

	Embryonic	Growth	Mature	Aging
Dominant				
Strong			• A	
Favorable			• B • C	
Tenable			• D	
Weak			• E	

FIG. 4.2.   COMPETITIVE DISPLAY

chains fall in the tenable and weak ranges.

The weaker your competitive position and the more mature your industry, the fewer are the strategic options. Figure 4.3 depicts what are the relevant strategic thrusts for businesses given their industry maturity and competitive position. As the industry matures, weaker competitors abandon the business. Tenable players, as an industry matures, generally are forced to turn around their business or abandon it. Favorable players are forced to select niches or develop their business selectively. Strong and dominant players generally have the widest range of options in terms of strategies open to them.

There Are a Limited Number of Strategies

In selecting strategies, the fourth principle of strategic planning applies: there are a relatively limited number of options. By strategy we mean a series of coordinated actions that direct resources. The resources a business unit has available to it are time, money, and people. In selecting from this relatively limited number of strategies, a business must consider its industry maturity and its competitive position.

We have developed 20 generic strategy options for a business in the food service industry. After being involved in a substantial number of strategic planning assignments for clients in all segments of the food service industry, we are fairly confident that these represent all of the options available to any competitor in the industry. These strategies focus on marketing, production, distribution, and whether to invest in or harvest the business. An example of each follows.

A marketing strategy might be initial market development as depicted in Figure 4.4. By that we mean to invest in creating primary demand for a new food service concept. Generally, this requires significant expense budgets, and some sort of marketing or technological advantage. It usually results in a negative cash flow due to high start-up costs. Companies pursuing an initial market development strategy generally capture market share. The risks associated with this strategy include significant expense exposure and the possibility of an incorrect de-

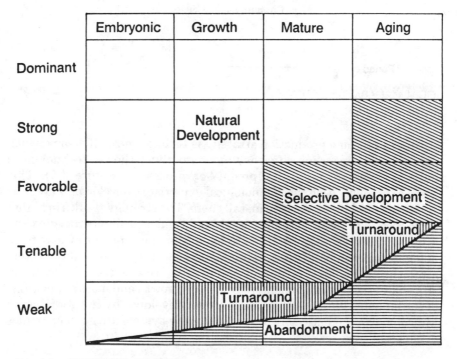

FIG. 4.3.   STRATEGIC OPTIONS

termination of supply and demand for the product. This strategy is typically undertaken by businesses that compete in embryonic or early growth industries. Wendy's International undertook an initial market development strategy with the four-unit Sister's Chicken and Biscuit chain they purchased.

Marketing Strategy:
Initial Concept Development

To Invest in Creating Primary Demand for a Brand New Concept

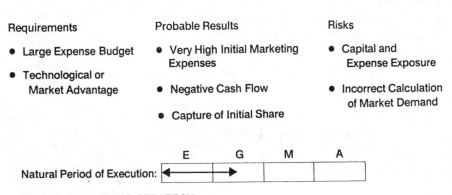

Requirements

- Large Expense Budget
- Technological or Market Advantage

Probable Results

- Very High Initial Marketing Expenses
- Negative Cash Flow
- Capture of Initial Share

Risks

- Capital and Expense Exposure
- Incorrect Calculation of Market Demand

Natural Period of Execution:

| E | G | M | A |

FIG. 4.4.   MARKETING STRATEGY

An example of a production strategy is technological efficiency which is to improve operating efficiency or productivity though technological improvements in plant, equipment, or processes (Figure 4.5). This strategy requires both the technological expertise to develop new systems and the capital investment to install them. The strategy results in higher fixed costs, but lower variable costs should generate higher margins and profits. Many firms are content to leave the development of new technologies to someone else and to implement the new equipment or system after the technology is proven. Generally we see the technological efficiency strategy implemented in the late growth and mature positions of the industry life cycle. The chain broiler developed by Burger King or McDonald's automatic soft drink portioning system are good examples of this strategy.

Production Strategy: Technological Efficiency

To Improve Operating Efficiency Through Technological Improvements in Plant, Equipment or Processes

Requirements	Probable Results	Risks
• Capital Investment	• Increased Fixed Costs	• Application of Technology May Not be Appropriate
• Technological Capabilities	• Decreased Variable Costs	
	• Increased Profits	
	• Little Impact on Sales	

Natural Period of Execution:

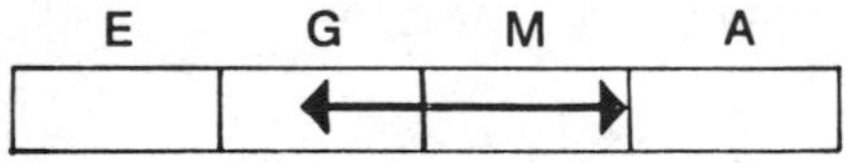

E   G   M   A

FIG. 4.5.   PRODUCTION STRATEGY

An example of a distribution strategy is market rationalizing where a firm prunes back the system to develop a more effective network. The requirements, results, and risks associated with it are indicated in Figure 4.6. Generally, this strategy seems to be natural in the very late part of the growth stage through maturity and probably mid-way through aging as companies seek efficiencies of operation to maximize cash flow. Jack-In-The-Box embarked upon a significant market rationalization emphasis when they decided to prune back their system by concentrating their efforts west of the Mississippi and closing units in the east. This was an effort to increase profitability and enhance their competitive position.

The fourth strategy area of investment or harvest (Figure 4.7) might best be characterized by an example of the Little Jewel strategy. With the Little Jewel strategy there is an attempt to strip the business to its most profitable piece, and re-invest the proceeds in successful operations. It requires cost-cutting analysis, decisions and commitment on the part of management, and divestment. It usually results in lower sales but increased margins. The risks associated with this strategy are that a company would abandon a unit or a portion of its business that could be turned around and contribute or it may result in a premature milking of the business. Typically, we see this strategy implemented by companies

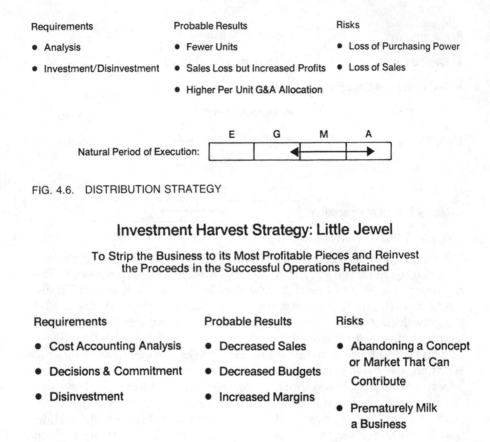

Distribution Strategy: Market Rationalization

To Prune the System to a More Effective Network; This May
Include Closing Unprofitable Units or Dropping Selected
Geographic Areas

Requirements

- Analysis
- Investment/Disinvestment

Probable Results

- Fewer Units
- Sales Loss but Increased Profits
- Higher Per Unit G&A Allocation

Risks

- Loss of Purchasing Power
- Loss of Sales

Natural Period of Execution:

E   G   M   A

FIG. 4.6.   DISTRIBUTION STRATEGY

Investment Harvest Strategy: Little Jewel

To Strip the Business to its Most Profitable Pieces and Reinvest
the Proceeds in the Successful Operations Retained

Requirements

- Cost Accounting Analysis
- Decisions & Commitment
- Disinvestment

Probable Results

- Decreased Sales
- Decreased Budgets
- Increased Margins

Risks

- Abandoning a Concept
  or Market That Can
  Contribute
- Prematurely Milk
  a Business

Natural Period of Execution:

E   G   M   A

FIG. 4.7.   INVESTMENT HARVEST STRATEGY

in the latter stages of maturity or aging and by competitively weaker
players within an industry. The Saga Corporation, in their institutional
feeding business, has been embarking upon a Little Jewel strategy as
they are slowly withdrawing from some institutional feeding and college

feeding situations. They are concentrating funds and manpower on more growth-oriented institutional feeding situations or in other businesses within the corporation.

Business Is More Condition Than Ambition Driven

The selection of strategy by a business unit is based upon the last principle: strategy selection should be more condition-driven than ambition-driven, i.e., a condition in which a business finds itself should determine the strategies the business pursues more than the ambitions of its managers.

Planning the goal setting must include analysis of both the internal and external conditions. For example, the managers of Del Taco may have had the ambition to become number one in the fast food Mexican segment. They acted on the ambition and built more stores in a shorter period of time than had ever been done before. However, they did not have adequate staff to open new units and volume at new stores never reached budgeted levels. The conditions Del Taco faced, both in the marketplace and their own internal manpower and financial performance, suggested that a strategy to become number one in the industry would be very difficult to complete successfully.

Consequently, Del Taco has basically retrenched and is concentrating turning around the business by improving existing units in current markets and not building new units or developing new markets. Thus, the managers at Del Taco analyzed the internal conditions of the company and the external conditions of the competitive environment. Based on that analysis, they determined new strategies and selected a revised course for the future of their company.

Strategy selection is a subjective management function that attempts to balance risk and reward. It is an analytical framework to assist managers in charting a long-term direction for their business. It is not a substitute for good management but, rather, one of the many tools a good manager must use.

It has been our experience that a business can implement only a relatively limited number of strategies. If a business is pursuing too many strategies, the chances are that none of them will be implemented well. This is one instance where less can give you more.

Strategic planning is a powerful management tool that is based on five simple principles that have been demonstrated with examples from the food service industry. This same process can be applied to any industry or company.

5

Corporate Strategic Planning for the Hospitality Industry: A Contingency Approach

Arie Reichel, Ph.D.

Today's business environment requires organizations to be flexible, adaptable as well as continually planning for the future. Mere adaptive or reactive approaches to economic, socio-political and other environmental changes often result in mediocre or low performance and in some cases, obsolescence and bankruptcy. Corporate success, on the other hand, is often associated with a future-oriented and systematic process of strategy formulation and implementation.

The intent of this paper is to present a strategic planning contingency framework for the corporate sector of the hospitality industry, with a special focus on future forecasts. The need for planning in this particular industry is apparent, as one must consider the high degree of price elasticity of demand and the high vulnerability to socio-economic and political trends, such as recession and local citizen unrest.

THE NEED FOR STRATEGIC PLANNING

Long range strategic planning (LRSP) has become one of the most widely discussed management concepts in the last decade. As noted by Rothchild (1980) over 300 companies increased the size of their planning staff by thirty percent over the past two years, and these same firms expect to increase their staffs by an additional sixteen percent within the next two years. In addition, a plethora of articles and books, written both by academics and practitioners in this area, has recently been published.

The systematic nature of the LRSP process, in addition to better corporate performance, is often associated with the reduction of environmental uncertainty, a proactive approach to managing the external environment, a methodical way for setting objectives and a high degree of coordination among organizational units and departments.

Reducing Environment Uncertainties

Rapid changes in the economy, government intervention, technological developments, sophisticated promotion methods — all seem to contribute a great deal to environmental complexity and uncertainty faced by top management in almost every sphere of business activity. A well formulated and successfully implemented strategic plan reduces uncertainty in several ways:

1. First, it requires an ongoing process of studying the environment of the corporation. This process, often referred to as "scanning" provides managers with information about events and trends that may affect them, whether directly or indirectly. This includes data about major competitors, availability of new technology, changes in public tastes, etc.
2. Second, in addition to data accumulation, LRSP assists organizations in exploring the consequences of various environmental conditions. Specifically, events or trends are categorized as being either threats or opportunities from the viewpoint of the organization. For example, a corporation doing business in the resorts industry may investigate the potential effects of cuts in tax rates on its revenues, or higher prices for gasoline may change the pattern of domestic tourism.

   Again, this can be considered either as a threat or an opportunity: a threat for a plan that depends heavily on long distance travelers and an opportunity for one operating closer to major cities.

Thus, LRSP serves as an early warning and monitoring system to alert the firm to potential environmental opportunities and threats. It provides the firm with ample lead time to formulate strategies to respond to anticipated changes, to "sell" these plans to managers at various levels of the organization, and to allocate resources necessary for implementing the selected strategy (Ang and Chua 1979).

Proactive Approach to Managing the Environment

In addition to its contributions to reduce environment uncertainties and to its early warning system, LRSP is the key factor in facilitating the adoption of a corporate proactive approach toward environmental conditions. Rather than just responding to external stimuli, corporations can actually "invent a future" (Steiner 1979). Top management may envision a desirable future and then develop strategies, plans and subsequent actions to mold their environment in order to create more favorable conditions for their profitability, growth, and survival. Thus, executives could take a more active role in the development of legislation favorable to their industry.

Objective Setting

One of the most important features of LRSP is its emphasis on setting organizational goals and objectives. While intuitive decision making may be associated with successful performance, it is often restricted to the short run. Given environmental and organizational complexities, success and survival in the long run relies predominantly upon a clear and systematic definition of goals and objectives. LRSP encourages executives to become more future oriented, and to avoid "muddling through" or utilizing a short run incremental approach to managing corporations. The necessity of defining the desired situation of the firm for the next five or ten years and the efforts to close the potential gap between the objective and the current situation results in overall organizational definition or direction, goals and results-oriented objectives. Managers at various levels in an organization that practices LRSP are constantly aware of objectives and performance criteria (Hofer and Schendel 1978; Odiorne 1979).

Coordination Among Business Units

In addition to objectives setting, LRSP facilitates better coordination among both business units within the corporation and various departments within each unit. For example, while discussing and formulating strategies, the food and beverages department is more likely to become aware of the needs, goals and objectives of its sales and marketing department and thus will be able to better coordinate their functions then if LRSP was not employed. This coordination also reduces the risk of misallocating resources. A well formulated strategic plan defines organizational priorities, thus assisting top management in allocating funds in accordance with the potential contribution, strengths and weaknesses of each business unit. A clear strategic decision to liquidate a specific property within the next two years will prevent unnecessary investment in upgrading its facilities.

In conclusion, LRSP enables top management to analyze both their present and future environment, to adopt a proactive approach in order to affect external events, and to better manage internal processes by setting performance objectives and coordinating among various levels and units within the organization. The merits of formal planning are well summarized by Vancil and Lorange (1975):

There is little doubt that formalizing the planning process is worthwhile, it ensures that managers at all levels will devote some time to strategic thinking, and it guarantees each of them an audience for his ideas. While formal strategic planning cannot guarantee good ideas, it can increase the odds sufficiently to yield a handsome payoff.

THE CONTINGENCY APPROACH TO STRATEGIC PLANNING

Striving to avoid environmental uncertainty, top management may formulate one strategic plan and enthusiastically adhere to it without realizing that some of the major assumptions or predictions are no longer valid. Moreover, in some cases, managers become "prisoners of their own strategy" — not being able to change their thoughts and actions. This may result in failing to meet periodic goals, and even in a threat to the survival of the corporation.

The contingency approach to strategic planning is based on the premise that even the most elegant and elaborated plan may become obsolete when environmental conditions change. Thus, it is necessary to develop a portfolio of referral blueprints, each based on different sets of future trends. This framework consists of the following phases:

1. Formulation of performance objectives, both at the corporate and business levels.
2. The construction of various future scenarios. Each would represent a different combination of economic, political, social and technological variables.
3. Based on the performance objectives, each scenario would serve as a foundation for a strategic plan. By the way of analogy, the various plans are alternative highways leading to the same destination. The selection of the appropriate highway depends on: (a) its conditions (environmental threats and opportunities); and (b) the ability of the corporation to move along a certain highway, taking into account its strengths and weaknesses.
4. Finally, top management must be committed to the implementation and administration of the selected strategy.

Setting Corporate and Business Objectives

Setting common objectives is one of the most important functions of the management process. Objectives serve as indicators of both future direction and actual performance of the organization. Well defined corporate objectives depict where the corporation is expected to be at a particular time in the future. It is also a performance criterion for top managers, a means to evaluate their accomplishments.

In long range strategic planning, corporate level objectives represent the overall direction and performance criteria of a diversified multi-business organization. Business level objectives, on the other hand, refer to the goals of a firm producing one product or a line of similar products with one particular market, for example, catering to only one distinct segment of hotel guests. Having several types of business, i.e., maintaining both "grand hotels" and popular motels, requires the formulation of corporate level objectives *and* business-level objectives for each unit.

As noted by Odiorne (1979), objectives should be challenging, realistic and measurable. Lacking these attributes, they cannot serve as motivators and performance criteria for managers. Goals such as "our aim is to satisfy our guests" may indicate top management philosophy, organizational mission, or simply a shrewd public relations campaign. On the other hand, a corporate objective of an annual 20% return on investment for the next five years is clear, measurable, and does not leave any grey areas for speculations.

Given well formulated corporate and business objectives, the next step entails formulating various future scenarios.

FORECASTING AND SCENARIO BUILDING

One of the most striking developments in managerial thought and action is the increasing awareness of the paramount role of a systematic study of future trends. As noted by McCarthy et al. (1979), regardless of the techniques or procedures being used, the main objective is to determine, as accurately as possible, the future state or condition of the corporate environment, or any segment of it.

It should be noted, however, that there are fundamental limitations in confronting an unknown future:

1. We cannot always be certain of future purposes, objectives and strategies.
2. We may not even know what questions to ask.
3. We may not know crucial cause-and-effect relationships, etc. (Lebell and Krasner 1977).

Probably the most useful means of organizing and systemizing long range planning in organizations is by the formulation of various future scenarios. A scenario can be described as a method used to explore the probability of future trends and changes in the firm's external environment. "Scenarios state: 'This is the way it will be; this is what is going to happen; this is what the situation will be at that future time'." (McCarthy *et al.* 1979).

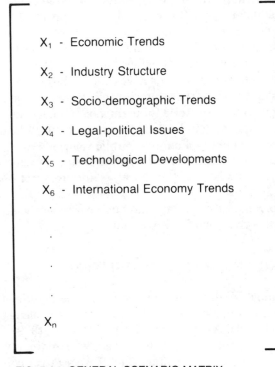

X_1 - Economic Trends

X_2 - Industry Structure

X_3 - Socio-demographic Trends

X_4 - Legal-political Issues

X_5 - Technological Developments

X_6 - International Economy Trends

.

.

.

.

X_n

FIG. 5.1.   GENERAL SCENARIO MATRIX

The first step in constructing scenarios is the identification of relevant environmental variable. Most scenarios usually consist of economic, legal-political, social and technological variables. Each industry or corporation selects different dimensions within each of the groups of variables.

Figure 5.1 depicts a general matrix format of a scenario. The scenario consists of several variables (X^1, X^2,. . .Xn), each depicting a major environmental force that may affect the firm either directly or indirectly.

Economic Forecasts

This factor should include general information about business cycles, possible recession or depressions as well as more specific data relevant to the hospitality industry. Thus, one would consider forecasting the following variables:

- Inflation and interest rates.
- Availability of consumer credit.
- Proportion of disposable income (especially important in the case of family vacations).
- Corporate slack — the tendency of major corporations to drastically curtail travel expenses when profits fall.
- Unemployment levels — regional as well as as national.

In addition, information about inputs and raw material should be included in the calculations, such as:

- Energy costs
- Costs of construction and renovation
- Food prices
- Labor costs

Industry Structure

This element in the scenario matrix represents predicting trends within the hospitality industry. It includes an assessment of potential strategies of direct competitors: those offering similar product or service. For instance, chain x, which caters to middle-class travelers and salesmen, puts an emphasis on uniformity of services. In addition one may seek information about market share and competitive positions of rival firms, trends towards diversificatiion and extent of foreign competition. Obtaining this type of information often requires some surveillance activities specifically trying to acquire as much data as possible about competitors, their customers or markets served, anticipated changes in service offered, primary policies and marketing techniques, including advertising and promotional tactics.

Some of the questions that should be included are: Are there major barriers to entering this industry? Is it likely that new firms will find this industry attractive? Are we to expect mergers and acquisitions? Is the industry moving toward an oligopolistic structure?

Another variable that has to be analyzed is the availability of trained employees. Note that hospitality employees may be pulled toward higher paying jobs in other industries after being trained at great expense.

Socio-cultural and Demographic Trends

These trends are probably the most crucial force to be considered by executives in the hospitality industry. Given that demand is very sensitive to price and disposable income, it is crucial for top management to assess the possible changes in the following factors:

- The population of the relevant segment (current and potential guests)
- Numbers of persons in each household
- Geographic distribution
- Patterns of travels and locations (whether annual, semi-annual, etc.)
- Proportion of disposable and discretionary income
- Changes in life-style, and general sociodemographic trends such as later marriages, fewer children and higher divorce rates are often associated with more leisure time and increased travel. Changes in the median age of the population may have a bearing upon the demand for a variety of services designed for a certain age group.

In addition, firms should examine changes in the values of the public. As noted by Wilson (1974), "It should be obvious that social moods, personal attitude and political action have become dynamic and determinative forces for business." This is true because of both external and internal impacts on the firm.

Externally, the impact on firms is manifested by means of government control over business and current and potential customers' attitudes toward business, as will be further explained later in the paper.

Internally, socio-cultural and demographic trends are reflected in employees' values, attitudes and behavior. The attitude of employees toward guests can significantly affect profitability and survival of hotels. Maintenance of rooms and quality of services (room, food and beverages) are crucial determinants of consumer satisfaction and loyalty to a specific hotel or a chain. Social unrest is another manifestation of employees attitudes, as was recently evident in several resort areas around the world. Thus, forecasts about such trends should be included in any scenario for strategic planning in the hospitality industry.

Legal-Political Issues

Legal-political issues are often referred to as the "softer" area, vs. the "hard" data of economic and technological forecasting. However, legal issues are of paramount importance to the hospitality industry, as well as to any other sphere of corporate venture. Constraints on corporate growth, corporate governance (accountability, disclosure of information) minimum wage laws, dealing with growing demands for job enlargement and more equality of opportunities, pressures from government agencies and unions, class action suits and the whole spectrum of consumerism, environmentalism, etc. (Wilson 1974) are but a few of the topics covered in the legal-political category. Moreover, EPA and OSHA cannot be ignored.

Any changes in the tax deduction policies for business travel and entertainment may have a significant effect on the hospitality industry. According to Serrin (1981), some estimate that if a proposal to eliminate deductions for business entertainment were passed, it would mean a 25% reduction in jobs in the New York restaurant industry, which employs 150,000 workers.

Technological Developments

The fifth factor in the matrix should include data about technological developments that may affect firms in the hospitality industry. Recent developments in computers, for example, changed the whole process of internal auditing in hotels, in addition to its reservation system. Moreover, several software programs available enable hotels to plan ahead capacity of rooms, manpower needed for maintenance and even to estimate the number of meals to be served by food and beverages departments.

Top management should always be alert to developments of technology that might be applicable to the industry. While it is true that there is usually sufficient lead time to enable firms to adopt new technologies and adjust to the resulting organizational changes, constant monitoring and forecasting technology will assure that a successful corporation maintains its position in the industry, and even increase its market share.

Internal Economic Trends

The last two decades have been characterized by increasing economic interdependence among the more and the lesser industrially developed nations. Rapid changes in the price of oil and gold have been closely associated with fluctuations in the value of the U.S. dollar, as well as other currencies. This, in turn, has significantly affected patterns of travel and travellers' expenditures. The flow of foreign tourists into the U.S. and their expenditures seem to be correlated with the relative value of the U.S. dollar. Thus, when the value of the dollar decreases, foreign travellers are more likely to select the United States above other countries, as their vacation destination. Goods and services offered here tend to be cheaper than in those countries with "stronger" currencies.

In addition to the influx in foreign tourists, a decline in the value of U.S. currency will keep Americans at home. Europe and other parts of the world seem to be beyond the means of many travellers. Consequently more Americans will travel within the United States.[1]

This inverse relationship between the value of the dollar and both foreign and domestic tourism expenditures is also evident when the value of the dollar increases. American travellers will be encouraged to spend their vacations abroad, while foreign travellers will find the U.S. to be relatively expensive.

In addition to international economic trends and the aforementioned scenario factors, each firm should consider other significant variables that may influence its operations either directly or indirectly. While most of the factors discussed so far can be shared by almost any organization in the tourism industry, and in other industries as well, each firm should consider introducing other factors, based on their particular economic, socio-political environment. Note that X7 through Xn in Figure 5.1 represent factors relevant to a specific firm. The decision to include these factors and their compositions is an integral part of the long range strategic planning process.

HOW TO GENERATE SCENARIOS

Most corporations utilizing scenarios for strategic planning employ experts who are first requested to construct a list of environmental variables, i.e., technological, economic, socio-demographic, etc., and then to comment on the likelihood of the occurrence of each event or trend.

Thus, the first step involves the selection of relevant variables to be included in the general matrix. While the matrices for most industries would probably include similar variables, it is the responsibility of each firm to ensure that their significant environmental variables are well represented in their matrix. For example, it is imperative for business in the hospitality industry to include information about patterns of travel and percentages of disposable income. This would be less relevant to the steel industry, to which Japanese competition is a major environmental constraint that will not be absent from any scenario.

---

[1]It should be noted, however, that this trend is general. It is possible to distinguish between various segments of domestic tourism expenditures who may react differently to the fluctuations in the value of the U.S. dollar. For a segmentation model of domestic expenditures see: Pizam and Reichel 1979.

The selection of these factors is the responsibility of top management, the unit of planning or the group of executives who are assigned to serve as an advisory board. In some cases, this task may be assigned to an outside consultant.

The second step involves the discussion and analysis of various scenarios. This is usually done by assigning different values to the variables, and the likelihood of occurrence of each. This enables the elimination of scenarios whose likelihood of occurrence is perceived as very small. Left with a probable scenario, one may choose to apply the method of contrasting scenarios, for example, a scenario that indicates major increases in unemployment vs. the one that assumes very low rates of unemployment.

INCORPORATING SCENARIOS INTO THE STRATEGIC PLAN

A careful formulation of scenarios is just one step in the long range strategic plan of a firm. There are several phases of the process, namely setting corporate and business level objectives, and them designing contingency plans based on the various scenarios. Figure 5.2 depicts the contingency approach to strategic planning.

Although it is an ongoing process, special emphasis should be placed on the objective setting stage. We defined objectives, as noted earlier, to serve as guidelines for performance and determine the direction toward which the efforts of the organization are being channeled.

The next stage consists of data accumulation, analysis and forecasting. Specifically, this is the stage when the scenarios are generated. The time horizon of the forecast should be correlated with the time dimension of the objectives. If one of the goals of a specific chain is to reach 90% of occupancy ten years from now, it is clear that forecasts should be made for at least the next ten years. One may attempt to contrast scenarios by choosing a "pessimistic" one and an "optimistic" one. The bright vs. murky futures serve as the contingent variables. Accordingly, at least two strategic plans should be formulated. A third one may represent the middle of the road approach.

In selecting the optimal strategy for each scenario, it is imperative to place long term objectives as the destination. By way of analogy, the various strategies available both at the corporate and the business levels are alternative highways leading to the same destination. The selection of the appropriate highway depends on (a) its conditions — in the strategic planning process, environmental threats and opportunities and (b) the condition of the car and the driver — the ability of the organization

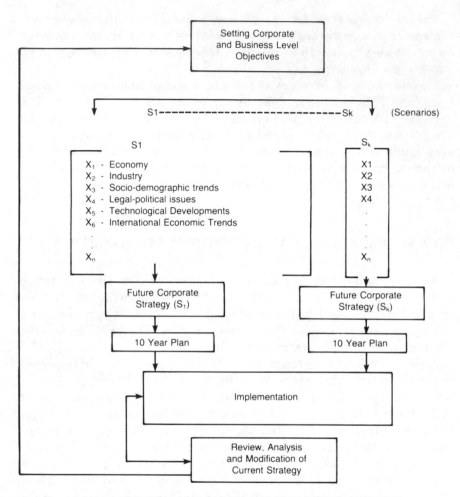

FIG. 5.2.   CONTINGENCY CORPORATE STRATEGIC PLANNING PROCESS

and its top management to move along a certain strategy, continually taking into account their strengths and weaknesses.

The plan includes a statement about services or/and products to be offered and the markets intended to be served. It is essential to specify the resources needed in order to implement each strategy, how to get them, and the way these resources will be allocated within the firm. Note that the two or three alternative plans share the same objective. They may vary, however, in terms of the products or services and with respect to available resources. A plan based on an optimistic scenario may suggest an expansion program that entails the acquisition of numerous properties. On the other hand, a plan based on a pessimistic forecast could suggest a concentration strategy emphasizing maintenance of present facilities and services without any acquisitions. A third alternative plan may specify a limited expansion within the United States only.

IMPLEMENTATION

One of the most important steps in the process of LRSP is its actual implementation. The likelihood of its success depends on applying several principles of management by commitment.

First, it is necessary that top management create the appropriate atmosphere needed to convey the seriousness of the process. Thus, they ought to express their belief in LRSP and to fully support the efforts required for ongoing planning, implementation, and maintenance. This may entail the training of executives to be more future oriented and able to formulate long range objectives and performance criteria.

Whether the process of planning begins at the top of the corporate headquarters or at the business or functional levels, it is of paramount importance that top executives manifest their full support of the efforts and resources involved in the entire process. Accumulation of data for the development of scenarios, setting objectives and analyzing the external environment and the strengths and weaknesses of the firm, require time, attention and devotion. Therefore, it must constitute an intergral part of the job expectation of every manager. A commitment to the planning process should be a key factor in a decision about pay raises and promotion. The actual attitude of top management is often expressed in the reward system of the firm, as opposed to formal statements. Rewarding managers not only for meeting objectives but also for supporting the planning process reflects the degree of commitment of top management.

Second, a smooth implementation of LRSP requires overcoming resistance to change. This phenomenon has been the cause of failure of numerous managerial innovations and organizational changes. Phychological predispositions and a fear of erosion of one's power base and authority combine to create a resistance to change which is a major threat to the introduction of any new system. It seems that a great deal of the resistance can be overcome when one is fully informed and acutely involved in the change process. Therefore, managers at all levels should be familiarized with the basic assumptions, principles and techniques of

the organizational change. By its very nature, LRSP is a type of participative management. This participation decreases the likelihood of
resistance to change and sabotage and encourages managers to actively
contribute to the success of the method.

In summary, the attitudes of top management, their involvement, the
long range oriented performance criteria they set, their commitment and
rewards for devotion will increase the likelihood of a successful adaptation
of LRSP. Non-committed attitudes and behavior, rewards directed
towards the short run performance and failure to explain the principles of
strategy formulation and implementation will result in failure, frustration
and deeply rooted negative attitudes toward LRSP in particular, and
other organizational changes in general.

SUMMARY AND CONCLUSIONS

The intent of this article was to present a strategic planning contingency framework for the corporate sector of the hospitality industry.
Strategic planning is often associated with the reduction of environmental
uncertainty, a proactive approach to managing the external environment,
a methodological way for setting corporate, business and functional level
objectives and a high degree of coordination among organizational units.

The contingency approach to strategic planning is based on the premise
that even the most elegant and elaborated plan may become obsolete
when environmental conditions change. The article suggests that a
portfolio of at least two long range strategic plans, each based on a
different scenario, be developed.

The planning process begins with the formulation of performance
objectives at the various levels of the organization. A well formulated set
of objectives depicts the overall direction and performance criteria of the
firm.

The next step entails the construction of various future scenarios.
Each scenario is a combination of factors including economic trends,
industry structure, socio-demographic trends, legal-political issues,
technological developments and international economic trends. Each
factor consists of numerous variables presenting forecasts about probable future events. Economic forecasts for the hospitality industry include
information about inflation and interest rates, unemployment levels,
energy and labor costs, and any other relevant variables. In addition to
the basic six factors, it has been suggested that each firm will add more
factors considered as meaningful for its long range plans.

In order to effectively manage all the information gathered, it is recommended to select at least two major opposing scenarios, as well as a middle of the road approach. Predicted on the performance objectives, each scenario serves as a base for the strategic plan. The selection of the appropriate strategy depends on objectives, the state of the firm, and its environment.

Finally, it is crucial to ensure smooth implementation. This requires total commitment of top management. These executives are required not not only to verbally support the planning process, but also to ensure that the rewards system takes into consideration both long run performance goals and the involvement of managers in the process.

Successful formulation and implementation of a strategic plan demands constant review, analysis and, if necessary, modification of current strategy. This is an ongoing process that requires executives in the hospitality industry to be on the alert, to keep examining their objectives, analyze their company, and scan their environment. In addition, top management has to train managers and employees at all levels to be aware of the changes and to make suggestions. Together they will practice future performance oriented participative management.

Management by Objectives—Update

George S. Odiorne, Ph.D.

In brief, the system of Management by Objectives (MBO) can be described as:

A process whereby the superior and subordinate managers of an organization jointly identify its common goals, define each individual's major areas of responsibility in terms of results expected, and use these measures as guides for operating the unit and assessing the contribution of each of its members.

The logical beginning point in the organization for MBO is at the top. The sequence in which objectives will be set and reviewed comprises a rudimentary calendar of events which occur in the organization over a two-year cycle on a continuing basis.

HOW TO SET OBJECTIVES

The first step in goal setting is to define the ordinary calendar of events which must occur in the organization where MBO is to become the prevailing management system. This entails, as is shown in Table 6.1, some events that occur prior to the beginning of the target year and some events which will occur during that year.

Management by Anticipation

This term is used to describe those goal setting actions which are required of staff departments such as personnel, accounting, legal, traffic, finance, controller, and other staff functions.

TABLE 6.1.   A RUDIMENTARY MBO STRATEGIC PLANNING CYCLE FOR BUSINESS
OR OTHER ORGANIZATION ON A CALENDAR YEAR OPERATION BASIS

Date	Event	Comments
July 1	Annual edition of the Five Year Plan and review of prior year's Five Year Plan.	Responsibility of the top man and all major functional (staff) heads, assembled by planning department.
October 1	Budgetary submission to budget decision group (for the following year).	Upward from all units starting with sales forecast, cost estimates, and profit forecast to budgeteer.
	Review, revise, approve final budget figures.	Executive Committee
January 1	Start the new budget year, release resources.	Issue detailed, approved financial targets in final form.
January 15 to February 1	Completion of individual operational objectives at all levels.	Sets standards for managerial performance for the year.
	Annual goals conference by managers of departments.	To share goals and devise teamwork.
	Annual Message of the President.	To give a challenge.
April–July 1 October 1	Quarterly reviews of individual results against goals and adjustments as required.	All managers at all levels.
April 15	Audits–Including program	Staff Departments
Monthly	*Meetings of the Executive and Finance committee to note exceptions and make corrective moves.*	
Passim:	Position papers for circulation and discussion and policy committee actions as major issues are noted.	By staff experts or any responsible manager or professional or functional group.
July 1	Repeat the process.	

Audit Information

This information, which includes program audits and overall reviews of the major strengths and weaknesses of each staff responsibility, should be reviewed to provide a basis for finding major opportunities and problems.

Five-Year Plan

The annual edition of the company five-year plan should be prepared for each of the major areas of responsibility. Thus the annual edition of the five-year personnel plan, financial plan, technical plan and the like should be prepared at a period some three months in advance of budget submission. For a company on a fiscal year starting January 1, the close-off date for the annual five-year plan thus would be about July 1 of the prior year. This permits opportunity to revise budgetary planning, move resources to new uses, find new funding requirements and make decisions about the abandonment of programs or plans.

Annual Budgets

With audit information reviewed and the annual edition of the five-year plan written and circulated, the allocation of resources can occur. It permits more rational commitments of resources, including the use of Zero Based Budgeting for support services and of Cost Effectiveness methods for facility and program decisions.

These three steps in Management by Anticipation are essential in the effective functioning of MBO in an organization. They provide for sound strategic objectives being in hand before efficient operational objectives are chosen. *Without strategic objectives stated in advance, measurable operational objectives may not be valid. You may simply be running a well-run bankruptcy.*

In formulating strategic objectives, the following points should be considered:

a. Strategic objectives should be stated in advance of budgetary decisions.

b. Strategic objectives should define strengths, weaknesses, problems, threats, risks and opportunities.

c. Strategic objectives should note trends, missions, and define strategic options, including consequences of each option.

d. Good strategic objectives will answer the question "are we doing the right things" in contrast with the operational objectives which define "how to do things right."

e. The emphasis in strategic anticipation staff goals need not necessarily be measurable but should use both words and numbers with clarity to define long-run outcomes sought. They are often established by groups such as the Board of Directors, management committee, personnel policy committee and the like. For example,"Burger King Corporation will become the leading seller in fast food operations by 1983."

As shown in Table 6.2, there are some specific questions which will be included in the strategic goals statement of every staff department and major business unit.

TABLE 6.2.   FORMAT FOR ANNUAL STRATEGIC OBJECTIVE STATEMENTS

1. Should be prepared three months in advance of budgeting decisions.
2. Should come up from below as proposed alternative strategies.
3. Should be prepared annually at *half-year*.

OUTLINE	COMMENTS

I. Describe the present condition,
   statistically and verbally
   (add your professional opinion) on:

  1. *Internally:* Strengths, weaknesses, problems?
  2. *Externally:* What are the threats, risks and
    opportunities you see?

II. Trends: If we didn't do anything differently in
  this area, where would be in $1-2-5$ years?
  (Do you like this possible outcome?)

III. WHAT ARE THE MAJOR MISSIONS? What are we in
  business for? Who are our clients? What is
  our product? What should it be?

	What would the consequences be?		
IV. WHAT ARE SOME OPTIONAL STRATEGIES?	contribution	costs	feasibility

  1. Do nothing differently

  2. _____

  3. _____

  4. _____

  5. _____

  6. _____

          (Press for multiple options)

Recommended Action Plan: To be turned into OBJECTIVES

HOW TO SET OBJECTIVES/OPERATIONAL GOALS

At the beginning of the operational year, each manager and subordinate manager sits down and conducts a dialogue on specific operational objectives for the coming year for the subordinate position. Prior to the discussion each reviews the present situation, the results of the most previous year, and some of the more likely requirements for change. Each thus comes to the discussion prepared to arrive at commitments and to assume and delegate responsibilities.

The boss is armed with information about budget limitations, strategic goals which have been agreed upon above, plus some information about actual results obtained the prior period.

The subordinate comes with some expectations and knowledge of his own performance strengths, weaknesses and problems as well as threats, risks and opportunities.

Management by Commitment

Operational management by objectives adds to the previous management-by-anticipation a new dimension which is a face-to-face relationship with the superior and through that superior the organization itself ...Management by Commitment.

Commitment means that the person makes some promise to somebody else whose opinion is important. This commitment is not general but specific, explicit, measurable and worthwhile.

Responsibility means that the person accepts full accountability for the outcomes which will be produced during the commitment period without reference to excuses or exculpatory explanations. This doesn't guarantee that the responsible person can't fail for reasons beyond control, but regardless, assumes a results responsibility. This implies a kind of adult behavior, professional effort and mature self-control in engaging one's work.

The superior is also committed. If the superior agrees in advance that the proposed operating goals are meritorious in advance, then those objectives must be agreed to be the criteria for judging performance at the end of the period. Such judgments could include salary adjustments and merit pay recommendations, bonus awards, appraisal, promotability notations and similar rewards for achievement. In accepting objectives in the beginning, the superior thus cannot apply capricious or *ex post* judgments.

The key to management by commitment is that the hard bargaining about what comprises excellence of performance is done up front, before the period begins and not after a year or so of effort.

The process by which the operating goals (commitments) are established consists of a dialogue and a memorandum. The dialogue is one in which each brings something. It is neither solely top down, nor solely bottom up, but a genuine discussion. It is most satisfactory when it is conducted on an adult-adult level rather than a parent-child model.

HOW TO WRITE OBJECTIVES FOR COMMITMENT

Operating objectives should comprise an ascending scale of excellence, by which the manager can administer certain ongoing concerns in managing managers. For the subordinate it should comprise a series of levels of excellence. As shown in Figure 6.1, this is best accomplished when the superior has criteria for making year-end decisions for purposes of compensation, personnel records, defining promotability and assignments, coaching and training subordinates, the administration of discipline and delegation.

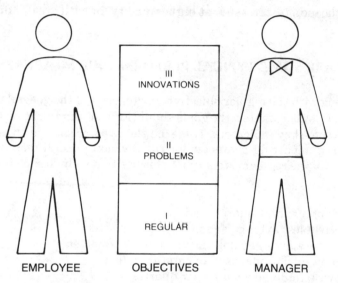

III
INNOVATIONS

II
PROBLEMS

I
REGULAR

EMPLOYEE   OBJECTIVES   MANAGER

FIG. 6.1

For subordinate, these five questions should have been answered or resolved:

a. What is expected of me? Let me know in advance.
b. What help and resources will be available to me in my work?
c. How much freedom may I expect, and what reporting times and forms should I assume?
d. How can I tell how well I am doing in my work while I am doing it?
e. Upon what performance bases will rewards be issued?

This is best achieved by writing goals in three categories as shown in Figure 6.1. Goals are defined in three major categories and should be written to cover all three.

Category I. What the *regular responsibilities* of the position will be. These are the ongoing, recurring, repetitive and measurable objectives of the job such as dollar volume of sales or units per shift.

Category II. What are the major problems which should be attacked and solved in this position during the coming period? A problem is a deviation from a standard which persists or which somebody important wants to have fixed.

Category III. What innovations will be attempted? These are not reactive but proactive goals. They are improvements, betterments. Projects which will cause the organization under the subordinate's control to operate better, cheaper, faster, safer, at higher quality, or with greater dignity to people.

WHAT ARE SOME TYPICAL PERFORMANCE MEASURES?

Starting with the regular objectives, Category I of the general manager and his key subordinates, the goals should lock the organization together through some key indicators. Table 6.3 shows some sample objectives of an ongoing, recurring character for the division general manager. The indicators of the regular category for this position include such indicators as:

- Cash on hand at quarter end
- Receivables, average age in days per quarter
- Inventory, average dollar level over the quarter
- Budget deviations, as % of capital budget
- Growth, in dollar volume per quarter
- Labor stoppages per year

The indicators are never standard, but the indicators listed were found to be common among a sample of fifty general managers. A study of Table 6.3 should highlight some of the features of operating regular objectives.

1. They are stated as *outputs for a time period.* Statements of *activities* are not objectives but means.

2. The actual numbers chosen as objectives should be stated in ranges. Start by defining the middle figure first, "normal realities." Let the subordinate set the optimistic or stretch objectives. The superior chooses the pessimistic figure. This figure comprises the *exception point* at which the subordinate knows that he should *notify* the superior that things are not going according to plan. The middle point is based upon history, upon estimates, industrial engineering studies or sales forecasts.

TABLE 6.3.   GENERAL MANAGER REGULAR-BASIC INDICATOR OBJECTIVES IN CATEGORY I

Responsibility		Level of Result Sought		
Output Indicator	Time Period	Pessimistic	Normal Realistic	Optimistic
1. Dollar volume of revenue per month	Qtr.			
2. Profit: R O I	Qtr.			
Dollar volume per month	Qtr.			
3. Cash at month end, dollars........................	Qtr.			
4. Receivables: Dollars month end	Qtr.			
Days	Qtr.			
5. Inventory: Number end, dollars	Qtr.			
Turn Over, Days	Qtr.			
6. Capital Budget % Deviation........................	Qtr.			
7. Labor Problems—Step 4				
Grievances..	Qtr.			
8. Share of Market %	Qtr.			
9. (Other) _____ .... _____				
_____ .... _____				
_____ .... _____				

RESULTS SCOPE SHEET

Target No.	1st Qtr.	2nd Qtr.	3rd Qtr.	4th Qtr.	TOTAL
1					
2					
3					
4					
5					
6					
7					
8					

3. When deviations occur, the subordinate should know it before anyone else, should know why the deviation has occurred, have taken corrective action where it is possible, and notified and requested help from above early enough.

4. On the other hand if the subordinate is attaining the middle level (normal-realistic goals), he or she should be left alone to operate without interference.

Table 6.4 shows what a page of written problem solving objectives Category II might look like, usually committing oneself to one or two major problems defining:

- The present level or condition
- The desired level or condition
- The time when it is to be corrected (brought to the desired level)

Category II objectives are also shown in Table 6.4. This is a statement of the present condition, the desired condition and some time frame for the proactive, innovative goals, perhaps including some stages of study or development.

TABLE 6.4.   OBJECTIVES IN CATEGORY II AND III OF THE GENERAL MANAGER

II. STATEMENT OF PROBLEM SOLVING OBJECTIVE

   A. Present condition or situation
   B. Desired condition or objective of the problem if solved satisfactorily
   C. Time commitments (always state as a range, pessimistic, realistic, optimistic)

III. STATEMENT OF INNOVATIVE PROJECT COMMITMENT

   A. The present condition or situation
   B. Innovation to be attempted
   C. Results sought (condition which would exist if the innovation were to work well)
   D. Time commitment (state dates, optimistic, pessimistic, realistic)

Organizational Objectives

The example given of the general manager's objectives, of course, must be supplemented by specific and explicit objectives for each of the key subordinates reporting to the general manager. The operations manager might have these regular (Category I) objectives to which he is committed:

- Average daily output per month
- Units per shift per month
- Indirect labor as a percent of direct per month
- Factory overhead as a percent of total per month
- Average quality reject rate per month
- Warranty and policy costs per month

- Step four grievances per quarter
- Overtime hours per week per quarter
- Hours of supervisory training per quarter

The sales manager, on the other hand, doesn't have the same as the general manager except for a few key result areas but rather defines those indicators which will cover the major indicators of output for a time period for his responsibility area. These might include such indicators as the following:

- Dollar volume per month per quarter
- Costs of producing the revenue per month per quarter
- New products introduced
- Dollar level of bad debts per quarter
- Days of sales training conducted per quarter
- New customers added per quarter
- Lost accounts per quarter

For each person reporting to the general manager, there would be indicators which are special to that position, but following a similar format. Indicators of output for the time period are stated in ranges and include problem solving and innovative goals.

HOW TO AUDIT AND REVIEW OBJECTIVES

Periodic Audits

Two forms of review and audit are important in MBO. The first kind of audit is the periodic audit. This is a financial audit of a comprehensive nature usually based upon a sampling of the realities of the situation. It can be done by professional internal auditors, or by some outside auditor, such as a CPA. Not only should program audits be performed periodically for financial results and practices, but for *program* operations as well.

Personnel audits and manpower audits for such matters as affirmative action, replacements of key persons, compliance with company or organizational personnel policy and similar matters including labor relations should be included in periodic audits. Safety audits against OSHA standards done internally may prevent unfavorable audits by OSHA inspectors from enforcement agencies.

Other current practices of the best run organizations include new forms of audit of programs. They might include technical audit, community relations audit, public responsibility audits, purchasing practices audits, and legal compliance audits for anti-trust or patent protection.

Continuing Review

Every manager having made commitments should be doing ongoing continuous reviews of his own performance. These reviews are observation and notation of actual results against the statements of objectives to which one is committed. They are of shorter time period and relate to the shorter time periods in which supervisory management gets daily, weekly, monthly and quarterly reports of outputs.

One of the major advantages of MBO is that it permits self-control by the manager against objectives agreed upon in advance. Self-control has some powerful motivational effects, for the tightest and most perfect form of control is self-control. Commitment is a means of motivation, which is considerably enhanced when self-correction is built into the system.

As shown at the bottom of Table 6.3, the manager should be able to post his own actual outcomes on the original objectives and send a copy to his superior. The function of the superior is to respond with help and resources when requested or when notified that exceptions are present.

Annual Review

At the end of each year, the superior and subordinate pull out the objectives prepared in advance and review actual results. This is a preface to defining new objectives for the coming year. Such discussions should be treated as important events. They should be done free from distraction, should deal with objectives, results, problems, deviations, and improvements needed. They should avoid personality discussions or adopting a manner which is exacting, hostile, judgmental or punitive.

With actual results against objectives in hand, the superior can make such personnel decisions as are required.

Part III

Financial Aspects

Capital Budgeting Practices in the Hospitality Industry—A Survey

Michael D. Olsen, Ph.D.

The literature in finance and accounting has frequently reported the results of surveys probing the capital budgeting practices of large U.S. corporations. This paper will focus on the results of a similar survey but is devoted to a specific industry segment, the Hospitality Industry. The survey investigated the capital budgeting practices of hospitality organizations and how they addressed the issues of risk, cost of capital, and cash flow determination.

A sample of 131 corporations was chosen for the study. The corporations were selected on the basis of information developed by the International Food Service Manufacturers Association and members of the financial officers group of the National Restaurant Association. Included were firms engaged solely in the food service and lodging industry in addition to diversified firms with food service and/or lodging subsidiaries.

Fifty-eight usable responses were returned for a 44.2% response rate. Responses were fairly evenly distributed in relation to the size of the firms' annual sales dollars which ranged from $1,600,000 to $6 billion. The wide range of sales and the distribution indicate that the results can be applied in general to a large proportion of the larger hospitality industry firms.

Respondents were classified in four categories of annual sales dollars: (1) less than $78 million, (2) $79 million to $197 million, (3) $198 million to $400 million and (4) $401 million to $6 billion. The purpose of the categorization was to permit determination of the suspected use of more sophisticated capital budgeting techniques by the larger organizations.

TABLE 7.1. CAPITAL BUDGETING TECHNIQUES BY ANNUAL SALES VOLUME

Capital Budgeting Technique	Sales Classification							
	Less Than $78 Million N = 19		$79 Million to $197 Million N = 14		$198 Million to $400 Million N = 14		$401 Million to $6 Billion N = 11	
	Primary Technique (%)	Secondary Technique (%)	Primary Technique (%)	Secondary Technique (%)	Primary Technique (%)	Secondary Technique (%)	Primary Technique (%)	Secondary Technique (%)
Payback	33	44	7	57	14	50	10	40
Accounting rate of return	16	33	21	7	21	28	10	20
Net present value	5	50	7	14	—	42	50	40
Profitability index	5	27	7	92	21	21	10	10
Internal rate of return	38	22	42	14	71	14	50	20

FINDINGS

Capital Budgeting Techniques

Respondents were specifically asked which, if any, of these capital budgeting techniques is used by their firm: (1) payback, (2) accounting rate of return, (3) net present value, (4) profitability index and (5) internal rate of return. They were asked to indicate which of these techniques they considered to be their primary method and which they considered to be their secondary method. Respondents frequently indicated that more than one technique served as a primary method and, similarly, more than one served as a secondary technique.

Table 7.1 shows that internal rate of return, a discounted cash flow technique, was the most popular primary method of capital budgeting used by firms at all levels of sales volume. Generally, the higher the sales volume of the firm the more likely it was that the firm used discounted cash flow techniques. The secondary technique most frequently used by firms at all sales levels was that of payback, a non-discounting procedure. Firms in the smaller sales categories, especially those with sales of less than $78 million, tended to favor non-discounting techniques such as payback and annual rate of return more than did the larger organizations.

Calculation of Cost of Capital

Table 7.2 presents the findings on how hospitality firms calculate the cost of capital. A plurality of firms, except those in the $79 to $197 million

TABLE 7.2. COST OF CAPITAL CALCULATION TECHNIQUE BY ANNUAL SALES VOLUME

Method Used to Determine Cost of Capital	Less than $78 Million N = 19 (%)	$79 Million to $197 Million N = 14 (%)	$198 Million to $400 Million N = 14 (%)	$401 Million to $6 Billion N = 11 (%)
Weighted average cost of capital	37	15	38	50
Risk free rate plus risk class premium	—	—	—	—
Cost of debt	18	23	7	—
Cost of equity	6	15	—	—
Measure based upon past experience	25	23	38	40
Expectations with respect to growth and dividend payout	18	30	15	—

Note: Column percentages do not total 100% as a result of some respondents checking more than one technique.

category, tended to use a weighted average cost of capital in calculating their discount rate. Some internal measure based upon past experience was frequently used by firms in all sales categories. The predominance of both these measures lessened somewhat, however, for those firms with sales below $198 million. For the smaller firms the cost of debt and anticipated growth in dividends shared in importance with weighted average and past experience as commonly used techniques in computing the cost of capital. Some respondents indicated the use of more than one technique but no provision was made in the questionnaire for prioritizing them.

TABLE 7.3.   METHODS OF ASSESSING PROJECT RISK BY VOLUME ANNUAL SALES

Method of Assessing Risk	Less Than $78 Million N = 19 (%)	$79 Million to $197 Million N = 14 (%)	$198 Million to $400 Million N = 14 (%)	$401 Million to $6 Billion N = 11 (%)
Probability distribution of cash flows	38	24	22	20
Covariance of a project's cash flows with cash flows of other projects	16	8	15	10
Subjective evaluation	61	62	78	70
Simulation	11	—	8	10
Sensitivity analysis	22	24	14	40
Risk models	11	—	7	10
Not assessed	5	15	7	10

Note: Column percentages do not total 100% as a result of some respondents checking more than one technique.

TABLE 7.4.   RISK ADJUSTMENT TECHNIQUES BY VOLUME ANNUAL SALES

Method of Risk Adjustment	Less Than $78 Million N = 19 (%)	$79 Million to $197 Million N = 14 (%)	$198 Million to $400 Million N = 14 (%)	$401 Million to $6 Billion N = 11 (%)
Increase required rate of return for high risk projects	38	23	21	20
Shorten payback period	16	7	14	10
Use expected values of cash flows	61	61	78	70
Subjective adjustment of cash flows	11	—	7	10
Risk is not taken into account	22	23	14	40
Some combination of the above	11	—	7	10

Note: Column percentages do not total 100% as a result of some respondents checking more than one technique.

Assessing Project Risk

Respondents were asked how they assessed risk in the capital budgeting process. It was discovered that the most favored approach by all firms, regardless of their annual sales volume as shown in Table 7.3, is the use of subjective evaluation. The only other approaches which approximated a degree of common use were the probability distribution of cash flows and sensitivity analysis techniques. The probability distribution method was most popular, after subjective evaluation, with those firms with annual sales of less than $78 million. Sensitivity analysis was quite popular with those firms doing in excess of $401 million.

Adjusting for Risk

It was assumed *a priori* that most of the respondents would attempt to assess risk so they were asked how they adjusted for risk when given the opportunity to do so. Table 7.4 shows that most firms in all categories use expected values of cash flow for purposes of risk adjustment. Surprising is the number of instances that risk is not even taken into account.

Reasons for Capital Rationing

Respondents were requested to identify the major reasons for capital rationing in their firm. Table 7.5 shows that firms in the smallest and

TABLE 7.5. VARIOUS REASONS FOR CAPITAL RATIONING BY ANNUAL SALES VOLUME

Reasons for Capital Rationing	Less Than $78 Million N = 19 (%)	$79 Million to $197 Million N = 14 (%)	$198 Million to $400 Million N = 14 (%)	$401 Million to $6 Billion N = 11 (%)
Limit placed on borrowing by internal management	38	21	21	40
Maintenance of a target earnings per share or price earnings ratio	11	42	14	10
Restrictive policy imposed upon earnings for dividend payout	5	—	—	—
Debt limit imposed by outside agreement, such as a bank or other lending institution	33	21	23	10
Debt limit placed by management external to the organization	5	7	7	—
Capital rationing not imposed	29	7	35	50

Note: Column percentages do not total 100% as a result of some respondents checking more than one technique or in two cases, did not check any technique.

largest categories of sales volume most often cited limits placed on borrowing by internal management as the major reason for capital rationing. Debt limits imposed by outside organizations, such as banks and lending institutions, was the second most frequently mentioned reason for rationing by the smaller firms. The incidence of this reason diminished as the firms' sizes increased in annual sales.

ANALYSIS

The hospitality industry has matured considerably over the past two decades as it has shifted from predominantly entrepreneurial business to an industry of large multi-unit organizations. This maturation process has created many organizations with large asset bases resulting in increasing complexities of management functions such as finance. The influx of professional management juxtaposed with this maturation has, no doubt, further contributed to this complexity by virtue of increased demand for more sophisticated analyses. Given this situation it was anticipated prior to the survey that practices in financial management, specifically capital budgeting, would be increasingly complex and sophisticated the greater the annual sales volume of the organization. In general the results of the survey tend to support this contention. These results are similar to findings in other industries (Klammer 1972; Fremgren 1973).

The current literature in financial management and accounting generally recognizes discounting methods as the superior capital budgeting approach. Internal rate of return, net present value and the profitability index are the three most frequently mentioned discounting techniques. Payback and accounting rate of return are less frequently recommended because they fail to take into consideration the time value of money. The results of this survey indicate that respondents generally favored the discounting approach over the less favored alternatives. This speaks well for the degree of financial management sophistication among the respondents.

In support of the notion that larger firms are more sophisticated regarding financial management practices compared to their smaller counterparts, it has been shown that, among the survey respondents at least, those firms in the less than $78 million category rely more heavily on non-discounting techniques. It is justifiable to speculate on why this might be so. One possibility is that since the firms are relatively small they may not be able to afford professionally trained and experienced specialists in sophisticated techniques like capital budgeting or financial management. It is also possible that for these firms these functions are more often performed by the chief executive who frequently has greater expertise in operations rather than he does in finance. Whatever the reasons for the greater reliance by smaller firms on the less favorable capital budgeting approaches, it appears clear that less sophisticated techniques do become relegated to secondary status as the firms' annual sales volume increases.

Greater sophistication in the methods used to determine cost of capital is also evident as firms increase in sales volume. Weighted average cost of capital is the approach usually accepted as the most sophisticated. The findings of this survey show that this was the most frequently used by the large firms. Past experience, however, continues to play a major role for all firms.

Methods of analyzing risk have also become more formal and sophisticated. Despite the availability of more complex approaches, subjective evaluation was the overwhelming approach used by most survey respondents. Contrary to the two techniques just discussed, larger firms relied more heavily on what can be considered the least sophisticated risk analysis approach, subjective analysis, while smaller firms tended to utilize a wide variety of techniques including the most sophisticated. One could conjecture that with bigness comes more security and less perceived risk and thus there is less need felt for sophisticated risk analysis techniques. In any case, the results of the study raise an interesting question as to why the larger firms seem to be fairly relaxed in their risk analysis techniques. Just as questionable is the percentage of firms that do not assess risk at all.

Similar results were obtained when respondents were asked how they adjust for risk. More frequently than the others, the larger firms indicated they did not take risk into account. Expected values of cash flows was the predominant method used by those who do adjust for risk. The determination of expected values of cash flows is one of the most difficult steps in the capital budgeting process. It may be that this difficulty contributes to the lack of use of more sophisticated techniques in risk adjustment.

Particularly interesting is the relatively large percentage of firms which do not experience capital rationing. In times of inflation, high interest rates and an unstable worldwide economic situation, it might be expected that capital rationing would be more prevalent. Further investigation into this phenomenon seems necessary.

CONCLUSION

Overall, the survey indicates there is a sophistication in financial management in the hospitality industry today that increases as firms grow in size and sales volume. The firms responding to this survey demonstrate an even greater degree of sophistication in key areas of capital budgeting than was expected by the researcher. In view of these findings, it is recommended that hospitality organizations and educational institutions preparing management personnel for the industry take into account this need for expertise in finance when designing management training and development programs or college curricula.

8

Zero-Base Budgeting: A Management Tool for Evaluating Hotel Expenses

James F. Downey and *James O'Keefe*

The need for an effective budget procedure is increasingly apparent in the lodging industry today. All hotels must adapt to an environment in which the allocation of resources presents a constantly growing challenge to the hotel management team. With properties facing decreasing profits, spiraling costs, constant pressure to hold down room, food and beverage prices, and increasing demands and costs for services, the lodging industry must seek ways to effectively allocate limited resources before a budget is prepared. One budget procedure the hotel management team should consider implementing is zero-base budgeting.

THE ZERO-BASE BUDGETING PROCESS

The zero-base budgeting process requires each hotel department manager to justify his or her entire budget request in detail, and places the burden of proof on this manager to justify why any money should be spent for any particular item. In other words, the budget for each hotel department is developed using a zero base rather the previous year's budget level. This type of budget procedure forces an individual manager to identify and analyze what goals and objectives should be implemented, what necessary operating decisions should be considered, and what changes should take place with regard to responsibilities and work loads, within a particular department.

In zero-base budgeting each department manager must prepare a "decision package" for each activity of operation. This includes an analysis of cost, purpose, alternative courses of action, measures of performance, consequences of not performing the activity, and benefits to the hotel. This analysis by alternatives method required by zero-base budgeting introduces a new concept in light of typical budgeting techniques used in hotels at present. Top management must first identify different ways of performing each activity — such as centralizing or decentralizing operations, or evaluating the economy of in-house laundry facilities versus commercial laundry services. In addition, zero-base budgeting requires that managers identify different levels of effort for performing each activity. They must identify a minimum level of spending, expressed as a percentage of their current operating level, and isolate in separate decision packages the costs and benefits of additional levels of spending for that activity. The procedure provides five benefits in preparing hotel budgets. It. . .

1. forces every department manager to consider and evaluate a level of spending lower than the current operating level;
2. gives management the alternative of eliminating an activity or choosing from several levels of effort;
3. allows trade-offs and shifts in expenditure levels among departments;
4. focuses on actual dollars needed for programs rather than on a percentage increase or decrease from the previous year; and
5. provides top management with detailed information concerning the money needed to accomplish desired results.

In traditional methods of budgeting the budget starts from an existing base. It may be a percent or it may be in dollars. In either case, the way it is usually done in hotels is to start from something that already existed and then add a percentage increase on top of that.

For example, you receive a budget that is given to you with instructions to make adjustments. You are only allowed a 5% increase so you have to adjust. This is putting the cart before the horse. With zero-base budgeting you start with a clean slate, or at zero. Each time you decide to do something different or intend to make adjustments to the budget you don't base it on last year; you base it on the needs of this year. This is the big difference between the traditional and the zero-base budgeting processes. No longer are you relying on what happened a year or two years ago, but on what you're going to be doing for the next year. Your thinking is directed towards the future, not what you did in the past. Certainly, you have to work from some kind of a base, but the idea is to instill a clean slate or scratch approach.

Another difference between the two approaches is that the zero-base budgeting process examines cost benefits from all activities rather than from just new activities in the traditional method. For example, the food and beverage department would like to install an automatic computerized bar system for the following year. That is a new activity or a new function that they would like to try out. The zero-base budgeting standpoint doesn't consider only the automatic bar system but everything else within the entire department as well. In other words, managers of each department have to justify their existence and how they are functioning in that department. Everyone gets into the picture. Department heads and those below them discuss what can be done to change or alter the approach that they have taken in the past. Instead of just talking about a computerized system, the talk centers around what already exists in the department. Is it still satisfactory? Can we go in another direction?. . .for every single function in the department. In zero-base budgeting you explicitly examine new kinds of approaches for old, as well as new, activities.

In traditional budgeting you are often given a more or less take it or leave it approach. Zero-base budgeting results in a choice for several levels of service and cost. Examination is made of new levels of service in regard to how the whole operation functions. The manager of the department gets together with everyone from the maids all the way up to the general manager. This process is simply saying we want to know what feeling everyone has about this hotel that can change or better the approaches we have now.

DECISION PACKAGE FORMATION

The most important step in installing a zero-base budget is to determine where decision packages should be developed within the hotel. This step identifies the managers who would be involved in the preparation of decision packages and determines the department levels through which a ranking process would proceed. Table 8.1 illustrates the type of analyses each manager within a hotel's marketing department would go through to develop a decision package and shows the variance in the types of activities that would be meaningful for that department.

In attempting to organize a decision package it is necessary to describe what it is. We want to know if there is something in the department that should change. What description can be applied to this service that should be changed or eliminated! Why change it or eliminate it. Justification for doing anything is the major element here.

The next step is to identify the benefits. This is the meat of the decision package. The example shows the benefit of saving $50,000 in advertising agency fees, but at the expense of reducing the marketing image of the hotel. The description is a justification for why the advertising would not be needed. Perhaps the hotel has established a favorable market image, has been in the market 3 years and doesn't need further extensive promotional expenditures. That is the description. The benefits are strictly economical; they will save $50,000.

TABLE 8.1.   DECISION PACKAGE

DECISION PACKAGE NAME:
Public Relations and Publicity

DESCRIPTION:
Combine efforts of in-house public relations and publicity department into one department, thereby eliminating outside advertising service.

BENEFITS:
Combining efforts saves expenses of outside service ($50,000 per year).

CONSEQUENCES:
Eliminating outside advertising service would increase responsibility of in-house public
relations and publicity department. Outside service termination would have minimal
negative sales impact due to favorable market status of hotel.

ALTERNATIVES:
Maintain outside advertising service at yearly rate of $50,000.

Combine efforts of in-house public relations and publicity department and outside advertising service.

The next thing that is needed in the decision package are the consequences of dropping the advertising. They must be identified. Yes, we
will lose market image but can we afford that at this time? If so, elimination may be justified.

The last step of the decision package is to list the alternatives. Perhaps
if the advertising is needed, why not do it in-house through the public
relations director? Or, hire someone on a smaller salary to come in and be
a part time advertising or promotion director to do the same as the
outside agency but at a lesser cost. This is a simplified example of a
decision package, but describes the process.

The entire process is communication, written and verbal. It is getting
people to justify why they exist. You may have a public relations-
publicity director, a convention sales director, a convention service
director. You may have 10 to 15 packages within one department. All find
out what it is that they can do to change, if there is a change to be made.

THE RANKING PROCESS

The initial ranking of decision packages should occur at the departmental level where they are developed in order to allow each manager to
evaluate the relative importance of his or her own activities. This ranking
process would then be reviewed at higher levels and used as a guide for
merging the rankings. At lower levels, the rankings would be reviewed
by an individual who would physically sort the packages in order of
importance. However, at higher levels the expertise required to rank
packages may be obtained from a committee. Committee reviews and
rankings are helpful when there are large numbers of decision packages

that cover activities with which a single manager is not intimately familiar. (See Table 8.2 for example of ranking form.)

TABLE 8.2.   DECISION PACKAGE RANKING FORM

Rank	Decision Package Name	Proposed Budget Allocation	Cumulative Total
3	Convention sales	$100,000	$100,000
4	Convention service	125,000	225,000
1	Public relations and publicity	75,000	300,000
2	Advertising	50,000	350,000

The committee would review all decision packages in detail or summary to become familiarized with the operation of that department.However, the committee may not rank all the packages but may concentrate instead on the lower priority packages around which the funding levels would be determined.

The final funding decisions for those activities using zero-base budgeting would be determined by establishing a cutoff level on each ranking. This cutoff level on each ranking would then be presented to the general manager for final decision making and funding.

MANAGERIAL DEVELOPMENT

Another important benefit of zero-base budgeting is in the development of managers. People have certain skills that are better or poorer than others'. Often people are promoted due to one or two particular skills that they possess. Zero-base budgeting identifies three specific skills that are important throughout an entire hotel. A person in the controller's office or an accountant possesses a technical skill. A person with an analytical skill can take a financial statement and tell you verbally the position of the corporation just by looking at it. The third skill is probably the most talked about and the least used. This is the skill of communication. A person may be well versed in technical and/or analytical ability but has difficulty when it comes to communicating an idea. Zero-base budgeting emphasizes communication skills as well as technical and analytical ones. All of these skills are required for running a zero-base budgeting process throughout the hotel.

DISCUSSION

Zero-base budgeting as a technique is fundamentally two things. First, it is anti-incremental. In this country, and almost every industry, we have all become habitualized into looking at our budgets and next year's budget in terms of how big a percentage increase can be gained over last year's. Second, it is anti-empirical. All that means is that in the hospitality industry, which uses zero-base budgeting extensively, as well as the utilities and electronic industries, we find a funny phenomenon: it has been done this way for x number of years and so what if the Japanese are catching up. We're just going to do more of the same and do it better. Somehow it will work itself through. This is really the empirical sense of the businessman: this is the way I have learned to do it, the way it's been done for 40 years and I am not going to change.

Look at the industries that have gone rather heavily into zero-base budgeting and you see some outstanding successes. Of course, it has had its failures too, but successes considerably outnumber the failures. There are industries that essentially have certain of the same characteristics. Markets tend to become saturated, get a little flat. There are caps on profits or caps on reimbursement, increased regulations and a high cost basis. A business that has essentially stayed away from new technology for a while has either not dealt with or essentially not wanted to deal in new technology. These are past characteristics of industries that are now starting to make use of this new budgeting tool.

Looking at the hospitality industry, there is a lot happening. On the revenue side there are caps on profits and a saturation market. There are also lots of regulations and a high cost base. There is a lot of new technology on the horizon that has the potential to really change the cost profile in this industry. These are reasons why this industry should use zero-base budgeting as a tool.

People who use zero-base budgeting dislike the term budgeting. This is not your classic budget. It is a program which is developed specifically for the department that has undergone the exercise. But mostly it is a management technique. It is an executive or financial management technique that takes a look at the organization. It forces a look at alternative ways of doing things. It encumbers the department or the division to look at the state of the art; to look at what is happening around it. How is the competition doing it? How does he do it for x cents a day when it is costing me y cents? When these questions come up, answers are needed. What is done about the answer depends on what is done in management.

It takes a week or so to teach people the idea of using a standard measuring performance and of measuring costs. Yet, it is a very simple analytical technique that every manager should be exposed to and use. There may be many lower and middle managers who have no experience with analytical decision making, a very vital process that takes place in zero-base budgeting. Traditionally, many non-managers are not affected by the setting of priorities on a business case basis. They are unfamiliar with this kind of approach of using alternate skills. Zero-base budgeting requires learning the use of basic analytical methods. That is the definitive nature of zero-base budgeting: setting priorities and working through the managers who will get together on a decision package formation, ranking these and handing it back to them.

You can modify the system. You do not have to go into it full swing. You can go into it in a piece-meal or part-time basis. Identify first what the priority items are in the hotel.

Next, there is communication. With zero-base budgeting people are forced to justify the way they exist today. They have to think about how they're doing, what they're doing, and what it costs and what might be a more effective way of dealing with certain situations.

Look at the process. First, what are the development planning assumptions? All those who do a budget have a planning assumption. It's very important in zero-base budgeting. Zero-base budgeting is a management game; a game played out within a set of rules. If the assumption is an expense reduction of 10% within a department because of this year's budget then that really is the object of the game. You're going to score the goal by dropping 10%. What is very important in planning assumptions is to be serious. You have a lot to do because this system will generate some pressures. If you really only meant 5% don't set up a program for 10%. It's very important to be consistent.

Secondly, you have to do what is called identifying the decision units. Decision units are a discrete activity within the department in which a complete package of services and associated costs will be identified. The package is directly influenced by management decisions. Look at a department and analyze what is happening. You will discover the influence of three to 15 to 20 things that occur in that department. Forming a decision package is to cluster those things together. Every department must be broken down into decision units. It is a management tool.

Difficult, perhaps, but the most dramatic cost savings comes in the costing of our processes. How do you look at items such as, for example, energy? Do you look at the cost of reservations or communications? The big processes within the organization are the most difficult jobs of zero-base budgeting because you're dealing with a lot of perceptual influences. These are the ones where enormous results are needed such as in energy, transportation or communication. These are sometimes the biggest problems.

In breaking down the decision unit, it is necessary to understnd three fundamental issues. First, understand the relationship of what you're paying to what you're getting. What are the services I am getting out of this department? Specifically, how much does each of these services cost and what is the real output? What different combinations or service and cost are there? This is very important for management to know even if output is exceeding input.

How do you analyze the decision units? Who does it? The manager of the unit does it. He is the one who has to understand it and has to deal with it. He should be assisted by someone from the finance department or by a consultant. But he has to rephrase the questions for his own application. Is the service necessary for the decision unit? This can be a shocker. In many cases where technology has changed over the last 10 years, sometimes it isn't.

Secondly, is there a better way to do it? This is a much more common question. If you haven't looked at the way you have been doing it for four or five years the chances are very good that there is a better way of doing it. What is a better way is a more effective way.

Finally, what different levels of the service and cost are possible?

These, then, are the three questions that managers are going to have to answer about the decision units in their department. This process is going to train them. It is going to expose them and their supervisors to a great deal of what has changed in the state of the art. The manager has to look at all the alternatives when he is performing this particular analysis. He has to go through a series of steps:

1. He has to describe what it is that is being done;
2. He has to develop output measurements;
3. He has to detail a major objective.

Developing alternatives is how you learn how you're going to achieve it and how you can do it better. There are always at least two ways of doing it different than the way you're doing it now. It's necessary to choose the appropriate one. Maybe change is needed, maybe it isn't.

The final step in zero-base budgeting is to outline the minimum increment of activity and service. Make a volume assumption. A minimum decision increment (MDI) is the smallest amount of funds you can keep in your department and still have a department. The minimum increment should be no more than 25% to 30% of an operations budget.

Having outlined the MDI you can proceed forward. What are the alternatives? You can eliminate. You can purchase versus in-house. You can make or buy. You can merge it. For example, the hospitality industry is very labor intensive yet there is a great deal of technology available or on the way. Microcomputers, today, can do in terms of reservation systems what was thought impossible yesterday. So one alternative may be new technology.

There are other alternatives for a better way of doing it: reduce the level of existing work using existing profits; change the organizational relationship. In certain cases you can do nothing but that decision should come only after looking at the alternatives.

What are the dangers of zero-base budgeting? Three ingredients seem to be present whenever there is a failure. First, someone tries to introduce a packaged program. They try to bend the company to fit the program. Every company is unique. The technique may be constant but the application has to adjust to the company.

Second, the senior management team waffles half way through the program. If management is not visible and consistent in this program it will lead to problems.

Third, is the person who says wait until you see what we are going to drop on you tomorrow! He will tell you how bad it is going to be and raise some very sensitive issues. Zero-base budgeting is not a program to ax people but sometimes it does. If it is necessary it allows you a rational, logical, and quantitative way to do it. The real intent of the program, however, is to find more effective, efficient ways to do the job at a reduced cost.

CONCLUSION

Hotel managers are faced with the problems of coordinating a broad scope of dissimilar activities within a single property. These activities must be balanced to ensure effective and efficient department operations, mandating the need for centralized coordination and direction. Zero-base budgeting meets management's divergent needs for centralized coordination and direction with decentralized operation policies.

In the long run, the most significant impact from the installation of a zero-base budgeting system within a hotel would occur in the middle and lower levels of management where department managers are required to evaluate in detail their planning, operations, efficiency and cost effectiveness on a continuous basis. This extra effort should improve the bottom line because high priority programs should be funded in part by improved efficiency and reduction or elimination of those current activities of less importance to the hotel. Ultimately, the guest should benefit due to the funding of priority programs without significant reductions in customer service.

9

Use of the Potential Cost Control Method for Food and Beverages

Hrayr Berberoglu

Many restaurant operators fail to control food and beverage costs effectively in order to insure maximum profits. Perhaps one reason for this is that many operators do not know what their costs should be.

A system which is used to maximize efficiency in this area is one which compares potential costs with actual costs. Potential costs are represented by percentages and are simply those costs established prior to a food and/or beverage function. In other words, the analysis compares actual costs (what happened after the food and/or beverage function expressed as a percentage) with what the cost should have been, also expressed as a percentage.

Potential costs, once established and updated on a monthly or daily basis, can provide the operator of a food service unit with the data to compare with actual costs and thus help determine whether the restaurant's cost performance is at the level it should be. Often enough, people refer to their food and beverage costs either in percentages or in monetary units and compare them to national averages compiled and published by large chartered accounting companies specializing in restaurant and hotel operations. The averages compiled and published by such companies may be helpful but it should be understood that no one operation can fall exactly into the national or even regional average cost percentage. Every operation is unique, since the costs and sale prices charged may vary.

In comparison to another similar operation, the advantages of the potential cost control system method can help in closing the cost gap between what costs should be and what they actually turn out to be. By comparing potential costs with actual costs the operator can determine whether or not the established control procedure is being followed. Whether the operation is a commercial food service, hospital or club is unimportant. What is important is that an established cost base can be compared with an actual cost to determine whether or not corrective action needs to be taken to bring the operation back on course.

In effect, for example, the food cost of a given food operation should be 35.0% and in reality, it is 36.0%. One knows by comparing both figures that the operation is not performing efficiently as far as these cost percentages are concerned. If, however, the potential cost indicates a food cost percentage of 35.0% and it actually achieves a cost of 34.0%, the operator knows by comparison that customers are not getting either the right portion size or quality, which is equally undesirable simply because of customer dissatisfaction.

Calculating potential costs for food and beverages is not as difficult as many operators may at first think. The following steps must be undertaken:
- establish the sales mix of foods and beverages sold;
- calculate the individual cost of every food item on the menu and the potential sales value of alcoholic beverages;
- update the costs based upon prices paid for goods purchased for sale and adjusting potentials when sales prices on menus are changed;
- establish potential costs of food and beverages separately;
- compare actual costs calculated based on inventories, and purchases minus credits, to potential costs calculated.

The techniques which are used to determine the potential costs can be found in many food and beverage costs control books on the market.

An example of how potential cost percentages for an operation are obtained is as follows:

	Sales Volume	Potential Cost in %	Potential Cost in $
Breakfast sales	$ 50,000	25%	$12,500
Lunch sales	100,000	28%	28,000
Dinner sales	150,000	30%	45,000
	$300,000		$85,500

The overall potential cost in dollars in this particular operation is $85,500 on a sales volume of $300,000. In percentages it would be:

% Potential cost = (Potential cost in $/Total sales) x 100

% Potential cost = ($85,000)/($300,000) x 100=28.5%

Let us look now at how one can compare costs and take corrective actions to alleviate undesirable discrepancies. For example, the revenue in the given operation is $300,000 and the actual cost in monetary units is $90,000 or 30.0%, but the potential cost percentage was set at 28.5%. To calculate the difference both cost factors are applied to the revenue as follows:

Revenue	Actual cost in %	Potential cost in %
$300,000	30.0%	28.5%

	Actual cost in $	Potential cost in $
	$90,000	$85,500

The difference in costs is $4,500 ($90,000−$85,500=$4,500) and this indicates that the operation in this particular accounting period has been deprived of $4,500 additional profits.

Clearly, a serious problem is indicated in this operation which must be thoroughly investigated. Once existing inefficiencies are identified corrective action can be taken.

The investigation must be conducted in two areas:

1) The Production side (portion size, overproduction, waste, consistency in quality and forecasting);
2) The Accounting side (are monies being properly credited on the registers and accounted for? Are the control systems working properly?).

On the production side all of the points mentioned above should be examined and analyzed on a daily basis for a certain period of time. A similar study should be undertaken involving every item being sold in the operation. Problems can be easily identified as a result of careful scrutiny in this area and can be remedied by implementing proper methods, i.e., standard purchasing procedures, proper specifications for merchandise being purchased, standard food recipes and production according to forecast of expected business. Failure to monitor these points contributes to excessive costs.

The accounting side of the operation needs investigating also when costs are higher than they should be. Here, the ordering system of waiters/waitresses, cashiering and deposits, along with the entry of the revenues to the accounting ledgers, have to be carefully studied in order to disclose any loopholes in the system.

Once both possible problem-based avenues have been identified and corrective action taken the processes begin over again, i.e., establish a workable food cost percentage, compare it with the actual cost percentage, and take corrective action if the result is not acceptable.

The changes instituted must, however, be monitored and their results evaluated again in order to ascertain whether the actions taken have been sufficient to remedy undesirable cost discrepancies. Control systems are only as good as the people administering them and, needless to say, all systems must be administered continuously, not intermittently. If administered effectively, potential cost control methods are both reliable and efficient. Every restaurant operator should apply them vigorously in order to increase the profitability and efficiency of an operation.

10

The Importance of Control Aspects in Casino Operations

Saul F. Leonard, CPA

This chapter discusses the control operation of a casino after it has opened for business or, in other words, how one makes certain that no employee walks off with any cash or chips; that one is getting an honest count; and that one obtains, with a year-end audit, an unqualified opinion from the CPA?

Though many readers may be familiar with controls in the hotel or restaurant business not many have been involved with casino operations, per se.

Controls of course, are the heart of any business or organization that deals in money. And, in the final analysis, what business doesn't?

Even if you the reader are not directly involved in the casino gaming business, you have probably visited, at one time or another, a gaming casino. As you stood there in the midst of that brightly lit opulence, with hundreds or thousands of people milling about, as dealers and other casino employees handle thousands of dollars in cash with apparent nonchalance and organized confusion, you might well have wondered: How can this five-ring circus be controlled?

Well, it can, and is, daily, in hundreds of casinos. Of prime necessity is to ensure that a well-planned system of internal controls is in place prior to the beginning of the casino's operations.

In both Nevada and New Jersey casino operators *are required* by law to have such internal-control systems and to file these detailed operational procedures with state authorities. These procedures, which must be approved by independent auditors, are carefully reviewed by state gaming commissions.

Unfortunately, some individuals have the mistaken impression that because a gaming casino's stock in trade is cash, or its equivalent, it necessarily follows that controls over cash are loose. Not so. There are many other businesses — including banks, savings and loan associations, retail stores and bars — where cash and its equivalents play just as significant a role in everyday operations, and are strictly accounted for on a daily basis.

In a casino operation the heart of the cash control system is the casino cashier's cage. All the money that flows through the casino's arteries pumps from it. In accounting for the assets of a casino cage, cash, chips and markers are all treated as if they were cash. A marker, incidentally, is a credit instrument a player signs when he is granted credit. All the funds in the cage are accounted for on an imprest basis — meaning all the funds or chips are recorded on a cash-advanced basis.

THE CASH CONTROL CYCLE

At the outset of any day or shift, the casino cage is equipped with a specified amount of cash and a specified quantity of chips.

In order for a casino table to have chips with which to operate, a specified number of chips will be transferred from the casino cage. These chips are accounted for by what is known as a "fill" slip, which records the transfer; a copy of the fill slip is deposited in the locked box attached to the casino table.

Next comes a player who wants to bet at a table. If he's playing for cash, he exchanges the cash for chips. The cash is immediately placed in the locked box attached to the table. If the player is betting on credit he signs a marker. One copy is placed in the locked box. The locked box is the key to cash controls at each casino table — whether it be blackjack, roulette, craps, or baccarat.

No one in the "pit" has access to the box. Pit bosses and other casino employees constantly monitor gaming tables to ensure that prescribed procedures are followed.

Upon completion of play, the customer takes whatever chips he has remaining to the cashier's cage and either exchanges them for cash, or uses them to payoff the marker, if one has been signed.

To complete this phase of the cycle, locked boxes are regularly picked up by security guards and taken to the counting room for checking and auditing. When the contents of the locked box are counted, the amount of win or loss is determined by totalling the amount of cash, plus the markers issued, plus the credit received for chips returned to the cage, less the "fill" slips received from the cage. This net figure reflects the table "win".

At this point, one may ask: "How can the operator or bosses be certain that none of the cash has been siphoned off?"

This brings us to another phase of controls that is becoming more and more sophisticated. This involves electronic surveillance systems, largely drawing on the use of closed circuit television cameras.

Most casino operators are generally reluctant to talk about these security systems. A typical casino in Atlantic City has approximately 160 closed-circuit cameras on 24-hour duty, covering every game being played in the house, and reaching into all corners of the casino, including the cashier's cage and counting room. The system also includes videotape recording systems, which routinely transcribe all the counting activities, plus any other desired activity. Cameras are so effective they can read the digits on a dollar bill.

In essence, what is emphasized here is that the control aspects of a casino operation are absolutely vital.

How effectively and how well these controls work, in the final analysis, depend upon the will and desire of top management.

From the accounting and systems point of view, we operate on the theory that every transaction must be either witnessed, proven, verified, analyzed or initialed — perferably with a combination of these steps.

Division of labor, or the separation of duties, is also paramount in any effective system of control. Employees that issue chips do not count them. Human control and constant supervision are vital. There must be an ongoing check of all transactions involving the purchase and redemption of chips and markers.

Equally important are the accounting functions, including the preparation and interpretation of financial reports and statistics.

It is this author's opinion that a gaming casino which maintains proper records, which operates by means of appropriate administrative and accounting controls, and is managed by qualified individuals is as auditable as any other business enterprise.

In other words, the auditability of a business does not depend upon the nature of the business, but rather on the manner in which it is conducted.

For the auditor a prime concern is the paper "trails" which are left to follow.

These trails result from the casino's system of internal controls, as previously discussed, and from the retention of complete and accurate records. Also essential is the availability of sufficient outside evidence.

In the paper control area, forms and other documentation must be originated, checked, and followed through, with appropriate check points along the way. Financial reporting comprises another factor in the area of paper controls and these are crucial for analyzing, evaluating and comparing operational results and trends.

An auditor's evaluation of the integrity of the records is based on assumptions he makes from numerous tests in significant areas. Since it is impractical for the auditor to examine every transaction, the tests provide a basis for conclusions. If the condition of a system of internal control is poor, or if a system is non-existent, then, of course, tests are of no use.

In auditing gaming casinos, the auditor's work has been somewhat simplified by gaming control boards in Nevada and New Jersey. Both of these states have mandated certain rules and regulations with which a casino must comply. One of these, as was mentioned at the outset, involves the establishment of detailed operating procedures. Another is a companion requirement that audited annual financial statements must be submitted to the Gaming Control Boards.

Additionally, copies of all letters submitted by independent accountants to their clients regarding internal control matters, whether involving weaknesses or suggested corrections, must also be sent to the gaming authorities.

Continued cooperation between the accounting profession and State Regulatory Agencies will lead to further refinements in casino controls — to the benefit of managers, owners and the public. We in this field are also working toward effectively standardizing procedures from state to state, so that owners with multiple casino operations will not be faced with new sets of regulations each time a new jurisdiction is opened up. In other words, casino operators will not have to reinvent the wheel for each new state.

In the final analysis, the development of a system to control cash receipts in a casino is the responsibility of management. The role of the independent auditor is to satisfy himself that the prescribed controls are adequate and to perform audit procedures to measure their effectiveness.

If such controls are inadequate or are not adhered to, the auditor may not be able to issue an unqualified opinion on the financial statements.

In conclusion, the most successful and the most profitable hotel/casinos are those in which management maintains a rigid set of controls, and does so with a sort of resilient, hard-headed determination.

In a major operation, this involves the cooperation of numerous levels of management, with day and night supervision.

Finally, equally important, in any operation, is a marketing program that will keep the customers coming back.

11

Information Systems for the Smaller Restaurant

Albert L. Wrisley, Ph.D.

Information systems in the restaurant industry have lagged behind those of other industries and behind the needs of the foodservice operation. The reasons behind this lag are numerous but probably stem from three major factors: the character of the restaurant business, the personalities of those who operate restaurants, and the fact that reliable data are expensive and time-consuming to acquire.

Purchasing, producing, and marketing the product of a restaurant may all occur in a very few hours, collapsing the time frame for control enjoyed by other industries and creating a short time span in which information can be collected and disseminated. This fact, coupled with the fact that foodservice firms maintain a large number of items in their raw materials inventory and produce a large number of finished products from their combinations (the finished products sold in a number of relatively small transactions), can often create a difficult control situation.

Further, the typical restaurant operator is not inclined by personality type to be as interested in the quantitative aspects of the enterprise as in the more subjective areas of marketing the product. These factors, in the main, affect the operator of a smaller restaurant in the same ways as they would the operator of a larger establishment. There is no advantage, from an information systems point of view, in being small except that better control may be maintained in the smaller establishment in spite of lack of information, through the simple expedient of physical observation.

Before the advent of electronic cash registers (ECR's), cost information for restaurants was hand compiled from a combination of payroll documents, physical inventories, mechanical cash register tapes, sales information gathered from guest checks, and production records. These data were costly to assemble and operators often followed the rule of not paying more for information than they felt they were losing by not having it, never certain where the breakeven point really lay..Records were gathered primarily to control cash and to develop food costs, usually monthly, as much for the purpose of creating accurate financial records as for control information. This information was lacking in both detail and timeliness and was often not available until several weeks after causes of cost variances may have occurred. When actual cost information was available, standard costs were not, because standard costs have to be developed from detailed recipe and payroll information that was simply too detailed to be gathered economically by hand.

THE ADVENT OF ELECTRONIC DATA PROCESSING (EDP)

The advent of ECRs (microprocessors) and mini-computers has made the ability to capture detailed information and to turn that information into timely management reports a reality. Initially utilized by the fast food chains, the use of microprocessors as point-of-sale (POS) devices has become prevalent in larger operations. Companies manufacturing and selling these devices have proliferated. Back-of-the-house (BOH) computers, with vastly expanded power and flexibility, have been used primarily in a few large companies, usually multi-unit organizations. These installations are factored specifically for the organization that uses them. However, the era of widespread use of BOH computer systems is at hand as a number of software packages hit the market.

There is concern on the part of smaller operators that computer-oriented information systems simply are not affordable. The truth may be that not only can they afford them but they *must* afford them in order to remain competitive and stay in business. This imperative has been additionally fueled by the effect of inflation on costs and selling prices, thus creating difficult problems in control of dollars even when unit sales may not have increased appreciably. With this scenario on the horizon, this chapter will be concerned with electronically enhanced information systems in the following purviews:

Why such systems may be needed;
What current systems can do;
What the results of providing better information should be;
How to calculate what the systems may cost and still be profitable;

Selecting and implementing the system;
all with the smaller operator in mind.

No attempt is made here to define the "smaller" food service operation as size is, of course, relative. Control can be as much a factor of menu size or service configuration as it can be of unit volume or dollar sales. Layout and number of service units or stations also affect control requirements. Size, then, is more important in the attitude of the food service operator and the feeling about the operation's ability to support information system costs.

SYSTEM NEEDS OF THE OPERATION

Some of the problems faced by food service operators that, in turn, create a need for better information are:

Insufficient data available;
Data not timely;
Data not organized and presented in a meaningful way;
Data incorrect and having no set standards;
Variances not available or calculated incorrectly;
Poor control over persons accessing the system.

Insufficient Data

Management has the responsibility for planning, menu development, inventory control, forecasting, cash management, production, staffing, service, quality control, sanitation, and maintenance; all of which is information-dependent in varying degrees. Few restaurant operators have either the data base or the appropriate reports from available data to be able to make the best decisions relevant to these responsibilities. Collecting, storing, and forming reports from multitudinous data are tasks that are difficult to achieve even with a relatively sophisticated information network.

Data Not Timely

The manager is faced with the need for immediate information to facilitate timely decisions in a fast-moving operation. Food or labor cost variances discovered weeks after the possible cause are of minimum assistance, as are sales data for use in forecasting future volumes.

Data Not Reported in a Meaningful Way

Reports are often not presented in a meaningful way. For example, food cost percentages have been traditionally relied upon to determine efficiency in the food production area. This measure alone does not reveal the number of possible causes of changes in food cost ratios which may range from operating inefficiencies to price, cost, and sales mix changes that remain unidentified. Thus food cost percentages are minimally useful for control.

Incorrect Data and No Standards Effect

Standard cost systems such as the "Pre-Cost-Control" system first described by Brodner, Carlson, and Maschal (1951) and reiterated by several others enable the operator to determine operating inefficiencies apart from the effect of price, cost and sales mix changes, and to discover the actual dollar contribution of each menu item and the total menu. Unfortunately, what appears so reasonable in theory turns out to be of questionable cost effectiveness, because the systems are dependent on the maintenance of current recipe costs. This, in itself, is a near impossible task without the help of computers. In addition, whole rafts of statistics on payroll ratios, individual server productivity, sales breakdowns, and product movement are needed, but can be obtained only with considerable effort and thus are largely foregone. Overall, operators lack meaningful standards because of the cost of calculating and maintaining them. Therefore they are unable to measure the variances that occur under existing conditions.

Poor Control Over Systems Access

Much of the current data available is compromised by unauthorized charges made by persons, either deliberately or accidentally. Cash and sales data are areas of frequent error. These problems, of course, can be problems of control as well as debasement of data thus creating a need for a better system.

If this listing of system deficiencies creates the suspicion that most operators do not know what they are doing such is not the case. However, it is true that they do not know in sufficient time and in sufficient detail what they *have done* to operate at optimum efficiency.

CURRENTLY AVAILABLE SYSTEMS

Systems currently available are capable of solving all, or nearly all, of the needs of the foodservice operator. Basically, electronically enhanced systems center around the use of electronic cash registers which may or may not be coupled to back-of-the-house installations, usually a mini-computer for other than very large operations. Detailed information is available from several sources. Levine and Van Wijk (1980) provide the most complete account. There is little in the literature on full-scale computer applications for restaurants although Balintfy *et al.* have pioneered in using computers in institutional food service, including computer-planned menus which meet established nutritional, cost, and preference constraints. Some early work was done by the author (Wrisley 1978) in computerized planning and control systems utilizing a large computer to provide standard cost data, actual costs, and variances as well as forecasting and purchasing algorithms. A more general discussion can be found in Kasavana (1978). It is sufficient for purposes of this discussion to briefly list what the various systems can do to provide information.

Capability of ECRs

ECRs collect, store, and report sales data and assist in cash and sales control. They may also provide payroll information and limited inventory control. It is possible to purchase an ECR or ECR system that will:

1. Price checks through pre-sets or price lookups (PLU);
2. Provide pre-checking;
3. Print at remote sites (kitchen and bar);
4. Maintain item sales by waiter, units, dollar volume;
5. Provide menu item totals and runout times;
6. Print checks, including printing previously entered items;
7. Summarize receipts by method of payment;
8. Track employee time, meals, and tips;
9. Prevent unauthorized access;
10. Provide limited menu explosion;
11. Provide limited inventory control;
12. Provide basic report summaries of all transactions.

Other refinements are obtainable in these microprocessors and the systems vary in cost from a few hundred dollars for the so called "dumb" terminals to master-slave systems costing several thousands. Basically, the above list satisfies the needs of most operators for front-of-the-house controls.

Back-of-the-House Systems

Back-of-the-house systems are normally based on mini-computers with central processing units capable of handling programs that can provide all of the back-of-the-house accounting functions. BOH systems can also integrate data collected from the ECRs with recipe and inventory files, creating a totally integrated information system that will, in addition to the information provided by the ECRs:

1. Prepare actual labor and supply costs;
2. Develop standard menu item costs from current food costs;
3. Calculate standard food costs;
4. Calculate variances;
5. Maintain current inventories;
6. Compile sales reports from terminals;
7. Develop forecasts;
8. Summarize data and provide statistical analyses;
9. Maintain the general ledger;
10. Maintain accounts payable;
11. Maintain accounts receivable;
12. Prepare payrolls.

Mini-Computer Capabilities

Mini-computers have the capability and size to drive large capacity memory units for data storage. Thus, they can provide actual and standard cost information including the calculation of variances by day, month, and year. This information was previously unavailable on a practical level. By polling (or through direct input) from the ECRs the minis can collect, analyze and report sales data in any desired configuration and then utilize the historical data to provide forecast information. Some provide forecast calculations, including the amount of food to be purchased to meet those forecasts. These systems are capable of providing statistical information in any desired format. Indeed, the tendency will be to provide more information than really needed if restraint is not applied.

In addition to preparing statistical reports in all cost areas the minis can also perform the standard accounting functions: maintaining the general ledger; providing financial statements; providing accounts payable and receivable programs; and calculating and preparing payrolls.

An additional feature for those who engage in direct mail promotions, or have considerable correspondence, is the availability of word-processing programs to facilitate those functions. Computer-controlled energy programs are still another capability.

COST CONSIDERATIONS

Obviously systems so versatile are not without cost. It is the affordability of these systems that most concerns the operator of smaller establishments. The general procedure for determining the dollar base at which investment in a system is profitable is quite straightforward; developing the data to be used in the procedure is somewhat more complex.

The general procedure for determining whether or not an information system is cost effective is to:

1. Select a system that meets pre-determined information needs;
2. Calculate the cost of the system;
3. Calculate the estimated savings the system should produce;
4. Calculate the incremental savings;
5. Determine the return the incremental savings represent, based on the investment in the system;
6. Compare this return with a pre-determined company standard.

If the standard is met the decision should be to purchase the system. If not, it is necessary to determine what levels of cost vs savings will be acceptable by means of successive interactions of the above procedure. Again, while the procedure is straightforward the determination of incremental savings requires carefully establishing system costs and savings.

System Costs

Costs must be determined for the following elements of the information system:

1. The system hardware
2. The system software
3. Programming
4. Training
5. Maintenance
6. Supplies
7. Capital costs
8. Additional labor costs.

When determining the system costs it must be made certain that all costs have been included. Equipment salesmen are prone to quote basic prices that may not include peripheral equipment, programming, or maintenance costs which the buyer might expect to be part of the package. An extensive coverage of equipment selection is given in Levine and Van Wijk (1980) and Marko and Moore (1980). Choosing a system requires a systematic, painstaking investigation, the complexities of which are beyond the scope of this paper.

System Savings

Cost savings can be expected to be found in the following areas:

1. *Cost of food sold:* through better forecasting, improved control of inventory, better cost information, faster selling price adjustments,

timely variance reports, and standard costed recipes and portions;

2. *Beverage cost:* through improved inventory control, more accurate pricing, reduced theft, and timely variance and product movement reports:

3. *Labor cost:* through employee productivity reports and timely payroll statistics; may also be some direct labor reduction in accounting/cashiering;

4. *Cash control:* through limiting access to registers, reduction in cash shortage;

5. *Sales control:* through increased income from pre-pricing and price look-up, checks priced and totaled by machine, and pre-checking.

The effects of the savings on each of these areas will have to be estimated and will, of course, vary from operation to operation. Obviously the establishment with poor current control can realize greater savings than one with little slippage.

Some Examples of Cost Saving

There are no definitive, published studies on cost savings. Because of differences in operations, they would probably not be particularly representative if there were. It is possible, however, to look at some specific examples to see what some companies have reported. Savais Restaurant in Chicago reported an estimated 8% savings with 4% from sales control and liquor pouring. A group of 60 Dunkin Donuts shops reported a 2½% savings on food cost after ECRs were installed. A McDonalds' change from hand to machine ordering resulted in an average sales increase from $1.00 to $1.60 per hour, a 1½ to 2% sales increase from pre-pricing, and a reduced average serving time from 4 minutes to 2 minutes. A consensus of operators and equipment purveyors spoken to by the author places average food cost savings at from 1½ to 4% following adoption of ECRs. It is presumable that the effect of totally integrated systems would exceed the above figures with improved inventory control as well as provide savings in the other areas mentioned.

All Benefits Not Quantitative

The real value of a total information system may be very difficult to measure quantitatively. This benefit is the increased efficiency that should be enjoyed by the manager or management team once they are freed from attempting to maintain cumbersome information systems. At the same time they are presented with timely reports that enhance their ability to make decisions and carry out programs resulting in increased sales and a greater cost savings in all areas for which they are responsible.

This is particularly true for the smaller operator who does not enjoy the staff support available to his larger competitors.

Calculating ROI

Once incremental savings are determined, the return on investment for the system can be calculated in line with company practice (for extensive coverage of this procedure see Marko and Moore, 1980). The basis for a decision on the system under study is arrived at by the procedures named. If desired standards of return are not met it becomes necessary to first decide if there may be non-quantifiable benefits of the system that should be given additional weight in the decision. If the answer is still negative, the process should be repeated with a less costly system.

SELECTION AND IMPLEMENTATION

In purchasing an information system for a particular operation the following steps should be taken to insure that the best possible system is purchased and implemented:

1. Analyze the present system for strengths and shortcomings. Determine if, properly utilized, it will do the job;
2. Ascertain the needs of the operation for information and develop equipment specifications to meet those needs;
3. Conduct a preliminary market search to find available systems;
4. Contact vendors for their presentations;
5. Request systems demonstrations from the finalists;
6. Re-examine needs and the ability of finalists to meet those needs (availability of service is an important consideration);
7. Conduct a financial analysis;
8. Choose the most suitable system and negotiate contract;
9. Have system installed by vendor;
10. Train operators to run system (Is this part of the vendor contract?);
11. Put the system on-line and wait for the inevitable "bugs" to appear. The better the attention to the previous steps the fewer the bugs.

This chapter has attempted to show that sophisticated electronic data processing systems need not be beyond the scope of the operator of smaller restaurant properties. In truth, a systematic analysis of needs and potential savings may well indicate that such a system is not only affordable but a definite requirement if optimum control with resulting efficiency and profit generation is to be achieved.

12

The Use and Interpretation of International Hotel Statistics

Eric Green

International statistics in general are usually collected as a part of various government functions and the cost of collecting and disseminating the data is often enough of a burden on public sector financing. Ultimately, it is a burden on taxpayers. In the case of hospitality accounting and consulting firms such as Pannell Kerr Forster the cost burden of statistical reports is on the partners of the firms around the world and ultimately, of course, on their clients who must pay those costs with their professional fees. Thus, statistical publications must serve two major purposes: the first is to provide a service to clients and the contributors who provide the raw data; and the second purpose is that the statistical data collected help the firm in its professional work as auditors and consultants. The strength of knowledge of the hotel industry of such firms is attributable to this relentless pursuit of data such as that published in the annual editions of *Trends in the Hotel Industry, International Edition,* by Pannell Kerr Forster which report on hotel operating results worldwide.

It is particularly significant that the 1974 edition of *International Hotel Trends* contained the reports of 205 hotels, all of which were provided by hotel companies based in the United States such as Hilton International, Inter-Continental Hotels, Sheraton Corporation and others. In the latest edition (1980) which summarizes reports of 400 hotels, roughly half of the number are from hotels not managed or controlled by United States based corporations. The change is indicative of the total change in the international hotel industry. Today, many more European and Asian hotel companies are involved and there is a growing willingness of international companies to contribute their operations results, always on a confidential basis, for inclusion in a statistical summary. Misunderstandings do arise, however, about such things as the data base used, the statistical validities, their basic purpose and the uses to which they may legitimately be put.

This chapter will explain some of the difficulties incurred in the collection of the figures, their presentation, and then will comment on their uses and interpretation.

UNIFORM DATA

The first problem, of course, is uniformity of the data. Not every hotel operator keeps books on the basis of the Uniform System of Accounts for Hotels recommended by the American Hotel & Motel Association. Those that do, generally speaking, have no particular problem in completing the questionnaire listing the data, but even for these companies the treatment of ad valorem taxes, such as value added taxes or sales taxes, and service charges that are handled differently in various countries can create acute problems. For example, some chains, for certain of their hotels, may report a negative payroll figure because they apply service charges to guests against the actual payroll paid to employees which is lower and results in a negative expense. By the same action the percentage of profit to revenue of these chains is greatly overstated in comparison with hotels that either do not make a so called service charge separately from the basic room rate or who regard the service charge as nothing more than an additional revenue item to be treated as revenue rather than a reduction of expense. These deviations can be straightened out provided that the data are carefully edited by employees who have access to the figures that must be adjusted. Unfortunately, that is not always the case and some arbitrary adjustments have to be made by the research department before preparing the final product.

Those who don't keep their books on the Uniform System of Accounts present acute problems of classification and in some cases the data submitted cannot be used at all. We therefore encourage everyone to adopt the Uniform System of Accounts for Hotels which was developed in 1926 and which has stood the test of time.

CURRENCY CONVERSION RATES

Another problem facing the compilers of statistical reports is the currency conversion rates that must be used. When international currencies were, in many countries at least, kept at fixed parities, distortions from year to year did not present a problem. In recent years the problems have been acute because of widely fluctuating exchange rates both within the calendar year and particularly from one year to the next. In converting the basic data in local currency into a uniform currency such as the United States dollar, it is necessary to avoid reporting currency fluctuations rather than fluctuations in hotel operating results. Every attempt is made to iron out currency fluctuations in presenting the results, but there are probably some distortions that are unavoidable. It is preferred to have the original data in the local currency so that year to year variations can be reported on that basis. Then, for purposes of overall summarization, results are converted to United States dollars while leaving the variations between two years as variations reported in the original currency.

SMALL SAMPLE SIZE

Another major problem in presenting the statistics is the very small available sample. This is not purported to be a statistically valid example of the hotel industry in various countries and areas for which data are published. It is an unfortunate characteristic of readers of reports that the printed word takes on a life of its own and for them is presumed to be more valid than the preparer ever intended it to be. Therefore, it is necessary to bear in mind that the figures published are not necessarily representative, though it is felt that they may be, of the results of the operation of any particular hotel.

Every attempt is made to secure a representative number of properties for a particular country for the data under each of the captions used. How many are reasonably representative is by no means a cut and dried matter and even if it were possible to decide on a number that would be statistically valid, it is of course by no means certain that contributions of that size could be obtained. Therefore, it is necessary to do with what is obtainable. A related difficulty is that a hotel may contribute figures in one year but, because of a change in ownership or some other reason, may not contribute them in the next. This makes it impossible to report the results of the same hotels over a long period of time. For any two consecutive years, however, only the same hotels are used.

USES OF STATISTICS

Having mentioned the problems of collection, analysis and presentation of the data, let me turn to the uses of the published material. Often we are in the business of preparing financial feasibility reports. Economists and governments are usually more interested in the economic feasibility of projects and that is sometimes reported on also, but ultimately most reports are to advise investors in tourism projects. For that purpose an accurate data base of financial expectations of tourist developments is indispensable. So one of the primary uses of the statistics is to provide a broad idea, on the one hand, of what the hotel industry in a particular area can do, in the second place, to make it possible to simplify the preparation of earnings projections for new or existing projects. Instead of a laborious line by line projection of every item of income and expense, it is possible to use statistical summaries as broad guides for the projections. This is particularly true for comparison with existing operations results for the purpose of pinpointing unusually good and unusually poor results. Therefore the statistical data are particularly useful for forecasting as well as for operational analyses of existing hotels.

The statistical results also provide a form of barometer of changes in tourism volume, the growing or diminishing appeal that a particular country has for foreign travel, a measure of the need for new hotels, the variations in principal expenses such as in the cost of merchandise for resale, the cost of energy, the cost of management fees and the cost of advertising and personnel.

Return on investment analysis is possible because the statistics show, in effect, the cash flow from operations available for return on investment. If these figures are related to a hypothetical investment, broken down perhaps among equity investment, government grants, and loan capital typically, a preliminary feasibility analysis can be made before an architect puts pencil to paper in a design phase. Much time can be saved by this kind of prefeasibility program.

Another important use is the tracking of hotel revenue and expenses against the general price level changes in the country concerned. For example, in the United States there is a quite extraordinarily close correlation between the consumer price index and the average room rate per occupied room over a period of 20 years. It seems that a major factor in the determination of room rates that can be charged is their relation to the overall price level. Though that is true for the United States, it has not yet been attempted to analyze those figures against the comparable indices in any other country. Now that there has been seven years of reporting international figures it could be a useful exercise to make that comparison. If there is a valid correlation in any other country it might serve as a measure of forecasting that country's future hotel rates. Such a forecast would be very helpful to many international companies. Unfortunately, under current inflation prospects, potential developers of hotels must look to the continuation of inflation to justify their projects. If the world is moving towards a lowering of inflation rates then more careful consideration of the investment that is warranted will be required.

Another use to which the statistics are put can be in support of requests for tax abatements and/or incentives of various kinds, particularly in those areas where there is low profitability. It is painfully true that in many parts of the world hotels that have been developed as a part of total tourism programs turn out to be financial failures because of inadequate demand, as well as poor management and excessively expensive operations. Though it might have been better for some of the projects not to have been built, there may be some economic benefits to the country as a whole, through the earning of foreign exchange, that would otherwise be unavailable to it. The availability of independently prepared statistics can be of great help in petitioning for relief and for securing recognition of problems that must be solved.

13

The Future Hotel Controller

Albert L. Wrisley, Ph.D.

This chapter on the hotel controller is the product of a panel discussion moderated by Jerome A. Solomon, Managing Partner, Pannell Kerr Forster, Boston, Massachusetts. The panelists in order of presentation were:

Paul Buckley, General Manager, Logan Airport Hilton, Boston, MA.
Daniel W. Ambrose, Area Controller, Sheraton Corporation, New York
John J. Walsh, Controller, Ritz-Carlton Hotel, Boston, MA.
Albert L. Wrisley, Ph.D., Professor, Hotel, Restaurant and Travel Administration, University of Massachusetts, Amherst, MA.

What follows is a transcription of the presentation of each of the panelists with minor editorial corrections. Taken together they present a thoughtful look at an area of hotel management that has been somewhat ignored in the past but has undergone changes that make it a vital management challenge and opportunity for the future.

INTRODUCTION

Jerome A. Solomon

I have watched the evolution of the hotel controller from the old hotel auditor who now appears to have been an uninspired non-decision maker compared to today's hotel controller, who is a vital part of the accommodations industry and the management team. The role of the old hotel auditor was to sit there with the daily transcript and the night audit and try to get them to balance. We'll never replace the manager's daily report in the hotel but today the controller plays a vital role in the overall management of a hotel, not just developing the historic financial data but in budgeting, forecasting, planning.

The hotel controller today is a fact controller, someone who should be looked upon to control and guide the destiny of the financial interests of the owners and management of the property. This is a new role that, as we step into the 80's, has to be pursued, learned, and played and played to the hilt because those sheets that come off the computer are vital to the organization and vital to its success. With those few brief remarks, I will introduce four gentlemen who have different interests and different viewpoints on the controller's job.

CONTROLLERSHIP: A MANAGER'S VIEWPOINT

Paul Buckley

In 1955, the controller was known as the auditor. He was considered a necessary evil, a non-productive overhead item, whose job responsibilities were something like this:

> The proper recording of the receipt and use of all merchandise, furniture, equipment and goods of any and all kinds to prevent misuse or loss. The maintenance of adequate control over the billing of sales and services and the receipts of cash; keeping the books of account and properly recording all the financial transactions of the hotel; maintenance of adequate records of authorized appropriations with the determination that all sums expended are properly accounted for.

I could go further with his job description:

> The auditor has unlimited rights of study and complete access to figures and facts. He can go into any department, ask any question and make any study he deems necessary. He must exercise reasonable tact. He should not give direct orders to employees except among his own immediate subordinates. He accomplishes his results with management through the respect in which his opinions are held. The auditor will submit his interpretation of the important facts revealed through the figures and ratios of the operating statements. Comments should also be submitted with respect to the hotel's budget. These should indicate whether the appropriations would prove sufficient, whether the undertaking will be completed by the date originally planned and whether any changes of importance seem desirable.

The auditor, then, was insensitive, unimaginative and negative. This was a person who both absorbed and was absorbed by figures. A pencil was his weapon. That's an accurate description of the controller, vintage 1955.

In 1980, job descriptions have changed and outside changes have influenced the job. Better operating results are demanded, strict labor contracts are enforced, payroll controlls must be instituted and followed up, and most necessarily, better forecasting must be done. In the old days, it was always the controller's fault when the forecast didn't come up right. Now, the controller advises the general manager, as his right hand in operations, on what seems reasonable — where corrections and adjustments have to be made and where proper controls have to be instituted. If today's controller doesn't act in that manner, he is not what I consider a controller to be. Attitude is more important than force.

The controller has to get out and be involved in the entire operation of the hotel. He can't just be responsible for the cashiers, whether they be in food and beverage or in the front office. He has to make sure that they follow along with every program. He has to be the watchdog. He has to characterize what I once heard from someone else: "Show me a controller that is winning a popularity contest and I'll show you a controller that isn't doing his job." He is put in that position to be the eyes and ears of management as part of the management team. He has to look at the financial results but he also has to be an advisor. He has to have that slight back seat behind the general manager. When you look at the organizational chart for a hotel the controller belongs up there on top as part of the top management team.

The regional controller coming into my property is not joining forces with the controller to tell me what I'm doing wrong. He'd better be coming into my property to tell me what we can do as a team for our own betterment. In the old days it was almost like a witch-hunt: "Here he comes, checking in tonight. Make sure everything is right. Be downstairs first thing in the morning — the ghoul is coming." Not anymore.

Today everyone in the hotel understands that a controller has access to every portion of the hotel — sometimes even more than a general manager does. What other department head can you name who has to get involved with every operational aspect of the hotel? The front office manager doesn't. You can be darn sure the housekeeper doesn't. The engineer doesn't. But, every payroll, every purchase order, every personnel organization form that channels through the hotel has to cross the controller's desk. He initials it, he initials checks, compares checks, and compares food orders. The controller has to be totally involved with the entire operation of the hotel. Otherwise, he's not what I consider to be the controller of the 1980s.

With Hilton today we have an executive committee that goes over the operating statement from front to back. And, I like to say to my controller, sometimes we read the edges because we might find something there that will help us to maintain a better operating profit mind and a better operating hotel. We frequently make reference to teamwork, to effort, to entire committees getting together to come up with the results we may need. This team must constantly weigh priorities. If you're the controller you have to be the advisor to the general manager. You may sway the control, sway the consideration because you are involved so deeply in the operation, and have far more knowledge and far more working background in some areas that could tip a current cash flow problem in the wrong, or the right direction. We must convert opportunities into profit and conduct our day-to-day efforts as though we own the business. This will automatically place us in the frame of mind to establish priorities and act with urgency.

CONTROLLERSHIP: A CHAIN CONTROLLER'S VIEWPOINT

Daniel W. Ambrose

The controller's contribution to a hotel operation is much different today than in the past. The hotel controller, however, still:

1. Protects the assets of the hotel;
2. Plans, organizes, directs, and controls a proper and effective accounting system;
3. Makes recommendations to management regarding the economic feasibility of various programs and projects.

These can be considered the basic functions of a hotel controller of the past, the present, and certainly the future.

Although controllers still do and will certainly continue to maintain responsibility over these basic functions, the hotel controller's department has been recognized as one that must be located in those areas of the hotel that facilitate accessibility to the hotel's management, the hotel's staff, and also to the hotel's guests.

For the most part, the hotel controller has been removed from the basic clerical functions as these have been turned over to qualified accounting assistants and supervisors. The controller reviews and evaluates.

The hotel controller of today has become a key member of the hotel's executive committee; he or she is now asked to provide the financial ramifications of most managerial decisions.

This evolution in terms of the controller's role in hotel operations has come about by direction from and guidance of either its corporate office, its parent company, or both. The framework for this guidance and direction is made up of many variables, some of which follow:

A. *The Companies' General Directions:* It has become apparent over the last several years that many hotel companies have slowly but surely been slipping out of the real estate end of the business and gradually moving toward leases, management contracts, and franchise operations. This requires the hotel controller to act as the company's representative in dealing with either the owners or partners. The ability to interface will continue to become much more of a prerequisite in the future in the placement of hotel controllers.

B. *Accountability:* The rules and regulations being placed upon the accounting profession not only from a basic accounting standpoint, but also from a procedural and reporting standpoint, have increased like never before over the last decade. The hospitality industry has felt the effect of much of this change, whether it be federal, state, or local or whether it be initiated by an independent agency like the F.A.S.B. (Financial Accountants Standards Board) or the A.I.C.P.A. (The American Institute of Certified Public Accountants). As controllers, we constantly become more involved at the hotel level in insuring that necessary changes, both operational and financial, whether directed from the corporate office or established locally, occur within the compliance guidelines and the designated time-frames.

Affecting the auditing standpoint (both internal and external) is the F.C.P.A. (Foreign Corrupt Practices Act) which was signed into law by President Carter on December 17, 1977. This law has given greater impetus to the audit function as a tool for management to assess the hotel's internal controls and its degree of compliance. Although the basic concept of this Act was for the purpose of strengthening the laws governing corporate accountability, this new direction in auditing has given the hotel controller a workable means of being able to evaluate the internal control systems within a hotel.

C. *General Economy:* With the prime interest rate sometimes exceeding 20% the days of the ten-day 2% cash discount are in the past. Today's hotel controller must become the Cash Manager. Cash forecasts daily, monthly, quarterly and yearly have become an absolute necessity to benchmark such things as: purchase of inventories, disbursement schedules, capital planning, working capital requirements, investment and borrowing. Certainly these elements and others affect the basic budgeting and forecasting processes. With more of today's hotel controllers becoming involved in management contracts and joint ventures the daily control of cash, both in and out of the operation, must be handled as if it were his own.

I think we could all agree that the clerical bookkeeper type hotel controller is a thing of the past and I have described several ways that I feel the present day hotel controller's role in the hotel's operation has come to change. What will the future bring?

First of all, technology will continue to improve and assist hotel management in all phases of hotel operations. It is only over the last ten years that hotels have begun to computerize various areas of the operation. During the 1980's we will find a variety of computerized systems in the majority of the hotels around the world. Today, although computerized hotel systems are still in the infant stage, there are already systems available for:

Front Office Systems —which handle reservations, check-in, cashiering, and accounts receivable;

Back Office Systems — for accounts payable, payrolls, and general ledger;

Computer Systems — that interface with electronic point of sale equipment, telephone systems, and energy and life safety systems.

In the very near future we will see computerized capabilities for such things as inventory controls, banking, and all types of financial reporting and analysis.

All this technology will save a great deal of time and manpower, provide speedy and accurate information, facilitate effective managerial reporting for the purpose of maximizing profits. This will necessitate that the hotel controller of the future become more familiar with data processing information systems. Such skills can be acquired not only through formal education, but also through on-the-job-training.

The hotel industry is becoming more "management company" oriented. For example, with the acquisition of the Sheraton Centre and Sheraton City Squire Hotels in New York City on January 24, 1979, the Sheraton Corporation engaged in its first joint venture partnership with the Equitable Life Assurance Society of the United States. Sheraton has since engaged in three more partnerships throughout the country and anticipates many more in the future.

These joint-ventures are very advantageous from a business standpoint for all partners concerned. However, they require that the hotel controller display strong managerial abilities since the majority of the inter-partner dealings are of a financial or accounting nature.

Finally, it is my opinion that, because of what appears to be the economic outlook over the next few years, our costs, especially energy costs and basic salary, wage and benefit packages for our employees, will probably rise at a rate faster than will be able to be recovered by raising prices. In order to maintain acceptable profit levels the hotel controller will assume a leading role in developing programs and systems, controls, and mechanisms, in whatever way or method necessary to assist in meeting the companies' profit goals. This ability to assist, advise, cooperate and become a vital part of any hotel operation is essential for the controller of the future.

THE CONTROLLER AND CONTINUING EDUCATION

John J. Walsh

The points made in Dan Ambrose's presentation hold true for the independent hotel as well as for the chain operations. I would like to discuss the hotel controller of the 80's from the viewpoint of his educational needs.

The controller of the 80's will be better educated than his counterpart was in the 60's. He should possess a well-rounded education and should participate in the industry's associations. He should be distinguished by new programs such as those of the International Hospitality Accountants and the CHAE (Certified Hospitality Accountant Executive). This latter program is just coming on board now. This program will blossom in the 80's and will be the basis for recognizing the hotel controller as a qualified professional. The program is being developed in conjunction with the International Hotel Accountants under Professor Metcalf of the University of Nevada-Las Vegas.

The hotel controller should participate in seminars as part of his basic education. There are important topics discussed in the trade magazines which must be read and digested. In order to keep up with all of this it is necessary to attend more seminars put on by professional organizations and universities in such areas as data processing, cash flow management, and taxes.

The hotel controller should be aggressive in human resources and in staff development. Controllers are only as good as their staff and a strong staff is a great asset to an operation.

Cash management will be a major part of the controller's responsibility in the 80's and needs special emphasis.

Data processing will be another important area. The computer will have established its place in the hospitality business of the 80's and there are no questions about its fantastic contributions. It even has its place in a small property. For the Sheratons and other large properties, total data processing will be essential in this decade. Only through data processing can we get the information necessary to operate efficiently.

The hospitality industry of the 80's has to realize, as it did in the 70's, the importance of professional education and the benefits to be gained from retraining all personnel, including executives. This is the key. You cannot simply graduate from a university, go into a position as a trainee and just sit there. The need is for continuing education, professional seminars and university courses. There are more and more of these available and they are the wave of the future.

Other than the basic things, such as cash management and managing human resources, controllers also must become involved in such areas as energy and security. Add to these the need to be involved in taxes, planning, budgeting, forecasting, special studies and insurance. These are all areas of operations in which the independent hotel controller must be involved. In order to do the job satisfactorily he has to have knowledge in all of these areas and these needs can be met only through the process of continuing education.

EDUCATING THE FUTURE HOTEL CONTROLLER

Albert L. Wrisley

The previous papers have developed a useful picture of the duties and continuing education of hotel controllers both now and for the rest of the 80's. I would like to discuss the need to develop a system of identifying and educating the hotel controller of the future, particularly by the four-year schools of hotel administration.

It is safe to say that, up until now, serendipity has had more to do with the making of a hotel controller than any conscious planning. Because of the fairly limited job description and purely advisory nature of the controller's position in the past, that route had seldom been considered as part of "Hotel Management." Now that the hotel controller has been firmly established as part of the management team, and salaries and prestige have kept pace with the concept, it is time to take a careful look at the recruitment and education of our future controllers.

Student Attitudes

One serious problem is that most hotel students do not visualize the hotel industry in terms of economics and finance. Rather they look more often at the glamour areas of front office, sales, and food and beverage. It is not always possible to determine just what the average hotel major has in mind for a career but it is usually fairly evident that he/she does not envision a life filled with financial statements, statistical analyses, and cash flow statements. Essentially, there exists a marketing problem, the solution of which must involve providing better information on the potential of the hotel controller position and the business education the position requires. In the past few years I have noticed an increased interest in this area on the part of students who are bright and motivated, but not particularly interested in operations. Unfortunately, there has not been a definitive body of information to which to refer them.

Need for Definitions

I would suggest that one very real need is for a good definition of the task and preferred educational profile of a hotel controller. What should the job entail in terms of ability and knowledge — including the proper course sequences in such as the accounting area? This is something that should be worked out by an industry/education committee.

Need for Industry Support

Another problem has been one of industry support. The accounting firms of PKF and L&H have supported the hotel schools for all the years that I have been connected with education, both as a student and as an educator. Recently, organizations such as Sheraton and the Ritz Carlton through Dan Ambrose and Jack Walsh have made it possible for me to spend time in their properties to prevent my teaching from becoming out-of-date. It is through this kind of cooperation by these organizations and others that we are able to provide meaningful and current education in our schools. More of this type of thing needs to be done.

In the past there was not the same imperative for industry/education cooperation because things really did not change very fast. I dare say that from the time I began my educational career at Cornell in 1946 until about 1975 I could have done a decent job of teaching without any refreshers from industry. Things simply had not changed much in the controller's department in all those years. Now the information explosion has caught up with us with a vengeance and we must help one another in providing new and creative approaches to the task at hand.

Need for Research and Development

This brings us to the subject of research and industry support for it. There has traditionally been very little R&D work carried on by hotel industry firms or, for that matter, by schools of hotel administration. Most hotel companies were not large enough to support in-house research and development programs and most hotel schools concentrated on the teaching aspect of university education. Some hotel organizations are now carrying out fairly ambitious research programs but are still hampered by the lack of facilities and expertise in the number of areas needed to carry on a first class program. Some of these include large research computer capacity, statistical expertise, laboratories, and availability of large research libraries and manpower. Universities that have these facilities often lack funds to carry out research. An even more difficult problem has been the feeling that all research must carry certain proprietary rights before the industry is interested in supporting it, and universities are dedicated to the universal dissemination of knowledge.

Perhaps it is time that the hotel industry borrowed the concept of university research and extension of that research to the field that has made U.S. agriculture the wonder of the world. With more and more faculty with research degrees teaching in the hospitality field the opportunity for this advancement in the sophistication of industry practices is at hand.

Using Industry People

Another potential tie-in between industry and education is to increase and improve the practice of utilizing industry speakers on campus. Perhaps the concept of visiting lecturers can be expanded with industry providing sabbatical leaves so that their top executives can spend a semester on campus—teaching and counseling students. There are many other possibilities for bringing current industry practice to the campus.

Off campus internship programs in which students spend a semester at work instead of at study is another form of possible industry/education cooperation, one in which the interning student is provided a rigorous and varied educational experience. This, of course, is not easy to give in a busy hotel operation.

Need for Teaching Materials

Those in industry should be aware that there is a continuing need for teaching materials from the industry. Sample financial statements, forms and procedures are samples of the kinds of materials needed. Cooperation in the writing of case studies for educational purposes is another area in which industry can aid the educators. I do not know what I would do if PKF and L&H did not provide me with multiple copies of their publications for distribution to my students. They are invaluable teaching tools.

Gifts

Students are not going to like what I am about to say, but say it, I must. The industry has always been quite generous when it comes to providing scholarships for students. My suggestion is that this money might benefit all students to a much greater extent if it were put to some other use. Library books, for one example, benefit all, as do gifts of equipment and endowments for chairs for additional faculty. Some hotels provide rooms for students and faculty during hotel shows and other educational programs. Without them we would lose many educational opportunities and we are most grateful.

These then, are some of the ways that industry and education, working together, can improve the education of controllers for the 80's. It is a task we can all look forward to with real anticipation.

14

The Economic Feasibility Study—
Panel Discussion

Eric Green

Eric Green.—Before we have any exchange of views, I think perhaps it would be just as well if we understood what we're talking about. Feasibility studies are of a relatively new origin in a sense. Nothing seems to get done today without a feasibility study being made. Often enough they get to be an excuse for not doing anything because nowadays they have to be followed up with environmental studies, social impact studies and a variety of other things. One politician that I remember, my local congressman in the New York area, said, "I know all about feasibility studies but I wish we heard more about desirability studies because what may be feasible may not necessarily be desirable, for a number of reasons." With that assumption, I think things do move rapidly in the feasibility study business.

Two years ago I wrote an article that appeared in the March 1979 *Lodging* magazine of the American Hotel & Motel Association. That article dealt with new requirements of the hotel feasibility study. Today, we want to talk not just about hotel feasibility studies, but any kind of a feasibility study that involves the tourism business. It could be for convention centers, it could be for tourism projects in general, or it could be for transportation.

I'm going to ask Alan just to run through a little bit of the major differences that exist in the various types of study, largely from the client's point of view, because the thrust of this presentation, this panel discussion, is differences, although we'll cover a pretty wide range. There is an important difference between feasibility studies required by the private sector for private investment purposes and those that are required by the public sector because the taxpayers' money is more involved.

Alan Hopper.—First, just a little background on what we do. We started this consulting business in the hotel and hospitality industry in London in about 1972. Today, our territory that we cover from London covers Europe, the Middle East and Africa so we tend to go trekking through those parts of the world. You can imagine certainly, from the Middle East and Africa aspects, that we're dealing with the Third World, developing countries that require a relatively low level of analysis and investigational studies. In Europe and certainly the United Kingdom our clientele is looking for a fairly high level of sophistication in analysis.

We had been doing "economic" feasibility studies out of London for about 6 years when we were joined by an associate, now a fellow Director, who had many years in consultancy. He has an academic background in economics. Within 2 or 3 days of arriving he made it abundantly clear to us that we were doing "financial" feasibility studies, as we didn't really address ourselves to the wider implications and ramifications of the economics of the project that we were looking at, and that of the local community and the local economy. To reach a common base of understanding, then, we should run through the key elements of a study and break it into the many subdivisions.

There are really three critical elements in a study. A hotel study is a logic process that one's applying. It would apply equally to a transportation study or to a condominium housing study. The first critical element is the location of the project, certainly as regards a hotel. If the concept of the hotel is for a city center property, 4-star or deluxe, addressing itself to the business market, it's really rather critical that the hotel is in a prime location to service the business traveler, as well as being relatively convenient for the central business district. If we are analyzing a project that was put to us by a client and it didn't satisfy these criteria, I think we would suspend the project fairly early on or we would advise him very clearly that it may be a good location for a hotel, but not a 5-star, deluxe hotel. We would try to steer him into something more appropriate.

On the other hand, one could be looking at a different type of hotel, a resort hotel in some area of the world and I'm thinking of one in Egypt where, because of the geography of location, it doesn't really matter whether the hotel is in the middle of town, on the edge of town, or five miles out of town, providing the site is adequate in size and the environment is one that can create a pleasant ambiance. Because of the nature of travel in Egypt you can transport your guests to and from the places of interest by coach very conveniently. In that case the site wouldn't be a particularly critical element. That phase is really a sort of micro-analysis, but Eric may want to talk later about a fairly heavy involvement he had in a large national tourism study on the Ivory Coast a few years ago. In that case the target was the whole country, focusing on identifying regions of the country which were the most appropriate areas to be developed.

In the area of market analysis, that's the next most critical area I think, one has to undertake sufficient research to satisfy oneself, and one's client, and the bankers, on the project, so that if the project gets built there will be sufficient support from the marketplace to maintain a reasonable level of income. If there is not sufficient market to justify the investment, one would want to inform one's client and explain why there isn't sufficient market support.

To give you an idea of the kind of characteristics that can impinge upon marketability, for example, many markets that one looks at are sensitive to the cyclical characteristics in business. I remember specifically looking at a project on Sardina in about 1972. It was really a most attractive location. The concept that the client was wishing to develop was second to none. The tragedy was that the market would only support the project from May through the end of September. There was really nothing you could do to stimulate the market off-peak because the weather conditions were so poor.

The most critical area of a study is the financial analysis and, as I put it here, the sensitivity analysis. I remember from my days in New York that one tended to go to the point of preparing a financial estimate, a revenue and expenditure statement of a project, and terminating the study there. In Europe the more sophisticated client wants to take the analysis beyond that point. He wants us to do a pre-financial feasibility evaluation, I mean by that he says "If I think of the project on this basis and that basis, and if the capital cost is thus and so, and if I get a tax holiday of this and so on, and put all the parameters together, does my anticipated revenue expenditure statement, my income before fixed charges, support the debt?"

In order to respond to this, we've moved into microcomputing to develop models that make our lives considerably easier. We start with a very straightforward financial statement with revenue, direct operating costs, and overhead costs, analyzed by department, giving us the income before fixed charges of the project after management fee and fire insurance. We're developing these estimates for year one through year five. We have variables that we can plug in. We can change the occupancy, we can change the room rate. We have a fair amount of flexibility in modifying the departmental operating performance. We have certain efficiency and inefficiency factors to fill in like marketing and administration in general. The net result of that computer run gives us income before fixed charges which, as you will appreciate, is the top line of our cash flow analysis. We try to make the model all-embracing for the needs of our clients, but inevitably one doesn't and one has to manipulate the computer. Let me explain in more detail.

At the top we have the capital inputs, the financing inputs of equity, and we're completely flexible on that. Then we have three loan parameters that we can use. Our clients might be financing the project on an export-import banking basis, or they might be using short-term commercial borrowing, or they could be using longer term finance if they can get it. Each of these loan packages within the model is very flexible. They have a length of up to 15 years and we can modify the repayment basis on each of those loans independently. We can repay the loans on a reducing balance basis, we can repay the loans on what we call an as soon as possible (ASAP). So, we take whatever net cash flow is available on the bottom line and plug that back into the loan factor to repay it as quickly as we can. This enables us to produce the various evaluated outputs that one might be interested in. It provides a net present value calculation, gives us a payback period calculation and gives us an internal rate of return calculation. One has the option of plugging in a terminal or residual value if one needs it. The other loan element that I didn't mention is on a standard mortgage type repayment basis. There is an inflation factor that can be built in here. There is an automatic tax calculation which calculates the tax on a given year and then plugs it into the following year on the basis that tax is paid one year in arrears.

The model is relatively simple in many ways. We plug in the income before fixed charges at the top of the cash flow and then we deduct items such as real estate taxes and the various interest payments. We have to deduct tax depreciation and, of course, this will depend on the regime that one's working in. In places like Egypt, it's a relatively simple regime. In the UK, rather more complex than I would imagine in the United States. It's a non-cash flow item. You only need to plug this in to determine what the tax liability is. The taxation element is computed and then the computer calculates the principal repayments on each of the loans. We have the option of putting in renewals, replacements or revisions as a cash flow expenditure.

This brings us down to the bottom line of the cash flow statement, net annual cash flow, or lack of it, as may occur. Later, simple calculations compute annual return on equity. This is something that we don't put in our reports, but it's an internal return evaluation, the loan cover of which, of course, is quite critical.

We sometimes have to remember, ourselves, that the final purpose of these studies is to advise people about financial results. We get involved in extensive market research in order to do that. In the final analysis, the question is what are the economics of either doing this or not doing it. This raises a very important question — what is the value or the cost-benefit relationship of having the study done? It costs a lot of money to have these studies done and a lot of time and effort goes into them. Are they worthwhile? I'll ask you, Peter. In your experiences with different kinds of studies, do you think it's demonstrable that there is a benefit to these studies?

Peter Walsh. — The most expensive feasibility study that I ever did was one on which we collected $288,000. But it was very much worthwhile because it identified several problems. It was not just a project, a hotel. It was for the government of the Kingdom of Jordan and it included 5 hotels and 1000 housing units on the Gulf of Aqaba. We had to identify the potential operating hazards of something brand new in a location where nothing existed. There were tremendous social impacts as well. It is a very strict Arabic-Moslem area where a girl in a bikini would have been a very big culture shock.

A lot of things came out. First of all, we were able to identify the infrastructural basic cost for preparing the area to accept the project; the cost would have been phenomenal. Even to get a work force or labor force to operate in this complex presented a tremendous challenge. While we were able to say the market is there, the demand is there, it became from a practical point virtually impossible to consider the project, to really develop it. An awful lot of money was spent to find this out but at least it straightened the record as far as the country was concerned and put what was then a very thorny issue in government to rest.

On the other hand, when someone may be building a $30 or $40 million property but hesitates to pay $10 or 11 or 12 thousand to have the market study done, to evaluate the type of market that will probably use the facility to modify that market, it is ludicrous. So I think the value of these feasibility studies is not just a question of values; it's absolutely essential.

We're not alone in this business and there are other firms. We are in a competitive situation. There is a healthy pressure to keep the fee competitive. A lot of clients who are looking at a project of medium size are really quite surprised by the fees that are charged. Unpleasantly surprised, especially if the findings are not positive for the project. Nine times out of ten we have an awful time with the client when we come in with a negative report.

That's an important point because, if it were not for the developers and the entrepreneurs of the world, obviously many things would never get done. It's very crushing if we come back and say "I'm sorry that your idea was no good" and then expect them to pay for that advice. It adds insult to injury. We have to give value for money paid. We are able to identify the key issues very quickly and therefore have a much shorter learning curve. If there is a particular difficulty on the assignment we can identify it sooner and get back and talk to the client sooner. Obviously, he pays less in the long run.

Our offices engaged in consulting, whether it be Calgary or London, develop a substantial library of printed material in what we call country files. These contain information from Afghanistan to Botswana. When someone asks us about prospects of tourism in Botswana, we can find out fairly quickly and give them an answer. The other aspect is our numerical data base. You've seen it manifested in publications such as *Trends in the U.S. Hotel Industry* and *International Trends* and *Town and Country* and the *Citywide Statistical Analyses*. By having access to this kind of information, one is bound to be much more accurate.

How do you use your consultants? How you get your best value from consultants? We encourage our clients to have a fairly high level of communication with us. If we run across a client who has a strong resistance to the fee, I always explain to him tht the amount of work that we do will be pretty much the same whether it's a small job or a large job. Although there will be some differences, one of the most expensive aspects of our work is putting the data down on paper. This is an expensive process. I have encouraged clients in certain situations to accept an abbreviated report, and to get together with us as often as possible so we can communicate the knowledge we have acquired verbally. It sounds silly, but many clients come to us not knowing what they want. I think it's very important that client defines the purpose of the study because it can affect the fee. If he really doesn't need a heavy report, it will be far better to define the kind of package that is right.

Another aspect of the feasibility study is that, in a way, it is an insurance policy. People who are investigating projects should pay some sort of premium for finding out whether or not they should risk very much larger sums. A difference arises rather quickly between what an individual developer is insuring against and what a government may be insuring against. Some governments have departments that are in the business of commissioning studies. That seems to be their main activity. In doing so they're looking to insure themselves against future suits or against future displeasure of their constituents when it is learned that large sums of money have been wasted on a project that has turned out to be a disaster. They are looking for two kinds of insurance, in a way. They're looking for insurance against making a bad decision, and they're also looking for insurance in case someone sues.

Government has sometimes different ideas as to what the word feasibility means. It could mean is it possible, and are the economic or social impacts desirable? I recently was involved with a project where the whole idea was entirely desirable except to a certain group of environmentalists living in the Alberta foothills of the Rockies. We have large parks, national parks, and protected areas and there are some individuals who feel that all of the Rocky Mountains should be protected areas that nobody should be allowed in except the grizzly bears. There is even a group up there called Alert, the Alberta League for Environmentally Responsible Tourism. The project we did was for the private sector but there was a tremendous amount of interface with government over questions of environmental feasibility. Was it socially feasible? The question being asked was whether by giving approval to this project, the government is sticking its neck out or doing something wrong? So, the requirement is somewhat different from whether or not the developer is going to make a dollar for his corporation.

Eric Green.—These are some of the complications that arise. On that point there is a new question that has developed in the last four or five years, that of impact on others. Today, if you build a new hotel or a new convention center or a new ski lodge the chances are that it's going to be financed somewhat by public money through taxpayer supported bonds or low interest rate bonds. If someone is already in the marketplace offering a similar service, he obviously doesn't want to have his life affected by public sector financed competition. An impact study is required to measure the effect on him. Alan, have you been asked much to do that in the United Kingdom?

Alan Hopper.—No, my reading of the situation is that it is more of an American phenomenon than a European phenomenon but I am sure it will come in the course of the next few years. But is it not a product of the way the industry has developed and the way the government has been responsible?

Eric Green.—Yes, I think that's right. Maybe I should say a few words on impact. The question of impact studies causes a great deal of concern. In the early days of franchising, almost all franchising organizations gave territorial rights sometimes over a very large area. The hotel chains quickly realized that they had given away more than they needed to because there was a demand for many more Holiday Inns or Hiltons or Sheratons.

Now most of the hotel chains will give a franchise only for a particular site or location, and they will reserve to themselves the right to give a franchise next door if they want to. The individual franchisees, who are then threatened with another hotel of the same brand near them, may feel this will affect their market and are quite likely to make strong protest regardless of whether they have a sound legal basis. If they have only the right to operate at a particular location one may assume they have no legal foundation for protesting, but it's not that simple. The franchising companies are anxious not to be the target of politicians and they don't want to dilute their own market too much. If they are going to wind up with too many of their own brand name everyone is going to suffer. There will be disaffection and the franchisees who may be powerful can cause another problem.

At that point the hotel chains, particularly, say "What are we going to do about this? If we are sued or if there is a lot of protest our best defense will be to say we've studied the financial impact on this particular franchisee here." Thus, the impact study was developed.

The requirements of the impact study are in some detail. How many points of occupancy will be lost? What will be the total effect on the profitability of that particular organization? Many of these are extremely difficult to answer because it isn't only a question of how many rooms, but of how well they are maintained, or even whether the room clerks smile. Are they efficient? Is the food good? You know you may lose business from a lot of other reasons than just having competition next door. So this is where the impact study caused us a lot of concern. Right now we're undertaking such studies, but we try to restrict them only to the market aspects rather than get involved with the subjective features of whether the carpet is clean or whether the housekeeping is good.

That brings us to something else that has happened in recent years more than in the past. That is the in-house consultants. Today, many hotel companies or airlines, for example, are perfectly capable of being their own consultants. Every large company in any field will have inside, in-house consulting not relying on outside independents.

Alan Hopper.—I think it comes back to the issue of objectivity or independence; they are related. We have seen over the last 15 years the rather rapid growth of major international companies. Once they have the momentum they take on the capability of doing their own analyses and feasibility studies. Fairly quickly they come face to face with two realities. On the one hand, these groups are structured within major companies such that their existence is inevitably related to performance. Their objective for a given year might be specified as bringing in 5, 10, or 15 management contracts. That would be the criterion, but nothing is said about the quality of the contracts or whether the hotel was in the right location. In some companies we have seen bad judgment on the part of the company itself in getting involved in a project they should never have been involved in. But, of course, the individual and the development group were committed to achieving a certain goal. It was quantitative, not qualitative. Once these properties become operational a rather long lead time, 2 to 3 years, occurs before it becomes clear how poor things were. There is then a review of the strategy and a determination of where the error lay.

The other reason for going to an outside consultant is that the consultant does not have an ax to grind. It is no skin off his nose whether or not the project goes ahead. Obviously, one does approach these things with a positive outlook but if it does not fly, with the criteria that prevail, you at least try to persuade the client that another alternative could be satisfactory.

Eric Green. — That leads to another thought, the developing role of consultants in some of these activities. What is happening now to a large extent is the need for multi-disciplinary studies, particularly in marketing projects for tourism. Your team must not only be people who are familiar with hotels, but also people who are familiar with transportation problems because part of the problem, particularly in the Third World countries, and the Caribbean in general, is that the transportation simply isn't there.

The airlines say, you build the hotels and develop the market and we will provide the transportation. The hotel says they cannot do that because there is no transportation. For these multi-disciplinary studies you need more experts, transportation experts. You need, of course, travel trade experts. You really need people such as the wholesalers or tour operators who are familiar with packaging. But I don't know of any organization that has enough demand for multi-disciplinary work to maintain all those experts on the payrolls. And so the tendency now is for people like us to combine with other consulting firms for a major consulting effort such as a tourism feasibility study.

Peter Walsh. — More and more in capacity with the *Travel Research Association* we have become involved with the totality of the players in the industry. It has been my belief, although there have been some extremely great improvements, that Canada still packages itself very, very poorly. Access to Canada for holiday information from overseas is difficult. There is a tendency to hide the Canadian Government travel representatives in embassies, where they are not very easy to find. I think that often we don't package our product very well.

Feasibility studies for resort projects are going to be more expensive than for a city center hotel. We have to go into these areas such as transportation, we have to go to the travel trade, we have to go out into the long distance markets, and that really drives the cost up.

Another thing we have found is that principles of the feasibility study are applicable not only to new projects, but also to existing facilities. Determining, if it was a single unit for example, what the future outlook for that property might be; helping to realign that property to changing markets; helping to make a buy-sell decision and to allocate a value to the property.

We've also found that feasibility study principles can apply to doing a complete review of a chain. That is something that we had the occasion to do in Canada. Not such a long time ago a certain railroad company had to make a decision as to whether or not, having built hotels along its railway line many years before, they were to stay in the hotel business or get out. We were asked to come in and do a total review, property by property, of all the hotels. Using the principles of the feasibility study, each property's markets were examined, its operations were examined, and the environment in which those properties were was examined. As it turned out, we did recommend that they sell or remove two properties, one with 330 rooms, another with 400 rooms. We advised them to sell those and concentrate in other areas and develop a plan for where they should be 5 years down the road, 10 years down the road, and roughly, the kind of money they will need to achieve this plan. I'm happy to say they have followed that plan perfectly and it's paying off beautifully.

There is another chain in Canada right now that has just asked that the same thing be done for them. I think they have 7 properties that they own and others which they manage. It's the owned properties that they're concerned with. Again, the same thing, the principle of the feasibility study, is used. The add-on in that case is the operational review and an evaluation of their personnel. An evaluation of their system means you need system staff working with you and again you get into this multi-disciplinary situation.

That is the market and I think that it is very real to have an outsider come in to do a review of the chain. It's very difficult for a chain to do it on its own. For example, if one of the properties is not doing well there's no point in going down and asking the manager why it is not doing well. He's got lot at stake; all the staff at the hotel have a lot at stake. And there are a lot of people that work at the hotel that have a personal interest. So you're not really necessarily going to get the true picture if you try to do that in-house.

When you do a feasibility study, you're making assumptions. It's up to the client whether or not your role stops the moment you hand over the report. That depends on a lot of factors. You can simply say "This is what this hotel should do, assuming good management, assuming aggressive marketing, assuming a strong staff." This is what 65% of feasibility studies say. Just because your client is a chain, doesn't mean that the

chain will not mess it up. This industry is a fraternal order, if you want to call it that. Once you're in the industry you are part of the gang. If you are not in the industry then there is no way you can "understand what it's all about."

Alan Hopper. — That's one of the reasons that we say it's important that we maintain our distance and objectivity. Otherwise we will find ourselves accused of two things. One is taking on management's role which our professional ethics don't permit us to do. Even more, we might be accused of having a financial stake in the future. We don't invest in our clients' projects, but on the other hand, if your're going to influence or make recommendations about the management company or the hiring of key personnel or other things like that, you may be perceived to have a financial interest. Then there would be no more independence.

Part IV

Operations Management

15

Improving Productivity in the Operations Function

Carl J. Bellas

If the 1960's and 1970's were the decades of growth, then the 1980's should be the decade of productivity. Companies of all sizes, in all industries, are working to improve the productivity of their organizations. In one study, a major management consulting firm asked CEO's to list their major concerns for the years ahead and consistently among the top ones were productivity and ability to cope with rapidly changing technology. The use of new technologies to improve productivity is common in the operations function of businesses where emphasis on productivity invariably increases the emphasis on operations where inputs are transformed into outputs.

In its simplest expression, productivity is the ratio of outputs to inputs, or the amount of output resulting from each unit of input. The identification and measurement of outputs and inputs causes problems for managers.

In the United States, the most widely used productivity ratios are based on labor inputs. This reflects a concern with the utilization of expensive and often scarce skilled labor. Innovation has been directed toward reducing labor inputs. In other parts of the industrial world capital and natural resources are the scarce and costly inputs and innovations that reduce their use have been emphasized. Today, capital and natural resources are scarce throughout the world. The innovative thrust in the United States is changing because of this and productivity measures are increasingly used to take into account the inputs of capital, energy and natural resources.

Outputs are easiest to measure when physical units are produced. Service industries, such as the hospitality industry because of the intangible nature of its product, have additional problems in measurement even if appropriate units of service can be determined. This chapter will concentrate on the factors influencing productivity in hospitality operations.

Traditionally, productivity has been linked to profitability. One way to increase profitability is to increase sales faster than increasing costs, or to reduce costs without reducing sales or, to put it another way, more customers must be served per unit of time (an increase in output) or less resources must be used to produce a given level of output (a decrease in inputs).

Input costs in the hospitality industry have continued to increase and the consumer is resisting attempts to pass along these costs. The effect of inflation on resource costs will continue to squeeze profits against pricing limits. Yet, replacement of unproductive and obsolete facilities is causing a drain on capital. Thus, productivity is an even more vital issue today than it has been in the past.

PRODUCTIVITY STRATEGIES AFFECTING OPERATIONS

In its strategic planning activities, a hospitality organization evaluates potential productivity gains in all functional areas of the business. At least four important strategies have their focus in the operations functions:
- Higher utilization of fixed assets;
- Reduced inventory investment;
- Increased return on new products;
- Increased revenues from the existing customer base.

Higher Utilization of Fixed Assets

Organizations place the great bulk of fixed assets in the hands of the operations function. The return on these assets must exceed that of alternative investments. For utilization of assets to be at the highest practical level, capacity planning is essential both prior to the specification and procurement of the assets and after they are in operation. Manufacturing industries are placing increased emphasis on capacity planning and developing new techniques to aid in capacity decision-making. The hospitality industry must develop improved methods to deal with its own unique situation in which backlogs rarely are permitted and thus capacity tends to be underutilized.

Higher utilization of assets can also come from better scheduling of personnel and even, where possible, of customers. Personnel scheduling techniques frequently involve only the quantity of employees but do not take into account an individual's productivity. Yet, inefficient personnel can limit the utilization of equipment, and investment in more efficient equipment may be justified only if it can be operated at capacity.

Reduced Inventory Investment

Any industry needs adequate inventories to avoid losing customers. However, over-investment in inventory requires excessive capital and incurs unnecessary interest costs. There is a real need to improve demand forecasts and to develop better systems for planning and controlling inventories.

At a time when values were increasing and unit costs decreasing due to scale economies, forecasting was frequently neglected or oversimplified.

Better detailed forecasting is now essential and more easily possible through the use of newer techniques and computer programs. Still, a data base is required and the need to have data collected often prolongs the implementation of a useful forecast. Even though forecasts are always wrong they do serve as guidelines for planning. Renewed emphasis must be placed on the system that plans inventory requirements, monitors changing conditions, and adjusts rapidly to meet changing conditions. Much remains to be done in this area.

Increased Return on New Products

Research and development of new products frequently originate in another part of the organization but operations plays a large part in determining the eventual return on the new product. The speed at which operations can get into production of the product at acceptable rates is often crucial to success. If a customer's first trial of a service or product results in dissatisfaction, the long run success and return on investment may be seriously hindered. Beyond the obvious need to provide quality and service at the time of introduction, the operations function must be capable of continuing to provide these elements throughout the product's life. To do otherwise is to shorten the product or service's life which may result in losses.

Increased Revenues from the Existing Customer Base

Revenue maximization is usually considered a marketing strategy but limitations are imposed by the products and services that operations can provide with its human and fixed asset resources. Physical layouts and specialized equipment may restrict the types of products that can be offered by an organization. Large multi-unit organizations may be able to effectively increase product lines by developing new items that can be produced efficiently in existing facilities but, to compete, smaller organizations may need to be more innovative in their product design. Thus, they require greater flexibility of production resources.

It is difficult to determine the extent to which companies that comprise the hospitality industry have developed the four strategies discussed. Each individual firm must ask itself where it stands in its strategic plans for productivity improvement within its operations function.

OPERATIONAL SOURCES OF PRODUCTIVITY INCREASES

Perhaps the most trite expression about productivity improvement is that "employees must work smarter not harder." Often, this implies that with better training and more motivation employees can be much more productive. It also over-emphasizes the importance of labor productivity. While some improvement is undoubtedly possible, working smarter will require better management and better use of technology. Several studies reported by utility firms found that approximately 50% of employee idle time could be traced to management's inability to provide material for the employees to work on.

The hospitality industry has historically used large amounts of low wage labor that is extremely transient. This fact of life is unlikely to change drastically, therefore, productivity gains will not come from a highly skilled, highly motivated, permanent labor force. What will be important are skilled management, management control systems, and technology.

Management

The large corporate hospitality firms have developed well publicized management training programs. In many instances these programs are available only to college graduates. While the programs include training in the operation of new, advanced equipment, it is unclear to what extent they emphasize productivity improvement via better employee selection, scheduling, and training. It appears that too many trained managers still lack well developed human relations skills and the ability to adapt to change. Nevertheless, in too many organizations, training is still nonexistent. Relying on an individual manager's natural ability to handle employee resources is extremely risky when attempting to develop a productive organization.

Management Systems

Without a definition and measurement of productivity in an organization no specific goals can be set. Control systems cannot be designed to monitor the progress toward attainment of goals. Most of the published material on productivity measurement in the hospitality industry comes from the academic community where studies have centered on the institutional food service industry. Researchers have at least tried to develop useful productivity measures.

The advent of affordable computer based information systems permits corporate headquarters to closely monitor the performance of its branch units. Other computer systems permit an organization to calculate the impact that changes in actual or projected resource costs will have on profitability and to alter product lines and prices accordingly. As better management control systems are developed and used, managerial performance may be improved, lessening the dependence upon the skill of the individual unit manager.

Technology

As information technology can improve the amount and quality of the management process, so too can technologically advanced production equipment improve product quality and operating productivity.

An informal telephone survey of equipment manufacturers conducted by the author revealed a belief that only about 15—20% of the potential for advanced equipment in the food service industry has been realized. Respondents cited the possibility of large potential labor savings where resistance caused by lack of trained personnel, service problems, and general resistance to change could be overcome. Some blamed the manufacturers who were unwilling to invest resources for product research and development. Most of the new equipment has been used by the large chains but new electronic based systems can also be justified by smaller operations.

CONSEQUENCES OF TECHNOLOGY

It is posssible to develop some scenarios based on new technology. Productivity will improve with the introduction of technology in the form of advanced computing systems or production systems.

There is a possibility that the new technology will be expensive and affordable only with large economies of scale. Return on investment will be possible only with large customer volumes and/or by centralizing some operations from many units. This places the large firm at a productivity, cost, and service advantage. In turn, the competitive advantage and survival of the smaller firm could be threatened.

If the pattern of computer development and availability is duplicated by other technologically advanced equipment, then the small firm will have the ability to improve its productivity. Small computer systems have only begun to penetrate the potential market represented by the hospitality industry's small and medium sized concerns. Low priced, cost justifiable production equipment may also have trouble gaining acceptance because of fears of maintenance problems, complexity of operations, or scarcity of skilled employees. Regardless, the new technologies can actually increase the competitiveness of smaller firms. Survival will be determined by the ability of management to recognize opportunities available to it.

Probably, technology improvement will continue, requiring less direct labor personnel but those who are employed will need to be more highly skilled and therefore better paid. This in turn will require better trained and better paid managers. Organizations and their units will have to reorganize to adapt to the new equipment. The evaluation of total factor productivity will be crucial to decision making. While there will be a concern for retaining a competitive advantage, managers must continually be aware of how others are improving productivity and adapt these improvements to their own organizations.

Finally, technology changes positions among current competitors and encourages the entry of new competition. In 1990, the industry leaders will be those who have adapted to the new technologies and increased their productivity. The emphasis will be on the operations function, but the innovations there will have major impacts on the entire organization.

16

Productivity Measurement and Improvement in the Hospitality Industry

Mel Sandler

As we are going to discuss productivity improvement, we must be certain that we have a common understanding of the terms we are using.

One organization states that productivity improvement simply means getting more out of what you put in.

More specifically, *productivity* is the ratio of output to input. The output is the related amount of work performed and/or total resource cost.

In manufacturing, productivity is often measured by ratio of the market value of goods *to* the costs required to produce them.

The output is most easily identified as a product or service that is purchased, used or experienced by someone.

The input involves many more factors and can be categorized broadly or in a specific incidence can be directed into minute categories of input.

For our purpose we shall use broadly constituted categories. They are in general:

Manpower	Materials	Machines
Capital	Energy	Methods and Systems

The quantity (and quality) of output is dependent upon how the input factors are combined, integrated, related to achieve an effectiveness and efficiency to approach desirable levels of output.

Although it is a simplification, productivity can be improved (or optimum levels reached) in five ways. They are:

a. Increase output more than input
b. Increase output without increasing input
c. Decrease output but decrease input more

    d. Maintain some output but decrease input
    e. Increase output and decrease input
        (National Center for Productivity 1975)

IMPORTANCE OF PRODUCTIVITY IMPROVEMENT

Productivity improvement has gained a measure of notoriety in recent months, for it is said to be the cure for our economic ills.

Productivity improvement can presumably have the following results:

Reduce inflation
Reduce unemployment
Maintain or improve our standard of living
Maintain a strong position in domestic markets
Higher *real* wages for all
Improved return on investment
More jobs and more opportunities for advancement
Future job security
Provide investment capital for making changes to keep up with new technology.
Build a strong position in international markets

These above apply to the service sector as well. Other methods of expression might be more appropriate to our sector.

Productivity improvement can achieve
    1. Increase in service levels at same cost
    2. Reduction in cost of services while maintaining equivalent service levels (quality).

These potential gains attributed to productivity improvement would suggest that this area of involvement and work should be a worthy effort with sufficient payoff for our energies.

PRODUCTIVITY MEASUREMENT —MACRO

Why has there been this major concern about productivity levels in the United States?

The United States has traditionally been a world leader in efficiency. This has permitted a prominent position in world markets, an increasing standard of living for our work force.

Productivity as measured by output per man hour has declined in recent years.

The average rate of increase in productivity (per hour) was 3.2% for the period 1948—1965.

This trend dropped off to 0.9% for the period 1973—1979. The latest data for 1980 indicates a further reduction in output per hour (Sommers 1978).

Certainly, the entire world has been affected by OPEC pricing. In the United States there has been considerable attention given to the burdensome cost of government regulation (environmental, OSHA, EEO, etc.) but it may be worthwhile to see how we have done compared to other nations.

Productivity change in 15 manufacturing industries which compares the United States, United Kingdom, Germany and Japan for the period 1969-1974 indicates (Anon. 1980C):

United States	2.7%
United Kingdom	4.1%
Germany	5.8%
Japan	9.8% (1960—1972)
Japan	5.2% (1972—1977)

More recent data indicate the United States still lags. For the period 1970—1979, we find (productivity growth):

United States   2.3%   West Germany   5.2%   Japan   5.2%

Attention has also been given to the rate of investment as a percentage of GNP. This statistic is important because it suggests the age of the production plant and its efficiency as well as the ability to renew resources. A comparison of 9 countries shows the United States investing 14% of GNP compared to 31% for Japan and 25% for Germany. The United States is low man based on this examination (Anon. 1980C).

On a macro level, the indicators used do provide a gross comparison of productivity changes. One can argue the relative merits of various measures but one will find that the trends are somewhat consistent.

POTENTIAL CAUSES OF UNITED STATES PERFORMANCE

Work Force Expansion

The growth of the work force in the 1970's resulted not only in a less experienced work force but also in a tendency to overstaff due to ease of staffing. Some also say there was an effort to fulfill social obligations by hiring females and minority group members.

This potential for less productive use of personnel may not be available in the 1980's since the work force growth will slow and the minimum wage has increased. Employers may have to adapt to getting more work done with a smaller work force.

Energy Costs

Not only have costs of energy increased but also more labor hours and effort have been expanded to conserve energy. In some cases, this diversion of labor and investment provided adequate returns but some feel it inevitably resulted in higher costs and less productivity.

CAPITAL INVESTMENT

It has been suggested that capital investment in the United States suffered due to the large labor supply. It was easier to hire additional employees compared to expending the effort and capital to keep production up. Also observers claim U.S. managers have been keeping their eyes on current returns (and stock market prices) rather than invest for the larger terms. Also, growth was conceived as a measurement of gross sales and gross profits which encourage growth by acquisition.

The average age of plant and equipment in the United States is 16-17 years compared to 12 years for Germany and 10 years for Japan (Anon. 1981).

RESEARCH AND TECHNOLOGY

A companion attitude toward capital investment is the approach to research and technology. Japanese industrialists have cited one advantage they have, their dedication to *long term* returns which has enabled them to rationalize continued "investment" in research and development (R&D), whereas the U.S. managers have been more concerned with profits today.

Companies and the federal government are able to install R&D cutbacks as the pain is not immediate and certainly can't be easily quantified.

GROWTH OF SERVICE SECTORS

Measurement of productivity is affected by the mix of jobs and their resultant output. Service jobs by their very nature are of relatively low productivity compared to manufacturing jobs. As society has changed (in style of living, affluence and standard of living), the service sector has grown and as a consequence, the overall measurement of output and input results in a lower rate of productivity growth.

EMPLOYEE MOTIVATION

Do employees work as hard today as they used to? This is a most controversial question. Lack of motivation can impact productivity and many companies have devoted their major energies toward improving motivation later.

STEPPING DOWN TO THE INDUSTRY
AND FIRM OR UNIT LEVEL

Industry Data

All the data up to this point in our discussion indicate that the United States is in trouble. We are losing our momentum, we are investing less in the future, we are doing less research and development, and we have less confidence in our ability to motivate our work force.

Data from industries and firms are collapsed into the overall calculations so in varying degrees we are part of the problem. I am not suggesting that everybody in our industry is a low producer, but at least we can suggest that productivity improvement requires continual effort by management.

A May 1975 Bureau of Labor Statistics (BLS) study of productivity in hotels and motels (Vrisko 1975) shows that output per man hour in the hotel-motel industry increased at an average annual rate of 2.5% between 1958 and 1973 compared to a 2.7% annual rate in labor productivity for the private nonfarm sector. The gains in productivity resulted from a growth in output of more than 75% accompanied by an increase of 20% in man hours.

The period from 1961 to 1967 was the most rapid growth period (4%), 1971 was a weak period and recovery occurred in 1972 and 1973.

During the period of 1958—1973 industry *output* increased at an annual average rate of 3.8%. Similar to the productivity measure, the average increase was not uniform. Output increased 5.4% for 1961—1967. Growth slowed in the late 1960's to early 1970's. 1971 was the low period and then growth recovered in 1973 (U.S. Dept. of Labor, Bureau of Labor Statistics, 1978).

Several general characteristics of the hotel-motel industry must be emphasized. Considerable labor must be available to merely operate rather than increase inventories, and thus becomes a fixed input. Another way of expressing this factor is that staffing in many job categories is not sensitive to demand changes.

The previously mentioned 1975 report does suggest that the industry has taken steps to counter and improve the productivity trend. Examples are the use of disposable items, no iron laundries, direct dialing telephone systems, automatic elevators, use of convenience foods, use of vending outlets, use of automated beverage systems and some electronic control equipment. Data processing and computers at this time were considered an application for large properties (500 rooms).

Industry customarily measures effectiveness by looking at Profit & Loss statement to determine profits. Certainly it is a reasonable objective to create a profit. Investors (and lenders) are equally interested in return on investment. There are probably some who are pleased when they can report that output increased or that productivity increased compared to prior periods.

Productivity ratios are helpful but do not permit an analysis that would lead to suggestions to improve productivity.

Inputs can vary according to:

- Degree of technological development
- Type of equipment used
- Quantity of equipment used
- Relationship of equipment capacity to utilized capacity
- Work flow and equipment layout
- Skills and training of employees
- Competence of management

Outputs, as mentioned previously, are the results of numerous internal and external factors such as: quality of product, market positioning, competition, weather, cost of gasoline, and general inflationary factors.

As part of a series of articles outlining the training program for management employees of a hotel company (Anon. 1980A) potential performance indicators are suggested as items to be considered in discussing performance goals

Key Indicators of Performance in Hotels

1. Quality of service. Methods of measurement include inspections, responses to guest questionnaires, study of complaint files and study of complimentary files.

2. House profit before repairs and maintenance.

3. Operating results compared to forecasts.

4. Departmental results compared to last year.

5. Number of rooms occupied.

6. Percentage of room occupancy.

7. Percentage of multiple occupancy.

8. Average daily rate per room.

9. Number of times average rate earned.

10. Total covers served.

11. Covers served per paying overnight guest per outlet.

12. Covers or rooms serviced per employee day: total, by outlet, by production area or other.

13. Average check: per cover by outlet, per meal period.

14. Comparisons of operating results with economic indicators or price level or currency exchange; adjusted indices for the country, city.

15. Sales growth by category. Rooms sales total and subdivided by category; conferences; food and beverages; outside catering; garage; casino; shops swimming pool, etc.

16. Sales growth by category compared to total sales.

17. Sales by category and/or department compared to room sales.

18. Contract sales by category: airlines, local companies, etc.

19. Sales per outlet or on average employee per day basis.

20. Accounts receivable to total credit revenue.

21. Average collection period.

22. Accounts written off as bad debts compared with charge sales.

23. Effectiveness of manpower productivity control system.

24. House profit before repairs and maintenance per employee day.

25. Payroll percentage for the entire hotel and for each department. For operating departments, compare to each department's sales; for non-operating departments, compare with total hotel sales.

26. Number of employees (employee day basis): total and by department.

27. Waiting time at outlets for service.

28. Number of guest questionnaires received per 1,000 guests.

29. Total value of inventories.

30. Inventory turnover, and trends in increases/decreases.

31. Heat, light and power costs per occupied room.

32. Maintenance and security of property and equipment as evaluated by technically competent personnel utilizing standard checklists.

33. Testing, evaluating and reporting on new products, services, facilities, techniques (in cooperation with home offices for chain properties).

34. Effects on guests and staff of internal and external building and rehabilitation programs (alterations, extensions, etc.) as measured by sales, covers, productivity, guest questionnaires, letters.

35. Return on assets utilized.

36. Improvement in scores of annual executive evaluations of department heads.

37. Promotion records.

38. For chain operations: evaluation of marketing cooperation, records of guest referrals.

39. Number of employees completing manpower development and training programs.

40. Extent of staff involvement in professional and trade association, charitable and civic groups (membership, attendance, offices held, achievements).

DIFFICULTIES OF PRODUCTIVITY MEASUREMENT

These indicators are valuable and provide a basis for discussion, goal setting and a degree of comparison. However, some managers point out the difficulty identifying the factors of productivity measurement which have been instrumental in the changes:

Examples are—

House profit—Result of outstanding marketing or general operating cost containment.

Average daily rate—Outstanding rate setting, upgrading room rates via sales or competitive influences.

Average check (food)—Good menu design and food production, or result of opportune purchasing or excellent sales work by dining staff.

Similar comments can be made about any indicators that are related to monetary measures. This problem affects both management and employees. The matter is most critical when trying to orient employees about the need for meeting certain productivity levels and providing a means for self-monitoring on an ongoing basis.

The principle we are suggesting is that the measure of productivity should be direct and simple, expression in non-monitary terms, and where possible, self-monitoring.

In an article entitled "Look to Consumers to Increase Productivity", Lovelock and Young (1979) suggest that hotels and restaurants have utilized customers to increase productivity via the use of self-service buffets, salad bars, etc. In-room coffee in some motor hotels has facilitated the peaks in morning coffee service demands in the restaurant. Some restaurants use customers to bus their own tables (normally in modestly-priced restaurants or cafeterias).

Their suggestions for identifying opportunities for improving productivity are in the area of systems and procedural changes. They are based on an analysis of what is being done now, why it is being done and its resultant effectiveness. The emphasis is on management's role in using resources effectively.

Hotel and Resort Industry magazine (Anon. 1979) reports on "Dunfey Hotels Enjoy Gains as Productivity Increases." It is interesting to note that the Dunfey productivity improvement study was not made out of desperation, but rather to make certain that the most efficient resources were in use.

The major steps of the program consisted of:

1. Development of forecasting techniques to serve as the basis for improved forecasting of labor requirements.
2. Development of departmental staffing standards, work routines and training in forecasting techniques. This included staffing

schedules applicable to varying volume levels.
3. Implementation and documentation of all procedures. In greater detail, the program planned to:

- Evaluate all work activities
- Establish a method of work measurement
- Forecast based on each work category
- Provide for a system of staff control via scheduling
- Train supervision to use work standards as a guide in making staffing assignment.
- Develop a system of feedback comparing performance with standards
- Provide for tight control of overtime
- Establish a means of communication of "unplanned" circumstances which would affect staffing
- Provide for a method of evaluating overall results of the program.

It is reported that the program paid off beyond expectations and was continued at other properties.

The essence of the program as I view it is:

- Management evaluated work activities to determine what had to be done, the method (including equipment and aids) to be followed, and the quality level.
- Staffing requirements were established to evaluate performance as well as a feedback system to the supervisor on how well he performed.
- Management tool on a commitment to make each supervisor aware of the information needed to staff effectively.

Holiday Inns reported that an industrial engineering approach in their property in Nashville, Tennessee resulted in savings in labor at the rate of $100,000 per year (Anon. 1978). In housekeeping alone, room productivity increased to 20 rooms from 13 to 14 rooms per day. This improvement resulted from an engineering study that redesigned a maid's cart as well as carefully determined steps in cleaning. Training (or retraining) was needed to make certain that the new procedures were understood and used. Additional improvements were made in the front office, laundry and restaurant.

The program determined what should be done, what tools and equipment are needed and how to assure compliance of procedures and standards. The final steps should be monitoring of the standards and procedures as well as considering further improvements.

In Theodore Levitt's (1971) well-known article "Production Line Approach to Service" a section is entitled "The Technocratic Hamburger." Levitt's thesis is stated in the forward to this article:

"We think about service in humanistic terms; we think about manufacturing in technocratic terms. This, according to the author, is why manufacturing industries are forward looking and efficient while service industries and customer service are, by comparison, primitive and inefficient. He argues that if companies stop thinking of service as servitude and personal ministration, they will be able to effect drastic improvement in its quality and efficiency." Levitt goes on to say: "But most important is the carefully controlled execution of each outlet's central function—the rapid delivery of a uniform high-quality mix of prepared foods in an environment of obvious cleanliness, order, and cheerful courtesy." "The systematic substitution of equipment for people, combined with the carefully planned use and positioning of technology, enables McDonald's to attract and hold patronage in proportions no predecessor or imitator has managed to duplicate." (p.44). . ."The entire system is engineered and executed according to a tight technological discipline that ensures fast, clean, reliable service in an atmosphere that gives the modestly paid employees a sense of pride and dignity. In spite of the crunch of eager customers, no employee looks or acts harassed, and therefore, no harassment is communicated to the customers; (p. 45)."

I am not suggesting that everyone go into the hamburger business but it demonstrates that management can determine the end product (and market), how to achieve it precisely and therefore accomplish both a quality product and a quantity that will represent optimum efficiency.

In a *Fortune* article entitled, "How Three Companies Increased Their Productivity" (Anon. 1980B), Burger King is presented as a company that has achieved a high level of productivity. The description is: "Every movement of each employee in a prototypical Burger King Restaurant is calculated and readjusted in time and motion studies...." This confirms again the principle that management must determine its needs and standards.

PROGRAM FOR PRODUCTIVITY IMPROVEMENT

There is sufficient evidence that not only is productivity improvement needed but does indeed go on. I recognize I have only reported on a few industry examples but the literature and my experience suggests that a program can be established in every organization (unit or property).

The principles are as follows:
1. Productivity improvement is a responsibility of management.
2. Responsibility should be placed on existing line and staff members.
3. Need for productivity improvement should be identified in a broad sense. (Beneficial in order to be competitive, enhance job security, provide a sense of satisfaction, etc.).

4. Productivity measurement should be explained and differentiated from profitability per se, although a linkage should be recognized.

5. Improvement objectives should be established (based on clearly defined measures) and review dates determined.

6. An awareness of opportunities for productivity improvement should be established by training in principles of work simplification, understanding of systems and the interdependence of factors of operation, and the ability to establish means of measurement.

7. Develop measurement factors and share data on existing levels to demonstrate the ability to use measurements.

8. Use rough estimates of measurement if precise measures become complex.

9. Measure "subunits" if possible, to permit better understanding and to facilitate improvements at every level of the organization.

10. Identify opportunities for improvements of modest amounts to effect the gains and to demonstrate that productivity improvement can be achieved.

11. Recognize that productivity improvement is the manager's responsibility. But this responsibility cannot be met without the understanding and support of his staff at all levels.

In summary, productivity improvement can be achieved if there is an understanding of measurement, if all resources of management are examined to achieve this improvement, and if the support of *all* employees is sought and used.

I feel that I must offer a word of explanation in closing. Since my field of interest and professional activity is human resource management, it might seem that I have not given sufficient weight to the area of motivation and specific personnel administration tools and techniques. I have purposely not included this area, as important as it can be, since I also think that management needs to set the stage for motivation, recognition, rewards, job enrichment, use of quality circles, bonuses, incentives, etc. by establishing goals, methods, systems, measurement and the desire to improve.

There are two quotes that apply to this topic.

1. Chinese Proverb—"Every journey of a thousand miles must begin with a first step."

2. Lord Kelvin (William Thompson 1824—1907) — "When you can measure what you are speaking about and express it in numbers, you know something about it; but when you cannot measure it, when you cannot express it in numbers, your knowledge is of a meager and unsatisfactory kind".

17

Operating the Traditional American Plan Resort

Stephen P. Barba

The traditional concept of American plan hospitality first evolved in New England some 150 years ago—in the White Mountains of New Hampshire, in the Green Mountains of Vermont, in the Berkshire Hills of Massachusetts, on Cape Cod and along the coast of Maine.

Resort destination areas developed throughout the Northeast in response to a genuine longing by many first-generation immigrants to discover a countryside that resembled their homeland. The New England resort areas developed in response to the needs of a very different clientele. While the *very* rich were building huge vacation mansions as summer homes in Newport, Rhode Island, the *less* rich, but still well-to-do, established families of the Northeast (today's country club set) were interested in traveling out of the city and into the country for extended summer vacations. The then excellent railway system (and soon after the automobile) enabled all Americans to relax and vacation in the country-side. A great number and variety of accommodations became available, many of which first developed from family boarding-house operations. The style of hospitality ranged from simple cottages and sportsmen's lodges to elegant inns and grand resorts, from the bargain rate to the exorbitant. Nevertheless, the American plan prevailed throughout; overnight rates covered all charges for accommodations, meals and use of facilities.

The quality and quantity of these American plan services varied according to the style and scope of each operation. Yet the innkeeper was always expected to serve as the host and provider in accommodating the tastes and needs of his house guests. New England innkeepers inherited the age-old custom of serving the local communities and the traveling public as "a friend along the road." The hospitable innkeeper welcomed a personal acquaintanceship with his guests and his guests expected no less of him. Each operation no matter how limited or expansive, was individually characterized by the nature of its innkeeper's personal sense of hospitality.

An inn directly reflects the personality of its owner/operator. The early resort innkeeper in New England distinguished himself and his property by the extra measure of hospitality he offered. Thus, the more enterprising resort innkeepers were known for especially clean and well-furbished rooms, bounteous meals three and often four times a day, efficient and friendly staffs.

Guests would spend their time walking, hiking, fishing, swimming in a dammed up stream or lake, or rocking on the front porch engaged in conversation with other guests. They had come to the mountains to enjoy the change of scenery, the fresh air, the pure spring water, and the pollen-free atmosphere. Later as the size and popularity of inns increased, they offered events during the day, musical and parlor entertainment in the evening, and a host of recreational and sports facilities. By the turn of the twentieth century some of the larger properties were offering full-size golf courses, tennis courts, polo fields, trap and skeet fields, bowling greens, and riding trails. Nevertheless, throughout the development and sophistication of the American plan resort, the most important feature of any property—no matter the size—was the quality of the cuisine. The meals were always bounteous; and having three such occasions to look forward to each day, it is sometimes a wonder to imagine how some guests could spend the whole summer on such a vacation.

The fame of New England's many grand resort hotels spread around the world. They truly were the original destination resorts; where guests could enjoy a luxurious lifestyle in a natural setting. American plan came to mean the deluxe, all-inclusive vacation experience. Once an American plan rate was accepted by a guest and his reservation made, he need not be concerned with incurring any major additional charges during his vacation. He was left to tip to his own discretion to insure prompt service from the hotel staff.

TODAY'S AMERICAN PLAN—A MISNOMER

Today the term "American plan" is a misnomer. American consumers are accustomed to dealing in a marketplace where the familiar merchandising practice would be more accurately described by the opposite term, "European plan." Americans now are more used to buying *a la carte*. Despite recent marketing techniques to sell "packaged" vacation plans (a concept offered only on European tours twenty years ago),

Americans are still wary buyers. They take heed from the ancient Latin maxim, *Caveat emptor,* "Buyer beware!" They want to know just what a package plan includes. They are notoriously poor bargainers and neither American buyers nor sellers are inclined to haggle once a price has been established. Any contrived vacation package today must be broken apart and spelled out as to the number days, the number of nights, the number of meals, the number of "complimentary" cocktails, the number of times for golfing or tennis or skiing, etc. As evidenced by the New England travel section of any Sunday newspaper, we innkeepers apparently now are all willing to comply with this trend by itemizing the ingredients of every resort vacation package we offer. The American comparison-shopper presumably is then able to determine which package is the best buy.

The open hospitality of the traditional American plan resort has all but disappeared today. The prospective tourist is much more likely to encounter *modified* American plan packages. They are modified to such an extent that not only is luncheon no longer included in the rate, but also the use of the recreation facilities and attendance at the entertainment events are frequently assessed more unless specifically mentioned to be part of the "special" package plan. Surcharges for playing golf and tennis, rental fees on bicycles, daily charges for poolside deck chairs and towels, cover charges for entertainment, American plan credit allowances on menus, 15% service charges—all are common expenses incurred in addition to any American plan rate today. Truly, the American tourist has good reason to study the terms of his resort "package vacation" very carefully.

Dinosaurs which roamed the earth's surface long ago were doomed to extinction primarily because they could not adapt to its rapidly changing environment. New England's historic grand resort hotels suffered almost unilateral extinction due to a completely opposite phenomenon. Karl Abbot recited in his classic story of New England hotel life at the beginning of the twentieth century, *Open for the Season:*

> An old story in the hotel world is, 'How to build a Bat Roost.' One has a popular hotel, but because of a slight depression or some other cause outside the hotel field, the hotel has a short run of poor business. The owners get nervous and demand that the managing director drastically cut expenses. The managing director, to please the owners, cuts out all *repairs* and *refurbishing,* cuts down on his *advertising,* and cuts his *payroll* to the point where the *service* is curtailed. The next step is to cut out the expensive items of *cuisine.* Because of these curtailments the business is a little poorer, so the managing director in order to attract business, cuts his *rates.* Because of the cuts, added to a *lower occupancy,* the *income* from the hotel is

much lower than it was before, so the whole vicious circle starts again. This goes on until there is no business left. And *then* one needs only break out all the windows to have a first-class bat roost.

In New England today only four grand resort hotels have survived. Each of these is located in New Hampshire: Wentworth-By-The-Sea in New Castle, The Mount Washington Hotel in Bretton Woods, the Mountain View House in Whitefield, and The Balsams in Dixville Notch. Each still possess its charm and graciousness. These huge arks of clapboards and shutters preside on large estates with accommodations for from 350 to 500 guests and almost as many employees. Their lists of facilities include golf courses, tennis courts, indoor and outdoor pools, alpine and cross-country ski areas, and miles of hiking trails over thousands of acres of New England countryside. The four are located in magnificent settings—one on the Atlantic Ocean and the other three high in the White Mountains.

How and why only these four grand hotels have survived is attributable to their four separate histories. In each case the major credit rests undoubtedly upon that hotel's own lineage of ownership and staff. The faithful service and hopeful attitude toward the future are all that separates these four from the many which disappeared. I can speak with definitive knowledge only about The Balsams. This summer I shall begin my twenty-third year of work there—the first twelve doing just about every job there was to do from caddy to elevator operator, bellhop to bartender; the last ten in management; and since 1978, as a full partner of the operating company which leases the hotel property from its owner.

The Balsams Grand Resort Hotel—One of the Last of Its Kind

The Balsams has operated for 108 consecutive years as a summer resort and for the past 15 years as a winter resort. It offers accommodations for over 400 guests and employs 300 people during peak season. It is situated on its own 15,000 acre private estate (which is more than 25 square miles) with a spectacular view of Dixville Notch. Eight hundred foot sheer cliffs surround the hotel complex, the only way in or out of the complex is through the Notch. The summer operation extends from mid May through to mid October.

From July Fourth to Labor Day a traditional "social season" is maintained when only family vacationers are accommodated. In May, June, September and October The Balsams caters exclusively to conventions, group meetings, and motor coach tour guests. There is virtually no mixing of group and social business in either portion of the summer season. In the winter The Balsams operates with its own Wilderness Ski Area from mid December to mid March. The winter clientele consists of families, singles, business and social ski groups, and small corporate seminars. During both the summer and winter seasons 30—50% of all employees live on the property. In between seasons for two months during both early spring and late fall, The Balsams does not operate. An indoor sports facility is in the planning stage, with the eventual goal of creating a year-round resort operation in the Notch.

I believe The Balsams to be the very last of its kind in continuing to offer its guests a traditional American plan hospitality. Balsams rates include three very extraordinary meals each day with a wide and varied menu selection. There is no extra charge for house guests to play either of the two golf courses or six tennis courts, or in the winter to ski either alpine or cross-country. Every guest is always welcome to use *all* facilities indoors or out *without* extra charge. There is a full schedule of daily events and activities such as professional golf, tennis and swimming clinics, guided nature walks, craft exhibits, scenic motor tours, a variety of contests and tournaments and a fully supervised children's program seven days a week. In the evening there are full-length featured films, a weekly lecture program, square dancing, piano concerts, live musical entertainment in three lounges; plus, two hotel emcees, a weekly staff talent show, and a variety of star performers (singers, magicians, concert musicians, and comedians) every week. Again, *everything is included.*

Operating a full-service resort with such an inclusive philosophy of American plan can be a very intimidating experience for both the potential guest and the businessman/innkeeper. Yet once a relationship of trust is. established, the full measure of success inherent in this style of hospitality can still be enjoyed by the guest and innkeeper alike. Potential guests must be convinced that there are no hidden surcharges in a rate which claims to cover everything. They certainly would not accept finding such charges on their bill at check-out time. We find that this assurance is best communicated to *potential* guests by *return* guests. Return guests promote The Balsams to their families and friends. Promotional advertising and literature are designed with the understanding that they will serve most effectively as a tool for Balsams guests to promote The Balsams in their own social spheres. As a result 45% of The Balsams' social clientele is comprised of new guests who had family or friends recommend this resort to them. To perpetuate this situation, every guest family who returns to The Balsams finds in their room a 16-ounce bottle of pure maple syrup with a short note of welcome hand-written on the custom-made label. In the same vein, each guest family who has returned to The Balsams for ten years receives a silver, Paul Revere pitcher engraved with an appropriate anniversary message.

A solid and well-established clientele is no more important than a trustworthy, dependable staff. The Balsams is able to offer 20% of its staff year—round employment and an additional 50% work both summer and winter seasons. Many of the Balsams staff are, in effect, full-time employees which is unusual for seasonal hotels. Thus many are native to the area or are now living here year-round. The loyalty and experience of The Balsams staff add an important dimension of consistency and continuity to a seasonal operation. Several cooperative education programs are maintained in the kitchen, dining room, and recreation departments with schools such as the New Hampshire Vocational Technical College, Johnson and Whales Culinary Institute, The American Culinary Institute, Holyoke Community College, Springfield College, and Ithaca College. In this manner, the spirit of professionalism is engendered in each hotel department by full-time year-round department heads and dedicated employees. The relationship long-time employees have with long-time guests is a very important contributing influence on the success of The Balsams. Throughout all the seasons of the hotel operation, guests and employees are enjoying the genuine pleasure in their reunion. This warm and friendly atmosphere is contagious and affects new and old, guest and staff alike.

In order to realize a complete and satisfying American plan experience, management must make a complete and personal commitment to both its guests and its employees. The future of The Balsams is completely in the hands of the people who care for it—ownership and management, guests and employees. To invest in its future, The Balsams invests in the people who visit and work there. The Balsams concentrates on its family clientele: the young families who vacation there make up the major portion of social and convention house-counts. Since the activities are included in the cost young, active people on budgets discover it to be the best buy for their money. They like the freedom and richness this style of hospitality affords them. No longer are Balsams guests accurately typified as "newly wed or nearly dead."

In the same way, no longer are Balsams employees accurately typified as "transient, seasonal, and untrained." There is a real opportunity for worthwhile employment with potential for advancement and professional technical training. Although there are still a number of employees who work just one season or part of one season, those employees join a staff, 70% of which works each complete hotel season year in and year out, and 20% of which has worked 10 years or longer.

The Balsams was at one time, and might be today, the most independent and self-sufficient resort hotel operation in the world. At the turn of the century The Balsams maintained a year-round system of 18 farms which provided almost all of the produce, dairy and meat products needed by the hotel during its 2½ month summer season. Although we farm very little now, The Balsams still maintains its own telephone company, harvests its own 15,000 acres of woodland, operates its own saw mill, runs its own laundry, conducts its own accredited culinary education program, and produces 70% of its own electricity and 100% of its heat by burning wood-waste (sawdust and bark) in its own cogenerating steam plant, thus saving more than 30,000 gallons of fuel oil every week in the winter.

The original and essential ingredient of American plan innkeeping involves the notion of the businessman/innkeeper providing for his guests as he would provide for himself. This aspect of New England's innkeeping heritage is fixed in the tradition of American plan hospitality. Yankee innkeepers have long been known for their independence, creativity and inventiveness, thrift, common sense and good and affordable accommodations.

In analyzing what factors are essential to The Balsams style of American plan, I have derived that the total experience is somehow more than the sum of its parts. The personal freedom and opportunity offered all guests for recreation and relaxation creates a special ambience and sense of comfort. Because the service and facilities made available to Balsams' guests are all owned and administered by Balsams Corp., it is not necessary to budget each department's operation with an uncompromising attitude toward profitability. Instead, budgeting exercises are commonly set up to work a proportional balance between such line items as golf cart profits and golf course maintenance expenses, beverage income profits and entertainment expenses. Most guest services are included in the daily American plan *room rate*, and so it is that figure with its predominantly fixed cost that is of greatest importance. The single most influential factor affecting this is the daily house-count. The Balsams develops its services, facilities, and programs on the optimistic premise that we are going to be busy. Therefore, our success will be measured directly by our occupancy. To operate at capacity is no more than 50% more expensive than to operate with half a house. Karl Abbott put it this way: "The resort innkeeper is primarily interested in a multitude of guests walking in and out of the front door, tariffs that will insure a profit, and the lowest cost possible consistent with good operation. And all this coupled with a gambler's instinct which would turn an auditor's hair white."

The Balsams and its three New Hampshire sister hotels are, sadly, all that remain to represent the glorious past when New England's many grand resorts brought American plan hospitality to its greatest heights. Nevertheless, today they still bear the standard. I sincerely hope and believe that they can carry on in substance the grand tradition of American plan hospitaltiy.

18

Hospitality and Heritage—A Profitable Partnership

Frank M. Go

With the expansion of mass tourism, the demand for accommodation and other touristic facilities has risen accordingly. More and more, accommodations and ancillary facilities are marked by a sameness in architecture, standards of service, recreation and food service. They are differentiated only marginally from other international counterparts by price and the extent to which they reflect the national image of the countries where they are found. This "pall of uniformity" as it has been called, is a syndrome frequently and justifiably attacked, but admittedly difficult to avoid. The approach in tourism has been in terms of volume, a conviction that more is better. Rarely have governments and corporate developers asked at what cost to society they produce volume.

The term "tourist pollution" has crept, uncomfortably, into the language, along with ecological awareness in general. It is a phrase that suggests a jungle of steel, glass and concrete hotels, tens of thousands of visitors and often the destruction of the very cultural inheritance that attracted the visitors in the first place (Anon. 1975).

It is becoming increasingly obvious to many observers, that the tourist industry is in danger of destroying its own foundations. Tourism now finds itself in a spiraling predicament: the greater the number of visitors that come in search of a country's assets, the more those cultural assets are endangered and threatened with obliteration. This is a problem now receiving attention from both governmental planning agencies and commercial interests.

THE NEED FOR AN ARTS AND HOSPITALITY ALLIANCE

During the past few years it has become obvious that the custodians of culture and the champions of the quality of life, of cultural values and treasures and of precious lifestyles will not let tourism interests concentrate so exclusively on old priorities. For these people there are values even more important than taxes, jobs and profits. Leaders in the hospitality industry and the government would be wise not to misunderstand them or underestimate them. "This concern for protecting the scenery, architecture, and native crafts of an area is not a marginal subject attracting the attention of a few intellectuals or culture vultures. It is the subject affecting the front line on which the bottom line of the travel business depends" (Patterson 1976).

The problem is that despite their common interests, those involved in tourism, design, the arts and community development often seem to operate in different worlds. The hospitality industry tends to be impatient with the environmentalists, preservationists intolerant to tourists needs, design professionals insensitive to the cultural landscape, planners unaware of the economic benefits of tourism. While decision makers and opinion brokers continue to operate in accustomed ways, a confluence of economic, cultural, and social forces has resulted in a potentially new outlook for cultural tourism. Often sparked by creative alliances among ordinarily divergent groups, the reclamation of historic, natural, and cultural environments has been supported by the commitment of the federal government to encourage preservation of the nation's heritage. The question is: Does the hospitality industry appreciate this forward momentum? And are conservationists willing to investigate how the cultural product serves and is served by tourism (Rifkind 1979)?

The difficulty in addressing these problems is that there has been so little contact between the advocates for natural and historic sites and the hospitality industry. Yet, the potential is there to form an integrated system to better manage the flow of visitors and to preserve the uniqueness of place (Rifkind 1979).

HERITAGE AREAS ATTRACT TOURIST DOLLARS

The market for hotel, food and related travel services is not static. Over a period it may grow by attracting customers from other premises, by creating wider interest and by the influx of more visitors or because of the economic prosperity of the area generally. The character of the market may change, necessitating changes in the standard of service and facilities (Lawson 1976).

Several changes have taken place in United States population demographics. The U.S. population is getting older. In the 1980's, the 25 to 34 age group will increase 42%. There will be more two-income households. In the last ten years, the number of two-income households has increased from three million to over 28 million. This population will be the best educated in U.S. history. Travel for cultural reasons usually increases with education. Thus, it could be fairly well assumed that artistic events and historical attractions will gain in importance because of the educational as well as the recreational experiences they afford.

Heritage themes already form the basis of major attractions in Canada, however there is still significant potentialfor further development. In the future the search for ways to fill one's leisure time with meaningful experiences will make history more popular than ever before. Enclaves of the past, similar to Colonial Williamsburg, Virginia; Mystic Seaport, Connecticut; and Old Tucson, Arizona may be very much in demand in the decades ahead (Abbot 1978). In a recent survey, one Western Canadian city found that 23% of its visitors ranked the local museum as the highlight of their trip. The Quebec area derives 35% of its Canadian tourist dollars from historical and cultural visits. New Brunswick, with a wealth of competing tourist attractions, draws almost 40% of its visitor dollars from heritage tourism. According to a recent Canadian Travel survey, 29% of Canadian tourism spending is attributable to visitors whose main activity is visiting historical and cultural sites. Fishing, the next most popular activity was found to account for only 15.2% of tourist expenditures.

American surveys have come to similar conclusions. The economic impact of tourism on New Orleans, for example, has been staggering. Annual tourism revenues generated by the Vieux Carre, the city's historic French Quarter, in 1979 were estimated at well over $200 million, and are still growing. Tourism revenues in Savannah measured $10 million a year before restoration work began there. Revenues have soared to $40 million after just six years of organized reclamation.

The total economic benefits generated by heritage attractions extend well beyond the measured impact. Even where the enjoyment of historic sites and streetscapes is peripheral to main purposes of a trip, it will still act as an additional draw, encouraging the traveler to stay longer and spend more (Galt).

RECYCLING THE PAST

The expressions of culture in an area which is attractive to tourists are one of that area's most valuable touristic assets. An important challenge for the hospitality industry is to make these cultural resources readily available to the visitor through proper development, accessibility and promotion.

A growing number of people are rejecting sameness. They want to be in a hotel that reflects the local heritage, that fits in with the environment and that is appropriate to the sense of scale and the sense of place.

Among the typical expressions of any society, there is one that is outstanding because of its permanency and its constant use: an area's own architecture. Tourism, as an activity of modern man, is very closely related to the product of architecture, not only because of the use given to it, but also, and mainly, because of what it represents as a cultural expression of nations. Nevertheless, we have forgotten this important component of our heritage not only as an expression of a culture, but, particularly, as an integral part of an authentic tourist area (Anzola 1972). Identification, listing and protection of buildings and monuments of historical and/or architectural merit is part of the planning functions enforced in a number of countries, albeit with varying degrees of effectiveness. Government departments concerned with the development of tourism have recognized the value of old buildings. Several companies have created hotels out of mills, warehouses, castles and palaces. An outstanding example of government policy to promote economic conservation is shown in the "Paradores" of Spain (Lawson 1976).

Fred Bosselman, a prominent attorney specializing in land use law, advocated that planners who must prepare an area for tourism should seek and preserve the qualities of a place that are "special". Although Bosselman (1978) admits that specialness is "an elusive characteristic", he insists that development must enhance a location's unique appeal, if it is not eventually to prove destructive.

COMMUNITY APPROACH

The late 1970's revealed an important trend that has enormous implications for the future of both cultural conservation and the hospitality industry: the turnaround of historic urban cores. There is a surprising return to neighborhood vitality in many North American cities. Residential neighborhoods, historic districts and large groups of buildings have been restored, and city streets have been freed from traffic and returned to pedestrians. Tourists have made these new public spaces the focus of their activities. New hotels can present a problem in the revitalized core. They are often unsympathetic in size, shape, and materials. Increasingly, countries which have experienced the damaging effects of haphazard entrepreneurial hotel building in the past are now limiting new hotels, apartments and associated construction to specific locations identified as being suitable for urbanization and tourism development. Local planning requirements are becoming more specific, stipulating height, capacity and constructional limitations; even in some areas dictating the basis of design and exterior materials to be used. Height restrictions may be applied to safeguard the prominence of famous buildings and monuments, to complement the scale and proportions of exisiting properties or to avoid changes in the landscape skyline (Lawson 1976).

Hospitality operators must begin to think in terms of creating hotels around a community. A hotel is part of a destination and therefore should reflect the indigenous qualities of the region. In a project built to attract a market segment to these indigenous qualities, the consumer, producer and society-at-large must be integrated into a matching product.

The time has come perhaps when hospitality operators must proceed on a new assumption: that they will be wanted by any given community only when they are willing to want what the community is (Hamilton 1972).

A FUTURE FOR OUR PAST

Exploring space is not necessarily an extraterrestrial matter. In an overcrowded world — and especially in heavily populated urban areas — it is existing space right here on earth that needs exploring most. In an era when cost effectiveness and energy efficiency seem to be the watchwords of industry, the success of entrepreneurs may depend not only on designing better structures in the future, but on making more imaginative use of urban space and surroundings as it exists today. Although there are no simple solutions to preserve cultural resources and profits, at least one option seems sympathetic to both tourism and historic preservation objectives. Indeed, the current high cost of construction has forced some corporations and entrepreneurs to consider adaptive reuse as a vehicle for entering profitable markets. Taking advantage of adaptive reuse may offer many economic, social, and cultural benefits. Among some of these are:

1. The sense of identification and belonging can be restored to the community;
2. The construction cost for an establishment can be substantially reduced;
3. The costs of financing and of maintenance of the establishment can also be reduced, which will make it possible to charge lower rates and be more attractive to the traveler;
4. Older buildings often have hidden assets. These hidden assets, either tangible, such as increased height, space, and volume, or

intangible, such as increased character and amenities all of which add to the value of the property;

5. The attraction to visitors who want to experience the pleasant sensation of getting to know the past;
6. Energy efficiency. Old buildings are virtual energy banks. Their heavy masonry retains heat. Restoration requires less energy than building from the ground up, which involves the multiple stages of demolition, manufacturing of new materials and construction.

There are numerous examples of hotel facilities constructed out of or within the shells of existing structures. Here follow just a few brief examples of how hotel operators have created facilities to fit the fabric of specific communities.

Example One: Amsterdam Sonesta Hotel

For years, Holland has been a model of rational planning. Ironically, Amsterdam's administration never developed a plan for the center of the city, even though controls were placed on the demolition of historic buildings and on the height of new buildings constructed in the core. Social and economic factors changed rapidly after World War II, and these had a devastating effect on the vitality of the historic center. Most of the buildings in old Amsterdam are in poor physical condition, with the exception of elegant houses located along the three central concentric rings. Restoration costs run very high. Local activist groups view new hotel construction as a negative development in the center of Amsterdam, especially since Holland's inflationary economy has put a further lid on expansion of the city's tourist industry. Even so there are a number of developers willing to invest in restoration (Finlayson 1980).

The Boston based lodging chain selected a site along a 16th century alley called "Kattegat", in the middle of a section of town that needed a facelift. But some residents wanted the site for a park. Only by agreeing to help improve the entire neighborhood, ultimately at a cost of $4 million was Sonesta able to pry loose the necessary permits. The structure is not new, but incorporates several monument houses in the heart of Amsterdam. The original foundation and key structural elements had to be retained resulting often in interesting, irregularly shaped spaces. The hotel is linked via an underground passage with a landmark 17th century Round Lutheran church, that lay vacant for lack of worshipers. The church was leased by Sonesta for one hundred years and turned into a convention center. This caused a storm of controversy. But critics were disarmed by the management, who staged Sunday morning concerts that have become a regular and popular feature of Amsterdam's cultural life.

Example Two: Benmiller Inn

Benmiller Inn and its related developments are bringing new life to one of Ontario's pioneer communities dating from the 1840s. What sparked the creation of the Hamlet of Benmiller in those far off days was the presence in one spot of all the natural resources vital to community survival, particularly a bountiful supply of spring-fed water and a large natural watershed. By 1885 Benmiller had become a miniature self-contained industrial center where the falling waters of Sharpes Creek turned looms, saws and millstones in no less than seven factories.

However, in the 1920s the march of time and technological change began Benmiller's gradual downfall. The great depression marked the beginning of the end of Benmiller's prosperity. By 1972 the turbine and wheels of the mills had ceased turning and Benmiller was a dying community. However, a few people were aware of the extraordinary natural beauty of this sleeping oasis just a few short miles off the beaten path. When the Gledhill Mill closed its doors the building was purchased, mill machinery removed and stored, and planning for renovation began. Imagination and much hard work have turned the Benmiller Inn into a distinctive country retreat. The Benmiller Inn conserves the best of the past and transformed it into something unusual. In the River Mill for example, two existing 1910 Barber turbines are producing sufficient electric energy to heat the water in the swimming pool.

Example Three: Delta's Barrington Inn

Like many of North America's older cities, historic Halifax is suffering growing pains. The old seaport's enthusiastic endorsement of the trend toward urban renewal is being aggravated by the city's location on a narrow peninsula. With land at a premium, the temptation was to cover the landscape with highrises. However, a unique experiment in one three acre site in the heart of the city proved that it is not necessary to tear down the old to make way for the new. Through a combination of public pressure, business pressure, and pressure from those engaged in historic renovation in the area, and the encouragement from Halifax City Council, a scheme was worked out whereby the historic character of the area would be preserved.

The new 200 room Barrington Inn which recently opened in this area signaled the start of coast-to-coast operations for Vancouver based Delta Hotels Limited, operators of nine other hotels located in major Canadian cities. A unique feature of the Barrington Inn is its location in a development which incorporates the restored facades of one of Canada's most distinguished streetscapes originally constructed in the mid 1800s. To fit in with this scenario, Delta Hotels originally intended using the existing walls of the buildings on the Granville Street side of the planned hotel. But the existing walls proved to be unstable. So, stone block by stone block, the unstable walls were dismantled. Every block was numbered and blueprints were drafted, showing where every number fitted into the walls. The blocks were cleaned of the grime accumulated through over a century and a half and were replaced in a new wall in the precise position they filled in the old wall. Although it is part of a spanking new hotel, this section of Granville Street looks just as it did in colonial days. The extra effort taken by Delta is an invaluable contribution to the heritage of Haligonians. Despite the historical and geographical variables, the recent trend toward renovation of older properties has one common characteristic: real profit potential—provided the conditions are right.

RESTORATION GUIDELINE

The formula seems simple enough. Start with an aging property. Add some fresh capital, a contemporary management philosophy and a proud sense of the past. But while the ultimate benefits of restoration can be substantial, so can be the risks (Barbaran 1980). It is therefore important for an organization to follow certain procedures to improve its chances for success in contemplated restoration efforts. Among the first things an organization should do are to define local preservation goals and issues, gather information on them, and seek out concerned individuals and associations who might be helpful and know what tools are available for implementing these procedures. The use of existing, old buildings that need no extension or major structural alteration, but do require complete modernization can be attractive rehabilitation investments, provided the buildings are structually sound. Location is also a critical factor: a hotel must be adjacent to activity centers, whether for business or pleasure. In a city, proximity to business activities and the market area can draw an abundance of guests to a nearby hotel. A feasibility study on market conditions within a given location can be critical tool in defining the risk and future potential for a renovated older hotel (Brown 1980).

Important tax incentives for the preservation and rehabilitation of historic structures were established by Section 2124 of the United States Tax Reform Act of 1976. The legislation amends the Federal Income Tax Code with the provision to:

1. Discourage destruction of historic buildings by reducing tax incentives both for the demolition and for new construction on the site of demolished historic buildings, and

2. Stimulate preservation of historical commercial and income producing structures by allowing favorable tax treatments for rehabilitation.

According to hotel owners who have taken advantage of the preservation provisions in the Federal Tax Code, tax incentives are influential
in determining the quality of rehabilitation work. The kinds of costs
allowable have been defined by the Internal Revenue Service as covering
most of the expenses within the four walls of a building. Architectural
and engineering fees, real estate commissions, site survey fees, legal
expenses, insurance premiums, developer's fees, and other construction
related costs can be figured in the tax deduction. Energy conservation
measures such as insulation or storm windows also qualify. Other
aspects of work common to hotel renovation projects include installation
of new heating, ventilating, and air conditioning systems, replacement of
antiquated elevator equipment, and construction of new fire stairs and
safety exits (Brown 1980). Restoration expenses can be deceptive. Aside
from unanticipated and costly problems that crop up during the process,
restoration work requires a great deal of time and highly skilled labor.

Still, the list of successful renovations may become endless, if economics continue to provide such clear cut opportunities for profit margins
and if the public retains its rather belated reverence for a period charm
(Barbaran 1980).

IN SUMMARY

The demands supporting development will lay even greater responsibilities on the careful planning of facility developers, if the impact on
our environment is to be minimized. Some companies oriented toward the
managerial and technological advantages of newly designed properties
prefer to ignore the opportunities restoration and renovation offer. There
are fortunately others who see money spent on a thorough facelift as a
preferable alternative, thereby attracting businessmen and tourists in
record numbers. Conservation means the best use of our scarce resources,
a plan for a future which wastes as little as possible. It will include using
many of today's buildings, but it will not exclude using new buildings.

One of the major attractions of any city is its individual character.
Historic buildings, when properly adapted to functional uses, provide
this special interest and stimulation, regarding the heritage and background of the community, for both local residents and out-of-town visitors.

The hospitality industry can make a valuable contribution to the revitalization of historic districts by paying more attention to protecting the expressions of the community in order to maintain and stimulate them. Individual developers can do this by creating facilities that fit the fabric of a community, for example through adaptive reuse. Adaptive reuse is more than preserving old buildings for the sake of sentiment and history. It is an attempt to incorporate and blend new buildings with older ones and to modify and use them to serve contemporary needs.

Today we are living with the planning decisions which were made yesterday. Tomorrow we will be living with what we decide today.

ACKNOWLEDGMENTS

With respect to historic renovation and restoration project examples discussed in this chapter, the author is indebted to Ms. Lisa Whitely, Innkeeper, Benmiller Inn, Goderich, Ontario; Ms. Ellen Novack, Director of Public Relations, Delta Hotels Ltd., Toronto, Ontario; and the management of the Amsterdam Sonesta Hotel, Amsterdam, the Netherlands.

Furthermore, the author wishes to acknowledge the assistance of Ms. Floy A. Brown, Educational Specialist of the Technical Preservation Services Division (Heritage Conservation), U.S. Department of the Interior.

RESOURCES

U.S. Department of the Interior
Heritage Conservation and Recreation Service
Technical Preservation Services Division
440 G Street, N.W.
Washington, D.C. 20243

The National Trust for Historic Preservation
1785 Massachusetts Avenue, N.W.,
Washington, D.C. 20036

Partners for Livable Places, 2120 P Street N.W.,
Washington, D.C. 20037

19

Hospitality and the Handicapped

Leland L. Nicholls, Ph.D.

Nineteen-hundred and eighty-one was proclaimed by the United Nations as the Year of the Disabled Persons. The aim of the Year was to encourage the rehabilitation of the estimated 400 million people who suffer from some form of physical or mental impairment. It is to be a time for understanding and communication in a many-faceted world. The handicapped are seeking respect for the fact that they are different: not fanfare or fuss, not pity weeping virtuous tears, and not disparaging remarks such as "it will do for the disabled." The hospitality industry can assist millions of handicapped people who live in a world often characterized by poverty, idleness, dependency, frustration and isolation to be part of a world of independence, security and skills with the confidence needed to take a full part in the rewards of the industry.

THE NEED

In 1979 instructors of the Hotel and Restaurant Management Program from the Department of Habitational Resources and the Stout Vocational Rehabilitation Institute at University of Wisconsin Stout and the National Restaurant Association recognized the need for a better understanding of the nation's handicapped population. The first real attempt to identify and inventory America's handicapped citizens had been made during the 1970 federal census. That census indicated that approximately 10% of all Americans have some physical impairment that limits their mobility. A decade later Schmitt (1981) reported the following characteristics of the disabled:

General Disability—36-50 million people;
General Mobility Problems—25 million people with 500,000 people

using wheelchairs;
Visually Impaired — 11.4 million people have some loss of sight,
1.4 million people cannot read newsprint with glasses,
500,000 people are legally blind,
100,000 people are totally blind,
121,000 people with visual handicap in the labor force;

Hearing Impaired — 15 million people,
1.7 million people deaf;
Mentally Retarded — 6.5 million people of which 90% are mildly mentally retarded.

Increased public awareness and the Federal Rehabilitation Act of 1973 have afforded many of America's 25 million mobility-restricted citizens meaningful employment and the subsequent discovery of the adventure of travel. The need has been recognized by industry and academic leaders for hospitality organizations to reevaluate the quality of existing services and offerings in terms of special needs of the handicapped individual. The implications for the hospitality industry are obvious but complex.

THE EFFORTS

It is prudent, for both economic and humanitarian reasons, not merely to tolerate handicapped persons but to welcome them. Recognizing this, many industry and government leaders have been involved in a variety of programs aimed at satisfying the needs of handicapped persons. Examples of these programs and actions have been delineated by Brodsky-Porges (1978):

Legislation:
- Establishment of the Architectural and Transportation Barriers Compliance Board (charged with encouraging, investigating and advising airports and train and bus stations to eliminate barriers preventing full use of such public facilities by everyone);
- Federal Aviation Administration and Civil Aeronautics Board ruling that domestic air carriers may not refuse passage to anyone, or practice price discrimination, on the basis of physical disability;
- Department of Health and Welfare's guarantee that every child in America has the right to a meaningful education;
- Federal Tax Revision of 1977 permitting lodging, food service, and related establishments an allowance of up to $25,000 for accessibility modification.

Travel:
- TWA became the first American carrier to offer a tour package designed specifically for the handicapped;
- Helping Hand Tours of New York and other travel agencies offer tours specially designed for the handicapped traveler;
- Amtrak allocated three million dollars to provide barrier free access to trains at 18 stations;
- Trailways and Greyhound allows the handicapped traveler one companion-assistant at no charge;
- Hertz, National and Avis all provide hand-operated automobiles at no additional charge;
- Cruiseships have modified a number of staterooms reserved for use by passengers in wheelchairs;

Restaurants:
- Braille menus;
- Modified seating arrangements;
- International House of Pancakes became one of the first restaurants to train employees in handling the needs of handicapped customers;
- National Restaurant Association's "Projects with Industry" aids the handicapped in finding jobs in the restaurant industry;
- Opportunity Village presents a special handicapped training program to meet the needs of the Las Vegas restaurant industry;
- Hoffman House-Henrici Restaurants in Wisconsin removed barriers to the entertainment areas of their restaurants;

Publications:
- The *New York Times* is among the many publications specializing in public awareness of the needs of the handicapped;
- Easter Seal Societies have for many years published guides to major American cities for the handicapped;
- The *Wheelchair Traveler* is an annually updated index of establishments accessible to the handicapped.

Lodging:
- The Holiday Inn chain plans to offer at least two accessible units at each of its properties;
- Howard Johnson and Ramada Inns publish indexes of their accessible features semi-annually;
- The Sheraton in Madison, Wisconsin has a long tradition of improving accessibility to handicapped people;
- There are more than 1,200 courtesy vans in the nation equipped with hydraulic lifts to accommodate mobility-restricted individuals;
- Lower liability-insurance premiums available for accessible hotels.

Education: The University of Wisconsin-Stout has done the following to educate its 1,000 majors in the hotel and restaurant management, food service administration and dietetics programs toward the needs of the handicapped:

- Created an upper level course in "Hospitality and the Handicapped Traveler";
- Devoted an annual tourism conference to the theme of the handi-capped traveler;
- Invited internationally recognized guest speakers to enlighten the faculty and staff of the opportunities and problems associated with being and accommodating the handicapped person;
- Developed for national distribution a 21-minute videotape with the National Restaurant Association on the subject of "Courtesy Needs of the Handicapped Traveler in Restaurants";
- Developed for national distribution a slide-tape series on the "Architectural Barriers of the Handicapped";
- Developed an extensive bibliography of reference material and sources of information on the handicapped.

The many needs, and the various ways they can be met, of the handi-capped are readily apparent. These needs have been raised to a conscious level by government, industry and academia but it remains only a beginning. It is beholden on all parties to continue to explore and provide for this very vital and sizeable element of our population.

20

The Measurement of Guest Satisfaction

Robert C. Lewis, Ph.D. and *Abraham Pizam, Ph.D.*

Most hospitality enterprises use some form of in-house guest survey. A national survey of hotel executives indicated that 92% of the respondents use this method of obtaining guest response on either a continual or a sporadic basis (see Chapter 25). Comment cards are frequently found in hotel rooms, restaurants, coffee shops and cocktail lounges. Responses are utilized as indicators of operating performance and measurement of guest satisfaction. They are also used by some hotels and hotel chains for "grading" management and for comparison purposes among properties.

These uses of guest survey responses mandate that the data collection method be one that is both highly reliable and statistically valid, and one that produces true measurements of guest satisfaction. When surveys fulfill these essentialities, they can be powerful tools for management action and planning as well as for measuring management. Unfortunately most, if not all, guest survey methods fail to meet these requirements. This paper describes the failings of present methods and then develops a new method of measuring guest satisfaction and management performance that overcomes most of the failings.

PRESENT METHODS

There are a wide variety of guest survey forms in use today but it is necessary to comment on only a few of them as they all share common faults. Figure 20.1 illustrates four forms currently used by major hotel chains. Form 20.1A uses an excellent to poor rating system for four different categories of the hotel with three or four elements in each category. This form is an ordinal scale of sorts but in actuality it is a gross

(A)

Please rate us

	Excellent	Good	Fair	Poor
CHECKING IN				
Reservation				
Front Desk				
Bellman				
YOUR ROOM				
Cleanliness				
TV Radio				
Bath				
Bed Furnishings				
RESTAURANT				
LOUNGE				
Name _____				
Food				
Beverages				
Service				
GENERAL				
Swimming Pool				
Parking				
Room Service				

(B) TO OUR GUESTS: A moment of your time in completing and giving this card to our Hostess will help us serve you better in the future. Thank You.

Date _____ Time _____ A.M. P.M. How Many in Your Party? _____

Server's Name _____ Are You: Local Out of Town

HOSPITALITY

Were you greeted as you entered? .... ____ YES ____ NO
Did the hostess host seat you? .... ____ YES ____ NO
Did server introduce her himself by name? .. ____ YES ____ NO
Were you thanked and invited to return? ...... ____ YES ____ NO

FOOD AND SERVICE

Was food served promptly? .... ____ YES ____ NO
Was your order correct? .... ____ YES ____ NO
Was food properly prepared? .... ____ YES ____ NO
Was hot food served HOT? .... ____ YES ____ NO
Did you receive smiling, courteous service? . ____ YES ____ NO

ENVIRONMENT

Did our staff have a neat, clean appearance? . ____ YES ____ NO
Were your dining area and dining utensils clean? .... ____ YES ____ NO
Was the restaurant clean overall? .... ____ YES ____ NO
Was the restroom clean and properly supplied? .... ____ YES ____ NO

(C)

	*****	****	***	**	*
Your arrival and reception					
a. Reservationist					
b. Doorman					
c. Registration clerk					
d. Bellman					
e. Telephone operator					
f. Cashier					
g. Garage					
h. Maid Service					
i. Concierge					
Entertainment and dining facilities					
a. Brasserie—Breakfast Lunch					
b. Brasserie—Dinner Night Owl					
c. Fairmont Crown					
d. Lobby Lounge					
e. New Orleans Room					
f. Room Service					
g. Squire Room					
h. Tonga Room—Bar					
i. Tonga Room—Dinner					
j. Venetian Room					
k. Catering and Banquets					

FIG. 20.1. GUEST SURVEY FORMS

(D)   Your constructive criticism is our most valuable source of information. If we did not meet your expectations in any area, your specific comments will help us to improve and update our services.

Exceeds Expectations   Meets Expectations   Below Expectations

Your Specific Comments are Appreciated

Doorman: _____

Garage: _____

Reception Desk: _____

Did you have any questions the receptionists were unable to answer?   Yes   No

Bellman: _____

Did you have to wait for service?   Yes   No
Did the bellman explain the hotel facilities and the use of the miniature bar?   Yes   No

Accommodations: _____

Was your bed turned down in the evening?   Yes   No
Were mints placed on your pillow?   Yes   No
Was ice kept in your refrigerator?   Yes   No

Telephone Operator: _____

Food and Beverage Service

Apple of Eve Restaurant and Lounge: _____

Greenhouse Restaurant: _____

Quorum Lounge: _____

Lobby Bar: _____

Room Service: _____

Was your order on time?   Yes   No
Was your order complete?   Yes   No

FIG. 20.1.   (Continued)

rating of various elements that defies meaningful interpretation or appropriate management action. In fact, it raises more questions than it answers.

Let us assume that a majority of guests check "fair" in any one of the categories such as "Front Desk." Does this mean the guest had a long wait to check in? Or that the clerk was surly? Or that the clerk couldn't find the reservation? Or that his/her uniform was dirty?

Consider "swimming pool." Too small? Too hot or too cold? No towels? Not open certain hours? Or "room service." Too slow? Too expensive? Forgot the cream? In other words, where does management take action to correct for the low ratings?

Given these ambiguities, how does management interpret the data in terms of guest satisfaction? Does excellent in some categories, good, fair or poor in others, mean the guest is satisfied? Will he/she return? Can management be held responsible or compared to other managements?

Figure 20.1B is a typical comment card used in the restaurants of a large hotel chain. This format provides strictly nominal categorization that is even less meaningful than the previous form. Consider the first question, "Were you greeted as you entered?" What does a yes or a no mean? Yes, I was greeted. In what manner? Politely, abruptly, cursorily, ...? No, I was not greeted. Does it matter? I was too busy talking to my companion to even notice. This same type of examination can be applied to all the remaining questions. Again, how does management tabulate the responses and correct for failings if, in fact, there are any?

Figure 20.1C solicits guest responses on what could possibly be construed as an interval level scale. Although the scale is inherently somewhat more meaningful than the others, what, for example, do three stars for "reservationist" mean, in terms of management action and planning?

Figure 20.1D is the most valid of the four formats pictured. Behavioral theorists have been able to substantiate a high correlation between satisfaction and expectation. This form also allows the guest to state specifically why or why not certain elements of the operation met expectations. Although management should be able to pinpoint the areas more closely in which to take corrective action, two problems remain. The first was mentioned in connection with form 20.1A: Is the guest satisfied or dissatisfied overall? Will he/she return? Which categories are important in making this determination? How do the expectations of one guest contrast with those of another guest? The second problem is one of tabulation. If numerous responses are received, as hopefully would be the case, many of them would require coding before statistical validation could be verified. This effort is both troublesome and time-consuming and frequently gets left undone, or is done belatedly, by a busy managerial staff.

On a much broader plane some companies have commissioned large scale studies of hotel guest profiles using random sampling techniques which in-house surveys do not use. The importance of various hotel facilities and the satisfaction of guests with certain hotel services derived from one such study (Anon. 1979) are shown in Tables 20.1 and 20.2. The response rate in this survey was approximately 35% from a sample of 5200 guests.

Table 20.1 shows that beds are very/somewhat important to 98% of the respondents, a friendly hotel staff is similarly important to 97%, the bathroom is important to 96%, but bars/lounges are important to only 68%. How does one interpret this data in a meaningful way? To be absurd, does it mean that 2% don't care about beds and 4% don't care about bathrooms? Or, would the 32% who don't report bars/lounges as being important be satisfied with the hotel as a whole, or even return, if there was no bar/lounge?

In Table 20.2 89.3% of respondents were satisfied with "reservation service" but only 66.2% were satisfied with bars/lounges. The correlation between importance (Table 20.1) and satisfaction is close to 100%. Does this mean that those who find services important also tend to be satisfied if they exist? What about those who don't find them important? Are they

TABLE 20.1.   IMPORTANCE OF VARIOUS FACILITIES IN HOTEL SELECTION

Item	Very/ Somewhat Important	Very Important	Somewhat Important
Beds	98%	84%	14%
Friendly hotel staff	97	77	20
Bathroom	96	72	24
Professional hotel staff	95	77	18
Safety and security	95	69	26
Towels	94	65	29
Housekeeping services	93	64	29
Price/Value	93	59	34
Restaurants	92	66	26
Reservation service	90	70	20
Check-in	86	51	35
Coffee shops	85	48	37
Size of room	85	33	52
Message service	83	55	28
Parking facilities	83	50	33
Location—near business	81	49	32
Check-out	80	47	33
Decor and ambience	80	26	54
Wake-up call	79	57	22
Bars/Lounges	68	34	34

TABLE 20.2.   SATISFACTION WITH QUALITY OF SERVICES IN HOTELS

Item	Total Satisfied
Reservation service	89.3%
Check-in	87.2
Check-out	86.2
Quality of Room Services	
Closet space	88.3
Safety and security	87.7
Size of room	87.4
Towels	87.2
Beds	86.9
Bathroom	86.7
Quality of General Services	
Housekeeping services	82.3
Wake-up call	81.5
Message service	73.8
Baggage handling	71.4
Room service	66.4
Laundry and valet	61.0
Recreational facilities	60.2
Courtesy airport service	53.4
Quality of Eating/Drinking Facilities	
Restaurants	68.7
Bars/Lounges	66.2
Coffee shops	66.1

Source: Profile of the Profitable Guest. Time Marketing Services, RR2141, Time, Inc. 1979, 12—14.

satisfied, or not? Do they feel they are unimportant? If 89.3% are satisfied with the reservation service and only 66.4% are satisfied with room service, which ones will return—or not return?

The previous rendering of semantic and statistical interpretation is more than just an exercise. Rather, it vividly punctuates the reality that most of the data collected on importance and satisfaction to the hospitality guest has serious problems for interpretation, meaningfulness and use for planning or action. In summary, the following problems exist with these guest survey methods:

1) It is difficult, if not impossible, to tabulate the data so that it has meaning. Eighty—six Yes's and 18 No's provide no revelations. Nor do 28 Excellents, 16 Goods, 20 Fairs and 6 Poors. Such data cannot validly be used to compare or rate management or to improve operations. Of course, if there were 86% No's on one item then that area would require immediate attention. On the other hand if there were 24% No's what would management do? Yet this might be the cream of the business being lost.

2) There is no measurement of the *relative* importance of the various categories, e.g., 98% might be dissatisfied with the swimming pool but completely unconcerned (in terms of returning) if they were completely satisfied with the cleanliness of the bathrooms.

3) Existing survey types are 100% operation or product oriented. While this information is important to management (if it can be interpreted), equally important is marketing orientation. Is the hotel satisfying the needs and wants of its target market?

There are other concerns with current in-house surveys in terms of statistical validity. These include the following:

1) Pragmatic validity: Are results useful as predictors of behavior?
2) Content validity: Does the measurement instrument capture the domain of the characteristic, i.e., is the domain of concern (satisfaction) the same as that being measured (operations)?
3) Construct validity: Is the instrument measuring what we think it is measuring? Is it actually measuring satisfaction, or operations, or is it measuring something else such as expectation, mood or expertise?
4) Sample validity: Is the sample truly representative of the population? Or, is it a response only from those who are truly satisfied or dissatisfied based, possibly, on singular experiences or expectations?

All of the above can easily be answered in the negative. The need is obvious for a more meaningful instrument.

WHAT A SATISFACTION INDEX SHOULD DO

A viable satisfaction index should measure dominant trends in consumer preferences, satisfaction and behavior. These trends are sufficiently pervasive that they should be obvious in any carefully executed survey. Conventional market research focuses on the major consumer trends, problems and opportunities that affect the company as a whole. Individual markets become the subject of investigation when the issues are important enough and the market size is large enough to justify the effort. A hospitality satisfaction index should provide reliable performance, decision and marketing information at the lowest level of market impact—the individual unit. By ensuring that each unit manager is aware of and able to respond to local market conditions such as consumer demands or competitive perceptions, the market position of the company as a whole is substantially enhanced.

A viable satisfaction index should provide straightforward information on performance and consumer needs and wants in the fundamental areas where management can take apropriate action.

There is a tendency in consumer research to want to ask every question that may be remotely relevant. After all, we need to know about *every* facet of the operation and the consumer. Yet, as seen in Fig. 20.1, hotels are pragmatically inclined to ask very few questions in order to facilitate response and interpretation. A viable satisfaction index should limit the number of issues that can be addressed at one time. It should be parsimonious in its application to facilitate both response and analysis, yet should encompass somewhere in its breadth all those elements that may have significance.

Many units in a chain have a great deal in common from a research perspective. Each unit is likely to have similar problems and opportunities that appear over and over again in different markets. Thus, a viable satisfaction index should be both unique to the individual property and, at the same time, able to be standardized for research and comparison purposes. On the other hand, comprehensive studies tend to end up in a filing cabinet rather than in use for decision making. If the goal is to encourage more informed decisions, it is better to conduct a few small studies rather than a single comprehensive one.

Conventional market research is often expensive and time-consuming to design, execute, and analyze. A viable satisfaction index should be tailored to an individual property in a short period of time, executed quickly, and the results analyzed and returned to management so that immediate and appropriate action can be take.

A viable satisfaction index should reduce the need for skilled research-ers. If the local manager can determine the major focus of the research such as service performance and needs, price, image, etc., the survey should employ a checklist format to suggest specific issues to the managers.

Finally, a viable satisfaction index should tell the organization whether the guest will or will not return, given numerous other alternatives.

A PROPOSED INDEX OF GUEST SATISFACTION

A study was undertaken for the purpose of creating an index of guest satisfaction that will redress the aforementioned shortcomings and fulfill the aforementioned requisites. The steps involved were:
1) Identification of the determinants of hotel guest satisfaction;
2) Calculation of the relative weights for each determinant, i.e., their relative contribution to satisfaction;
3) Development of an index that is parsimonious and readily usable by management in its application and analysis; easily adaptable to an individual chain, hotel and/or target market; yet comprehensive in its breadth and statistically valid and reliable.

Method

A series of focused interviews were conducted with hotel guests in order to identify which variables of hotel satisfaction/dissatisfaction were important to them. The findings provided the basis for a questionnaire consisting of 41 determinants of guest satisfaction with hotels in general to be rated on a 1 to 5 scale of importance. An additional question measuring the overall satisfaction with a specific hotel stay was added to serve as the dependent variable.

The questionnaires along with a cover letter were placed on guest pillows the night before check out in three different and varied types of hotel. At check out time each guest was reminded to submit the completed questionnaire. This method of administration differs significantly from the existing ones where the guest comment cards are placed permanently on a chest of drawers or night stand. The results indicate that this method increases the response rate and reduces the probability that only those guests who are highly dissatisfied or highly satisfied will respond.

In order to develop a parsimonious instrument it was necessary to reduce the number of determinants of satisfaction. The 41 variables with their guests' ratings were factor analyzed to accomplish this. This statistical procedure produced a set of dimensions or factors consisting of variables that have large communalities among themselves. These dimensions are then used to develop the final instrument of limited size. When a problem dimension is identified, the variables comprising that dimension are then used in a similar limited instrument to identify the specific problems. Thus both parsimoniousness and breadth are obtained by use of the index.

For example, in one hotel the original 41 variables when factor analyzed produced the following 11 dimensions:

    I) Room & Bathroom Quality
    II) Room & Bathroom Cleanliness
   III) Front Desk Services
    IV) Prices — Relative and Actual
    V) Restaurants — Availability, Quality, Services
    VI) Professionalism of Staff
   VII) Convenience and Availability of Services
  VIII) Room Service
    IX) Prestige & Aesthetics of Property
    X) Sport Facilities
   XI) Bathroom Condition and Maintenance

Scores for each guest on each factor were computed as the first step in calculating the relative weights for each determinant variable. These scores represent the summated ratings of each guest in a factor or dimension. The factor scores were then regressed against the overall measure of satisfaction for the hotel. This procedure produced coefficient weights which were indicators of the relative importance or contribution of each factor in determining satisfaction at varying levels of significance. For example, in the hotel mentioned above, the following three coefficient weights significant at .05 were derived:

I) Room & Bathroom Quality .42

VIII) Room Service .33

VII) Convenience and Availability of Services .25

Thus it can be seen, in terms of relative contribution to overall satisfaction, that Dimension I (Room & Bathroom Quality) was 27% more important in determining total satisfaction than Dimension VIII (Room Service) and 68% more important in determining total satisfaction than Dimension VII (Convenience and Availability of Services). Other weights and their relative importance are obtainable for the remaining eight dimensions. Similar weights are obtained for the variables within each dimension.

Use

The final instruments to be used by the hotel are developed using the significant dimensions or those considered to be important and/or of concern to management.

For purposes of illustration assume that the five dimensions shown in Table 20.3 are of concern and that guest response means on a scale of 1 to 5 are also as shown in that table with the bottom half showing mean

TABLE 20.3.   SATISFACTION INDEX BY DOMAIN

Domains	Weights	1 to 5 Rating	Possible	Weighted Ratings	Possible
Room & bath quality	.308	5	5	1.540	1.540
Room service	.262	4	5	1.048	1.310
Convenience/availability	.172	3	5	.516	.860
Sports facilities	.150	2	5	.302	.750
Staff professional	.108	1	5	.108	.540
	1.000	15	25	3.514	5.000
Satisfaction level		60%		70.3%	
WITH REVERSED RATINGS					
Room & bath quality	.308	1	5	.308	1.540
Room service	.262	2	5	.524	1.310
Convenience/availability	.172	3	5	.516	.860
Sports facilities	.150	4	5	.604	.750
Staff professional	.108	5	5	.540	.540
	1.000	15	25	2.492	5.000
Satisfaction level		60%		49.8%	

TABLE 20.4.   SATISFACTION INDEX BY VARIABLE WITHIN DOMAIN

Domain: Room and Bath Quality

Variables	Weights	1 to 5 Rating	Possible	Weighted Rating	Possible
Room decor	.496	5	5	2.480	2.480
Room size	.182	4	5	.732	.910
VIP rooms	.145	3	5	.435	.725
Bath size	.112	2	5	.224	.560
Bath decor	.065	1	5	.065	.325
	1.000	15	25	3.936	5.000
Satisfaction level		60%		78.7%	
WITH REVERSED RATINGS					
Room decor	.496	1	5	.496	2.480
Room size	.182	2	5	.366	.910
VIP rooms	.145	3	5	.435	.725
Bath size	.112	4	5	.448	.560
Bath decor	.065	5	5	.325	.325
	1.000	15	25	2.070	5.000
Satisfaction level		60%		41.4%	

ratings in reverse order of those in the top half. Two things are achieved. First, it is learned not only which dimensions are weak from an operational viewpoint but also what their importance is in relation to overall satisfaction. Second, an overall satisfaction rating is revealed. Using conventional methods overall satisfaction is seen as 60% in both examples. Using the weighted index, however, satisfaction is 70.3% in the first example and 49.8% in the second. Obviously there is a significant difference in the trend of guest satisfaction and potential return rate.

For further illustration assume that the hotel now wishes to determine what are the problem areas in the dimension of Room & Bathroom Quality and that it was previously found that five variables comprise that dimension. The same procedure shown in Table 20.3 is followed, and the findings are as shown in Table 20.4.

The analysis previously discussed is applied and does not need repeating. The use and implications for management are readily apparent.

Still another important finding is available to management through the use of the index. The simple addition to the questionnaire of one or more demographics, purpose of stay or other questions, presents the possibility of determining satisfaction for a particular market segment. For example, a hotel management that has always had a largely male and/or business clientele might want to know how it is satisfying a small but growing female and/or pleasure traveler clientele. Responses from one segment can be easily isolated and compared to those from another segment.

DISCUSSION

The use of the weighted index proposed here to measure hotel guest satisfaction provides a quick measure of overall guest satisfaction at various points in time. It identifies those domains where satisfaction or dissatisfaction occur and, further, identifies the individual variables which comprise each domain and are the causes of satisfaction or dissatisfaction. The instrument used is easily completed by the guest and easily tabulated and analyzed by management. Results can be used with validity and reliability for rating management, locating operational flaws, determining guests needs and wants, determining marketing positions to target markets, tracking trends, comparison among properties, measuring improvement over time and other purposes of managerial interest.

The satisfaction index proposed here diverges from existing measures in the following aspects:

1) It is a tailor-made index specifically fitting the type of hotel to which it is to be applied and the market segment that it serves. For example, the composition of the indices for mid-city hotels, resort hotels, convention hotels and budget hotels will differ. This composition will also vary according to the demographic and psychographic segments served by those hotels.

2) Only those factors that have been found to be empirically related to overall guest satisfaction are included in the index. Factors are eliminated that by themselves might show high or low guest ratings but are not correlated with overall guest satisfaction with a hotel stay and therefore are not as consequential.

3) Each satisfaction factor in the index has a differential weight which indicates the contribution of that factor to overall guest satisfaction. In other presently used measures equal weights are assumed so that, for example, the availability of a sauna is as important to overall satisfaction as is the quality of the food in the restaurant, the efficiency of the check-in/check-out procedures, and so forth.

4) The index is parsimonious and therefore easy to administer, code, and analyze. Its parsimoniousness is not achieved at the expense of sacrificing important factors or variables. The reduction in the number of variables and factors is achieved through two empirical steps: a) Factor analysis which combines many variables into fewer common factors; and b) Multiple regression which correlates the factors with overall satisfaction and eliminates those that have no or low correlations.

The problems of obtaining a probability sample and low response rate in the use of in-room guest questionnaires is inherent in the use of the proposed index as well as in the use of other measures. The alternative is research conducted in a different manner using standard sampling techniques. There are, however, other problems inherent in that method, not the least of which is the high cost and the delay in obtaining useful data. To overcome some of the equal probability sample problems in the use of the index, the authors recommend imposing certain conditions on its use:

1) It should be used sporadically or intermittently. There is little doubt that in-room comment cards have become so commonplace in hotels that they are usually ignored except under very irate or very favorable conditions. If guests encounter these instruments less frequently they may be more inclined to use them, especially when they are conspicuously placed, such as on the pillow, and when the cashier specifically asks for them at check-out time.

2) Offer a reward for completion and return of the instrument such as a free drink in the bar or a free continental breakfast. Even if the cost of these items was fifty cents, the cost per 1000 responses (a more than adequate sample size) would be $500. Ten times a year would equal $5,000, relatively inexpensive. The alternatives are the current methods with their invalidities and unreliabilities, or a full-scale research study that would probably cost close to $10,000 for a one shot approach, a smaller sampling and time and delay factors which could obviate the results.

The authors have no hesitation in stating that their proposed index is the best method developed so far, all things considered, for hotel managements to understand their customers.

ACKNOWLEDGMENT

A version of this paper was published in the Cornell Hotel and Restaurant Administration Quarterly, November 1981.

21

The Influences of the International Visitor on the U.S. Lodging Industry

Bunny Grossinger

This chapter discusses some of the effects the international visitor has had on American lodging industry and comments on some of the changes that have occurred in servicing these special guests. Obviously, there are discernable service differences that they present, some of which are quite different than we might have orginally expected.

Let us briefly examine language needs, as a typical example. In 1980, the major thrust of overseas business came from the United Kingdom. Normally, we might assume that these guests present the least amount of difficulty in hosting, since ostensibly we share a common language. We have found, however, to our surprise, that English and American dialects very often can be quite dissimilar.

One cannot help but be reminded of the story of an elderly gentleman who decided to take a trip abroad. Since it was his first trip, the travel agent recommended that his destination should be the United Kingdom, eliminating a severe case of culture shock. Our traveler landed in Preswick and spent his first evening in the country in a typical English inn where bed and board are supplied. Upon showing him to his room, the maid kindly suggested that if he wanted to, he could have a "lay in" in the morning and then he could "knock her up".

Needless to say, the gentleman curtailed his trip since his age and inclinations were somewhat threatened by what he presumed to be an overgenerous offer on the part of the staff!

Now. . .the point of the story is not to denigrate the morals of the English working class, but to indicate that there are very specific differences between peoples. That difference is important for us to recognize and acknowledge.

As we look forward to hosting an anticipated 23.5 million guests from abroad in 1981 (an estimated 7% increase over 1980) we do so with considerably more skills and sophisticated techniques in marketing and servicing than in our recent past. We do not claim to be where we will be eventually, however, having learned a great deal from the guests themselves. We are a lot closer to those goals than we were when first confronted with the explosion of international tourism in 1973.

This influx of welcome but puzzling new business presented a complexity of service problems for American operators and while we may have been dazzled by the statistics, we were totally ill-equipped to handle "the people". It quickly became evident that to operate successfully, new skills appropriate to the international market had to be learned. The service areas needed to be redefined and augmented.

A considerable amount of learning has occurred in a reasonably short span of time, and for those world-wide counterparts of the "doubters from Missouri", there is ample evidence that Yankee ingenuity does not suffer in translation.

Our first step was to understand what the problems were. After proper analysis, we divided them into two components, marketing and service. Operators wisely opted to tackle the service areas first, recognizing that guest satisfaction is the primary source of repeat business and word-of-mouth the most effective form of advertising.

The prospects offered by the flip side were too risky to delay resorting to remedial aids until better systems could be devised and put into place.

As the representative of the U.S. lodging industry, the American Hotel and Motel Association turned to its own members for help. It culled information from hotels with a history of dealing with international guests and therefore learning what is needed and what was available. Matching this data with studies done by U.S. Travel Service, foreign carriers and tour operators on VISIT U.S.A. travel profiles enabled us to produce excellent guidelines

We found that service problems fall into three distinct categories: language requirements, special services needs and marketing requirements.

LANGUAGE REQUIREMENTS

Today we understand and are filling more satisfactorily the primary needs for better language capacities. These needs fall into three areas: written, visual and oral. We propose that written information be available in five languages — French, German, Japanese, Spanish, and Italian. It is advisable to follow a system based on the assumption that nobody can read English, thereby making it mandatory for all vital information that an operator must know about the guests and the guests must know about the hotel to be printed in those five languages. Multi-lingual personnel should be hired whenever possible or appropriate for a given property. The availability of a language bank from the hotel's personnel can often be not only surprising—but very useful. The community can offer resources through colleges, graduate students and in some cities, highly sophisticated volunteer groups.

In the United States, we have a foreign language deficiency. As we become more involved in the international marketplace, we are learning that it is costly to be hampered by the lack of language proficiency. The hospitality industry regards this as one of the areas of concern. We have taken a stand that now requires us to support better language training schools and ultimately, we hope to bring influence upon the academic community in order to have them re-establish foreign language require-ments for degree credits.

International signs and symbols appear with more frequency, in public places such as airports, post offices and federal buildings, but their use is not universal. Our highways need better signs. We need more roadside information centers again with multi-lingual maps and tour instructions. Certainly our national and state parks offer an immediate challenge since they are extremely popular to the international visitor and can present a serious problem for someone literally "lost in the wilderness".

Multi-lingual tour guide operators, park guides, bus-tour guides or any service people that come in contact with the international guest, particularly women and children who are less prone to speak or under-stand English, should be available. One has to be reminded that the ability to speak English is not a guarantee of the ability to read it. Adjustments must be made to take care of those situations.

Visual language offers some creative opportunities to speak through the eyes. Buffets, food displays, dessert trolleys or pictures depicting an item on the menu for the day not only help the guest but can stimulate sales. They are equally mouth-watering to your American guests.

Finally the question of language identity. Some hotels favor the use of a foreign flag worn in the lapel of the personnel who speak the language of the country that the flag represents. I do not favor that system as I think it is very limited. Many people speak French who are not from France and cannot even identify the French flag. Also, many countries, particularly in Central and South America, speak Spanish but are extremely national-istic about their own flag. I prefer the Smithsonian color-coded system which uses five established colors to identify the specific language assigned to that color. The infinite possibilities that the adoption of just this system offers are mind boggling and could offer standardizations across the country insuring immediate recognition and eliminating the confusion of having to re-adapt to a new system at each stop.

SPECIAL SERVICE NEEDS

One of the most irritating service problems that the international visitor has encountered in this country is the inability to exchange currency on the premises. We have gone a long way in remedying that. Today most of the major chains have established their own currency exchange desks; smaller hotels are using the services of international money houses such as Deak/Perera, who buy and sell money on a daily quoted rate. Generally, there is a significant improvement in the banks who have become more amenable to handling these transactions.

A continuing problem involves the reluctance on the part of the American operators to accept international credit cards, foreign currency and vouchers as a form of payment. Emotionally, it is difficult for them to take on trust (funny money) or to accept the word of an unknown operator from Frankfurt on the Main or Henley on the Thames. There are practical considerations, too. Even those who accept vouchers, waiting 60 to 90 days for payment on an already discounted rate, can make this an unprofitable market in which to be involved. The industry must come up with better ways to do business. We are exploring with American Express the possibility of a guaranteed system and with payments based on a shorter time period. This system, when perfected, would allow for a satisfactory transaction for the guest, the tour oeprators and the American properties. However, it is still on the drawing board, and cannot be specified as to when it will be operative.

Bell Telephone has responded to the industry's requests for easily identifiable multi-lingual creative phone instructions. They provide, upon request, a display box for the reception area that contains cards with national flags, easily identifiable by the guests. The card explains in their language how to direct dial abroad and how to use our system. One of the problems is that hotels using our system have difficulty in obtaining refills. Better delivery services with the telephone company are being explored.

Again, at our request, Bell is experimenting with an international phone facility at the point of arrival inside the customs area. Upon arrival, the visitor will be able to contact, through a multi-lingual button on the phone, someone to place the call either here or abroad. This facility is in the experimental stage and restricted to one terminal.

Some hotels offer very elaborate in-house services along with attractive international ambience, while others can only provide the basics.

The important factor is that the services are being offered and they continue to improve.

MARKETING TO THE INTERNATIONAL VISITOR

There is no doubt that selling in the international market is quite different from domestic methods. In order to deal internationally, one cannot "go it alone", and it is expedient to form alliances and create new consortia of common interests.

The operator's community is the place to start since the destination is always the primary attraction. Once the destination becomes an attractive choice on an itinerary, then the individual property located in that destination becomes a consideration. For example, guests coming from Germany do not say, if they are touring the United States, that they will go to America to visit the Sheraton Hotel in Boston. Their decision to go to America and then to Boston will be based on the attractions that Boston holds for them. Their choice to stay at the Sheraton Hotel will be made only to the extent of the marketing efforts the Sheraton Hotel has made either to convince their travel agent or to promote word-of-mouth recommendations that they have heard from their friends about the desirability of staying at the Sheraton Hotel in Boston.

Therefore, it is critically imperative to find partners in the travel profession. First one must comprehend the systems that create the machinery to stimulate and maintain the flow of traffic, and then develop working relationships with the professionals who maintain that machinery. Multi-destination packages offer new opportunities for marketing properties, particularly those not located in the immediate vicinity of a gateway city. One can not overemphasize the desirability of entering into such agreements. These agreements in many cases may lead to opening new domestic markets as well.

If operators are in the international market, they must have the commitment to do business on a year-round basis. By providing the tour operator with guaranteed room allotments, based on seasonal rates with tiered rate structures and guaranteed rate schedules for an 18-month period, one allows the wholesaler to have the necessary requirements to put together a package and allow for sufficient lead time to market it.

Selling techniques must be improved as well. Today, any hotelier who is a serious competitor for business outside of the United States must adopt fundamental requirements in the conduct of that business. It is essential to have a professional approach when making sales calls, including such tools as personal business cards that include a Telex number and multi-lingual brochures with information about the property and its location. Repeated and personal calls to overseas buyers are as mandatory as annual trade visits to I.T.B. and Pow Wow.

Successful marketing today must be target marketing; specific people with specific interests to specific places. Therefore, the most significant change we can make, with long-lasting implications, is to reappraise which are our target markets and to understand why people visit the United States. What attracts the international visitor to the United States is the very vastness and the variety of our continent. The adventure that accompanies being a part of big, bigger, biggest is a powerful lure. America marches to a distinctive beat and to a larger drummer, one in which our neighbors from all over the world wish increasingly to share. Our national parks, our pop and fine arts, our museums and our range of climates offer a variety attractive to many international visitors. Yet those who come for the first time will need reassurance of comfortable and safe accommodations and social and cultural acceptance at our hotels and motels.

The American hotel and motel industry can have the privilege of opening up America and its universality to the international visitor but it must reinforce marketing, service, and value. Good information must be followed by credibility. Networks of common interests must unite in order to provide imagination in planning programs and insuring variety, service and value for their money. These are the lynch pins of our industry.

As we begin to understand this and make our infinite possibilities available, we will insure our continued place in the world market as a prime travel and business destination.

22

Changing Trends in Food Purchasing

Hrayr Berberoglu

For many years the majority of restaurant operators have purchased goods required for their operations from specialized purveyors regardless of the quantities involved. This practice, as we know it today, has led to two important facts: First, expensive gas and labor are needlessly wasted; second, accounting departments of purveyors and operators, as well as purchasing personnel of purveyors and receivers of restaurants and hotels, require more hours than if larger quantities were purchased or if many items were obtained from one supplier.

Both of the above facts have contributed to increased wholesale prices. As better educated people enter and influence the hospitality business they are realizing that by placing large orders both purchase prices and labor costs are reduced. However, with storage space at a premium, large orders can be placed only by large operations or institutions which have warehouse space to accommodate large quantities of food, beverage and other deliveries. Purveyors also recognize the savings in delivery and labor costs. Consequently, purveyors slowly but surely have started to impose minimum quantity limits for delivery free of charge. Below these set amounts modest charges are being imposed for delivery or the prices of small quantities of goods delivered are increased.

Conventional purchasing methods have had to be changed. Purveyors have added additional lines of merchandise to their inventories in attempts to increase sales and decrease warehousing and delivery costs. Raw materials costs evenly distributed over a wide range of goods have diminished on a per unit basis. Frozen foods, for example, have become increasingly available. More varieties of items have been developed and freezing techniques and packaging materials have been improved to prevent quality deterioration in the flavor of frozen foodstuffs.

These practices provided additional opportunities for purveyors to increase sales while another important change was taking place. Skilled European cooks were no longer as readily available as they had been ten years earlier and this necessitated that operators look for more pre-prepared convenience foods. (A convenience food is defined as a food product which is partially or wholly processed, canned or frozen, portion packed or in bulk.) Using these items requires fewer cooks in the kitchens and less skilled help. Using convenience foods also reduces storage space requirements because of the reduction of bulk where waste has been previously removed.

NEW TECHNIQUES

Some purveyors have emerged who have created the one-stop purchasing concept. These "full-line distributors" offer staples; frozen, processed or unprocessed foods; paper goods; disposable items; and, in some instances, even fresh meats and produce. Many small operators have found it advantageous to purchase most of their needs from such suppliers since one telephone call is all that is needed to place the purchase order. Similarly, the purveyor has advantages. Because of the large quantities ordered the price can be kept competitively low because delivery costs are less and accounting costs are reduced considerably.

Still another technique has emerged which benefits hotel and restaurant chains. This is the establishment of subsidiary jobber companies by large chain operations. Due to consolidated quantities ordered these firms can deal directly with manufacturers of foodstuffs and equipment and thus eliminate the wholesaler. Smaller operators, however, are not able to take advantage of the subsidiary jobber technique. This has led to the development of still another innovation in co-operative purchasing. A company is set up which solicits restaurateurs to join their association. Restaurateurs who apply are financially scrutinized and sound operators gain admission into the association. The restaurateurs provide estimates of their annual use of staples. The association tabulates the required quantities which aggregatively represent considerable amounts. The association then negotiates with purveyors for lower prices based on the volume size.

The future of purchasing will allow for more changes and streamlining except for a few foodstuffs which cannot be dealt with successfully by huge corporations or frozen food suppliers. These items include fresh produce and dairy products. However, even in these categories many changes are occurring, e.g., nondairy coffee cream and simulated cheeses are now being processed and have excellent keeping qualities.

In spite of all this progress still more changes need to take place.

Clearly there are several reasons:

1) Skilled labor is becoming both more expensive and, in some cases, non-existent;
2) Due to increased land and/or rent costs kitchens are being built smaller;
3) Delivery costs continue to increase;
4) Profit margins of restaurants are shrinking in both percentages and constant dollars.

CHANGES COMING

These reasons will contribute to several profound changes in the restaurant business. In all likelihood they will include:

1) Fewer menu items;
2) Smaller food production staff;
3) Improved food production equipment;
4) Better and more efficient ways of purchasing goods.

In 1981 there are a myriad of convenience foods available on the market, which were either not available or not popular for purchase a decade ago. Some of the more exotic of these include frozen desserts; ready-cooked and frozen dishes designed for microwave oven cookery; prepared, powdered or dehydrated sauces; crepes; and frozen prepared coffee. This is only a small fraction of convenience foods now on the market. And more and more items are being added to the already long list on a regular basis. Operators must keep themselves constantly informed of new developments relating to the availability of such products. Many feel, however, that the quality of convenience foods is not as high as the quality of foods prepared on the premises from scratch. There is little doubt, exceptions notwithstanding, that this is true.

Frozen foods, for example, are not usually the equal of freshly and skillfully prepared dishes but, nevertheless, do not require a highly qualified staff and high quality foods. These attributes are often difficult if not impossible to come by today and in the future will be even more difficult to find. There will always be a small market which will demand and get fresh products skillfully cooked and graciously served, but the price to be paid will be well above the means of the average consumer. Today's restaurants frequently make greater profits from large volumes than from small volumes , as is the case with fast food operations like McDonalds, Kentucky Fried Chicken, Pizza Hut and others.

A potential future purchasing system may work as follows: Every unit operation will have a computer terminal. This terminal will be connected to an analog central processing unit where the computer will be programmed to do the following:

- At the insertion of a punched card analogous mechanism the terminal will either print out or display on a screen a selection of prices for goods on the market, along with their specifications, offered by three or four purveyors;
- The operator will select the purveyor from whom he wishes to purchase and punch in the names of the foodstuffs, the quantities, specifications and delivery date and time;
- Upon delivery, the foodstuffs will be verified and inspected. The acceptance thereof will be communicated via terminal to the purveyor;
- Once the acceptance has been received by the purveyor the invoice amount will be communicated to the bank of the restaurateur. The bank will credit the amount to the account of the purveyor and debit the account of the restaurateur.

This ordering procedure will take only minutes instead of hours and the accounting will also take only minutes which replace the hours of entering ledgers, writing checks, mailing, and so forth.

The hardware and software for the above system already are available. All that is necessary is to organize an affiliation of the businesses that would participate in the process. Eventually, many more similar cost cutting ideas will evolve such as delivery systems to serve various purveyors operating from one warehouse functioning as a single supplier for many companies. The Brewers' Warehousing Company in Ontario, Canada, is operating in this manner today.

Operators today must more than ever be alert for new items which are potentially and profitably usable and accepted by the public. Moreover, they must study their present purchasing system; evaluate it; and search for ways to make it more efficient and less costly in the years ahead.

23

Assessing Bottle Sales Values—Theoretical Analysis Using Different Portion Sizes[1]

Jack D. Ninemeier and *G. Kent Stearns*

Procedures for resource control require that performance standards be set and that actual results of the operation be measured. Corrective action is required when the variance between standard (planned) performance exceeds actual operating results by a predetermined variance. The traditional bottle sales value method of beverage income control incorporates these concerns and procedures. Standard anticipated sales income estimates are established for each brand of liquor. The amount of expected sales income is determined by summing the sales values represented by all liquor bottles emptied at the bar and returned to the storeroom during the issuing process. A comparison is then made between the standard, expected sales income (represented by the sum of the standard sales values for each empty bottle) and the actual income received as determined from the sales register tapes and from count of money in the cash drawer. Corrective action becomes necessary when the variance between the standard sales value and actual income exceeds a predetermined level.

After the standard sales values for each brand of liquor are established, and if these values are reasonably accurate, this basic approach can provide a useful method to control beverage sales.

It is obvious that the accuracy of the method rests with the ability to

[1]The authors wish to thank the management of the Royal Sonesta Hotel, New Orleans, Louisiana, for their cooperation in providing sales and other information necessary for this study; and Mr. Donald Hardenstein, then an HRT student and currently Manager, Convention Sales for the Greater New Orleans Tourist and Convention Commission, for his assistance in gathering data used in the study.

determine the correct bottle sales values for brands of liquor being issued to replace empty bottles. If, for example, the actual sales values for some types of liquor are understated (actual income should be *more* than the amount represented by the standard sales value) the control system is affected; more income will accrue than anticipated. This difference represents an amount of income which can be misused without being recognized by the control system. Alternatively, additional amounts of beverage products can be used for non-income generating purposes (such as overpouring or providing free drinks) without being observed through the control system.

Conversely, if the actual sales value of some types of liquor is overstated (actual income should be *less* than the amount represented by the standard sales value) the control system is likewise affected; "paper losses" will occur which cannot be reversed through analysis and physical corrective action procedures.

PROBLEMS WITH TRADITIONAL APPROACH

Problems with the traditional bottle sales value method of beverage income control most generally arise both during the initial planning stage (when expected bottle sales values are initially determined) and during the routine operational stage (when standard income is being assesed).

Planning problems occur during the process of estimating bottle sales values. Bottle sales values are essentially determined by calculating a weighted sales value for each ounce of each brand of liquor. This ounce value, once developed, becomes the basis for establishing a bottle sales value for each brand; the ounce value is multiplied by the number of ounces in the bottle to yield a bottle sales value for each brand and each bottle.

The weighted sales value is affected by the sales mix of drinks served with differing ounce sales values. For example, when the sales value for gin is established, it will be affected by the number of ounces sold at highball price and the number sold at cocktail price[2]. Normally, the sales value per ounce in a cocktail is lower. If a one-ounce highball sells for $1.50, the price of a one-and-one-half-ounce cocktail may be set at $1.75 or $2.00. Therefore, as more one-ounce drinks are sold, the bottle sales value

---

[2]Highballs are generally drinks made with only one liquor to which a non-alcoholic mixer (such as soda, tonic, water, etc.) is added. A cocktail is generally a drink containing a larger portion of one liquor (such as Martini, Old Fashioned and Manhattan) or a drink made with two or more liquors. Based upon the sum of standard sales values for all bottles of each liquor class issued to the bar at the end of a shift.

will be higher ($1.50 ÷ 1 ounce = $1.50 per ounce) than when more one-and-one-half-ounce drinks are served ($1.75 ÷ 1½ ounce = $1.17 per ounce).

The problem, then, which occurs during the initial design of the system involves planning for procedures needed to accurately establish the standards. For example, beverage officials may use inconsistent, inaccurate or inappropriate techniques to determine:

- How beverage sales mixes should be calculated.
- Times when analysis of drink sales should be undertaken.
- Lengths of required observation periods.
- Number of total drinks which must be observed to establish accurate sales mix patterns.
- How to count beverage sales when prices differ during low, regular and high pricing periods.

Beverage planners need detailed assistance regarding procedures to establish the weighted sales values which become the basis for the control system. It is a paradox that a basically simple system to *use* is dependent upon seemingly complicated techniques necessary to accurately develop the control standards. Likewise, the sheer volume of work involved in keeping track of drink sales for a large number of brands found in most beverage operations dissuades many beverage officials from implementing the system. Since the task is large and complex, errors can be made when separate information must be kept and analyzed for each liquor brand.

The second problem occurs during the routine operational stage of the control system. This concern essentially involves the need to assign a separately established sales value to each brand of liquor as a replacement bottle is issued. This is necessary to estimate standard income applicable to the time period (usually shift). In the average beverage operation, using seventy or more liquors with seventy or more differing bottle sales values, the task of determining the standard sales values for all liquors issued can be a time consuming activity. This a most serious matter since the time consumed directly relates to how practical the system is; as more time is required, the system becomes less practival from the perspective of the beverage manager. This, of course, correlates with willingness to implement and maintain the control system.

METHOD TO RESOLVE PROBLEMS
WITH TRADITIONAL APPROACH

A variation of the bottle sales value control method has been suggested by Stearns and Ninemeier (1980). It provides definitive procedures to estimate weighted sales values with a predictable confidence of accuracy.

It additionally simplifies the task of calculating standard income at the time of beverage issuing. Weighted sales values are determined through procedures recognized as a result of computer simulation of drink variations based upon sample observations. This yields guidelines which inform management officials about the number of drink observations necessary and also suggest the degree of confidence which can be placed upon the accuracy of sales values established as a result of the process.

The suggested method simplifies both the process of estimating bottle sales values and calculating standard income because beverages are classified by class of liquor (House, Call, etc.) rather than by brand of liquor. This results in a need to collect information for perhaps only two and seldom more than five categories of beverages. This is much more practical and simple than the seventy or more separate tallies needed when liquor is classified by brand. Our study indicated that the revised approach was feasible when there were two basic types of drinks (Highball and Cocktail) and two classes of drinks (House and Call). Drinks contained either one ounce or two ounces of liquor. It was recognized, however, that these parameters limited the applicability of the simplified method.

PROCEDURES FOR PRESENT STUDY

The present study was undertaken to explore whether additional variables could be included within the proposed revision to the traditional Bottle Sales Value Control Method. A public bar (LeBooze 2) in the Royal Sonesta Hotel in the New Orleans French Quarter was chosen for the study. Guests can enter this bar directly from Bourbon Street, a high pedestrian traffic route. It is not accessible from the interior of the hotel.

The property has a sales structure of five drink types (Highball, Cocktail, Cordial, Special, Cocktail plus). Drink sizes are 1.25 oz., 1.75 oz., and 2.50 oz. Three drink classifications are utilized: House—liquor used when drinks are ordered only by liquor type; Call—liquor used when drink is ordered by liquor brand; Premium—liquor which is a more expensive call brand.

This information is summarized in Table 23.1.

Since these drink characteristics are different from those used in the earlier study, it was believed that analysis of beverage service at the property could help to enlarge the number of situations in which the simplified method could be applied.

Procedures were designed to tally and record all drinks served over several representative time periods. The objective of this process was to determine the actual weighted sales values of all liquors served at the facility. This information was used as the base for computer simulation. The resulting analysis was used to assess the number of drink observa-

TABLE 23.1.   PARAMETERS USED TO CATEGORIZE DRINKS FOR SALES VALUE PER BOTTLE CALCULATIONS

Type of Drink	Definition	Number of Ounces	Price Period[1]	Price By Class House	Call	Premium
Highball	One liquor with mixer such as coke, water, soda	1.25	Low Price[1]	1.00	1.85	2.35
			Reg. Price	1.65	1.85	2.35
Cocktail	One liquor with one juice or mix	1.25	No Price Change	1.85	2.35	2.35
Cordial	A liqueur served alone	1.25	No Price Change	2.25	2.25	2.65
Special	A drink made with more than one liquor or more than one juice	2.50	No Price Change	2.80	2.80	2.80
Cocktail Plus	Martini, Manhattan Old Fashioned	1.75	No Price Change	1.85	2.35	2.35

[1]There is a cocktail hour special price charge for highballs.

tions which would be necessary in the real world to develop bottle sales values with an acceptable degree of accuracy in similar situations (five drink types, three drink classification, two pricing periods and two different drink sizes).

Basic procedures used to collect, analyze and interpret information follow:

- The actual beverage operation was observed during hours which represented both busy and slow periods and low and regular price periods.
- A coding sheet was used to record each drink served during the observation periods according to drink type, class and liquor brand, ounce size of drink, drink price, and pricing period.
- A base of 1038 actual drinks served was established. These drinks were tabulated over an approximate cumulative 38 hour observation period. The actual drink count and percentage of total of all drinks served is shown in Table 23.2.

TABLE 23.2.   FREQUENCY OF DRINKS SERVED BY TYPE AND CLASS

Type of Drink	House Number	Percentage	Call Number	Percentage	Premium Number	Percentage[1]
Highball	256	24.7	269	25.9	127	12.2
Cocktail	151	14.5	12	1.2	33	3.2
Cordial	26	2.5	60	5.8	25	2.4
Special	19	1.8	10	1.0	13	1.3
Cocktail Plus	10	1.0	24	2.3	3	0.3
Total	462	44.5	375	36.2	201	19.4

[1]Percentage of total drinks (1038) served.

To test the sampling effect a computer simulation program was utilized to randomly select drinks from the various categories in order to calculate the resulting bottle sales values. The "actual" weighted sales value represented by the base of drinks actually observed was compared with simulated drink sales mixes. This process yielded information about the range in accuracy of resulting bottle sales values which occurred when the number of observations was varied.

CONCLUSIONS

Several conclusions can be drawn from the present study. Each confirms the findings of our previous study which suggested that the simplified bottle sales value method—attaching standard income expectations to liquor by class rather than by brand—is useful in an expanded range of operational variables.

Conclusion One

As the number of drink observations increases, the accuracy of resulting sales value estimates increases.

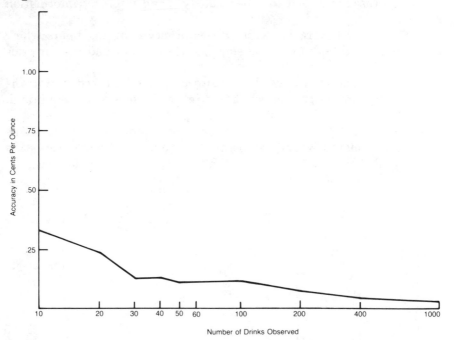

FIG. 23.1.   HOUSE LIQUOR: PREDICTABLE ACCURACY OF SALES VALUE PER OUNCE
Actual Sales Value Per Ounce Will Be Plus or Minus This Limit 95% of the Time

Data for House, Call and Premium classes of liquor is presented, respectively, in Fig. 23.1, 23.2 and 23.3 below. These figures present the accuracy (expressed in terms of cents per ounce) of sales value estimates when differing numbers of drinks are observed. For example, Fig. 23.1 (House Liquor) indicates that if 50 total drinks are sampled, the resulting sales value per ounce estimate will have an accuracy rate at the two standard deviation level of 12¢; that is, 95% of the time the actual sales value per ounce will be the standard value plus or minus 12¢. As the number of observed drinks increases to 200 the resulting sales value per ounce estimate will have an accuracy rate at the two standard deviation level of 8¢. That is, in 95% of the time the actual sales value per ounce will be the standard value plus or minus 8¢.

Accuracy rates at the one standard deviation level (67% confidence) are, of course, also available. However, the researcher judged that the lowered accuracy range would not be meaningful or helpful to most food and beverage management officials. It is, for example, extremely difficult to generalize about, plan for or attempt to control when data are only applicable in approximately 67% of the occasions. Therefore, information throughout this paper is directed to the two standard deviation confidence level.

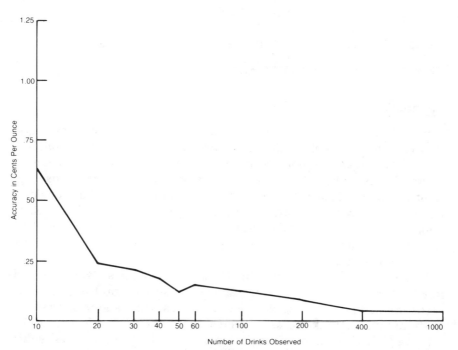

FIG. 23.2.   CALL LIQUOR: PREDICTABLE ACCURACY OF SALES VALUE PER OUNCE
Actual Sales Value Per Ounce Will Be Plus or Minus This Limit 95%of the Time

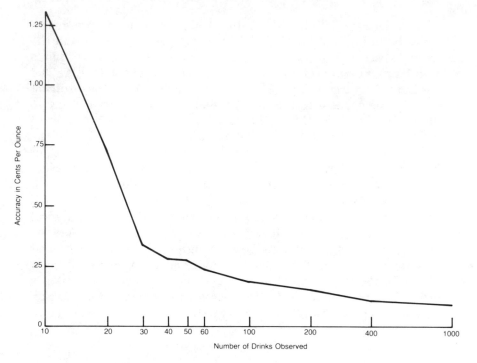

FIG. 23.3.   PREMIUM LIQUOR: PREDICTABLE ACCURACY OF SALES VALUE
PER OUNCE
Actual Sales Value Per Ounce Will Be Plus or Minus This Limit 95% of the Time

Conclusion Two

Knowledge of accuracy levels in sales value per ounce estimates eases the task of utilizing bottle sales value standards in routine operation. It is possible to express standard deviations as a percent of variance across all liquor classes. When this is done, one variance range can be used to compare standard and actual income. For example, rather than considering variations from standard sales values separately for each liquor class (House, Call, Premium) one variance can be developed. As would be expected the range of variance drops as the total number of drinks observed increases.

Findings derived from combining the three liquor classes are presented in Fig. 23.4. Note that the percentage of variance in total sales volume between standard and actual sales levels decreases (more accuracy results) as the number of drinks observed increases. For example, when 50 drinks are sampled the standard deviation is 5%; if standard sales value estimates are based upon this sample size, the actual sales value will be the standard sales value plus or minus 5% on 95% of the occasions.

When standard sales values are based upon a sample size of 200 drinks, the actual sales value will range from 3% more to 3% less than standard sales value 95% of the time.

This has very important and practical implications which are illustrated in the following example.

- If only 50 drinks have been sampled, there is a 5% accuracy factor. Therefore, if total standard sales at the end of a shift[3] are estimated at $500.00, the range of actual sales is the standard sales plus or minus $25.00; the range of actual sales will be from $475.00 to $525.00.

- If 400 drinks have been sampled, there is a 1.8% accuracy factor. Therefore, if total standard sales at the end of a shift are estimated at $500.00, the range of actual sales is the standard plus or minus $9.00; the range of actual sales will be from $491.00 to $509.00.

- It can be seen above that the beverage manager who has sampled a larger number of drinks when bottle sales value estimates were established realizes greater accuracy (less variance between the standard income and the range of actual income). Tighter control (which is the objective of implementing the bottle sales value method) becomes possible.

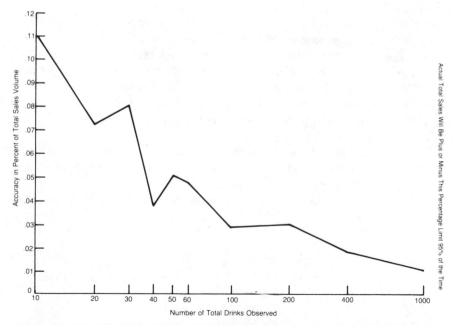

FIG. 23.4.   ALL LIQUOR CLASSES: PREDICTABLE ACCURACY OF TOTAL STANDARD SALES VALUE

Conclusion Three

The simplified bottle sales value method can be used in an expanded number of beverage operational structures with a predictable degree of accuracy. Tested variables which have been utilized in the sampling and simulation process include:

Drink Types—
  Two (Highball and Cocktail)
  Five (Highball, Cocktail, Cordial, Special, Cocktail Plus)
Drink Classes—
  Two (House and Call)
  Three (House, Call and Premium)
Ounce Sizes—
  Two sizes (1.0; 2.0)
  Three sizes (1.25; 2.50; 1.75)
Pricing Periods—
  Two (regular price and low price)

SUMMARY

The findings presented from the pilot study have significant implications for beverage control practices. For cost and time effective implementation, however, it is necessary to develop other parameters. Research is presently being conducted in the following areas:

- Assurance that other variables, such as differing portion sizes, beverage sales prices, and use of more than two pricing structures, do not affect the accuracy of resulting bottle sales values.
- Development of recordkeeping and control forms necessary to determine and use bottle sales value information in an on-going beverage control program.
- Determination of means to most effectively provide assistance to beverage management officials desiring to know proper sampling size and other procedural requirements.
- Determination of the process necessary to cost-justify use of the control system.

24

Convention Negotiations and Contracts—
A Panel Discussion

James Abbey, Ph.D.

Question: Can hotels quote firm room food and beverage rates two to four years ahead? If not, what is a reasonable time for the hotel to quote in writing the firm rates for:

  guest rooms—months prior to the convention;
  public space—months prior to the convention;
  food & beverage—months prior to the convention?

John Russell: Normally we quote guest rooms 12 months ahead, public space 12 months and food and beverage 3 to 6 months. Basically we don't like to quote any further ahead than that. Just like you don't know what the price of a car is going to be next year, to quote more than 12 months ahead is a little ridiculous. I do understand Al Sear's problem, where he has to do a budget based on a contract that he negotiates with the hotel. So what we attempt to do, from a customer's standpoint, is to give him some kind of projection of what his room rates will be based on present rates.

It is very difficult for us to make any commitments beyond one year.

Al Sears: I have no problem getting a 12-month quote on rooms. In the food and beverage area, I like to give flexibility to catering. I know you go to a supermarket weekly and things are jumping. If you cooperate with a hotel you are going to get a good deal. The guy that comes in and raves that he wants a definite rate quoted—six months ahead. Well, the hotel is going to react accordingly.

Question: What time of the day is best to negotiate?

Bob Keilt: You should negotiate when you are fresh. The customer should have the same advantage that you have. He should be sharp, clear and not worn out. I know one way of negotiating is to wear him out until he'll say yes to anything, but that doesn't make a good contract.

Question: There is such a rapid turnover in personnel at hotels and among meeting planners. Is it important who signs the contract? Should the contract include a *warranty of authority* clause stating in effect that the signers are authorized agents of the two parties and are empowered to bind their employers to all provisions in the contract?

Bob Keilt: If it makes the customer happy then I think it's good. It makes for a better climate to negotiate and I see nothing wrong with indicating that an authorized individual sign the contract.

Question: As a meeting planner, do you prefer to negotiate with the Director of Sales, a Sales Manager, or the hotel's General Manager?

Al Sears: The Director of Sales seems to have the best handle on the property. I know the industry really well, and I pride myself in dealing with people and not buildings and most of the directors of sales know me and it's a lot easier for me to deal with them.

Question: Can a planner insist the hotel hold all function space?

Al Sears: I ask for all space when I begin to negotiate and then as we come down the home stretch I generally work with the convention service department and catering on space that they assign. I do insist that I have control over who is in that public space. Now, if they call me up and say Boston University wants to have a prom on Sunday night, I've got no problem with that; they are out to make a buck too. And I would just like to know who is going to be in there and I'd like to have some control over it.

Question: Do gratuities belong in the contract or is there a general industry understanding on a 15% service charge?

Bob Keilt: Why not? It's part of the agreement and it should be specified and if a hotel doesn't tell the customer he should feel free to go to the Chamber of Commerce or the local hotel association and with a little salesmanship he could probably get a copy of the contract to read. It should not be a secret.

Question: Are hotels willing to negotiate food guarantees? Twenty-four or 48 hours ahead? Five or 10 percent over?

Maxine Kaplan: We would like to guarantee 48 hours ahead and we will set 5% or 50 above the guarantee, and of course everything is updated 24 hours in advance.

Question: It seems a good policy to review reservation pickups at

periodic intervals: 90 days, 60 days and 30 days ahead. Should this procedure be part of the contract?

Al Sears: Definitely. I even get a weekly report the last two months. Most of your housing bureaus send you a computer printout starting every two weeks, starting 90 days ahead, and when you get into the 60 days area you get it every week, and it gives you a good feel. One of the things I do like to negotiate as far as reservations are concerned is that cancellations be thrown back into my room block until my cutoff date.

Question: To service a group effectively, the convention service manager must receive a tentative program with a reasonable lead time. Should the contract include a clause to this effect?

For example, a clause stating "the meeting group agrees to furnish a tentative schedule six months in advance and a detailed program 45 days in advance of the convention. If the hotel does not receive the program in the above specified time, the hotel shall provide space on an availability basis."

Does such a clause seem too stringent?

Maxine Kaplan: Well, I think it would be an ideal situation if it could be observed all the way. I think it is a little too stringent depending on the type of organization. Flexibility on the part of the meeting planner and the hotel is always very important and if the convention service department is doing what they are supposed to be doing, they are in contact with the meeting planner and should have a good schedule to go by at least six months ahead.

Al Sears: I'm troubled with the words detailed program. I have speakers that don't get their AV requirements in until 30 days before. When you are using free speakers in the industry then you can't push them too much. If detailed programming means AV and all that, I'll have trouble. Right now, I've sent in a copy of my Dallas program to San Francisco so that they can have an idea of the space I'm using this year. Again, you have got to have flexibility. We have to work together.

Question: If meeting space is complimentary, is setup labor also provided by the hotel at no cost?

Maxine Kaplan: We do not at this time charge; however, there is a trend to charge for special schoolroom setups, audio-visual platforms, and anything that goes beyond the norm. Of course, that too has to be negotiated.

Question: Should the contract include a clause about settling the master account? For example, "75% of the calculated master account must be paid before departure".

Al Sears: Seventy-five percent is too high; however, I am willing to send a deposit to cover some of the cash flow problems. You don't know what that master bill is going to be like. It's a lot easier for me if we come to an agreement in advance that I will advance a deposit of $10,000—$15,000. I do this with convention centers all the time. This is one of the problems. The hotel industry has a reluctance to put a deposit policy into effect. They insinuate we'd like to have you do this, but no hotel group has the courage to take that initial step. I don't think you would have a big problem with meeting planners if all of a sudden the hotel said, we anticipate that you are going to spend $20,000 by your previous records, we want 10% in advance. I don't think the average meeting planner would have a problem with that, if he is being realistic. But, nobody has the guts to pick it up.

John Russell: A definite date should be agreed upon by the hotel and planner as to when the master account should be paid. Let's face it, hotels don't want money to come between our friendship. However, we would like to be paid in a reasonable time. Maybe a reasonable time is a week or two after. This should be included in the contract. The problem we run into occasionally is when the master account gets over into the 30 day and 60 day accounts, where they are disputing $3000 on a $250,000 bill. And they are just using that $250,000 as their cash flow.

Question: Some planners request the hotel provide a final occupancy report showing the arrival and departure patterns, as well as the amount of money the hotel received from his people in areas such as room service, boutiques and food and beverage functions. Is this a common request? Might it be part of the contract?
Al Sears: Yes, and we do insist on post convention reports and a post convention meeting. I'm not an expert and I don't profess to be one. I pick up a lot of tips here and there where I can save money and I try to give some honest objective criticism to the hotel in the areas where I see problems.

Question: When exhibits are part of a convention program should the hotel protect itself in the contract from exhibit theft and/or accident liability?
Bob Keilt: Every hotel that works with exhibits should have a hold harmless clause written into the contract. Frankly, I think that you owe it to discuss it with your customer and I think the customer or the majority of them buy insurance and it's not that expensive to cover themselves.

Question: Several hotels and meeting planners suggest an arbitration clause should be included in the contract. Such a clause states that in the event of a dispute both parties will submit to arbitration. Both parties agree in advance that the arbitrator's decision will be final and legally binding. Do you favor arbitration clauses?

John Russell: I'd favor a penalty clause as opposed to an arbitration clause. In arbitration, who is going to arbitrate and when do you decide on that? How long is it going to take to arbitrate? I mean you could have a case that could be 1, 2 or 3 years long, whereas a penalty clause is right up front.

Al Sears: I don't favor arbitration clauses. I have the same worry as John: who is going to arbitrate? The industry is getting complex enough. I think one of the keys to the industry is when you are negotiating, you know the people you are negotiating with, and you know how realistic they are.

Question: What is the liability of the hotel in the event of overbooking? Should there be a penalty clause favoring the meeting group holding the hotel liable for non-performance?

Al Sears: I had one serious overbooking situation about seven years ago. The hotel came out and they worked and they worked hard. The entire sales department was out there, on Sunday afternoon, explaining the situation. They did something that I wouldn't have the courage to do. They stood in the lobby of the hotel and they asked people, "if we give you a discount rate, a considerable discount, would you double up?" They got people to double up that I never thought would double up. They had hotels in the outlying area and they paid their transportation the entire week.

It was just a problem that the meeting grew. The hotel figured, we'll get a little hungry; we'll take more and more reservations and then they had a serious problem on their hands. We were able to sit down in the three day period and iron out the whole situation. We saw it coming. We knew it was going to be a problem and it was handled very well. Again, I think it's the professionalism. I hate to see this industry becoming so inflexible, that if you overbook you are going to pay me $25 per room.

We've got to be realistic about it. It's a two-way street. As far as an overbooking clause, I think, it would be great but I don't see who is going to gain from it. I really don't. In certain times and certain areas it might work out. Corporate meetings planning is another world from association meeting planning. I don't have the control over my attendees that corporate meetings are going to have.

25

The Relationship Between the Strategic Planning Process and the Service Delivery System

Alex F. De Noble, C.P.A. and *Michael D. Olsen, Ph.D.*

Significant fluctuations in our economic and social environment have spawned an intense interest among food service executives in learning new and effective ways for strategically planning and managing their operations. Such factors as rising food and fuel prices, the shift towards more working wives in America's households, and skyrocketing interest rates have all had a definite impact on how firms choose to run their operations. In addition, the decade of the 1980s promises even more changes in the environment that will seriously affect the way we presently conduct business operations. In the long run, those firms that are flexible enough to adapt to the demands the environment places upon them will have the best chance for continuing in operation and maximizing their potential.

This notion can be related to the topic of proper layout and design of service delivery systems of hospitality industry facilities. The basic tenet is that organization and unit design considerations should reflect management's attempt at trying to match the firm's internal strengths and capabilities to overall trends and fluctuations within the environment.

The purpose of this chapter is to present the findings of some exploratory empirical work conducted to assess the state of the art of strategic planning practices among the nation's top food service operations. Further, it will discuss how these findings specifically impact on service delivery systems by citing examples of various problems relating to service delivery design.

FRAMEWORK FOR SURVEY

Two underlying concepts prevailed throughout the duration of the study. First, in developing a viable service delivery system, the organization must design it so that it will coincide with the type of demands the environment places upon it. This presents an important question that has confounded business oriented researchers for years. What is the most important determinant of the firm's ultimate organizational and unit design: the *objective* contextual nature of the environment or management's *perceptions* of the contextual nature of the environment?

The position taken in this study is that determination of design is based on management's perceptual viewpoint. It is our belief that firms will organize, more often, in accordance with the way their top management views the nature of the environment. If management's perceptions are closely in tune with actual trends in their environment, they will successfully design their units so as to be able to meet routine types of demands, as well as to be able to handle potential future shifts in those demands. Alternatively, if management's perceptions are widely divergent from the state of the actual environment, unit design will be inefficient and incapable of surviving environmental fluctuations in the long run.

The key issues, then, focus on how well top management perceives what is happening in the overall environment and how well it can forecast potential environmental influences on a particular operation.

A second related concept underlying this specific research endeavor is the distinction between an *operations manager* and a *strategic manager*. According to a prominent researcher in the business policy field (Ansoff, 1977), an *operations manager* is one who is "a change absorber, cautious risk taker, convergent problem solver, skillful diagnostician, coordinator and controller of complex activities". Ansoff describes a *strategic manager,* on the other hand, as one who is "a change-seeker, risk propensive, divergent problem solver, and skillful in leading others into new and untried directions". Therefore, strategic management is concerned with adapting organizations to the environment, while operations management is concerned with operating within that environment. In the long run, a firm needs to develop an optimum mix between the two if it expects to survive in dynamic changing times.

Considering these two concepts, the hypothesis for the present research was that top management may be demonstrating a narrow *operations* perspective in dealing with the environment and in plotting its company's future direction.

METHOD

Questionnaires were sent to 130 of the nation's top food service chains. The survey instrument contained 22 questions aimed directly at finding out how participants scan the environment for relevant information, how they actually perceive their environment, and who within the firm participates in the strategic planning process.

Only 27 usable responses were returned so no meaningful statistical analysis could be performed. However, the plotting of response frequencies and their analysis permits the drawing of tentative conclusions. The figures contained in the following tables represent the percentages of those who responded, on the scales indicated, with a specific choice as an answer. The number of participants responding (with a rank answer) to each category is also provided.

FINDINGS

Table 25.1 shows the categories of information about the environment that food service executives consider in their business operations. Respondents were asked to rate the significance of these categories on a scale of 1—5 with one having the most significance and five the least significance.

As shown in Table 25.1 an overwhelming majority of those responding to the questionnaire primarily seek environmental information specifically affecting their segment of the industry (96.2% ranked it either first or second). Current activity in the overall industry is also considered highly important — 85.7% ranked it either first or second. Relevant technological innovations and current activity in the overall environment appeared to be less important to the respondents than industry specific information. Concerning leads on acquisitions, mergers and joint ventures, the respondents clearly indicated that such information was least important to them.

TABLE 25.1.   TYPES OF INFORMATION SOUGHT ABOUT THE ENVIRONMENT BY RESPONDING FIRMS IN PERCENTAGES

Type of Information	n	Most Important 1	2	3	Least Important 4	5
Current activity in industry environment	21	33.3	52.4	14.3	0	0
Current activity affecting the firm's industry segment	26	73.1	23.1	3.8	0	0
Relevant technological innovations	20	10.0	20.0	35.0	30.0	5.0
Current activity in overall environment	23	8.7	17.4	34.8	34.8	4.3
Leads regarding acquisitions, mergers and joint ventures	12	0	8.3	16.7	16.7	58.3

Table 25.2 presents the results of a set of questions designed to assess how respondents perceive the environment of their customers, competitors and suppliers. For each category, participants were asked to react to statements concerning the degree of stability (certainty/uncertainty) and complexity in the environment. The stability dimension refers to such items as: changing customer tastes and preferences; the extent of competition and the availability of reliable suppliers. The complexity dimension, on the other hand, refers to the *range* of environmental activities such as: the number of different market segments served by the firm, the number of direct competitors and availability of substitute products confronting the firm, and the alternative sources of supply available to the firm.

In aggregate, the respondents appear to be mixed in their perceptions of their customer environment. A little over half think that their consumer environment is stable and certain, while the reminder perceive this environment to be characterized by frequent changes. Most of the respondents did indicate however that they perceived their customer environment to be complex.

Concerning their competitors, a majority of the respondents perceived this environment to be unstable, uncertain, and highly complicated. On the other hand, they were mixed in their perceptions of the supplier environment, with 63.6% agreeing that it was stable and certain while 55% felt that it was complicated.

The tentative conclusion that can be drawn is that the environment is indeed a perceptual issue. In most cases, in each environmental category, respondents were as likely to agree to the environment being certain and simple, as they were to its being dynamic and complex. We have no way

TABLE 25.2. HOW RESPONDING FIRMS PERCEIVE THEIR CUSTOMER, COMPETITOR AND SUPPLIER ENVIRONMENTS IN PERCENTAGES

Category	n	Strongly Agree	Agree	Disagree	Strongly Disagree
Customers					
Stable and certain	27	3.7	48.2	33.3	14.8
Simple and uncomplicated	26	3.9	19.2	34.6	42.3
Competitors					
Stable and uncomplicated	25	0	28.0	60.0	12.0
Simple and uncomplicated	25	0	24.0	56.0	20.0
Suppliers					
Stable and certain	22	4.5	59.1	31.8	4.5
Simple and uncomplicated	20	0	45.0	40.0	15.0

of determining which perceptual view is most likely to be correct. However, it is intuitively obvious that a comprehensive perception is critical in the decade of the 1980s.

Table 25.3 provides information as to which functional areas the respondents felt were most important in the actual strategic management process of the firm. Based on a 4-point scale from 0 (no involvement) to 3 (total involvement), the respondents were asked to rate the degree of involvement in the strategic management process of executives from each of the five functional areas of marketing, accounting, finance, R&D and operations.

TABLE 25.3. EXECUTIVES FROM FUNCTIONAL AREAS INVOLVED IN THE STRATEGIC MANAGEMENT PROCESS IN PERCENTAGES

	n	No Involvement 0	1	2	Total Involvement 3
Marketing	27	7.4	7.4	55.6	29.6
Accounting	27	25.9	7.4	51.9	14.8
Finance	27	11.1	7.4	44.5	37.0
R&D	27	40.7	25.9	22.3	11.1
Operations	27	14.8	0	29.6	55.6

The results indicate that executives from the operations area seem to be the most involved in the responding firms' strategic management process. A large majority of the participants (85.2%) ranked this function on the upper end of the scale. Other functional executives from finance, marketing and accounting were also significantly involved, though to a lesser extent. An important point to note here, however, is that R&D executives in the responding firms seem to be the least involved in the strategic management process. Another majority of the respondents (66.6%) indicate that executives from this functional area have little or nothing to do with the strategic management process.

DISCUSSION

The results of this study support the initial concern that food service executives may be placing too much emphasis on operations and not enough on strategic decision making. Referring back to Table 25.1, it appears that food service executives are concerned primarily with events directly related to their particular segment of the industry. Most respondents, for example, appeared to be extremely interested in industry specific information, while downplaying technological innovation and events occurring in the general environment. Strategic-oriented managers, on the other hand, are most often primarily concerned with how they can take advantage of opportunities in the environment, given the risks involved and the company's own internal capabilities (Ansoff 1977). This strategic viewpoint requires that management take a much broader perspective of the environment than that of just industry specific information.

Second, with regard to how top management perceives the environment (Table 25.2), the responses may indicate symptoms of much greater long run problems. Over half of the participants perceive their customer and supplier environments to be stable and certain. In light of the present state of the economy, these may be dangerous assumptions to make. If management does not perceive these problem areas, it is highly unlikely that they will plan for any future contingent fluctuations in these areas.

Finally, in terms of the way food service firms go about developing strategic plans, Table 25.3 indicates that the most involved personnel in the overall strategic planning process were executives from the operations function. The potential implication here is that the strategic planning process may be too narrowly focused; i.e., most of the emphasis will be placed on maintaining the status quo over a short run period. For a firm that wishes to strategically adapt itself to a changing environment, more input will be needed from managers of other functional areas such as R&D and finance.

IMPLICATIONS FOR SERVICE DELIVERY DESIGN

The implications of these findings to problems of service delivery design can be best viewed by specific example. Two cases from a recent report published by Olsen and De Noble (1981) were selected for this purpose. These cases both involve the fast food segment of the industry, but the universal implications for all firms presently engaged in designing or redesigning their service delivery system are evident. The first example deals with problems presently confronting the Wendy's hamburger chain; the second discusses the barriers preventing Burger King from entering the breakfast market.

Wendy's

Wendy's, the number 3 chain in the fast food segment of the industry, experienced a high degree of success during its initial years of operation from 1969-1978. In this time span, Wendy's grew at an extremely rapid pace by using a cookie cutter approach in reproducing its "old fashioned" theme unit almost 2000 times. Founder Dave Thomas attributed his initial success to a service delivery system which offered a limited burger menu, utilizing fresh instead of frozen products. An important aspect of this service delivery system was a new *technological innovation,* the drive-through window. This window significantly increased the potential demand that could be placed on the system by offering the product to a whole new segment of the market. Since the introduction of the drive-through window, all other major chains have begun to use similar types of set-ups. This illustrates the importance of technological innovation to the food service industry.

Around 1978, however, Wendy's bright picture dimmed. In the ensuing years, the company had experienced a series of sales declines which caused it to flirt seriously with operating losses. One suggested reason for that dilemma was that Wendy's had not attempted to keep up with changing trends in the environment. During its earlier rapid growth years, Wendy's management spent so much time opening new units that it almost completely ignored the changing trends in the environment. Today Wendy's is faced with a unit design that may be obsolete in light of a dynamic environment anticipated in the 1980s.

In an attempt to modify its present unit design to meet new customer preferences, Wendy's has recently added a salad bar in some of its stores. This salad bar, though serving to expand present menu offerings, was instituted by Wendy's at a very high price. For example, the actual location of the bar is in a place that was previously used to seat six customers. This and other attempts to change Wendy's unit design in reacting to the environment comes only at considerable expense.

This situation might not have been so severe if Wendy's had taken a broader, long range perspective of the environment earlier. The need to scan the *overall* environment continually for clues of trends that may lead to specific implications for an individual company is evident. A more systematic, continuous environmental scanning approach is more appropriate than trying to play "catch up" by instituting structural changes later.

Burger King

Another example of how technology can have an impact on the demands placed on a service delivery system by the environment is Burger King. In trying to gain increased utilization of their basic service delivery unit, many chains have attempted to expand into both the dinner time and breakfast markets. Burger King, in this endeavor, is presently years behind the leaders, McDonald's and Hardee's in the breakfast market. One reason for this difficulty is that Burger King units are primarily designed with a broiler system instead of a grill. The broiler is not suitable for cooking traditional breakfast items. The company's R&D

people must find ways of utilizing the existing technology to cook breakfast items, or modify the system by adding equipment that will be able to do the job. In either case, Burger King is placed at a decisive disadvantage against the leaders in the breakfast market.

CONCLUSIONS

The purpose of the research reported in this chapter was to gain some insight into the state of the art of strategic planning practices among the nation's top food service operations. In summary, the study has revealed indications that food service executives may be placing too much emphasis on the operations perspective while plotting the course of their companies' future growth.

Also, the results support the notion that executives utilize a limited view of their environment. A good number of food service firms appear to seek primarily industry — related information as opposed to trends in the overall environment. They perceive their customer and supplier markets as fairly stable and certain, and they make greatest use of operations executives in developing their strategic plans. As the examples of Wendy's and Burger King indicate, a narrow perspective on any aspect of the environment can lead to serious implications.

If this sample is representative of the state of the art of the strategic planning process currently existing within the food service industry, it is obvious that developing better planning methods is necessary. Specifically, more emphasis should be placed by food service executives on trends in the overall environment which may impact on future operations. In addition, a greater role needs to be given to a company's R&D executives in formulating future long range plans. Technological innovations significantly affect the performance level and capacity of competing service delivery systems. Finally, managers must recognize that their customer, competitor and supplier environments *are not* stable and certain, and *are* subject to drastic changes that could cripple an operation that fails to anticipate such occurrences.

Part V

Human Resources

26

Future Manpower Projections of the Hospitality Industry

Chester G. Hall, Ph.D.

The hospitality industry which feeds, houses and entertains the American public is both people-dependent and labor-intensive. Its hotels, restaurants and other establishments are operated to meet people's demands and lifestyles. When customers' requirements change, the industry must respond and adjust to the changes. At the same time, the industry needs millions of people to staff its establishments and provides jobs and income as well as opportunities for advancement and even proprietorship. When manpower supplies change, numerically, qualitatively or both, the industry must also adapt to these changes.

This chapter is concerned with the manpower prospects of the hospitality industry during the two decades between now and the year 2000. The first section of the chapter focuses on the industry and its current manpower situation and examines governmental and industry estimates of employment and the occupational outlook. The second section deals with the national manpower situation, demographic developments and projections of population and the labor force. The final section considers the effect on the industry of projected demographic and socio-economic developments and suggests actions which may be taken to insure a supply of manpower which is both adequate numerically and of high quality.

Because of the substantial size of the foodservice industry segment within the hospitality industry, as well as availability of data and projections, foodservice is the principal subject of this chapter. The manpower concerns of foodservice are assumed to represent those of the entire hospitality industry. Since two of every three foodservice employees in 1981 are females, the term "manpower" obviously has no sexual connotation.

239

STAFFING THE INDUSTRY

A Service Society?

For years, we have been told that the United States is on the road to becoming a service society. It is true that over the past thirty years, America has experienced a rapid shift away from a mass industrial society. Whereas 65% of the people working in this country in 1950 were in the industrial sector, today that figure is around 30%. But the shift of most jobs has not been to service occupations. Rather it has been to what are called information occupations—those involved in creating, processing and distributing information, including education, government, banks, and stock and commodity markets. In 1950, the number of workers in the information sector was 17%; it now exceeds 55% of the labor force.

Table 26.1, excerpted from the November 1980 U.S. Department of Commerce statistics, shows employment and projected employment in the service industries sector. As in the past, employment is projected to increase, but the rate will be slower. Relative to total national employment as well as to that in the information sector, it will remain flat. In 1969, 18.1% and in 1978 20.3% of all jobs were service jobs. These figures are projected to reach 22.3% in 1990 and only 23% in 2000.

The character of service jobs has changed over the years and will continue to do so. The principal growth has been, and will continue to be, in health services occupations. A large number of people work in fast food jobs today, and we have few domestics; but the post-industrial society is not the service society which many have predicted. Since 1979, the primary occupation in the United States has been that of the clerk. Two years ago, the clerk replaced the laborer, just as the laborer replaced the farmer in the first decades of the twentieth century.

TABLE 26.1. EMPLOYMENT AND PROJECTED EMPLOYMENT, SERVICE INDUS-TRIES, 1969–2000

	Employment (Thousands)				Average Annual Growth Rate (Percentage)	
	1969	1978	1990	2000	1969–78	1978–2000
United States	15,503	20,630	27,310	30,727	3.2	1.8
New England	1,017	1,326	1,651	1,777	3.0	1.3
Mid East	3,573	4,330	5,347	5,666	2.2	1.2
Great Lakes	2,710	3,550	4,656	5,128	3.0	1.7
Plains	1,183	1,614	2,093	2,333	3.5	1.7
Southeast	3,168	4,207	5,636	6,511	3.2	2.0
Southwest	2,258	1,752	2,452	2,899	3.7	2.3
Rocky Mountain	363	567	864	1,047	5.1	2.8
Far West	2,148	3,143	4,398	5,105	4.3	2.2

Source: U.S. Dept. Commerce, Bur. Economic Analysis (1980).

Industry Employment

The current *Foodservice Industry Pocket Factbook,* a handy compendium developed and widely distributed by the National Restaurant Association (NRA), states that the industry in 1981 consists of 546,000 units, split between two categories, Commercial Feeding and Institutional Feeding, plus an unspecified number of Military Feeding units. The Commercial Feeding category consists mainly of "Eating and Drinking Places" (a term used by the U.S. Department of Labor for most restaurants and commercial establishments), followed by "Foodservice Contractors," "Hotel/Motel Restaurants" and "Others" (vending, retail, recreation, etc). "Eating and Drinking Places," the *Pocket Factbook* tells us, are mostly small businesses, 94% of them having annual sales of less than $500,000.

Table 26.2, based on Bureau of the Census data, indicates the number of "Eating and Drinking Places" in business and the total employment in such establishments in 1972 and 1977. Both national information and information from one state representing each region listed in Table 26.1 are shown. On a national basis, total employment increased by 1.1 million from 1972 to 1977, and the number of paid employees per establishment rose by 3.5 employees. If a similar five-year growth in the number of establishments and in employment can be assumed to apply to the period from 1977 to 1982 (a conservative estimate), approximately 4.9 million paid employees will be required to staff the 310,000 establishments which will be open for business next year.

Data comparable to those on "Eating and Drinking Places" are not available with respect to employment in the other components of the industry (Institutional Feeding and the three Commercial Feeding segments which are not "Eating and Drinking Places"). College and

TABLE 26.2. EATING AND DRINKING PLACES, ESTABLISHMENTS AND EMPLOYMENT

	Establishments with Payroll		Paid Employees		Paid Employees Per Establishment	
	1972	1977	1972	1977	1972	1977
United States	287,250	298,614	2,635,114	3,759,222	9.1	12.6
Arizona	2,975	3,586	32,996	50,823	11.1	14.2
California	31,196	33,875	304,381	443,162	9.8	13.1
Colorado	3,799	4,537	42,998	67,551	11.3	15.0
Florida	9,706	11,452	116,454	178,812	12.0	15.7
Illinois	16,110	16,408	157,412	213,616	9.8	13.4
Massachusetts	8,324	8,625	91,606	108,748	11.5	12.6
Nebraska	2,829	2,792	22,185	32,733	7.8	11.7
New York	28,175	27,520	219,678	252,700	7.9	9.2

Source: U.S. Dept. of Commerce, Bur. Census (1977).

school feeding employment data, for example, are often included in educational statistics; those for hospital feeding are usually hidden somewhere in the totals for health care employment. Estimates of total sales for each component are, however, provided by NRA's *Foodservice Industry Pocket Factbook.* Assuming that the ratio of the number of employees to total sales for the other industry components approximates that of "Eating and Drinking Places", there are 2.5 million employees in Institutional Feeding, "Foodservice Contractors," "Hotel/Motel Restaurants" and "Others". Adding this to the 4.9 million in "Eating and Drinking Places", foodservice employment in 1982 can be projected at about 7.4 million people.

Some validation for such a projection is found in a study which the NRA conducted in August 1975, wherein foodservice employment was estimated to be approximately eight million people, including both part-time and full-time workers. The conclusions of a more substantial follow-on study, conducted for the NRA in 1976 by Market Facts, Inc. of Chicago, were published by the NRA as *1976 Foodservice Industry Employment.* This study, based on national sampling, also found that eight million people were employed. The two surveys on which identical estimates were based were both made during the summer, a season when foodservice employment traditionally peaks and college and high school students are most available to the industry for vacation employment. Both studies also reported that approximately half the industry's jobs were part-time.

The 1976 study found that three million foodservice employees that summer were students. Of these, 2.6 million were full-time students, consisting of approximately equal numbers of college students and high school and grade school students. Surprising to the researchers, but highlighting the dependence of the industry on student employees, 1.5 million students worked in the industry on a year-round basis. This was about 18.7% of the industry's labor force.

The 1976 profile of foodservice workers provided no surprises. About 53% of the labor force was under 24 years of age; two-thirds of these were under 20. Workers in the age-group from 25 through 54 constituted 33% of the work force, and 14% were over 55.

Industry Occupations

The U.S. Department of Labor annually publishes the massive *Occupational Outlook Handbook,* listing a variety of occupations and offering brief job descriptions. As a part of the Department's up-dating and revision process, each year the Department asks a number of organizations, including the National Institute for the Foodservice Industry (NIFI) to

TABLE 26.3.   FOOD SERVICE OCCUPATIONS

Occupation	Number Allowed 1980	Average Annual Openings 1978–1990
Bartenders	324,000	22,000
Cooks/chefs	985,000	86,000
Dining room attendants	267,000	14,000
Food counter workers	426,000	34,000
Kitchen helpers	761,000	23,000
Waiters/ waitresses	1,558,000	70,000
Total	4,321,000	249,000

review the sections covering foodservice occupations. This review process provides another approach to estimating industry employment.

Table 26.3 has been developed from the texts of the foodservice job briefs sent to NIFI for review in December 1980 and from additional Bureau of Labor Statistics estimates on average annual offerings by occupations. For some reason, the revisions of the job briefs this year do not include a brief for Dishwashers. Statistically, dishwasher jobs were combined with those of Kitchen Helpers, although the job brief for the latter does not mention dishes or pots.

The foodservice occupations listed in the *Handbook* and in Table 26.3 do not include managers and proprietors, cashiers, food checkers, clerical and administrative personnel, or maintenance personnel (electricians, technicians for heating, air conditioning, etc.) who work in the industry. In a section of the *Handbook* which discusses all management jobs, mention is made that foodservice managers and proprietors constitute one-seventh of the total restaurant work force. There are also other general statements about some of the other job categories. Overall, an estimate that the industry is staffed by between 7.4 and eight million workers, including full-time and part-time, is not inconsistent with the *Handbook's* statistics or job descriptions.

THE NATION AND ITS MANPOWER

The Baby Boom

In a ten year period which started in the mid-1950s, more than 42 million babies were born in the United States — better than 4.2 million a year. In 1961, births peaked at 4.35 million. This phenomenon, the post-World War II "baby boom", is the top part of the curve in Figure 26.1.

Probably few events during the twentieth century will have such far-reaching consequences for American society as this surge in American

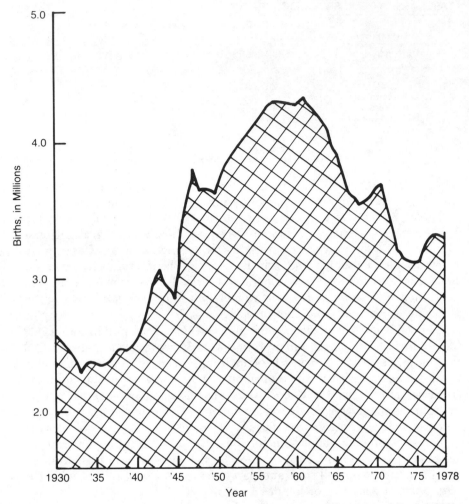

Masnick and Bane (1980)

FIG. 26.1.   ANNUAL NUMBER OF BIRTHS (1929–1978)

fertility. Like a wave, the baby boom swept over American society and its institutions, which were accustomed to a smaller and more orderly flow. It brought many changes, notably to housing, education, work, healthcare, entertainment, and hospitality. It certainly shaped the development of the foodservice industry in the 1970s, providing unprecedented numbers of young customers demanding food away from home and vast numbers of young potential employees seeking full-time and part-time jobs. The baby boom made possible the growth of the fast food segment of the industry as we see it today. As the baby boom ages, its influence will continue to be felt.

Almost twice the number of babies were born during the period 1955 to 1965 as had been born to the older generation during the 1930s. Particularly significant with respect to manpower projections, the number of births since 1961 has declined and has stayed at a lower level. In 1975 only 3.1 million births were recorded, and the total has remained between 3.1 and 3.4 million a year ever since. This is not at as low an annual level as was experienced during the 1930s, but like the baby boom, it has important implications for population and labor force projections.

Tables 26.4 and 26.5 show, for males and females respectively, the movement over time of the population groups whose years of birth are graphically presented in Fig. 26.1. They are based on the more detailed tables published in the Department of Labor's magazine, *Monthly Labor Review* (Fullerton 1980).

The foodservice industry should be concerned with two features of these population dynamics.

The first and most important of these features will be the sharp decline in the 1980s in the number of both males and females in the age group 16 to 24. This is the inevitable consequence of the drop in the birth rate which occurred in the 1960s after the baby boom. High schools have already experienced major declines in enrollments, and competition for students (and in fact survival) among colleges and universities is visibly increasing. Males and females born in the peak birth year 1961 will enter

TABLE 26.4.   U.S. POPULATION (MALES), 1975–79, PROJECTED TO 1995 IN MILLIONS

	1975	1975–79	1979	1979–85	1985	1985–90	1990	1990–95	1995
16 and over									
total	71.4	+5.0	76.4	+5.5	81.9	+3.3	85.2	+2.8	88.0
16–24	16.8	+0.9	17.7	−1.3	16.4	−1.7	14.7	− .7	14.0
25–54	36.6	+2.8	39.4	+5.3	44.7	+4.5	49.2	+3.0	52.2
55 and over	18.0	+1.4	19.4	+1.4	20.8	+ .6	21.4	+0.5	21.9

Source: Fullerton (1980).

TABLE 26.5.   U.S. POPULATION (FEMALES), 1975–79, PROJECTED 1995 IN MILLIONS

	1975	1975–79	1979	1979–85	1985	1985–90	1990	1990–95	1995
16 and over									
total	79.9	+5.2	85.1	+5.9	91.0	+3.8	94.8	+3.2	98.0
16–24	17.7	+0.7	18.4	−1.4	17.0	−1.7	15.3	−0.8	14.5
25–54	39.3	+2.7	42.0	+5.3	47.3	+4.7	52.0	+3.1	56.1
55 and over	22.8	+1.8	24.6	+2.0	26.6	+0.9	27.5	+0.8	28.3

Source: Fullerton (1980).

their twenties this year. The decline can be expected to intensify in the second half of the 1980s and to continue through the 1990s, although the angle will be less sharp.

The second important demographic development during the 1980s (and to a lesser extent, the 1990s) will be the swelling of the population in the central age groups. While the teenage ranks thin, millions of people born in the post-World War II baby boom will reach and move into middle age. As Tables 26.4 and 26.5 show, the population in the age group 25 to 54 will grow substantially. Among the implications of this development, as pointed out by Flaim and Fullerton (1978), is that "the labor force, in general, will be more mature, composed of persons with considerable work experience, and supposedly, very productive. In terms of potential output this development should tend to offset, at least partially, the effects of the numerical decline in labor force growth during the 1980s."

This development will also continue in the 1990s, although not as strongly as during the 1980s.

The Labor Force

Every other year, as a part of its continuing program of economic projections, the Bureau of Labor Statistics prepares national labor projections. These include projections of "labor force participation", a term which officially means being at work or looking for work. But whereas population projections, particularly those for the short term, can be made with a degree of certainty since they deal to a great extent with people already born, labor force growth is a function not only of population trends but also of trends in participation among various population groups (defined by sex, age and race).

The Bureau's 1980 labor force projections are in their usual form of three scenarios, one each for high, middle and low rates of growth, to 1995 levels of 135, 128 and 122 million people respectively. The areas of agreement among the three scenarios, rather than their differences, are of value for our purposes.

One area of agreement is the observation that by 1985, because of the changing age composition of the population caused by the baby boom and swings in births over the past 50 years, the number of persons in the labor force in the 1980s will increase substantially and will in fact exceed all those not in the labor force, including babies. For the same reason there is agreement that by 1985, more than 70% of the labor force will be in what the Bureau calls the prime working-age group (25-54).

A second area of agreement in all three scenarios is that more than two-thirds of all labor force growth between 1980 and 1995 will come from increased participation by females. Most of the growth will occur in the prime working-age group (25-54), where the increase in the proportion of employed females in that group will more than offset the projected decreasing proportions in both younger and older age groups of employed females. In 1975, 46% of all females were in the labor force; by 1985, this is projected to increase to 56.4% under the middle-growth scenario.

A third area of agreement is that the black labor force (both male and female) can be expected to grow at a rate almost twice that of the white labor force. This principally reflects the fact that for some time the black population has been increasing at a rate higher than that of whites, and the assumption is that the higher fertility rate of blacks will continue through the period of the projection.

Women and Jobs

The jump in labor force participation of women projected in everybody's scenario for the remainder of this century will not be a new phenomenon. Since World War II the rise in such participation, especially of wives and mothers working or looking for work, is visible and well publicized. But sociologists are now concerned with more than labor force participation, which includes, after all, women who spend only small amounts of time and energy at work as well as those pursuing full-time careers.

Masnick and Bane (1980) point out that, from their study of the data, the increase in the number of employed women will not only represent more participation in the labor force, but will also represent a revolution in what they call "attachment" to employment, particularly among women born after 1940.

"Attachment" to work is measured by the extent to which a woman's involvement in her work is substantial and permanent — in other words, how she feels about work and about herself as a worker. "Permanent attachment", which is defined as working at least seven years out of ten, does not currently characterize most women. But, Masnick and Bane report, such a work pattern does apply to about half the married women in the age group 18 to 47, and this is expected to continue.

Figure 26.2 shows the age patterns of labor force participation rates for women since 1940, plus one representative and typical age pattern for men (1970). The men's pattern is a simple curve, with participation rising gradually to the mid-20s, levelling off until the mid-50s, then falling gradually after age 55 and more steeply after 65. The women's participation rate curves, in contrast, show an "M" pattern, rising until the early 20s, falling until the late 20s (the childbearing and child-rearing years), rising again until the middle 40s and falling during the 50s.

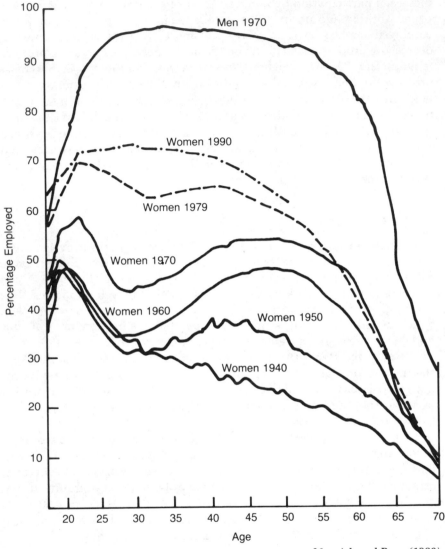

Masnick and Bane (1980)

FIG. 26.2.   LABOR FORCE PARTICIPATION RATES FOR MEN AND WOMEN BY AGE (1940−1990)

Age Data For Five-Year Period, Urban Institute Projection

The age patterns for women show that labor force participation rates have been rising since 1950 for women of all ages between 20 and 55. But they also suggest, in the 1979 and 1990 projections, that the participation pattern may be changing, with the "M" dip for women in their 20s and 30s gradually flattening.

Masnick and Bane conclude that it is not impossible to predict that future labor force participation rate curves for women will not only be the same shape as those for men but could well approach the levels of men as well. The 1990 women's participation rate pattern in Fig. 26.2 does assume that shape.

"The disappearing 'M' curve could be expected to indicate a new life-course pattern for women, one of high and continuing attachment to the labor force even through the childbearing period" (Masnick and Bane 1980).

In point of fact, a person who works only for a few hours each week is reported as in the labor force and employed. Similarly, a mother who leaves her job for a few months or a year around childbirths can think of and report herself as temporarily out of work or unemployed and be counted in the labor force.

Today's very high participation rates in younger generation women reflect the attitude that considerable attention to the duties of motherhood is not inconsistent with attachment to and participation in employment.

THE INDUSTRY'S FUTURE MANPOWER

Manpower Requirements

Essential to considering the manpower prospects of the foodservice industry in a period of dramatic demographic changes is having some idea of the industry's manpower requirements, the number of employees who will be needed. There is no guaranteed method of estimating this, and there are relatively few known quantities compared with a large number of economic, demographic, social and cultural unknowns. Since NIFI is not an agency of the federal government, we do not have the luxury of offering three scenarios with which to hedge our bets.

Accordingly, one projection is offered, based on the following assumptions:

1. The foodservice industry will grow at a moderate rate to the end of this century, with the exception of fast food chains, whose overall growth will tend to be slower. In *Fast Food — The Endless Shakeout,* securities analyst Robert Emerson (1979) predicts that these chains will grow only until the nation is fully saturated, probably within the next five years. This seems to be a good possibility, especially with our aging population, although Emerson's time estimate may be too short.

2. The industry will remain labor-intensive, without major applications of automation and without much, if any, increase in productivity. Its

manpower requirements will grow at about the same rate as the industry itself.

3.   Although the average age of foodservice employees and the ratio of female to male employees will change over the years, the ratio of full-time to part-time employees in the industry will remain approximately as currently constituted.

4. Service industry employment will increase at an average rate of about 1.8% per year through 2000, but increases in health and related occupations concerned with an aging population will constitute most of the gain.

5. The foodservice industry share of the national increase in service industry employment through 2000 will produce an average rate of growth of about one percent per year.

6. The NRA's estimate that the foodservice industry employs eight million people is an acceptable 1982 base to which to apply a statistical forecasting.

Using the above, it is projected that:

1. In 1986 (short-range), the foodservice industry will require 8.32 million employees to staff its establishments;

2. In 1991 (mid-range), 8.75 million employees will be required;

3. The industry's manpower requirement will pass the nine million employee mark in 1994; and

4. In 2000 (long-range), 9.42 million employees will be required to meet the demands of the early twenty-first century public.

Adapting to Change

The American population will increase through the end of this century, and the labor force will also grow, at times faster than the overall population. There will be large numbers of potential foodservice employees and many will be needed. The industry's ability to recruit, train and retain a sufficient number will depend to a large extent on how well it adapts to changes in the age and sex make-up of the labor force.

During the 1980s the most important demographic change will be that caused by the aging of the large year-groups born during the baby boom and of the smaller year-groups born after them. From now through 1985, the supply of teenage potential employees will drop sharply. From 1986 until 1990, when people born at the end of the baby boom will observe their twenty-fifth birthdays, the supply of potential employees between 20 and 24 years of age will drop sharply. The supply of potential employees 25 and older will increase all through the 1980s.

During the 1990s, increased numbers of women who are working and seeking employment will bring the most important demographic change affecting foodservice manpower. Some of these women will be members of the baby boom generation moving into the prime working age group (25–54). Others will be women who are motivated by generally increased participation of women in the labor force, plus, in many cases, increased attachment to employment as a life-pattern.

Recruiting Replacements

Throughout the 1980s, with many fewer high school and college students and the number of teenagers in the labor force declining by millions, where can foodservice operators go to find replacements? Five years from now, where will they seek replacements for young adults aged 20 to 24 when the number of available members of that age group is substantially reduced?

Finding an answer to these questions involves two steps. The first is identifying alternative population groups which are projected to grow in size and participation in the labor force and whose members (defined by sex, age, and race as well as special qualifications) offer a potential for satisfactory performance in foodservice jobs and careers. The second is organizing and conducting a recruitment program focussed on attracting and hiring members of the identified population groups.

There are four such groups:

The first is not really an alternative population group. Rather it is a continuation of current recruitment of teenagers, but with a strongly increased emphasis on minority youth, principally black. Because of the historically higher birth rate for blacks than for whites, this age group will not decline at nearly as pronounced a rate as that of white teenagers. In fact, although the birth rate of the black population has been slackening, the total number of black youths is projected to rise slightly during the 1980s. Both young black men and women can be expected to benefit substantially from reduced competition for jobs among youths in general, and their labor force participation rates should increase. Foodservice must recruit to obtain its share.

The second alternative group, recognized already by fast food chains, contract feeders and other foodservice companies, consists of men and women 55 and over. Some wish to continue to work rather than retire, perhaps as a result of recent changes in mandatory retirement legislation. Others may have already retired but wish or need to work. This may be on a full-time basis, or part-time, to earn up to the limit they can while receiving Social Security benefits. In 1981, this is $5500. Older workers have some significant advantages: they are more stable and more mature, have a lower turnover than younger workers going off to school and require much less supervision.

The third alternative population group with considerable potential for the industry consists of handicapped men and women of all ages, particularly the employable mentally retarded. Many handicapped workers are already employed in productive, satisfying and stable foodservice jobs, and employer reports are generally excellent. Increased attention to training and supervision is required for handicapped workers, particularly new employees, and their jobs should be structured to fit individual capabilities. Managers, supervisors and fellow employees often must be prepared to accept and work with handicapped employees.

Substantial interest in improving training and expanding employment of the handicapped exists in the industry today. The NRA's successful three-year-old "Projects With Industry" placement program and the Wisconsin Restaurant Association's sponsorship of the "Kitchen Helper" training program are examples.

The fourth alternative population group, men and women of the expanding prime working-age group, between 25 and 54, will increase in number each year in this century. The cost of employing people in this group will obviously be higher than that for teenagers and young adults they may replace. However, if with their maturity and work-experience, such workers also bring somewhat increased productivity which makes possible a compensatory reduction in the number of employees, employers will find advantages in hiring them. Competition for available jobs may also intensify because of "crowding" within the population group, possibly increasing interest in part-time job opportunities offered in foodservice.

Important to success in attracting personnel in all four alternative population groups, but critical for the prime working-age groups, will be programs designed for women. As pointed out before, women will account for two-thirds of labor force growth in this age-group. Over five of every eight foodservice employees are women now, and the percentage will surely increase at every job level, especially in management, including top management. In 1974, about 21% of the graduates from baccalaureate programs in hotel and restaurant management in the United States were women. In 1980 this had risen to over 38%, and the upward trend should continue, as will women's expectations.

Training and Retaining Employees

Whether or not the industry succeeds in finding and hiring a sufficient number of employees, foodservice operators will have to compete with other employers to keep the people they recruit. What might be done to train and retain personnel who are qualified for their jobs, motivated to perform them and interested in staying?

Several years ago, under contract to the U.S. Department of Labor, the NRA conducted an extended program of systematic research concerning the major manpower problems of the foodservice industry. *How to Invest in People, A Handbook on Career Ladders* (Natl. Restaurant Assoc. 1973), was a product of the research. Its conclusions and recommendations seem to me to be as relevant for the remainder of this century as they are for today.

To quote in part from the foreword to *How to Invest in People:*

"An underlying condition — a key factor in producing the foodservice industry's extremely high personnel turnover rate and extremely low productivity rate   was identified by the research. This was a general dissatisfaction among industry employees with their career opportunities, a widespread feeling that employers did not care enough about them to 'invest in them' and a feeling   there is 'nowhere to go' in the industry and no training provided to help employees up the career ladder—even where such ladders exist.

"The industry clearly needs ways to change these attitudes, but to do so it has to change itself, particularly in its treatment of employees.

"Our research has suggested some of the ways. The industry must invest in people just as it does in facilities and equipment. Employees must be trained and be offered visible career opportunities. An employee should be able to see where he or she may go after entry and be assured that there are no dead-end jobs, no dead-ended people" (Natl. Restaurant Assoc. 1973).

The best way to insure that increased attachment to employment becomes attachment to employment in foodservice is for the industry to demonstrate increased attachment to its people.

27

The Use of Human Resources in the Hospitality Industry—A Survey

Abraham Pizam, Ph.D.

The hospitality industry is a "people" industry. Its major product is a service that is delivered "by people for people." Therefore each hospitality manager is involved in "people management." "People management" or personnel management is too important to leave to the personnel department and its staff. The personnel policies and practices which are usually established by personnel specialists determine not only the type and quality of superior-subordinate relationship but in the final analysis the success of the entire organization.

This is why it is imperative to identify and analyze the personnel policies and practices prevalent in the hospitality industry today.

Therefore the objective of this study was twofold:
1) To analyze current personnel policies and practices in metropolitan hotels.
2) To examine the influence of the hotel size on its personnel policies and practices.

METHODOLOGY

Sample: One hundred thirty-three hotels of 200 rooms or more, located in the metropolitan areas of Boston, New York and Philadelphia were selected via systematic random sampling using the 1979 American Hotel and Motel Association (AH&MA) Hotel Red Book. Forty usable questionnaires or 30.1% were returned.

Instrument: The research instrument was a forty—four item questionnaire containing two types of information:

1) Current personnel practices and policies used in the respondents hotels (31 questions).
2) Data concerning the profile of the hotel (13 questions).

The personnel practices and policies studied were:
   a) Compensation
   b) Performance Evaluation
   c) Promotion
   d) Training

ANALYSIS

Frequency distribution analysis was performed for the purpose of describing the personnel policies and practices used by the respondents. Pearson product moment correlations and one way analysis of variance analyses were conducted to test for the influence of hotel size on personnel policies and practices.

RESULTS

Personnel Policies and Practices

Hotels' Profile — The hotels in our sample had an average of 590 rooms and a median of 450 rooms. Though only hotels with 200 rooms or more were contacted the returns indicate that 7.7% had less than 200 rooms. This may suggest that the information contained in the AH&MA Red Book was not accurate as far as number of guest rooms. 12.8% of hotels had more than 1000 rooms.

The number of employees reported averaged 390 with a median of 300. The ratio of employees per room averaged 0.66.

The hotels in our sample reported an average annual sale of $1.01 million and a median of $775,000. This figure should, however, be interpreted with caution since 43% of the sample did not respond to this question.

Sixty-four percent of the respondents reported not having a personnel department at all, a staggering figure considering the size of these hotels and the complexity of their operations.

However, when we analyzed the existence of personnel departments in relation to the hotel size we found that the larger hotels tended to have personnel departments while the smaller ones did not, as is evident from Table 27.1.

The average personnel department annual budget was reported to be $296,000 and the median $203,250.

TABLE 27.1.   THE EFFECT OF HOTEL SIZE ON EXISTENCE OF PERSONNEL DE-
PARTMENT

Group	A. Employees				
	Mean Number of Employees	Standard Deviation	Degrees of Freedom	F	N
No Personnel Department	179	147	1		14
				10.1*	
Personnel	513	347	36		24

Group	B. Guest Rooms				
	Mean Number of Guest Rooms	Standard Deviation	Degrees of Freedom	F	N
Do Not Have Personnel Departments	357	177	1		14
				6.98**	
Have Personnel Departments	721	496	37		25

*$p > .01$
**$p > .05$

Compensation Policies and Practices

Method of Determination—The most prevalent method of determining
employee compensation was reported to be the union contract. 62% of all
respondents had a union contract which specified the method of determining compensation, 19% reported wage surveys as their major method, 5%
position description, and the remainder cited corporate guidelines and
other miscellaneous methods.

Discretion to Determine Individual Employee Compensation — Table
27.2 lists the organizational levels in the hierarchy which determine
individual employee compensation.

As can be seen from the above, corporate and upper management has a
very significant amount of discretion to determine individual employee
compensation levels not only for managerial positions but for skilled and
unskilled employees as well. In the opinion of this author, this indicates a
high degree of centralization of decision-making and lack of delegation of
authority in personnel matters.

TABLE 27.2.   DISCRETION TO DETERMINE INDIVIDUAL EMPLOYEE COMPENSATION

	Upper Management (%)	Mid Management (%)	Skilled (%)	Unskilled (%)
Corporate	93	26	11	9
Upper Management	7	74	60	54
Mid Management	—	—	23	20
Supervisor	—	—	6	17

Bases for Salary Increase — Three bases for salary increases were reported by the survey participants: merit, union contract and across the board raise. The most common used was a combination of the three — 42.5% reported using all three bases followed by merit only (22.5%), followed by a combination of merit and across the board (20%) and last by across the board only (10%). The high incidence of merit as a base for salary increase was surprising since two-thirds of the hotels had union contracts. One would expect that under unionization merit will be supplanted by seniority. Apparently this was not the case in our sample where only 2.5% used a combination of seniority and across the board raise as a base for salary increase.

Methods of Pay Increase — Six methods of pay increase were reported by the respondents. These were: promotion, across the board increase, production piece, commission, other incentives and merit increases. The prevalence of their use varied according to the employee classification as seen in Table 27.3.

TABLE 27.3.   METHODS OF PAY INCREASE[1]

	Promotion (%)	Across the Board (%)	Increase Production Piece (%)	Commission (%)	Other Incentives (%)	Merit Increases (%)
Management	47	31	0	31	33	36
Supervisors	36	50	6	6	22	36
Skilled	33	80	14	6	17	25
Unskilled	33	81	6	3	11	22

[1] Multiple responses give rise to totals of greater than 100%.

Overall, promotion was stated as one of the most popular methods of pay increase and the most used for managerial employees. This deficient practice of using promotions to increase an individual's pay, which has been coined "The Peter Principle", stands against all modern practices of human resource management. While this practice has been discontinued in many industries, it is unfortunately still prevalent in ours.

The preferred method of pay increase for supervisors, skilled and unskilled employees was reported to be "across the board". This method, while easy to administer, is improper to use by itself, because it does not reward individuals according to their performance. Only a small proportion of the respondents used commissions and increase in production piece pay as a method of pay increase.

Commission Pay—Fifty-five percent of the hotels reported having some form of commission pay for the following jobs:

Front Office Manager 61%

Group Sales 22%

Banquet Sales & Beverage Manager 17%

The average commission rate reported for the above was 5.6% and the median 2.4%

Employee Benefits — Table 27.4 lists the ten most reported employee benefits by our respondents, in order of popularity.

TABLE 27.4.   EMPLOYEE BENEFITS

	Vacation (%)	Health Insurance (%)	Paid Holiday (%)	Workmen's Compen- sation (%)	Sick Leave (%)
Management	97	92	92	90	90
Non-Management	100	95	95	97	82

	Life Insurance (%)	Dental Insurance (%)	Pension (%)	Profit Sharing (%)	Stock Purchase (%)
Management	82	68	51	21	18
Non-Management	85	49	69	13	13

The reported average value of management benefits per employee per year was $2181 (N=17) and for nonmanagerial employees $1662 (N=18). These figures are well below the national average for all industries which amounted to $4692 in 1977—a very disquieting fact (Chamber of Commerce of the U.S.A. 1978).

Looking at Table 27.4, two other conclusions can be made, (1) that the proportion of hotels having pension plans for their employees is smaller than the national average for all industries (69% compared to 91%) (Bur. of Natl. Affairs 1975); and (2) that the proportion of hotels having life insurance plans is lower than the national average (which is almost 100%) (Am. Coun. of Life Insurance 1978).

Employee benefits in the respondents hotels were not equally distributed. Forty-five percent of the sample reported that the benefits are determined according to the employee's level in the hierarchy (the higher the level the higher the benefits and more of them). Twenty-three percent reported that the benefits are determined according to the seniority of the employee and 19%, a combination of the two.

One particular benefit which is extremely common in our industry and was widely reported by our respondents is free or reduced meals. Ninety-five percent of the hotels reported having this employee benefit. The average annual meal cost per employee was reported to be $324. Apparently this is not the actual cost but the accounting cost that is allowed by Social Security regulations.

Performance Evaluation — Almost all hotels represented in our sample used some form of periodical employee performance evaluation. The reported figure, 90%, is even higher than the national average for all industries (84%) (Bur. of Natl. Affairs 1975).

The median frequency of evaluation was reported to be every twelve months for all employee categories. The most preferred and used methods of evaluation were written forms followed by personal interviews. None of the more modern advanced methods such as BARS, MBO or Assessment Centers were utilized.

Promotion — Respondents were asked to rank the following five factors in determining an employee's promotion: Past job performance, length of employment, expected job performance, present job level in hierarchy and other.

Table 27.5 lists the average results obtained.

As evident from the above table, the most important factor in determining a person's promotion is his past job performance. This finding again lends support to the existence and practice of the "Peter Principle" in the respondent hotels. These hotels seem to promote people basically on the basis of their past job performance and not necessarily on the expected performance in the new job which may be totally unrelated to the past job.

The individual exerting the highest influence in an employee's promotion was found to be his direct supervisor—with a mean influence of 37%, followed by upper management (mean=28%), followed by mid-management (mean=24%), and terminating with corporate management (mean=14%). This finding once again indicates that in these hotels a significant amount of personnel discretion is concentrated in upper management's hands.

The favorite policy of promotion and hiring in our sample hotels was "from within". Eighty-five percent responded they promote and hire

TABLE 27.5.   RANKING OF FACTORS DETERMINING PROMOTIONS

Factor	Mean Rank (1 = Highest; 5 = Lowest)
Past job performance	1.66
Expected job performance	2.61
Present job level in hierarchy	3.14
Length of employment	3.27
Other	4.17

from within. In a majority of hotels (65%), employees can skip levels and every promotion carries with it an increase in pay (75%). Last item on promotion was related to the impact of civil rights laws on promotion procedures and policies. Ninety-two percent of our sample responded that civil rights laws had no impact upon promotion policies or procedures. This is indeed impossible to believe. We interpret it as either being one of those questions that was answered more with a "social desirability" or "lip service" attitude in mind or simply was misunderstood.

Training of Employees — Almost half (42%) of the hotels in our sample were not involved in any form of employee training. This figure is staggering and by itself is a cause for serious alarm. One cannot understand how today's hotels can manage and operate without some form of formal training for their employees.

In those hotels that have some form of training, the person who determines its needs is usually the General Manager, the department head or a combination of both, as seen in Table 27.6.

TABLE 27.6.   WHO DETERMINES TRAINING NEEDS

Position	Frequency in %
General Manager & Department Head	31
Department Head	28
Personnel Manager & General Manager	17
Other	24

The most frequently mentioned method of determining training needs was external management consultants (25% of the sample) followed by past experience (21%) and observation (21%).

Though, as we mentioned before, 42% of the hotels did not have any formal training for their employees, they did have (97% of them) a job orientation program.

The orientations were conducted by either the personnel manager and his department (40%), by the department head (26%), by the immediate supervisor (14%) or by the training director (11%).

A majority of the hotels reported that they encouraged their managerial staff to enlist in any off-the-job developmental courses that are related to their job, such as: management skills, AH&MA courses, employee relations, etc. However, only 84% of those companies pay for external job related courses for their managers and 43% pay for their non-managerial staff.

Finally, only 27% of the hotels questioned had a person in charge of training—full or part time.

The Impact of Hotel Size on Personnel Policies and Practices

To test for the impact of hotel size on personnel practices and policies, a series of Pearson product moment correlation coefficients and one way analyses of variance were conducted between various personnel practices and policies and two measures of hotel size: number of employees and number of guest rooms.

Following are the only variables that were found to be significantly correlated/associated at the .05 level with hotel size:

1. *Frequency of Evaluation*—For most types of jobs in the hotels it was found that the larger the hotel size the higher was the frequency of performance evaluation. The correlation coefficients ranged from a low of 0.30 in the housekeeping department to a high of 0.37 in the kitchen department.

2. *Promotion Decision*—The larger the hotel, the more influence have lower level managers on their subordinates' promotion. Or in other words in the larger hotels promotion decision making is more decentralized than in smaller hotels.

3. *Personnel Department* — Hotels that had a personnel department were significantly larger than hotels that did not have such a department (mean number of employees of 374 compared to 147, with an F ratio of 10.1).

4. *Training Director* — Hotels that had a training director position were significantly larger than the ones that did not have such a position (mean number of employees of 678 compared to 271 with an F ratio of 12.7).

5. *Job Orientation Program* — Hotels where the training director conducts the job orientation program are larger than the ones where such programs are conducted by department head, personnel director or supervisor (mean number of employees of 1142 compared to 258, 358, and 490 respectively, with an F ratio of 8.0).

None of the many other personnel practices and policies was found to vary according to the hotel size. Or in other words, the same practices exist, more or less, regardless of the hotel size.

CONCLUSIONS

Overall this study found that many of the personnel policies and practices found in the respondent hotels were simply outdated and unsophisticated as indicated by the following:

1. Only large hotels have been found to have a personnel department (mean 513 employees).

2. The personnel department budgets were relatively low (mean $296,000 per year).

3. Personnel decision making was found to be concentrated in the hands of upper and corporate management — an indication of authoritarian management.

4. The "Peter Principle" is still widely practiced.

5. There exists a preference for "simpler and easier to administer" methods of pay increase such as "across the board". This is done in order to avoid confrontation with employees and unions.

6. There is a paucity of employee benefits. Those that do exist in the industry average lower than in other industries.

7. Though there is wide use of employee performance evaluation, the methods used are archaic and unsophisticated.

8. There is high preference for "Promotion and hiring from within", a practice that brings about organizational calcification.

9. Lack of involvement in job training.

10. One would have expected that at least the larger hotels would have more sophisticated policies and practices, but with few exceptions, this was not found to be true.

The findings, if true for other hotels as well, should be a cause for serious concern on the part of academics and practitioners alike. Our industry is a labor intensive one where the quality of the service is highly dependent on the attitude of the employees. Employes attitudes — to a large extent — are molded and shaped by human resource management practices and policies. Inappropriate or insufficient policies can create, in the long run, negative employee attitudes which will result in poor service to the guests.

ACKNOWLEDGMENT

Special thanks are given to Laura Richardson and Donald Goldsmith who assisted with the collection of the data for this study.

28

The Future of Hospitality and Travel Industry Management and Education: Structures, Trends, Strategies, and Needs

Atid Kaplan, Ph.D.

During the next few years there will be some massive changes in the hotel industry's structures, strategies and management. These will be the result of several influences: maturation, concentration, lifecycle position and the effects caused by more traditional (i.e., processing and manufacturing) industries taking over or entering the hospitality and travel field. The effects and implications of these and other factors will be discussed here. But the overriding conclusion is that this industry has to upgrade management techniques and training programs for new management and existing managers, radically change its organization structure and hire, train and use technologically skilled people for both line and staff positions within the industry.

One factor, that will cause most of these changes, is the movement of nonservice firms into this industry, through a combination of takeovers, mergers, bailouts, and new ventures. These nonservice industries are attracted by the recent high growth rates, high cash flows and opportunities for expansion which their own, more mature industries no longer have. What these firms do not realize is that the hospitality industry has moved very sharply and quickly from the growth stage of the lifecycle into the maturity stage, as gauged by such standard indicators as increased competition, lower profits, greater concentration, etc. This shift in lifecycle stages has been caused as much by external factors as by internal factors, e.g., the petroleum situation, lower discretionary incomes, changing travel habits as well as changing age patterns and market demographics.

Another major change is the disappearance or overthrow of founder-entrepreneurs in major chains. The founders built on the basis of growing demand, good quality, service, and properly run operations and grew up with the industry. The high growth rates and high demand for the services did not require very sophisticated strategies; basically it was sufficient to get there first, with the most.

The original founder-entrepreneurs built in an era where labor, capital and energy were cheap, an era which no longer exists. Competition has become more intense. It has adversely affected operations since profit margins have decreased and the "good-old-boy" approach cannot survive in the emerging era of sophisticated management and increasing competition. In some cases there have been takeovers by nonservice firms; in other cases, internal management revolts. In other situations, management has upgraded itself and changed with the changing times. But pressure from both the market and the shareholders has forced and will force the remaining founders to either step down, or adapt.

This is very similar to the situation faced by the manufacturing industries some time ago when companies that were started by engineers were eventually taken over by marketers and are now in the hands of legal, control and financial people, thus reflecting different priorities which occur at different stages of the lifecycle.

In the future other companies in the hospitality field will be affected by an increasing number of takeovers and mergers caused in part by increased competition, both quantitative and qualitative. In addition, changing consumer demographics and an aging population will positively and negatively affect some of the resorts and hotel chains. The hotel chains will be hit harder because more and more travelers will be using public transportation and package tours.

Fast food chains will also be affected. Those that are aimed at the younger market are seeing this market slowly aging and changing their tastes. Some firms are becoming more sophisticated, e.g., a sequence which might start as a plain hamburger then a rather fancy hamburger and then, a business man's sophisticated hamburger with wine and beer and may end up with hamburger, bearnaise and vintage wine served on linen. The present organizations that are geared to the youth market will find that the size of this market will drop considerably over the years and they will have to diversify, adapt, retrench or go under.

As these mergers, takeovers and revolts continue, the demands on management will increase, since business will be larger and more complex. These organizations will be more difficult or even impossible to manage using present day organizational structures. New structures will have to be accompanied by decentralization—so that local needs, interests, and desires can be taken care of—and by increased reliance on large staffs of technologists and analysts. Another factor that may complicate structures will be increased direct labor costs at all levels and shortage of unskilled and semi-skilled labor.

The effect of the above mentioned factors will be the emergence of a new type of generalist manager. This manager will no longer be the old "hands-on" experience manager, up from the ranks, but rather a highly skilled professional who is trained not only in vagaries of the industry, but also in general management. Other change inducing factors will be more competition and stronger competition. At the same time, there will be fewer companies competing because, inevitably, as an industry hits the maturity stage of the lifecycle, there is a shakeout. Changing consumer tastes caused by changing demographics will require different types of technology, plant, research and organization to meet new consumer needs. As companies increase in size, their control problems will become more complex. Thus, there will be a need for more sophisticated planning and strategy.

In this industry, strategic aspects have largely been ignored over the long term. Most companies operated on short term planning cycles based on their ability to open new operations. This was appropriate in situations where primary demand was increasing constantly. Now that primary demand decreases or stabilizes (as in more mature industries) it is more difficult to enter markets and far more careful planning and analysis is required.

In the future there will be less of a personal type of management, and an increasing reliance on paper, technology and therefore on staff. This will be accompanied by an increasing technical and automated process within the industry.

What are the implications of this? Fundamental changes in organizations with a greater reliance on staff, more highly skilled staff specialists and a decentralization of operational control in certain organizations will be required. The maturity and concentration of the industry will result in lower profits. How can one prepare for these changes?

Several actions could be taken, such as:

1. An increased upgrading of present management knowledge of tools and techniques (as developed for some of the other industries and adapted for the hospitality industry).
2. Increasing concentration on marketing as well as changing attitudes in management.
3. Introduction of long term strategic planning.
4. Sending managers back to school for MBA's, as well as specialized courses in their areas of expertise.
5. Starting new programs in business schools and hotel schools aimed at producing more staff-trained managers as opposed to line op-

erators.

6. Increasing expenditures on research and development for new technologies, markets, products and management tools.

The results will be major changes in recruiting and training of new people coming into the industry where, rather than going through the food and beverage, the front-of-the-house, control, sales, etc., they will tend to advance more through a specialist stream as opposed to the generalist. Anyone interested in general management will have to be in that area from the start, as opposed to flitting back and forth between various departments. The structure for management will be shaped less like a triangle and more like a square. In other words, people will advance through their area of specialization (See Fig. 28.1 and 28.2).

Instead of moving, say, from food and beverage manager to executive assistant manager of a hotel, they'll probably tend to move up from food and beverage manager of one hotel to a slightly bigger hotel, to food and beverage manager of the biggest hotel in the chain or Vice-President of Food and Beverage. They will also tend to accumulate specialists helping them. One already sees this pattern emerging in the controller positions.

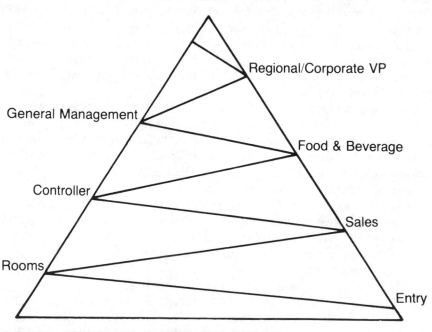

FIG. 28.1.   PRESENT MANAGEMENT GROWTH MODE

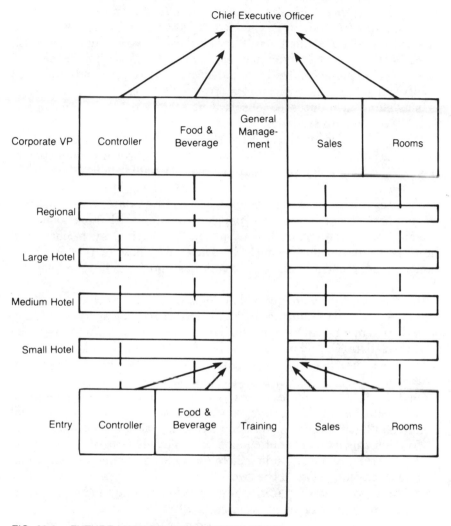

FIG. 28.2.   FUTURE MANAGEMENT GROWTH MODE

Thus the management strategy for the 1980's will be more long term, more carefully thought out, based on indentifiable market demands, the competitive situation, the organization's capability and the environment in which it operates. This, in turn, will affect the nature of management and the operating strategies management will select.

If one accepts this premise of changing managerial needs and more generalized, upgraded management skills one is then forced to reexamine many cherished concepts. It is ironic that when leading business schools are broadening their outlook in line with the changing nature of business environment, this industry seems to be getting more parochial in its outlook. There is a strident chorus in industry, 40 years out of date, still living in the founder-entrepreneur era, calling for more "relevance" and "hands on" experience. They are aided and abetted by underqualified faculty whose sole claim to fame is often a 2—5 year stint in industry, passing along their outdated, obsolescent, traditional, vocational operational knowledge to students.

It is the opinion of this author that in the new era of increasing concentration, specialization, mechanization and growing competition, most of the university-level, four-year vocationally-oriented programs are obsolete.

The need today is for managers who are up-to-date, aware of their environment, technologically capable of dealing with new tools and techniques, entrepreneurial, conceptual, innovative, systematic and multi-disciplinary in their outlook. They must have a firm grasp of modern management tools and techniques and be able to implement them.

The hotel general manager will no longer have the powers of a ship's captain nor a need to know the intimate details of every operation. Many of the departments will be controlled by outsiders, head office or regional staff specialists. He will manage by coordinating people and skills rather than having detailed knowledge. His vision must be broad rather than narrow and deep.

Obviously this cannot be achieved overnight. It is rather an evolutionary or revolutionary change over time. Those that will not adapt will fall behind and be absorbed by more modern competitors or outsiders.

How will this management change be achieved?

1. A return of free standing hotel schools to business schools and closer cooperation between the two.

2. An upgrading of traditionally vocation-oriented faculty or their replacement by management oriented faculty.

3. An increasing cooperation with top management levels in industry to help them adjust to new realities.

4. Greater outreach by hotel and restaurant management schools to serve the industry's needs.

5. A possible faculty/executive interchange program whereby faculty members trade jobs with their industrial counterparts — not so much to perpetuate present day methodologies but rather seek grounds for improvement.

6. An introduction of: Environment of Business, Government and Business Strategy, and Business and Society courses into Hotel and and Restaruant Management curricula.

7. Increasing emphasis on tourism courses as the umbrella and

overview of the total hospitality and travel industry.

8. A series of Industry/Academe seminars, workshops and conferences which will act as idea filters and exchanges at all levels of management.

9. Increase research by both academe and management in order to see what current general business research is adaptable.

10. A flourishing of entrepreneurship programs for those graduates who wish to go out on their own.

11. Increasing cooperation with other elements in the tourism industry through acquisitions, trade associates, workshops, etc.

12. Internship training programs geared to exposing students to both work situation and management, to new tools, techniques and concepts.

It would be naive to hope all these will occur either simultaneously or immediately. However, if one does not try, even with a strategy of creeping incrementalism, the entire industry will be absorbed by outsiders.

Far too many educational programs are geared to meet yesterday's vocational skill needs. The industry has never really felt happy with advanced management concepts. That is why so many of the "hooking bulls" in the industry, i.e., the successful innovators, were outsiders: Thompson of Fleet, Henderson of Sheraton, Wilson of Holiday Inns, Kroc of McDonald's and, of course, Conrad Hilton. These aliens broke the dated mores and folkways of the industry, many of which we have never excised from the tablets of stone.

There is far too much emphasis on how to cook, write an airline ticket, make a bed, and so on. Whereas we should have students conceptualizing or analyzing whether they should cook, buy ready cooked, contract out or whether the operation needs any food service whatsoever.

The industry will require graduates capable of solving problems using state-of-the-art business knowledge and technology rather than waiting, as we have in the past, for someone to rewrite a concept with the word Hotel, Restaurant or Tourism in the title. Students must be trained to take this modern research, literature and technology and be able to apply or develop it for our industry. By the same token, they should broaden their scope and realize that most of our industry's problems are exactly the same as other service industries': location, inflation, management and government regulations and interference.

Finally, professionalism is an issue which must also be addressed. Usually professionalism is a term associated with rigid peer-control, disciplinary structure, licensing and other restrictive measures. However in this author's opinion it is unlikely we will see the type of professionalism that one sees in lawyers, CPAs, MDs, etc. After all, the best judges of performance are not necessarily peers but stockholders, bankers and customers.

29

Executive Chef—"Key Man or Dinosaur?"

Wayne C. Guyette, Ph.D.

The demands of fiscal exigency and societal change have become increasingly pressing concerns within all segments of the hospitality industry. As a response to these concerns, upper management has become more familiar with issues within the areas of manpower planning and organizational design. As a consequence, traditional processes and individual roles are being reexamined to determine their current and projected relevancy to the operational health of the hospitality industry.

However, while this reexamination is laudable, few concerted attempts have been initiated to review the role of the executive chef in order to determine his organizational role at the unit level.

Therefore, this chapter will attempt to determine the current role of the executive chef and whether or not that role will remain essentially the same in the future as it is today. Will that role decline in importance or will that role need to be redefined so that it can be more contributory to the attainment and maximization of the organizational goals?

This chapter will respond to these questions by first establishing a current frame of reference and perspective through a review of the chef's current status and availability as well as his managerial operational skill levels as perceived by himself and his employers. The prospects for future manpower planning decision-making will take into account emerging trends and possible corporate responses to the environmental conditions discussed.

For purposes of the chapter, an executive chef is defined as the individual who, on a daily basis, has managerial responsibility and authority for the operation of the culinary department. His title may be Executive Chef, Chef des Cuisine, Working Chef, or Chef.

Traditionally, the majority of chefs have been drawn from Europe. However, with the devaluation of the American dollar to European currencies and changing immigration laws, increased numbers of European trained culinarians have opted to remain in their own countries. Additionally, many European trained culinarians, who have been working in the United States, have elected to return to Europe.

Responding to the demand for culinarians, the American education system has, over the past fifteen years, dramatically increased the number of culinary arts programs offered by secondary and post-secondary educational institutions. Nevertheless, any cursory reading of the trade press reveals numerous advertisements for "European trained" chefs. Therefore, one must assume that many hospitality organizations regard European training as highly desirable for their Executive Chefs and other culinarians. This preference for European trained culinarians can be traced to the high degree of craft skills internalized by the

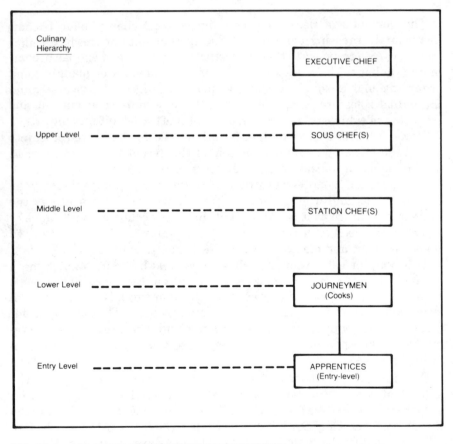

FIG. 29.1. CULINARY DEPARTMENT ORGANIZATION

individual through European culinary apprenticeship programs. These programs are typically based upon repetition and meritocracy. The Guild System, under which the apprenticeship programs operate, are traditionally founded upon a quasi-master/servant relationship. Consequently, an authoritarian role model is established for the young, impressionable apprentice. As a result, the apprentice internalizes this authoritarian role model as acceptable and, in later years, attempts to emulate the associatd behavior characteristics. Such authoritative and autocratic behavior further perpetuates the long held view of many that chefs are tyrannical, erratic, prima donnas. One can easily understand why many managers go out of their way to avoid confrontation situations with their chefs. Since American culinary departments have been dominated by chefs with these learned behavior characteristics, the system and the behavior patterns become self-perpetuating.

However, the key issue for upper management should not be one of geographical training or perceived stereotyping; the issue should center upon the desired role that the chef should ideally fulfill for the property. Herein lies the crux of the problem role definition. The promotional ladder for becoming a chef, as shown in Fig. 29.1, indicates a dependency upon how qualified the culinarian is as a craftsman. Consequently, culinarians promoted to the position of Chef, Working Chef, or Executive Chef are viewed by their employees, peers, and upper management primarily as qualified craftsmen. Yet, by function, they are promoted and removed from the craftsmanship level to a level requiring performance as managers with all the complex skills that position encompasses.

THE STUDY AND ITS RESULTS

In an attempt to determine how effective chefs are in fulfilling this management role, the author conducted during the summer and fall of 1980 two national studies directed at hotel executive chefs in cooperation with the School of Hotel, Restaurant and Tourism Administration and the Division of Business and Economic Research at the University of New Orleans. The first study cosponsored by the American Hotel and Motel Association was designed to determine the perceptions of hotel general managers toward their executive chef's managerial and operational skills. This study cosponsored by the American Culinary Federation (a federation of 10,000 executive chefs) was similarly designed to determine the perceptions of hotel executive chefs toward their own managerial and operational skills. For purposes of the study, managerial skills were defined as those skills perceived to be appropriate to the executive chef's responsibility and authority. And, more specifically, the skills which center upon their ability to employ resources to accomplish the organization's goals and objectives. Operational skills were defined as those skills which were considered to be either technical or craft related.

The study utilized a questionnaire format composed of four main sections: demographics, managerial skills inventory, operational skills inventory, and environmental issues. The managerial and operational skill sections presented a series of statements with two six-point Likert-type scales. The first scale focused upon the desirability of the skill, and the second scale focused upon the degree to which the skill was currently being practiced. The last section, environmental, was designed to determine perceptions toward various topical issues of concern to general managers and executive chefs.

The instrument was pilot tested and mailed to 425 hotel general managers and 425 executive chefs employed at the same properties. One hundred and twenty-nine instruments were returned by general managers

TABLE 29.1. RESPONDENTS' PROFILE

	General Managers Respondents (N=78) (%)	Executive Chefs Respondents (N=86) (%)
Age of executive chef		
20 years or less	—	—
21 to 29	13.1	19.5
30 to 39	43.5	52.9
40 to 49	25.0	17.3
50 to 59	17.1	10.3
60 years of age or older	1.3	—
Executive chef's formal culinary training		
American culinary apprenticeship program	20.0	10.2
European culinary apprenticeship program	52.2	43.0
Vocational-technical program	11.0	15.9
Two-year community/junior college	4.5	9.1
Four-year college/university	7.5	10.2
Other	3.0	12.5
Type of property		
Resort	18.4	17.4
Convention	42.1	43.0
Metropolitan	34.2	32.6
Other	5.3	7.0
Gross food sales		
$299,000 or less	—	1.2
$300,000 to $599,000	2.7	1.2
$600,000 to $999,000	5.3	6.0
$1,000,000 to $1,449,000	12.0	12.0
$1,500,000 to $1,999,000	9.3	16.9
$2,000,000 or more	70.7	62.7
Full-time culinary employees		
19 or less	14.8	2.3
20 to 39	28.4	41.4
40 to 59	23.0	29.9
60 to 79	5.4	11.5
80 to 99	5.4	8.0
100 or more	23.0	6.9

TABLE 29.2.   PLANNING SKILLS

	Percentage by Category				
	Very Poor	Poor	Fair	Good	Very Good
General managers	1.5	8.1	27.1	46.4	16.9
Executive chefs	—	0.5	8.9	44.9	45.6

	Ranking	
Skill	General Manager	Executive Chef
Make firm decisions	1	8
Develop workable short-range plans	2	8
Listen and understand directions	3	1
Correctly interpret the organization's policies/procedures	4	3
Write marketable menus	5	9
Correctly identify and successfully solve operational problems	6	7
Develop workable long-range plans	7	4
Set realistic (attainable) goals/objectives	8	5
Generate realistic department budgets	9	6

(30.4%) and of those 78 (60.5%) were found to be usable. Eighty-six (60.6%) of the 142 (33.4% response) instruments returned by executive chefs were found to be usable.

The profile of the typical chef studied, as shown by Table 29.1, indicates that the chef was between 30 and 39 years of age, European-trained, employed by either a convention or metropolitan hotel having over $2,000,000 in gross food sales, and supervised between 20 and 59 culinarians.

It was found that the general managers and executive chefs generally agreed as to what constitutes desirable managerial and operational skills. However, the perceptions of both groups toward the degree to which these skills are currently being practiced varied significantly, so that a consensus was not evident.

Planning Skills

Regarding planning skill, 90.5% of the executive chefs rated their performance in this critical area to be either good to very good, as opposed to general managers who rated their executive chefs' current planning skills at 63.3%—as seen in Table 29.2.

General managers rated their chefs' skills to be the lowest in the areas of budget generation, setting goals and objectives, and developing workable long-range plans.

Relative to chefs' ratings of themselves, managers rated the chefs higher in decision making and menu writing; they rated chefs lower in long-range plan developing, setting goals/objectives and generating budgets.

Organizing Skills

More than 87% of executive chefs rated their organizing skills as good to very good while 61% of the general managers rated these same organizing skills as good to very good, as seen in Table 29.3.

TABLE 29.3.   ORGANIZING SKILLS

| | Percentages by Category | | | | |
	Very Poor	Poor	Fair	Good	Very Good
General managers	1.4	8.6	29.0	42.5	18.5
Executive chefs	0.1	1.1	11.7	41.2	45.9

| | Ranking | |
Skill	General Manager	Executive Chef
Promote positive attitude toward property	1	5
Schedule work assignments	2	1
Generate cost effective recipes	3	13
Generate cost effective menus	4	8
Delegate responsibility to subordinates	5	12
Recruit an effective culinary staff	6	17
Generate proper purchasing procedures	7	11
Train culinary workers	8	6
Promote food conservation	9	4
Promote positive employee morale	10	7
Prevent employee complaints/grievances from occurring	11	16
Delegate authority to subordinates	12	15
Organize an efficient catering department	13	2
Generate proper inventory procedures	14	10
Generate standardized recipes	15	14
Train supervisors	16	9
Initiate work simplification methods	17	3
Successfully select new employees through effective interviewing techniques	18	18

General managers rated their executive chefs' current organizing skills lowest in the areas of interviewing, initiating work simplification procedures, training supervisors, generating standardized recipes, and generating proper inventory procedures.

Relative to the chefs' rating of themselves, managers rated their chefs higher in culinary staff recruiting, recipe generating, and responsibility delegating; managers rated chefs lower in initiating work simplification procedures, organizing efficient departments, and training supervisors.

Directing Skills

When asked to rate their executive chefs' directing skills, 58.3% of the general managers and 87.3% of the chefs rated them as good to very good, as seen in Table 29.4.

TABLE 29.4.   DIRECTING SKILLS

	Percentage by Category				
	Very Poor	Poor	Fair	Good	Very Good
General managers	2.1	8.2	31.4	43.1	15.2
Executive chefs	0.6	1.6	10.5	40.6	46.7

	Ranking	
Skill	General Manager	Exec. Chef
Supervise minority workers	1	2
Supervise female culinary works	2	6
Supervise young culinary workers (29 years of age or younger)	3	5
Effectively deal with his own job-related stress	4	12
Promote positive employee morale	5	21
Maintain effective employee discipline	6	1
Effectively resolve conflict between culinary workers	7	20
Effectively communicate with upper level management	8	17
Successfully deal with customers cn a one-to-one basis	9	21
Develop team work	10	3
Enforce safe work habits of employees	11	4
Communicate effectively through the spoken word (disregarding English as a second language)	12	15
Effectively communicate with peers (other department heads)	13	19
Effectively resolve conflict between culinary workers and culinary supervisors	14	10
Motivate culinary workers	15	7
Counsel employees on job related problems	16	8
Enforce the use of standardize recipes	18	20
Motivate supervisors	17	16
Enforce positive sanitation practices of employees	19	11
Correctly handle employee complaints/grievances when they occur	20	13
Communicate effectively through the written word (disregarding English as a second language)	21	18
Enforce effective portion control procedures	22	14
Use different leadership styles when appropriate	23	22
Counsel employees on non-job related problems	24	23
Conduct productive department/staff meetings	25	25

The directing skills rated lowest by general managers were: conducting productive department/staff meetings, counseling employees on non-job-related problems, use of different leadership styles, enforcement of portion control procedures, and written communications.

Relative to the chefs' ratings of themselves, managers rated their chefs' performance higher in promoting employee morale, resolving conflicts, dealing with customers, communicating with upper management, and dealing with their own stress; managers rated chefs lower in motivating workers, counseling employees, enforcing sanitation practices, handling employee complaints/grievances, enforcing safe work habits, and developing team work.

Controlling Skills

This category elicited the most frequent instances of consensus between the two groups. However, executive chefs continue to rate their current performance significantly higher than their employing general managers;

87.5% of the chefs rated themselves good to very good at these skills, while only 60.8% of the managers rated them good to very good. (See Table 29.5).

The skills rated the lowest were in the areas of controlling utility expenses, controlling labor costs, reduction of employee absenteeism, and turnover.

In general, the rankings were very similar by both managers and chefs. Managers rated chefs higher in appraising supervisor performance and reducing work turnover; they rated chefs lower in controlling labor costs.

TABLE 29.5.   CONTROLLING SKILLS

	Percentage by Category				
	Very Poor	Poor	Fair	Good	Very Good
General manager	1.6	6.5	31.0	42.8	18.0
Executive chef	0.3	0.5	11.7	40.9	46.6

	Ranking	
Skill	General Manager	Executive Chef
Control food cost at acceptable levels	1	1
Reduce supervisory turnover	2	2
Appraise culinary worker performance	3	3
Appraise supervisor performance	4	6
Initiate operational and procedural changes effectively	5	4
Reduce culinary worker turnover	6	8
Reduce employee absenteeism	7	7
Control labor costs at acceptable levels	8	5
Control and reduce utility expenses	9	9

DISCUSSION

During the past year the author has conducted numerous two-day Executive Chef Managerial Development Workshops sponsored by various hospitality corporations and Chefs' associations throughout the United States. The data which have subsequently been collected during these problem-solving workshops clearly verifies the findings presented here. In addition, it was found that a majority of the participating chefs suffer from a lack of identity which has been fostered by their employing organizations. They typically do not know the full extent of the role upper management would like them to fulfill nor have they been made aware of their current performance as viewed by their superiors.

To summarize findings, it was found that managers and chefs generally agree as to what constitutes desirable managerial and operational skills. However, the perceptions of both groups toward the degree to which these skills are currently practiced vary significantly. The chefs ranked their own planning, organizing, directing, and controlling skills higher than their employing managers.

To rationalize these dramatic differences, it might be appealing merely to make the statement that poor managers often overrate themselves. Apparently, a number of organizations have accepted the view that chefs are, and will remain, poor managers and must, therefore, be considered expendable dinosaurs. Their solution to the "problem" is quite simple, remove the dinosaur and replace him with a kitchen manager. The management of the kitchen, they maintain, need not be vested in the hands of a highly skilled craftsman. Furthermore, if menus are cyclical, set, or centralized at a corporate level, the primary role of the kitchen manager should center upon scheduling skilled or semi-skilled station supervisors. They maintain that this system reduces labor costs while providing a consistent, standardized product.

While innovative, this system may be faulted for a variety of reasons, such as: it reduces the opportunity for culinarian upward promotion and mobility; perpetuates performance mediocrity; reduces the opportunity for an adequate unit level response to local market competition; stifles creativity; encourages employee turnover; and, most of all, it is designed to respond to a symptom rather than a problematic causation. If the chefs' managerial skills are less than desirable, the organization, not the chef, is at fault.

Our industry continues to promote a culinarian to the position of chef purely on the basis of his craftsmanship skills. Once promoted, it does not provide him with opportunities to increase his knowledge and understanding of contemporary management practices. As the research findings demonstrate, the system which trained him and the system which provided him his on-the-job craftsmanship skills and promotions has not been effective in eliciting from him *or* from upper management either an interest in, or a commitment to the management development of executive chefs.

As highly skilled craftsmen in managerial positions, it is reasonable to speculate on the chefs' attemp to emulate behavior characteristics exhibited by previous chef role models encountered during their early training. This attempt to emulate the role model, coupled with few opportunities for formal managerial development, probably contributes to the chef's unconscious self-isolation from contemporary management processes. As a consequence, chefs avoid situations which would bring attention to their managerial deficiencies and resist experiences which might increase and improve their understanding of contemporary management practices.

As a result of the discrepancies existing in a chef's management knowhow, chefs are generally restricted to lateral promotion opportunities. When chefs are promoted to higher levels of managerial responsibility, such as Director of Food and Beverage, retraining must occur or the managerial descrepancies remain.

A review of the organizational structures in use by various hospitality segments indicates that upper management, consciously or unconsciously, has effectively insulated itself from the executive chef and his managerial problems. These organizational structures generally perpetuate the continuance of the executive chefs' managerial discrepancies.

From a very basic perspective, the hospitality industry offers two main services—food and lodging. The executive chef occupies a pivotal role in that his contribution determines client acceptability of the product served. While, to a great extent, this contribution is craft or technical related, his primary role is as a department manager with all the attendant managerial functions and responsibilities. The importance of the role is self-evident. Unfortunately, upper management has seriously abrogated its own responsibility in recognizing the importance of that role. Upper management has deluded itself by viewing the executive chef merely as a craftsman and as a unique individual to be humored and catered to because of some ill-conceived self-perception of what and how that role should be played. Upper management's patronization of the chef due to stereotype perception merely perpetuates an already untenable situation.

SUMMARY

Depending upon the property and industry segment, the future role of the executive chef may take three possible paths.

The first path, declining importance of the executive chef, will no doubt occur if upper management *does not* upgrade the managerial skills of their executive chefs in response to technological change and mounting economic and societal pressures. Failure to respond will not resolve the need and will only create a managerial void which will need to be filled. Since this managerial void still must be filled, new positions will need to be created, and the organizational structure will have to be redesigned in order to incorporate the new positions.

The second path, the systematic obsolescence of the executive chef, will occur as a result of a very conscious attempt by upper management to replace the executive chef (seen as a technocrat) with a kitchen manager. The kitchen manager *will* probably be regarded as a management generalist as opposed to a specialist. The kitchen manager's responsibilities will encompass the four broad functions of management with direct control over the culinarians. These culinarians will be regarded as technicians.

The third path, key man or key role, will occur if upper management reexamines the role of the executive chef and, as a result, redefines the role to recognize its key *managerial* position within the organization's profitability. Such recognition will result in strategies for the professional growth and development of the executive chef.

As the hospitality industry moves from adolescence to maturity, the concept of organizational reexamination for purposes of continuity becomes even more critical if a healthy, vibrant environment is to be achieved. No longer can the industry afford the luxury of traditional responses to contemporary concerns. The role and performance of the executive chef remain traditional while contemporary responses to that role remain to be seen.

30

Working with Seasonal and Temporary Employees

James S. Overstreet, Ph.D. and *Don C. Dodson, Ph.D.*

INTRODUCTION

Managerial theory and practice traces its roots to the Sumerians, the developers of a written language. Since that time, management thought and practice have focused upon the needs of the times, from early Roman Catholic Church record keeping on clay tablets to Diocletian's reorganization of the Roman Empire. With the advent of the factory system, centralized production led to the development of new management methods, techniques and strategies for motivating employees to produce more with greater quality. Beginning with early factories and scientific management to the current billion dollar corporation and modern behavioral theories, managers faced with continuous technological and social changes have had to cope with increasingly complex factors to be effective.

No present student of management can say precisely where management thought rests today — only the future will reveal our place in management history. It is safe to conclude, however, that modern managers and teachers of management rely on some combination of the old interfaced with new ideas and new strategies to meet current needs. A review of twentieth century management thought clearly reveals that most of the literature focuses on the permanent, full-time employee. Although there have always have been seasonal employees, very little research or systematic investigation has been devoted to this subject.

During the past two or three decades an increasingly mobile American society has placed new demands on the hospitality industry. A more affluent population, more leisure time, better and faster transportation and/or a need to escape the pressures of modern life have all contributed to the growth of the hospitality industry. Modern lodging facilities, restaurants, and recreational/leisure time organizations have replaced the old "Mom and Pop" courts and roadside cafes.

Most hospitality organizations must hire temporary or seasonal employees to meet seasonal demands, and while this workforce is important to organizational success, management systems are most often designed with the permanent employee in mind. Programs and techniques directed toward increasing employee motivation, satisfaction and performance are generally based on assumptions about the needs and goals of the long-term employee. Far too often, major reward structures and personnel programs, e.g., retirement and fringe benefits, appraisals, and promotions, have little meaning for the temporary or seasonal employee.

A review of the literature, analysis of course offerings in colleges and universities, and an examination of noncredit training programs indicate that the subject is not one of systematic investigation. While some organizations obviously provide various incentive plans and have developed administrative procedures for seasonal workers, little empirical research has been conducted or published. To help fill this void, a mailed questionnaire was used to gather preliminary descriptive information

TABLE 30.1.   DESCRIPTION OF SEASONAL EMPLOYER SAMPLE

Variable	N	Percentage
Number of participating firms	131	
Mean number of seasonal workers	35[1]	
Firms by number of seasonal workers		
0-10	78	59.5
11-25	23	17.6
26-50	13	9.9
51+	17	13.0
Number of busy seasons per year		
1	77	58.3
2	34	25.8
3	20	15.2
Average length of busy season:	4.4 months	
Type of business		
Lodging	32	24.2
Restaurant	10	7.6
Fast foods	2	1.5
Retail outlet	26	19.7
Amusement/Recreational	18	13.6
Theme park	5	3.8
Service	10	7.6
Other	28	21.2
Type of firm		
Independent operation	86	68.8
Franchise	9	7.2
Part of larger corporation	25	20.0
Other	4	3.2

[1]Does not include two very large firms reporting 1800 and 2500 seasonal employees. Including these would change the mean size to 65 seasonal employees.

about the employment and management of seasonal employees. The survey was sent to all business firms located in a major coastal resort area with a limited number sent nationally to major theme and amusement parks. Given the exploratory nature of the survey, the decision was made to gather data from several business types employing seasonal workers rather than extensively surveying a particular industry.

SURVEY RESULTS

Table 30.1 contains a description of those firms responding to the questionnaire. As indicated, approximately 60% of the firms reported employing 10 or fewer seasonal workers, with only 13% reporting over 50 seasonal workers on the payroll at any one time. Of these largest firms, all but one reported being in the amusement/recreation or theme park business. The types of businesses comprising almost 80% of the sample were those in the lodging, retail outlet, amusement/recreation and other categories. Some of the business types included in the "other" category were aviation, building, charter boat, banks, etc. Firms checking both the lodging and restaurant options were listed under lodging, leaving "restaurants" to represent stand-alone operations. Almost 90% of the firms described themselves as being either independent operations or part of a larger corporation.

In looking at a profile of the seasonal workers employed by the sample firms (Table 30.2) it was found that the bulk of these workers were either college/high school students or regular seasonal employees. Moonlighters

TABLE 30.2.   RECRUITMENT OF SEASONAL EMPLOYEES

Source	Percentage
Classification of seasonal employees	
High school students	28.8[1]
College students	30.6
Housewives	9.6
Retirees	7.8
Moonlighters	7.7
Regular seasonal employees	14.7
Other	.7
Recruitment of seasonal employees	
Newspaper ads	26.4[2]
State employment agencies	11.2
Private employment agencies	0.8
Word of mouth	71.2
Radio ads	1.6
Trade journal/association	0.8
Walk-ins	44.8
Other	12.8

[1]Percentage of total number of seasonal employees reported by 151 firms.
[2]Percentage of firms using this source reported by 125 firms.

TABLE 30.3.   COMPARISON OF SEASONAL AND PERMANENT EMPLOYEES

Dimension	Percentage of Respondents Replying[1]		
	Somewhat/Much[2] Lower	About the Same	Somewhat/Much[2] Higher
In *comparison to your permanent employees,* how would you rate your seasonal employees on the following dimensions?			
Performance	46.8	48.4	4.8
Absenteeism	20.1	50.8	29.1
Reliability	50.4	40.7	8.9
Motivation	54.0	33.9	12.1
Training needs	18.5	29.0	52.4
Situations needing discipline	5.6	51.6	42.8
Personal problems	16.3	51.6	32.3
Supervision needed	5.6	21.8	62.6
Unexpected resignations	11.2	30.6	58.1
Importance to success of firm	39.5	50.0	10.5
Level of pay for summer work	44.3	51.6	4.0

[1]Total number of respondents was 125.
[2]Percentages for "Somewhat" and "Much" responses were combined in this figure. Those interested in seeing these percentages broken down may contact the authors.

TABLE 30.4.   COMPARISON OF SEASONAL AND PERMANENT EMPLOYEES BY FIRM SIZE

Dimension	Percentage of Respondents Replying[1]		
	Somewhat/Much[2] Lower	About the Same	Somewhat/Much[2] Higher
In *comparison to your permanent employees,* how would you rate your seasonal employees on the following dimensions?			
Performance			
$0-10^3$	43.0	50.0	7.0
11−25	43.5	56.5	0.0
26−50	61.5	38.5	0.0
51+	53.0	41.2	5.9
Absenteeism			
0−10	22.2	59.7	18.1
11−25	17.3	34.8	47.8
26−50	15.4	61.5	23.1
51+	17.6	29.4	52.9
Reliability			
0−10	40.8	49.3	9.8
11−25	56.5	26.1	17.4
26−50	69.2	30.8	0.0
51+	64.7	35.3	0.0
Motivation			
0−10	52.8	33.3	13.9
11−25	52.2	39.1	8.7
26−50	53.8	30.8	15.4
51+	64.7	29.4	5.9
Training needs			
0−10	19.5	34.7	45.8
11−25	17.3	17.4	65.2
26−50	23.1	23.0	53.9
51+	11.8	23.5	64.7

Table continued next page

TABLE 30.4.   (continued)

Dimension	Percentage of Respondents Replying[1]		
	Somewhat/Much[2] Lower	About the Same	Somewhat/Much[2] Higher
Situations needing discipline			
0–10	7.0	63.9	29.1
11–25	8.7	43.5	47.8
26–50	0.0	46.2	53.9
51+	0.0	11.8	88.2
Personal problems			
0–10	19.4	55.6	25.0
11–25	21.7	43.5	34.8
26–50	7.7	53.8	38.5
51+	41.2	58.8	
Supervision needed			
0–10	8.4	23.6	68.0
11–25	4.3	21.7	73.9
26–50	0.0	38.5	61.6
51+	0.0	0.0	100.0
Unexpected resignations			
0–10	15.2	43.1	41.7
11–25	8.6	21.7	69.6
26–50	7.7	84.6	
51+	0.0	5.9	94.1
Importance to Success of Firm			
0–10	41.7	50.0	8.3
11–25	39.1	43.5	4.3
26–50	38.5	53.8	7.7
51+	29.4	52.9	17.7
Level of Pay for Summer Work			
0–10	36.1	59.7	4.2
11–25	52.2	43.5	4.3
26–50	38.5	53.8	7.7
51+	75.0	25.0	0.0

[1]The number of respondents was 125.
[2]Percentages for "Somewhat" and "Much" responses were combined in this figure. Those interested in seeing these percentages broken down may contact the authors.
[3]Number of seasonal employees.

holding down part-time jobs, retirees and housewives did not accout for a large percentage of the workers. It could not be determined if this particular percentage breakdown was a function of the summer resort area sampled, or indicative of the seasonal workforce in general. As indicated in Table 30.2, most of these workers are recruited by word-of-mouth methods or selected from walk-ins.

In addition to these general descriptive data, managers were questioned as to their perceptions of seasonal employees. Using a five point Likert-type scale designated Much Lower, Somewhat Lower, About the Same, Somewhat Higher and Much Higher, managers were asked to compare their seasonal and permanent employees in terms of their motivation, performance, reliability, etc. Table 30.3 contains the results of these comparisons. The "Much" and "Somewhat" responses for each dimension have been combined. As shown, seasonal employee performance, reliability and performance are seen as lower by a large percentage of firms, while training needs, disciplinary actions, personal problems, supervision needs and unexpected resignations are seen as higher. Only absenteeism is seen as higher and lower by equal numbers of firms.

These data are broken down by firm size in Table 30.4. Analysis of those differences between responses of the larger and smaller firms indicate that while the differences are not always consistent nor significant, they suggest that the larger firms generally have greater difficulty with seasonal workers than do the smaller firms. In all four size categories, a large number of firms see their seasonal employees as being less important to the success of the firm and report paying these workers less for similar work.

In addition to these comparisons, managers were asked about special programs being used to deal with their seasonal workforce. A representative selection of these programs are provided in Table 30.5. Many of these programs, or something very similar, were mentioned by many of the firms sampled. As can be seen from the responses, most of the special programs are directed at those special problems mentioned by many of the firms, i.e., absenteeism and early resignations. Almost all of the programs involved the use of extrinsic rewards, e.g., parties, gifts, bonuses, etc., as the means to getting desired behavior. Only a few mentioned such intrinsic factors as "asking advice", making them "a part of the team", etc.

DISCUSSION

Recognizing the preliminary and limited aspects of these data, the results cannot be considered as conclusive evidence. However, the initial impression is clearly one of widespread disenchantment on the part of most managers. While many firms are attempting to develop policies and procedures for managing seasonal employees, the data in Tables 30.3 and 30.4 indicate these programs have met with limited success. Comments made by some participating firms suggest a view of seasonal workers as necessary evils to be confronted each year.

While there are constraints and additional problems surrounding regular seasonal employment situations, the potential likely to be found in regular seasonal employees, students, housewives, etc. would seem to belie the idea that seasonal workers are somehow destined to be less motivated, reliable, etc. There is reason to believe that the state of the art as indicated by the survey results can be improved. First, research into the motives and characteristics of seasonal workers as well as the practices of the more successful firms would serve to improve the state of the art.

TABLE 30.5. SPECIAL PROGRAMS FOR MANAGING SEASONAL EMPLOYEES

Question	Response
Do you have any special programs for rewarding/motivating your seasonal employees?	• Bonuses for improvement • Quarterly supper meetings • If satisfactory, up to one week's pay at end of season • Employer of the month—if they have worked 2 continunous months • Bonus for no days missed during busy season • Give them days off when they want, ask their advice—part of "team" • Film-training session, cookouts, etc. • Allow them to purchase merchandise at cost • If work is superior to permanent employees, then seasonal employee gets the permanent position manent position
Do you have any special programs for retaining your seasonal employees for the whole season?	• Opportunity to work full time • September bonus for those who work entire season; 5% of seasonal earnings • Not hired unless they agree to stay entire season • Good pay and working conditions • Employment contracts • Excellent pay • No—programs tried have failed
Do your seasonal employees present any special problems?	• Training and indoctrination • Early leaves before Labor Day • High turnover, unreliable, housing • Honesty, lateness and attendance (easy to get a new job in area) • Much time required to find best position for new employees • College students tend to be immature • Want to design their own schedules • Stealing, schools differ in closing/ /opening in each state • Play/work ratio interferes with attendance and motivation • Seasonal employees must be accompanied at work because training is too expensive, dangerous, and time consuming • How can a young man or woman be motivated when they know they'll leave in September?
Do you feel you could use additional training/information in managing seasonal employees? employees?	• Yes—Could always use more training in management • Yes—Motivation and supervision

Obviously this further research and exchange of information is needed. Secondly, improvement could come not by the development of new knowledge, but rather by the application of existing management and behavioral techniques.

TABLE 30.6.   PROSPECTS

Recruitment/Selection
- Attempt to identify more "local residents" for seasonal jobs.
- Investigate school/work programs in high schools and universities.
- Look into workers with periods of unemployment paralleling busy seasons, e.g., teachers, construction workers, etc.
- Develop statistical predictors of likely absentee/resignation problems.
- Look for match of worker interest/job responsibilities.

Scheduling
- Job sharing using part-time seasonal workers
- Develop weekday/weekend crews, e.g., using students on weekdays, housewives, moonlighters on weekends
- Use job rotation to maintain variety, sharing of enjoyable/unenjoyable jobs.

Training
- Use pre-employment training/orientation for seasonal employers
- Improve supervisors training skills
- Train supervisors in Behavior Modification techniques (OB Mod)
- Make supervisors aware of "self-fulfilling" prophecy

In Table 30.6 we have suggested several ways to apply existing knowledge to the seasonal employee problem. While many firms may have tried or are presently trying some of these suggestions, the others may also be of benefit. The suggestions deal basically with first, which people are chosen and how their work is scheduled; and secondly, how they are supervised. Of particular interest in this second group is supervisory training in the use of operant conditioning and reinforcement to change behavior (Organizational Behavior Modification—O.B. Mod.). This reinforcement approach has proven highly effective in situations dealing with permanent employees, and holds even greater promise in situations involving short-term seasonal employees. Supervisory training in this area is highly recommended. Finally, given the negative perceptions held by many managers, awareness of the self-fulfilling prophecy, i.e., people behave as they are treated, may do a great deal to improve the climate surrounding the manager/seasonal worker interaction.

In conclusion, while the survey results indicate widespread disenchantment on the part of many managers in dealing with their seasonal workers, there are many prospects for improving the state of the art. While these prospects will not solve all the problems in managing these employees, they will go a long ways toward increasing the performance of this important group of workers.

31

Training with a Systems Analysis Approach

Lothar A. Kreck, Ph.D.

It is the intent of this chapter to look at industrial training from a systems analysis perspective. It is not a survey of present training efforts in United States businesses. Rather, it constitutes an attempt to place and delineate within the system framework certain training models and classifications potentially useful to the overall effort of changing or improving the behavior of people in industrial organizations. However, before doing so at least two terms need to be defined: 1) what is a system and 2) what is meant by training.

SYSTEMS

A system can be looked upon as being an organized assembly of parts to form a purposeful and integrated whole. The parts can consist of stars, mountains, rivers, human beings, machines, buildings, or many other elements and are combined to form such systems as the universe, galactical systems, social systems, transportation systems, communication systems, electrical systems, respiratory systems, and molecular systems. System thinking is a way of organized thinking, system analysis is an organized approach to analyzing a situation, and systematic planning is a step-by-step progression in the planning process. All systems have an objective, a purpose. Some maintain the present state, such as keeping a certain temperature or controlling the speed of a machine; and others can be deliberately designed to bring about a new state, e.g., higher sales, or more and better trained personnel. The sole justification for the existence of a system is its objective. Since systems are often assigned more than one objective, conflicts will arise if not one overall objective is spelled out, subordinating the remainder of the objectives and compromising among objectives. Another property of a system deals with its design. Only the system which is specifically designed for the stated objective will come closest to reaching that objective (Jenkins 1976). Furthermore, all systems have sub-systems which, as in any hierarchy, are subjected to the power of the system to which they belong. Although there exists this downward power structure, sub-systems more often than not influence the system (and incidentally also other sub-systems) in that the output of a sub-system becomes part of the input of the system (and/or sub-systems), e.g., the quality of the training of middle-management may have a significant bearing on the performance of the organization as a whole. This signifies two important points about the relationship between a system and its sub-system(s): 1) resources needed by the sub-system which enter the sub-system as inputs are controlled by the system and not the sub-system; 2) the sub-system, a weaker system, by its output has the potential to influence the output of the more powerful system. However, the important lesson to learn from the above is that systems and sub-systems cannot be regarded in isolation. This is not only true for many of the daily management tasks, such as planning and problem solving which is often done in isolation (Kreck 1978), but applies equally to the training function. Departmentalized thinking in management is inefficient and harmful to any organization; integrated thinking and acting is what is called for in the future.

TRAINING

Before discussing the necessary inputs, it would be helpful to state what is meant in this chapter by training. It does not include the change which goes on in an individual despite the lack of any training efforts by the organization or what McFarland (1974) calls ". . . patterns of informal or unprogrammed changes. . . ." It means instead deliberate efforts of pre-planned changes, both in a formal or informal mode to meet the needs of the organization. It is unfortunate that most of the changes in behavior of the employees in the hospitality industry today occur in "patterns of informal or unprogrammed changes." Can this be one of the reasons why large service organizations are taken over by manufacturing concerns where much more formal training goes on and that top managements in the hospitality industry are replaced by manufacturing executives?

Inputs

In order to accomplish any objective (output), resources (inputs) have to be planned for and made available. The type of inputs depend on the objective to be achieved, as does the amount of each input assigned to the objective. The transformation of the inputs into the output is the process.

To implement training, the following inputs will be considered and discussed: information, personnel, time, finances and facilities. The order listing the inputs is of little importance. In this discussion the present system is regarded as a sub-system of a larger or wider system. For reasons of clarity the larger or wider system will be called System I and the sub-system System II.

Information.—At least two categories of information are necessary; one deals with organizational matters and the second with subject matters.

First of all, information is required about the need for training. The need can appear in a shock-like fashion, unexpectedly, in the form of observable undesirable symptoms or it can come through systematic evaluation. A number of possibilities for the latter include: interviews, group conferences, surveys, tests, management requests, job performance analysis, merit rating, personnel records, business reports (e.g., financial statements, employee turnover reports), long-range organizational planning, especially with regard to expansion, new technological demands on personnel, changes in the product and service delivery, replacements for retirement, termination, promotion and transfer. Once a training need is established the desired output has then to be determined, and the new or improved behavior specified. If the need is established through the observation of undesirable symptoms, the standard for the desired output, expressed or inferred, must be known in the organization already, if not in System II then in System I. It can be stated with little hesitation that actual performance can only be measured if a standard exists at all and an undesirable symptom expresses performance below standard by its very definition.

On the other hand, if the need has been established through evaluation of the organization, standards for training will be laid down for System II which are part of an extension of the standards in use in System I. For example, to run a large hotel successfully (objective of System I), certain inputs have to be specified, among them the desired behavior of the general manager. While for System I the behavior is an input, it has to be specified as an output standard of the training system, System II.

A few more words should be said about this most important subject of standards, specifically the expression of standards. For all practical purposes, all standards should be expressed in numerical terms, e.g., percentage, seconds, dollars, ounce, inch, or in such final terms as "all" or "none." At first appearance that does not seem to be possible, but on closer observation it is indeed possible if the idea is laid to rest that one behavior (a "good" manager) has to be expressed by one standard. If one considers what makes a "good" manager and lists the attributes on one side, such as "turns in a profit of 12%;" "receives no more than 3 complaints per month;" "keeps employee turnover to 25%;" "finalizes all (100%) required reports within the allotted time," etc., and lists the numerical values in the fashion indicated, one has accomplished this task.

So far in the discussion of organization-related information, the need for training has been detailed. The second type of information deals with the trainee: Whom to train? The success of any training often depends on the right selection of trainees. What is "right" is not easily answered. In some methods of training, trainees may be presented with certain tools, e.g., principles. Assuming that the trainee had all intentions of using the new tools but could not activate the new behavior because of organizational pressure by superiors or peers, was he or she the "wrong" trainee?

In the preceding section information concerning organizational matters was brought up. To conclude information as an input it must now be discussed in regard to the subject matter of training. What information is necessary for the training process? There are at least two groups of indispensable information. First is the subject material to be covered in the training periods, e.g., functions of management which are often found in company manuals, audio-visual aids or in professional books and journals in the form of principles.

The second group of information deals with the training expertise. In other words, is sufficient knowledge about training available to carry out the planned training? Included are such subjects as learning principles, designing training plans, training types, methods, and aids, resisting training, communication techniques and barriers.

Personnel.—After information, the second input is personnel: Personnel to be trained must be available and there must be personnel to conduct the training. The question "whom to train" has been touched on before. To define what type of trainee is desirable and to have these individuals available is not necessarily the same. There are situations where all definitions must be disregarded and the next best person is assigned (or hired) to be trained. This is especially true in developing countries (Kreck 1969). It goes without saying that the preferred way is the planned management of human assets. Most organizations try to fill positions from the inside. If this is not possible, trainees are hired from the labor market.

Time.—Time represents the third input. It must be regarded from at least two perspectives. When is the overall job supposed to be finished? This can be crucial when it must coincide with, e.g., the opening of a hotel. Needless to say, a detailed overall training plan has to be available in that instance. It can be supported by some devices such as PERT (Program Evaluation and Review Technique), CPM (Critical Path Method) or IRM (Instant Review Method) (Kreck 1969). The second perspective is concerned with the availability of trainees for formal training sessions, away from the job, and at regular intervals, e.g., every second Wednesday from 3 to 4 p.m. Organizational demands, such as higher occupancy, special functions, higher production demand, no-show of personnel or shift rotations can tax any serious commitment to training by top management.

Finances.—The fourth input concerns the availability of finances. A commitment to training is also a commitment to fund this function, with what has become a scarce resource—money. There is a multitude of competing needs in any organization at any time. It is knowledge that training efforts are the first to be cut in troubled times. Why is this so? There seem to be at least two reasons for this. The results of training efforts are often a) not immediate and b) are difficult to measure when compared to dollars of sales or number of items produced. It is simply difficult in adverse times to defend an expenditure, the results of which are not very visible, difficult to measure and not immediate.

Finances are needed for such items as the compensation of trainees, for both inside and outside trainers, the facilities, and supporting staff.

Facilities.—The last input deals with the training facilities and is a function of the previously discussed input, finances. In this group belong the physical facilities, the resource material and training aids, among others. How much the facilities contribute to the success of training is not easy to determine. The lack of minimum facilities can certainly detract from the success of the efforts especially when they become barriers to communication, e.g., a noisy training environment.

This concludes the enumeration of the necessary inputs. It should be again pointed out that in the present training task, for which the systems analysis approach is used, the inputs are made available by System I, and assigned to the subordinated System II. Inputs are always scarce, on top of which information is never complete. It is under conditions of scarcity and a lack of complete information that many systems must function. As if this were not sufficient to deter systems from performing at all, the environment in which the systems function imposes certain restraints, a point which will be brought up again in the next section.

Process

In the process part the available inputs are utilized to produce the planned output, in this case the desired new (or improved) behavior of the trainees. It is the actual training phase following the pre-training phase.

The overall output has previously been clearly defined, with the help of behavioral terminology (Mager 1962) and quantitative standards. For example, the required output is twelve service persons for a French type restaurant in a new hotel to be opened in two weeks. The personnel must be able to demonstrate French service (100%), must be able to explain the menu (100%) and must function within policies and procedures (not more than one misconduct per 12 months). It goes without saying that "policies and procedures" in themselves should be a collection of quantitative standards. Here is another example. The planned promotion of a general manager to that of area vice-president should include a period of training since the behavior of the latter differs from the former. If this is not done, chances are that an effective general manager becomes a mediocre vice-president or an effective director of food and beverage a mediocre general manager. The new behavior of the vice-president, to be available in three months, should include the ability to achieve an overall profit of 15% of sales with no unit achieving less than 12%, to keep labor turnover at less than 25%, to act within policies and procedures (not more than 3 infractions per year), to successfully demonstrate a command of the principles of management (not more than 2 deficiencies per year) and to operate within legal and socially acceptable boundaries (100%).

It now becomes clear that it is unlikely any two trainees will have the same background. This is true in the above case of the service personnel and perhaps even more so in the case of future vice-presidents, assuming that an effort is ever made to find out. It was previously pointed out that the gap between present behavior and new behavior constitutes the training need or the training task. The training task can therefore very likely vary significantly between two trainees.

Training Tasks.—A training task is in reality not one but several tasks. A task can be broken down into categories. One way of doing this is expressed in the following three categories: 1) skills, 2) concepts and

3) attitude change. There are basically four types of skills: motor skills such as manual skills; verbal skills, such as addressing guests in a certain way; sensory skills, such as recognizing desirable or undesirable properties in foods and alcoholic beverages, especially wines; and reasoning skills such as are needed for problem solving and decision making. The second category, concepts, will deal with items such as management principles, French service (the idea, not the technique of serving) and "legal and socially accepted boundaries". With some reasonable and professional efforts, success in the above categories is almost certain. Not so certain is success in the last category, attitude change. How does one permanently change another person's behavior to become more hospitable, more service oriented? Or, how does a supervisor become genuinely more employee oriented? The task is equally difficult for the service personnel as for the vice-president.

Different hierarchial levels require differing amounts of training of one or all of the above categories. However, the necessity for motor skills seems to regress as the person moves up in the hierarchy and the demand for concepts, such as management principles and also reasoning skills seem to increase. The knowledge of management concepts and reasoning skills of a captain are minute compared to the motor skill requirements. This seems to make sense if one considers that captains supervise perhaps 4−6 persons, are supposed to work actively with them and are not required to make any decisions which will effect the conduct of any organizational unit, except that which they supervise. On the other extreme, presidents of hospitality chains, for all intents and purposes, do not need any service skills and are not required to possess any. Their areas of expertise lie in management concepts and reasoning skills. This speaks also very clearly against the idea of promoting, for example, a food and beverage manager of a relatively small food and beverage operation in a hotel with perhaps 80 employees in food and beverage to the same position in a larger operation with perhaps 400 employees in the department, without the benefits of prior specialized training. The new requirements in managerial concepts and reasoning skills, especially in problem solving and decision making, are simply not congruent in many cases with the present knowledge of the person to be promoted or transferred to the larger property.

Intensity.—Besides clearly deciding on the categories of changes, it is important for the trainer to determine in advance the degree of intensity of knowledge needed. For example, in a given situation, should the trainee merely be familiar with the principles of delegation and planning or should the trainee be able to actually apply the principles? This is an important consideration because the category of change and the intensity required will determine the training types, training methods and training aids.

Training Types.—The category of changes and the intensity is now determined. Next a decision has to be made as to the training types. There are basically two: on-the-job training and off-the-job training. It should be emphasized again that this discussion centers only around the organization's deliberate efforts in pre-planned behavioral changes. In managerial training it is customary to decrease the off-the-job training as a person rises in the hierarchy. Some of the reasons are certainly the need to cover a position and the cost of non-productive labor. Other arguments favor this trend. The first one deals with management principles. If a person is familiar with management principles—a big "if" indeed—the only way to master the concept is practice. It can only happen on the job. Another argument for on-the-job training is that there is no need for adjustments from the training situation to the work situation. The argument against on-the-job training is the fact that because of organizational demands, training will be short changed.

As far as nonmanagerial training is concerned, especially training for manual skills and concepts, off-the-job training is in most cases superior. Thus it is cost efficient with regard to long-term benefits for the organization, e.g., the absence of ill-will created in guests by trained service personnel. Other advantages are that trainers, often the trainees' supervisors, are available and not called away; training sessions are not constantly interrupted by the demands of business; trainees are not confronted with embarrassing situations because of a lack of job knowledge; and finally, training sequences can be better planned and followed.

Training Methods.—Once the type of training has been decided upon the appropriate training method needs to be selected. On-the-job training methods include assistant positions, special project assignments, multiple management, job rotation and junior board appointments. Off-the-job training often consists of lectures including programmed instruction; problem solving conferences; case studies; role playing, skill drills; counseling (can also happen on the job); business simulations; communication games; T-groups; transactional analysis; in-basket games; and a game called Apex, developed by C. Kepner and B. Tregoe, which includes elements of games, in-basket and role playing.

The next question is: What training method is appropriate for the training needs? Training need classifications were discussed earlier. They were: motor, verbal, sensory and reasoning skills, concepts and attitude change. Of the methods mentioned above, only skill drills are suitable for motor and sensory skills. Verbal skills can again be acquired by skill drills but also in certain communication games and role playing. Reasoning skills have the greatest choice of training methods. For on-the-job training they are: assistant position, special project assignment, multiple management, job rotation, and junior board assignment. Off-the-job training includes: problem-solving conference, case study, business simulation, communication games, in-basket games and Apex. Here lectures are appropriate because more often than not concepts might be involved and the only suitable training method seems to be the lecture and its derivatives. Lectures are presented in seminars on or off the premises, college courses and derivatives such as programmed instruction, and supervised or unsupervised reading of professional texts and journals.

A word of caution about using an outside source for training: the outside source constitutes a separate system with its own input, process and output and unless that system's output delivers what is planned for by System II, the results can be less than satisfactory.

Finally, there is the elusive training need of attitude change. Common industrial training methods include role playing, counseling, T-groups, transactional analysis, and to a degree some of the on-the-job methods such as assistant positions, multiple management and junior board assignments. To acknowledge the different demands, the training task requires that proper methods are selected and that the level of intensity is specified if training efforts are to pay off.

Training Aids.—Any training can be helped by the proper selection of training aids; these include visual, audio and audio-visual aids. Training aids should function as such and not replace the training methods. Also, aids, e.g., films and video-cassettes, are more effective if they are close to the conditions as they prevail in the organization in which they are utilized. If the trainees cannot associate themselves and the work environment with the visual stimuli of the aid, a tendency can develop for trainees to avoid the behavior change situation, which is often a stressful situation anyway.

Resistance.—Despite the fact that training often brings significant benefits to the organization as well as to the trainee, really strong feelings can exist against training on both sides. A supervisor complains that the trainee leaves the job to participate in a training session when the workload is heavy, or wonders what new-fangled ideas the trainee brings back and how to squash any new idea. The peer fears that the trainee will be promoted while in the meantime the peer has to do the trainee's job as well. The trainees do not like to be evaluated, to be roused from their comfortable position, and wonder how the training sessions will be, will they like the trainer, and the other trainees, and wonder also why they should change the behavior in the first place, the present self-image is in balance, doesn't need any improvements, complain about the free time it might take away, if it will be worth the efforts and exertion. And between a supportive top management on one side and less enthusiastic supervisors, trainees, and trainees' peers on the other stand the trainers in their staff role.

An official, upward pressure is exerted by top management for training and a lot of behind the back downward pressure by the other side with the trainer and his livelihood caught in the middle. To succeed in this organizational game requires a survival instinct, tact and tenacity in spite of the fact that most trainers like what they do, often with a religious conviction, and a desire to contribute to the organization.

Barriers.—If these were not sufficient difficulties, other potential barriers have to be recognized and at least partially removed during the training session: barriers which will hinder communication. These can be divided into two groups: physical barriers which are easily recognized and removed, such as foreign noise, distance to source, inability to receive, speech defects, special language, too dark, too hot or cold, poor air quality. The second group involves psychological barriers. They are not easily recognized or removed because the causes may not be readily identifiable. Among them are power and status relationships among trainees and between trainer and trainees, the "climate" or present relationship, differences in values, standards and attitudes, individuals' habits of thought and action and information "ownership". This happens when one person has some information that someone else needs but the "owner" is unwilling to share it. Because training happens through some form of communication, recognizing and removing barriers before training sessions start as well as during sessions is vital.

Controls.—It was said earlier that inputs are used in the process part to bring about the desired outputs. Finances and time seem to be especially important. They should not exceed the scheduled amount, separately or together. Pre-planning as well as progress checking is important to stay within the allotted amounts. Very often finances influence the time available for training and not vice versa. Instead of asking what time is needed to train the employees for the opening of a new hotel, the pre-opening budget contains one item, called "employee training," and this sum is often divided by the amount of the employees' starting salary; the result is the training periods available for the different departments. Since the training system (System II) has to coordinate actions with other sub-systems, as well as with System I, in

addition to other outside
construction company), car
and ever present activity if
conclude on opening day.

Environment.—At least on
and this deals with the germa
one hand, the elements of the e
of a system, as are inputs. On t
considered a part of the system
influencing a system, e.g., System
one] of which can produce a chan
1976)." Although System II is a su
"shielded" from System I's environ   constant changes brought about by tl   ystem I have
influenced System II in the past and   the future. It is for this
reason that, in the process part of System II, environment changes, more
often in the form of restraints than not, should be mentioned. Here are
some examples 1) legal restraints: The law prohibits discrimination
based on race, color, religion, sex, national origin, or age. The trainee
and trainer selection process can thus be influenced; 2) economic restraints, such as the particular composition of the present labor market,
the influence of labor unions, the shareholders, the competition, and the
business cycle; 3) social-cultural restraints such as religions. For example, certain religions do not allow their members to touch particular food
items and alcohol, degrade manual labor, outrightly prohibit some labor
tasks, and require prayer sessions during the work day. Other social-
cultural restraints are the status of women, the level of education and in
general the degree of social acceptance of the members of the hospitality
industry in a society (Kreck 1969). Finally, restraints arising out of the
political orientation of a society include the absence of a free choice of
occupation. Employees are assigned to jobs by the government.

It is then that under conditions of limited personnel, time, finances
and facilities, in addition to less than complete information and restraints imposed by the environment, System II has to perform to
produce a pre-determined output.

Output

The result of System II's inputs, including the efforts of the people
involved and the frustrations created in many industrial organizations,
is its output, the objective of the system. Earlier it was said that the only
reason for the existence of any system is its output. That applies equally
to System II. Outputs are defined in the output part of the model. They

...contain quantitative requirements often to be ...certain time frame. The fundamental question is: ...output been accomplished? This is answered in an ...basic system: the feedback control part.

Feedback Control

It is important to understand that feedback control belongs to the sphere of communication: it collects information about the output of System II, processes information and passes it on to System II. It can also be called a system since it uses certain inputs (the output standards of System II as well as information), processes the same and communicates the results as output to System II.

Contrary to manufactured goods as output, evaluating the new or improved behavior of supervisors or managers cannot be done with one look. Except for the time frame and perhaps the number of trainees, other standards have often to be observed over time in actual performance on the job. This necessitates setting up procedures for the collection of relevant information that has the potential for answering the question: Has the training been successful? In addition, the information must be factual, observable with one of the senses, and not containing opinions or hypotheses which distort the evaluation process.

The relevant information is now received and is being compared to the standards in regard to, e.g., the time frame, the total number of trainees and performance on the job. Paradoxically, it is not uncommon to establish a tolerance at this point regarding the standards and the performance for the simple reason that it is easier for a superior to live with a subordinate's performance just a fraction below the standard than to repeat the training of the subordinate or to set up a different training program for him or her again.

Once the standard, the output, has been reached, the objective of System II accomplished, then the purpose for the existence of the system passed and the time come to abolish the system. For example, the opening of a new hotel is a case in point. The day the hotel opens, pre-opening training activities terminate and so does the system. This does not mean that training as such will not continue. It means rather that a new system has to be designed with its specific output standards and required inputs.

On the other hand, if the information shows that the output has not been reached and the objectives not accomplished, the life of System II continues. There are a thousand and one possibilities for a system not reaching its objectives. Among these are not enough finances, too little time, poor facilities, poor selection of trainees, ineffective trainers, desired objectives which are too ambitious, faulty selection of training types, training methods, training aids, lack of understanding of training techniques, discrepancies between the training efforts and the organization (training vs. post-training), and underestimation of the force of the environment's restraints.

It would seem that feedback control depends highly on the collection of information and comparison with standards which could be described as a mechanistic function. This is probably the extent of intellectual involvement where the standards have been met. A totally different picture prevails if the standards have not been reached and a problem-solving sequence must be initiated. There is nothing mechanistic in this activity; in contrast, it calls for the most serious, intellectual involvement of management. It is a creative activity, based on a high degree of experience and deep understanding of organizations and the systems approach. Finally, it may also require courage if some recommendations or orders are less than popular to some elements of System II.

Recommendations or orders will go out to modify the inputs, including modifying output standards, and/or to the process part with the goal of finally matching the desired output with the observed output, at which time the system ceases to be.

CONCLUSION

An attempt has been made to present the training function of an organization as an orderly process by placing it within the framework of a system. Included in that system is the feedback control, which can be regarded as a somewhat mechanistic device in cases where no improvements are called for in the system or as a highly intellectual and innovative device in cases where deficiencies have to be located and improvements to the system recommended or ordered.

The particular approach incorporated models and categories relevant to the training process, suggested a particular flow pattern, and demonstrated the effective linkage of activities concerned with training.

[This contribution is an extract from a more detailed study available from author.]

32

Training for Skilled Human Resources

Lynn Dykstra

Tourism is BIG Business. The economy may be slow, construction financing may be difficult, yet thousands of new hotel rooms will come on the market in the next few years. Over 30,000 new rooms are projected just in the next three to four years. Each new hotel means quality rooms, fine restaurants, banquet and convention facilities, and, above all, service. The rooms must be filled, quality room and food service provided, and skilled staff assembled. The success of each of these properties will depend largely upon how well skills-level staff perform their jobs—both those who are in the "back of the house" and those who have face-to-face contact with the paying guests. Millions of investment dollars depend upon the skills-level staff.

Major hotel operators are spending millions of dollars to market these new and existing properties. Will the paying guests who respond to these marketing efforts find a level of service which meets these expectations as projected in the marketing plan?

The responsibility for satisfying these expectations lies to a great degree with the skills-level employee who has direct guest contact: the waiter, the waitress, the room cleaner, the cook, the front office clerk, etc. Some of the most sophisticated planning ignores the fact that over 70% of the employees are in this skills-level category and have guest contact. The need to train skills-level staff properly is evident; and yet it is one of the most frequently overlooked areas of importance.

Because of the difficulty of finding pre-trained staff we need to train our own employees. We will discuss successful ways to train staff and have them understand their role in the overall goal of guest satisfaction, increased sales, and return clientele.

DEFINITIONS

When we discuss skills-level training we mean teaching the technical skills necessary to effectively and efficiently perform one's job. We include in this technical skill training, the means to perform one's job with courtesy, a positive attitude and an understanding of appropriate guest service. Such training occurs on-the-job and/or in short term classroom sessions. Some positions in our industry require more technical skills training than others. It takes longer to train a professional cook thoroughly than it does to train a professional room cleaner. It may take longer to train a front office clerk or cashier than it does a food server. Although there are various levels of skills training, the important point is that the same program development principles apply.

BASIC PRINCIPLES

Successful training begins at the top. Management must make a positive commitment to training—otherwise it simply will not succeed. When the employee knows that the management supports the program this makes the job easier. A positive climate must also include a high level of respect for the skills of employees. That is, their importance in the overall organization plan must be recognized.

Training programs do not have to be sophisticated and include the latest cliches in program development. They have to be practical, results oriented and well planned. Just as the successful marketing program is practical, results oriented and well planned, so must training. They go hand in hand—yet, more frequently than not, are considered separately.

A training program is on-going. It is not successful if it is hit or miss. There has to be initial planning, implementation and follow-up. A basic plan includes:

1) defining the overall objectives
2) developing specific performance objectives or standards (that is, to detail what the trainee will be able to perform at the end of the training)
3) developing course outlines and lesson plans
4) selling the benefits to the employee
5) presenting the training
6) following up with a built-in program evaluation

The development of performance objectives can be done by a thorough evaluation of the job functions, the results to be accomplished and the time frame for completion. It is of great importance to involve the skilled worker at this level of program development. Not only will the skilled worker be in a better position to define the functions of the job and contribute suggestions toward the training objectives, but when the actual training is to take place, he or she can be a great help in selling the program to those who are not so skilled and will benefit from the training.

Our industry has a challenge to standardize basic training formats. Training plans and programs with uniform performance objectives have not existed in the past. When we at National Culinary Apprenticeship Program began two years ago to design systematic performance objectives for the training of professional cooks for a three-year modular program, we found a lack of uniformity in the instruction of the basics of classical cuisine in today's kitchens. Since then, we have established effective national performance objectives and training standards applicable to all phases of the kitchen operation of full service restaurants, hotels and clubs. These standards provide uniformity of training. They are flexible enough to be used by the smaller restaurant or the larger hotel operation and are accepted by the industry. We are beginning to see the results of this work, because employers who hire graduated culinary apprentices are aware of their basic skills. The quality of the program is respected and the training results speak for themselves.

AUDIO-VISUAL AIDS

The same need for uniform training standards exists at all levels of skills training and thus must be developed to insure overall success.

In addition to developing detailed performance objectives, course outlines, lesson plans, handbooks for the executive chef trainer and other materials for the National Culinary Apprenticeship Program, we found a gap in the audio-visual aids which are currently available to our industry. Following is a description of what was discovered.

When setting apprentices' standards for certain segments of the related instruction which complements the on-the-job training, we wanted to include audio-visual aids explaining the preparation of foods before the actual cooking process stage. We discovered that there is a wealth of material on the cooking process, but nothing on how meat, fish, poultry and vegetables are prepared for the particular cooking method. We are now producing audio-visual aids which fill this gap. We have developed a uniform format and personalized it for use in each separate property or each chain. The advantage of these programs is that they benefit regular kitchen staff in addition to being used by the apprentices. We have developed them as sound/slide productions with the flexibility of being converted to video. Again, this principle is easily adapted to all skills-level training.

BENEFITS OF PROPER TRAINING

The initial cost factor of proper training is quickly offset by the benefits it produces.

Proper training results in the following:

1) guest satisfaction
2) increased sales through positive word-of-mouth advertising
3) a proven work force from which to draw when seeking applicants for promotion and additional responsibility
4) a decrease in absenteeism
5) a tremendous cost savings in staff turnover
6) a staff with a positive and secure attitude regarding their ability to perform their job skill
7) a decrease in disciplinary actions

The cost savings alone are enough to offset the initial cost of training programs and the overall benefits are quickly measureable. We have found the training format developed by National Culinary Apprenticeship Program has produced the following:

1) a system of training, adaptable by any large or small food service operation
2) a positive means to motivate individuals through high-quality training acknowledged throughout the industry
3) a successful track record in retention of selected apprentices
4) graduates who have become full-service operation second cooks, sous chefs and some on their way to becoming executive chefs

Skills-level training must have a total commitment from top management. It must complement the marketing programs; it must be well-planned and organized with specific goals which reflect the basic objectives of the operation. Successful programs can be uniform in their basic goals and training approaches. This is not only a cost savings for individual properties, but a time savings for the trainees. Just as the industry is adopting uniform performance objectives for training culinary apprentices, it is beginning to do so for other skills-level training needs. The initial cost factors of such a program are quickly offset, if the program is well-planned, thorough and includes on-going evaluation.

We all know the difficulty in getting pre-trained employees. Through the National Culinary Apprenticeship Program, the industry has taken a positive step to insure that a successful system exists and functions effectively. The need to expand this approach to all skills-level areas is next, because we know that unless we train our own employees, no one else will.

Part VI

Marketing

33

Current Practices in Food Service Marketing

Robert D. Reid

In the last ten years, the food service industry has experienced a period of continual growth. Several new chains such as Wendy's and Steak and Ale have achieved national attention. Food product firms such as General Mills, General Foods, and Pillsbury have invested heavily in the food service industry. In light of this period of expansion, what is the state of the art in food service marketing?

This chapter represents a survey research effort in food service marketing. The survey has several objectives:

1) to access the manner in which selected marketing activities are performed within various segments of the food service industry;

2) to ascertain the number of personnel involved in the performance of marketing activities within food service firms;

3) to determine the degree to which consultants and internal departments other than the marketing department are utilized in the performance of marketing activities;

4) to examine the advertising budgeting techniques and advertising expenditure patterns within the food service industry;

5) to determine the most widely accepted growth strategies for the next ten years;

6) to determine the extent to which written short-term and long-term marketing objectives are established by food service firms.

METHODOLOGY

A sample of 90 firms was selected for this study. The selected firms were all members of the National Restaurant Association (NRA) Marketing Executives Group. The survey instrument and a cover letter explaining the purpose of the study were sent to each member of the NRA's Marketing Executives Group. A copy of the instrument is in Table 33.1. The marketing executives included in this study represented independent, franchised, as well as chain-owned food service firms. Annual sales of these firms ranged from $1 million to in excess of $100 million.

From the 46 responses to the survey, 43 were usable, a 47.7% response. A vast majority (74%) of those individuals responding to the survey represented chain organizations, while the remaining respondents represented independent firms (15%) and franchised firms (11%). The most significant results of the survey are presented below.

RESULTS

Personnel

The firms responding to the survey indicate that the job title of the individual with the major responsibility for marketing decisions was most commonly the Vice-President of Marketing, the Director of Marketing or a Vice President. In a small number of firms the individual with this responsibility is the Chief Executive Officer or the Controller.

Slightly more than one half (55%) of the responding firms employ fewer than 5 individuals with job responsibilities directly related to marketing, 35% employ between 6 and 15 individuals, and 25% employ more than 15 individuals. Those firms with annual sales in excess of $100 million are more likely to operate larger departments, as 20% of these firms employ more than 30 individuals in the marketing department or division.

Advertising Practices

Those firms responding to the survey indicated a variety of practices related to: (1) percentage of the firm's sales budgeted for advertising; (2) methods utilized to establish an advertising budget; and (3) pre-testing of advertisements.

Over two-thirds (67%) of the firms responding spend 3% or less of their gross sales on advertising, while 25% of the firms spend between 3 and 5%, and 8% of the firms spend in excess of 5% of total sales on advertising. It appears that those firms with annual sales in excess of $100 million spend a higher percentage of total sales for advertising. Of the firms with sales in excess of $100 million, 59% spend less than 3%, 30% spend between 3 and 5%, and 11% spend in excess of 5% of total sales for advertising.

The most widely used method for establishing an advertising budget is to base the budget on a specified percentage of sales. This method is used by 45% of those firms responding to the survey. The objective and task method, wherein a firm establishes specific advertising objectives and then budgets a specific amount needed to achieve each objective is favored by 24% of the responding firms. Ten percent of the responding firms simply budget an amount which the firm's management considers affordable. Over 20% of the firms favor a combination approach, relying on more than one of the methods previously discussed. None of the firms utilizes the competitive parity method, a method which attempts to maintain a stable advertising position relative to major competitors.

Pre-testing of advertisements is not a common practice among food service firms. Pre-testing is more widespread among those firms with annual sales in excess of $100 million than it is with those enjoying less than $100 million in annual sales. Twenty-nine percent of the firms responding with sales in excess of $100 million pre-test more than half of their advertising. None of the independent firms responding to the survey pre-tests more than half of their advertisements. Of those firms with less than $100 million in annual sales, 8% pre-test more than half of their advertisements.

TABLE 33.1.   QUESTIONNAIRE USED IN SURVEY OF CURRENT MARKETING PRACTICES UTILIZED BY FOOD SERVICE ORGANIZATIONS

1. What department or division within your organization has the major responsibility for marketing activities? _____ .
2. What is the job title of the individual holding major responsibility for marketing decisions? _____ .
3. How many individuals with direct job responsibilities related to marketing are employed by your firm? _____ .
4. What percentage of your firm's gross sales is budgeted for advertising? _____ %.
5. What specific method does your firm use to set an advertising budget?
    □ Percentage of sales method (predetermined percentage of projected gross sales)
    □ Competitive parity method (budget an amount to maintain current position vis-a-vis competition)
    □ Amount affordable method (budget an amount which the firm is able to spend based on project revenue and expenses)
    □ Objective and task method (identify specific objectives, then budget the funds necessary to achieve each objective)
    □ Other, please specify _____ .
6. What percentages of your firm's most recent advertising budget are allocated to the following media?

| | Percentage of Advertising Budget |
Media	
Television	
Radio	
Newspaper	
Magazines	

TABLE 33.1   (Cont.)

Outdoor/Transit
Direct mail
Other
(please specify)

Total = 100

7. Does your firm pre-test advertisements prior to placing them in various media?
    □ Rarely (0−20%)
    □ Some of the time (21−49%)
    □ Most of the time (50−79%)
    □ Almost all of the time (80−100%)

8. If your firm pre-tests advertisements, what method(s) does your firm use?

_____

_____

9. Which of the following methods(s) does your firm use to evaluate the effectiveness of advertising?
    □ Monitor sales of total menu mix
    □ Monitor redemption of print media coupons
    □ Monitor sales of specific menu items which have been advertised
    □ Test sales volume in specific geographic areas
    □ Other, please specify _____

10. Which of the following best describes your firm's growth strategy for the next ten years?
    □ Market penetration (increasing sales volume in present markets without adding new units)
    □ Market development (selling current menu mix while adding new units)
    □ Product development (adding new menu items within current units)
    □ Integrative growth (purchase firms which supply food service goods and services)
    □ Conglomerate growth (purchase non-food service firms)

11. Which of the following market segmentation criteria is (are) used by your firm? (Check all that apply)
    □ Demographics (age, sex, income, occupation, education)
    □ Consumer behavior (purchase behavior and trends)
    □ Geographic (areas where consumers live and work)
    □ Other, please specify _____

_____

Please place an "X" in the box which best indicates the department or area which is responsible for the performance of the activities listed in the left hand column. If the activity is performed internally, is it performed by the marketing department, another department or jointly? If the activity isn't performed internally, is it performed externally to the firm or in a manner which is a combination of internal and external? If your firm doesn't undertake a specific activity, please place an "X" in the column labeled *Activity not Performed*.

Activity	Internal Department			External to Firm	Combination Internal/ External	Activity not Performed
	Marketing	Other	Joint			
12. Determine current market share						
13. Establish written short-term goals and policies						
14. Establish written long-term goals and policies						
15. Develop overall marketing plan for the firm						
16. Establish menu item prices						
17. Collect information on competitor prices on ongoing basis						
18. Evaluate pricing policies on ongoing basis						

TABLE 33.1   (Cont.)

19. Develop overall
    advertising plan
20. Create and place
    advertising
21. Evaluate the effectiveness
    of advertising
22. Evaluate customer's
    wants and needs
23. Study profit trends in
    markets by product
    categories
24. Develop new menu items
25. Test Marketing
26. Site Selection
27. Evaluate the firm's
    product life-cycle

28. What type of ownership best describes your firm?
    □ Independent
    □ Franchised independent
    □ Chain owned
    □ Chain headquarters
    □ Other, please specify _____.
29. For your firm's most recent fiscal year, indicate the gross sales volume.
    □ under $500,000
    □ $500,000−999,999
    □ $1,000,000−2,999,999
    □ $3,000,000−4,999,999
    □ $5,000,000−9,999,999
    □ $10,000,000−24,999,999
    □ $25,000,000−100,000,000
    □ more than $100,000,000
30. What percentage of your firm's gross sales is budgeted for all marketing and sales
    activities? _____%.
31. What percentage of your firm's gross sales is budgeted for the development of new products
    and services? _____%.

Strategies for Growth

During the 1960s and 1970s many food service firms experienced
rapid growth. New units were built and new markets were penetrated.
To date, the 1980s have been a decade of high interest rates, high rates
of inflation and a greatly reduced rate of growth for the food service
industry. Specifically, what are the most favored growth strategies for
the next ten years? Over a quarter (27%) of those firms surveyed have
adopted a strategy of market development, such as selling current menu
items while adding new units. Sixteen percent favor a product development strategy, such as adding new items to the menu in an attempt to
increase sales. Ten percent of the firms responding to the survey indicate that market penetration was the most favored strategy. They focus
on increasing unit sales and not building new units. However, nearly
half (47%) of the responding firms have adopted a strategy which combines two or more of the following: market penetration, market development, or product development. None of those firms responding indicate a desire to expand by acquiring a non-food service firm.

Performance of Specific Marketing Activities

Determining their current share of the market is most frequently performed by those firms with annual sales in excess of $100 million, as 90% of these firms perform this activity. Determining share of market is undertaken much less frequently by those firms with annual sales of less than $100 million. Twenty-five percent of all the food service firms surveyed utilize the services of a consultant to determine share of market.

Ninety-five percent of the firms surveyed have established written short-term marketing objectives. The responding firms indicate that these objectives are formulated most frequently: (1) by a joint effort involving both the marketing department and another internal department (46%); or (2) solely by the marketing department (38%). In 10% of those firms responding the services of a consultant are used to assist the firm in the formulation of these short-term objectives. Those firms with annual sales in excess of $100 million show a higher utilization of consultants than do those firms with less than $100 million in sales. A smaller percentage of firms have established written long-term marketing objectives than have established short-term objectives. Whereas 95% of the firms have established written short-term marketing objectives, 84% have established written long-term marketing objectives. Long-term marketing objectives are more likely to be established by those firms with annual sales in excess of $25 million than by those with annual sales of less than $25 million. Ninety-five percent of those firms with more than $25 million in sales establish written long-term marketing objectives, whereas 66% of those firms with less than $25 million in sales establish written long-term marketing objectives.

All of the firms responding to the survey establish an overall marketing plan. Nearly two thirds (64%) of these firms rely solely on the marketing department to perform this activity. In 21% of the firms, the marketing plan is developed jointly by the marketing department and another internal department. Fifteen percent of the firms utilize the services of a consultant who works with the firm's personnel to develop the overall marketing plan. Independently owned firms are much less likely to utilize consultants than are chain organizations.

CONCLUSION

This study represents a beginning survey effort in the food service marketing area. The conclusions discussed in the paragraphs which follow need to be researched further.

First, marketing as practiced by food service firms today has reached a level of professionalism. Most firms have adopted written marketing objectives in an attempt to plot the future direction of the firm. A variety of marketing activities are being performed such as determining share of market and pre-testing of advertisements.

Second, the fact that vice presidents often hold the final responsibility for marketing decisions indicates that the marketing function has established itself firmly within the framework of food service firms, in the same manner as operations or finance. Most food service firms employ between 3 and 15 individuals in the marketing department, another indication that marketing has established itself as an individual department.

Third, most food service firms have not yet adopted the more sophisticated marketing techniques commonly used by product oriented firms. For example, the percentage of sales method was indicated as the most common technique used to establish an advertising budget. However, more sophisticated methods such as the objective and task method are being used by food service firms with annual sales in excess of $100 million. Currently only a small percentage of food service firms pre-test advertisements.

Fourth, as might be anticipated, in larger food service firms the marketing department takes a more active role. Larger firms, defined as those with annual sales in excess of $100 million, show a higher utilization of long-term marketing objectives. These firms were also more likely to determine share of market and utilize the services of consultants than those firms with less than $100 million in annual sales.

Further research needs to be done in food service marketing. While additional information is needed concerning the practices of all food service firms, particular attention should be given to those firms with annual sales in excess of $100 million. These firms, because of their large asset base and higher level of sales are likely to implement more complex marketing practices which the rest of the industry will then begin to emulate.

34

The Growing Distance Between the Buyer and the User: Channels of Distribution

Michael A. Leven

In 1972 a report written by the hospitality accounting firm, Laventhol & Horwath, contained the following caveats:

1. There is little doubt that the potential within Europe as a source for tourism to the United States is great, that America is still seen as a highly desirable vacation location. Economically such a vacation need not be beyond the bounds of what much of the mass market would be prepared to pay.

2. As a secondary consideration hotels should prepare for new business and the new markets that will eventually develop. However frustrating it may be, there is little the lodging industry can do to hasten the availability of such new sources of business other than to join with other interested parties [I repeat, "other interested parties"] in making its needs and position heard in political quarters.

3. There is some evidence to suggest that air travel for the pleasure traveler is in the mature phase of its life cycle and as such may have developed into a commodity item rather than a highly differentiated product.

4. The foreign tourist market is highly price sensitive in choosing between vacation alternatives.

5. Marketing to tour operators and organizers rather than to the general public should be marketing policy.

6. Personnel and staff should be prepared to provide standardized products of adequate quality and adjust services to cope with mass

arrival and mass departures, full occupancy, and provide streamline service to many tourists who are unable to speak English.

7. Be prepared to adjust prices, accommodations and meals to suit the high volume, low-cost concept and price the services only slightly above variable costs to provide a contribution to fixed expense which might otherwise go unabsorbed.

These quotes appeared in 1972 and some of us, in fact most of us, have not yet begun, 9 years later, to pay attention to or to take action on the extraordinary changes and the extraordinary conditions that were prognosticated and are now affecting our industry and our livelihood. In this chapter I will highlight the areas that we should be concerned about and the areas that we *absolutely must pay attention* to so that development of our business in the future is assured.

CHANNELS OF DISTRIBUTION

Channels of distribution is a marketing term. In the hotel business it means simply the path by which a business firm or guest finally executes a reservation to use a facility. An agent or a tour operator, a reservation system, a referral system, a secretary club are examples of channels. For example, if you were in the retail business and you wanted to purchase goods for the store and you weren't able to purchase direct from the manufacturer, you would perhaps purchase from what you would call an area jobber. The area jobber then becomes an individual in the channel of distribution from the supplier to the individual receiving the goods. On the supply side, if you were the manufacturer trying to get your goods to the retail store, you might use a jobber for that purpose.

The customer, of course, has to pay the price for moving the product from the manufacturer to the middle distributor to the retailer. All of this adds to the cost of doing business and adds to the consumer purchase price. As an example, I once visited Korea on business and managed to get to the factory that produces Rawlings baseball gloves. I bought three baseball gloves for $5.60 each. The same glove sold in a sporting goods discount store in New York for $36.00. I bought directly from the manufacturer but between the manufacturer and the retail outlet channels existed, each of which has to make a profit, thus creating an end of the line retail price of $36.00.

The same thing has happened in our industry. Twenty years ago a travel agent was an uncommon source of business for a commercial hotel; so uncommon, in fact, that many hotels refused to pay attention them and today some still do not. Travel agents were recognized as somewhat important, a necessary evil, in the distribution system of a resort business off shore, not domestic. Actually, we would have preferred to forget that they existed at all. At the same time, tour operators, airlines, corporate reservation systems, corporate traffic departments and other similar distribution channels also did not receive a great deal of attention. The hotel industry suffered then and does today from the "marketing myopia" syndrome defined in Theodore Levitt's (1960) widely acclaimed article on why businesses fail. Marketing myopia is presented as the failure to see oneself in the big picture. It represents introspective rather than external marketing philosophy.

Many would identify this industry as the hotel industry. Perhaps more would identify it as the hospitality industry. But very few would identify our industry as the travel industry. This omission pinpoints the same mistake that created failure for the railroad industry and is helping to create failure in the airline industry. We are part of the travel industry and we must understand it, watch it, bend to it, take action and participate in its development and potential if we are to reach our success potential. Levitt's article emphasizes that the railroad industry failed because its leaders thought they were in the railroad business rather than the travel business. Today we are a part of this travel business and the channels of distribution are far more complex between the customer and the hospitality industry.

There is an old cartoon in which Pogo states, "We have met the enemy and they are us," not the customer and not the distribution channel—us! We have paid little or no attention to the fact that being in the travel industry requires a sensitivity to what is going on in the other elements of the travel mix. We cannot be afraid of change but need to take advantage of it for our benefit. In 1829 Martin Van Buren, Governor of New York, wrote the following to President Andrew Jackson:

The canal system of this country is being threatened by the spread of a new form of transportation known as 'railroads'. The federal government must preserve the canals for the following reasons: 1), If canal boats are supplanted by 'railroads' serious unemployment will result. Captains, cooks, drivers, hostelers, repairmen and lock tenders will be left without means of livelihood, not to mention the numerous farmers now employed in growing hay for horses; 2), Boat builders would suffer and tow-line, whip and harness makers would be left destitute; 3), Canal boats are absolutely essential to the defense of the United States. In the event of the expected trouble with England, the Erie Canal would be the only means by which we could ever move the supplies so vital to waging modern war.

For the above-mentioned reasons the government should create an Interstate Commerce Commission to protect the American people from the evils of 'railroads' and to preserve the canals for posterity. As you may well know, Mr.

President, 'railroad' carriages are pulled at the enormous speed of 15 miles per hour by engines which, in addition to endangering life and limb of passengers, roar and snort their way through the livestock and frightening women and children. The Almighty certainly never intended that people should travel at such breakneck speed.

Of course, in spite of Van Buren's "marketing myopia," we elected him President; his letter needs no further elaboration.

On January 29, 1981 a Travel Weekly "Month in Review" article contained the following information:

1. The CAB proposal authorized the ATC and scheduled airlines to pay travel agents commission on official government travel bookings. Under this ruling travel agencies are now permitted to reimburse certain expenses of the corporations' employees who operate in-plant travel agency locations.

2. The air traffic conference reported that four travel agencies received appointments to operate at airport locations.

3. President Carter signed into law a foreign convention tax bill allowing business deductions for meetings if they are reasonable.

4. Competitive marketing case hearings finally get underway—competitive marketing, net fares, variable commissions are major topics of discussion.

Environmental changes and impacts of this type are going on every single day. Needless to say some of these items directly and absolutely affect the hotel industry and the channels of distribution from which it gets its business. Do we still believe we are in an industry that can continue to pass on all increased distribution costs to our customer? Or will we, like the airlines, reach a point in time where the increased pricing will cut off the demand for our services, allowing budget substitutes to dominate the market? Obviously we can pass on costs to those customers who must be in a particular location at a particular time, but that only represents about 50% of the so-called indicated hotel-travel base. The other 50% is discretionary travel. Understanding these particular channels of distribution surely will lead us to develop marketing and operational strategies that are more different and responsive to today's environment.

CHANGING CHANNELS

Let me be more specific about some of the absolutes in the distribution system that are changing today and bear watching.

The Travel Agent

His role has moved from a distributor of our resort product to a distributor of our commercial hotel room. The present position of the travel agent in in-plant corporate involvement indicates that in the next few years he will be a major factor in our commercial business. This means commercial business will be subjected to commissions and increased costs. This travel agent whom we didn't want to pay commissions to for individual or group business has now emerged as the major factor in the commercial business area.

Today some travel agencies control enormous amounts of bookings for hotel rooms. Some use the corporate rate and some use a commmissionable rate. If we are not aware of their impact and if we don't act upon it, we will not understand our pricing, cost structure and marketing capabilities of the future.

Changes can occur very quickly and very substantially.

The Airlines

The airline and CAB marketing cases referred to previously may mean that the airlines will soon sell bulk tickets at a discount directly to major operations and corporations. The airlines will have different commission structures for different types of agents. Thus, the airlines are now a major factor in our distribution system today. They take many of our reservations and transport most of our traffic.

Are we aware that that is going on in the airline part of the travel industry? We say it's the airline business but, in fact, it's the travel business. What is happening to the airlines directly absolutely affects how many beds we sell, how many meals we serve, how many drinks we pour. The airlines can be marketing arms, or they can be marketing destruction in any particular destination area. A change in their rate structure, their equipment, their management, or their fare structure affects the hotel business and the others in the distribution system. The interdependence of all the channels becomes more and more obvious.

The Tour Operator

The channel of distribution recognized in the 1972 Laventhol & Horwath article is the tour operator. Laventhol & Horwath warned that we would have to work with tour operators. Yet, how many of us do? How many of us know how tour operators work? What is important to the tour operator? What does he run his business? What we do know is to price and deal according to *our* needs. Do we really understand the tour operators' needs? I submit that if we are unable to understand the basic needs of our distribution channels that we will be unable to have those channels deliver customers to us. The spector of the early 1970s and the oversupply of hotel rooms bodes ominously on the horizon. Many of the cities in the United States today are perilously close to where they were in 1974. We have been euphoric about the late 1970s with what we have been able to do with our rates. Today we charge $100 for a room that was $26 in 1978 and the customers seem to be absorbing it—well, at least they seemed that way until the last few months. Of course, we can always blame the economy. Will as many people be traveling? Do they want to pay the freight or will they buy a car instead? We blamed the economy in 1974 and that didn't help when the bank foreclosed. The spector of the early 1970s, the euphoria of the late 1970s, and the early returns on the 1980s suggest that these are going to be very difficult times and we will have to come to grips with the travel agent, the airline and the tour operator.

ADDITIONAL CHANNELS

There are other channels to think about, such as government travel. A large part of our business today is government travel. It used to book us directly; now the government has authorized travel agents to handle their travel.

Some airlines, small fleets of carriers like Midway Airlines and Southwest Airlines whom you may have never heard of before, are now in the business of discounting their tickets for government travel. Thus, feeder airlines have become part of the distribution channel and this tactic is going to continue to grow as the major scheduled carriers get out of the unprofitable short-haul business.

Are there hotels whose rate structure and empty room capability could handle government business if delivered by Midway Airlines on an incremental "fill the empty room" basis? Certainly, but is there anybody who has talked to Midway Airlines about building a seat and a bed program for government people? Probably not. If you look at them as blocks in the road between you and the customer, they will work against you.

Some additional channels are on the horizon: your own 800 number service, perhaps a satellite system, a computer system, a manual system. Manual systems are a major channel for us. If AT & T is allowed to raise its rates on WATS lines by 60%, will you be able to maintain the same channel of distribution, or will it move to another channel? In other words, will you develop another channel of distribution or will you just try to pass on the cost of doing business to the customer? Can we risk reaching the point where the non-price-sensitive business man, the bottom 50% of our business, is going to say travel costs too much and choose to have a satellite TV meeting. Some chains have been successful in tele-conferencing activity but a $500 rental for a ballroom for the day is never going to replace the profitability of a couple of hundred sleeping rooms. Further, you don't need a hotel ballroom to have a tele-conferencing situation; eventually it can go right into the company headquarters office.

What is happening to the corporate traffic department and what changes can we expect in that channel of distribution? In-plant agencies are coming in and the corporate traffic department is on the way out. However, if the CAB marketing case rules the other way, the travel agent could be out of in-plants and the corporate traffic department could be back in.

We cannot react passively, rather we must look for the opportunities. We need to stop having a kind of myopic approach to our business and get up on top of the opportunities that are presented to us by a myriad of exciting changes that are going on.

PROACTING INSTEAD OF REACTING

Today, we're buried in the day-to-day situations such as someone's got this problem and someone's got that one; we have OSHA, the EEOC and all the other kinds of regulations; we have fire safety, food cost and droughts. We have this and that and we're buried in both.

Fifty-two years ago Mr. Edward C. Romine, CPA for Horwath and Horwath in Toronto, made the following observation:

The ability to control income, food costs and operating expenses is no longer the most important factor in the hotel business for regardless of how efficiently your hotel is operated it will not be successful unless sufficient sales can be obtained. Knowledge of sales and sales method is indispensable to the hotel business. In fact, success is now largely measured by the ability to sell a hotel's services. With all due respect for the claims of our advertising friends, advertising alone will not solve this problem. Every successful business man today is devoting more attention to distributing his product than to producing it. We are in a buyer's market—a race for the guests where the position of the business promotion managers begins to creep into the hotel industry. He must first of all be a salesman. Knowledge of the hotel industry is of secondary importance. In the future much more attention will be given by successful hotel men to sales promotion and merchandising.

In spite of Mr. Romine's warning in 1929, myopia once again set in. Today, there isn't a choice any more. The vice president and general manager of at least one hotel in Hawaii spends 80% of his time going to the civic association banquets. And if he is successful, he is successful because he cannot depend on his sales department alone. It is a day-to-day job; and part and parcel of that job is not paying attention to the nitty gritty of our business, but paying attention to the big picture in the channels of distribution and what is happening to them.

Publications worth reading are Monthly Review, put out by *Travel Weekly*, with news of the travel business, and the travel management newsletter published weekly by the Official Airline Guides. The travel management newsletter lists the events in air transport, travel agencies, tourism, hotels and other relevant areas. Third, read on a regular basis one of the travel/trade publications, such as the *Travel Agent* or *Travel Weekly*. Last, *Travel Weekly* publishes each January an economic survey of the travel industry which runs the gamut of government, travel agents, cruise business, airlines, world tourism, and so forth.

If you do not have time for all this reading, make sure that someone does it all for you. More than that, spend some time keeping up with what is happening in the travel industry, the industry on which we are dependent for our future. Take the time to learn the elements of the channels of distribution because we are very, very far from our customers. Our customers' decisions are being controlled by more than just the individual user today more than ever before, and that gap will continue to widen in the future.

Consumers will continue to play the starring role, but who are our consumers? They seem to be taking many different roles at various purchasing levels. Consumers may be wholesalers, industrial buyers, retail buyers or purchasing agents so that the buyer is not the actual user, as was mentioned before. The real purchasing influence may lie somewhere else. For example, a student is a user of education but the buyer is the parent who pays the tuition.

An organization cannot plan unless it knows something about the market universe in which it operates, or plans to operate, and the needs of the consumer or channels of distribution it serves. Environmental forces have changed markets overnight and competitive strategies have mercilessly undermined less astute marketers.

The consumer has become more sophisticated and more inclined to examine alternatives. Only by dealing with a market plan and understanding channels can we hope to be effective in the overheated atmosphere of today's marketplace. The market universe can turn up hidden opportunities as easily as it can swallow others. It is our mandate to find out how to minimize the risk of failure and how to maximize our knowledge and planning for the certainty of unpredictable change. To paraphrase an old saying, there are really three kinds of industries: (1) the kind of industry that makes things happen; (2) the kind of industry that watches things happen; and (3) the kind of industry that wakes up and says, "What happened?" Let's not allow the travel industry to be the industry that says, "What happened?"

35

Positioning Marketing for Its Future Role

Sig S. Front

If you look at the history of any business you find that good marketing is the truest barometer of whether a company or corporation has done a good job over the long-haul, both in comparison to its competition and as a measure of its success. No matter what business you are in, or what phase of it you control, marketing is as important as any function that falls within your responsibility and authority. Yet the higher up the ladder many executives go, the less time many spend in the marketing functions. It is as if that particular responsibility falls to people either further down the ladder or younger in the organization, and often without the full support and guidance of the best minds higher up in that organization.

Perhaps we are not giving marketing the attention that we should. In the final analysis two things are completely inseparable: marketing and profits. The right profits are not necessarily the profits we might be making, but the ones we could be making.

Certainly, many will contend that we have a pretty good chance of doing greater and better things than ever in the future. In the decade to come, millions more people will travel because they are going to have more time and money and more of a desire to go places. If we take more of the fear out of travel, of just going to a restaurant, of making reservations, or of getting tickets for entertainment or, simply, if we take the mystery out of travel and activities within the hospitality business, we will increase the amount of business each of us does in the future. We'll still be competing with other industries for the discretionary dollar, but each of our businesses should grow. The question is whether you will get your share. One thing will determine that. *Marketing!*

MARKETING AS A BUSINESS GENERATOR

The hospitality business is like farming because we actually sell futures. A farmer plants his seeds in order to harvest a crop months later. The commodity market bets on that farmer's capability and luck. There's no difference in the way we deal in futures. We are as much in the commodity market as a farmer but we have a lot more going for us. The difference is that our seeds are our sales people and we reap a harvest from what those people plant.

A corny analogy? Perhaps, but it fits. What other business can sell group business, catering and banquet functions, trade shows, exhibits, major association business conferences, tours and sundry business as far in advance as we do in the hospitality industry? Many hotels around the world are now booking as much as 25 to 30% occupancy at least one year in advance. In some cases that business is on the books 5 and 8 years in advance for those hotels or resorts with large conference facilities. No matter what phase of the industry you are in, that's quite an insurance policy for business.

At the same time one of the most important responsibilities you have is to see that your business has been positioned and that everything possible has been done to market your services 100%. How much do you know about the marketing mix of your business? Do you know where your customers come from and why they are utilizing your services instead of someone else's? There is a great deal of talk about this in the industry, but how many, as individuals, spend time thinking about it, participating in it, and helping to make the marketing function actually happen?

Some years ago there was a hotel company that was building a large new magnificent hotel and spending top dollar to do it. One of the top executives who had come out of the controlling and financial side of operations decided to reduce the size of the sales department. He felt that the hotel would produce enough business on its own because of its magnificence. The Director of Sales and Marketing of that hotel could not get his boss to give him the kind of sales staff that he felt was needed to produce year-round occupancy to its maximum potential.

At a meeting where the subject was discussed, a vice president of the company said to the top executive, "Let me ask you a question. What do you think it would be like after having built this magnificent new hotel, if you had not provided an electrical plant for the building? What would it be like to not be able to turn on the lights, run the air conditioning and so forth?" "What's that got to do with it?" replied the executive. "Well, you're about to leave out a generator as important as electricity is for the lights and air conditioning. Sales and marketing are nothing more than a generator and you can't do it on a halfway basis. You have to have

100% availability of lighting and air conditioning; you also have to have 100% availability of marketing of the rooms." He got the point across and it's a crucial one to always keep in mind.

MARKETING'S FUTURE ROLE

Let's focus on the future and how we can personally affect it. How are we going to contribute to tomorrow and its mix of business? Not our company or co-workers, not our university, but we personally. It is what we do that makes a difference. Each of us can make a tremendous difference if we want to.

What form might marketing take in the future? Will it be a hard sell situation? You bet it will. We've got to do it with quality, flair and the excitement that people are looking for in their lives. This is our business and it is our energies and creativity that will make the difference in what happens tomorrow. That means what happens in 1985, in 1989, in 1995 is going to have our own creative stamps on it.

People tell us that there are going to be many differences in those years. I don't doubt that. Certainly, we'll have computers doing more things than anyone can imagine. But it will still be a world of people. In fact, by the 1990s the people we will serve might be completely bored with computers, electronic gear, robots and other devices. A human being at the front door, the reception desk, behind the bar or seating us at a good restaurant may be a welcome relief.

The hospitality industry could well be an oasis in a desert of electronic impartiality. In the early 1990s even gas stations will be completely unattended. Your car that won't use gas will be automatically energized, cleaned and programmed in a one-stop computerized auto-park. When you are flying you will be accompanied by hundreds of people, possibly a thousand or more. Your luggage won't be on the same aircraft that you are on. It will be sent ahead to be waiting for you when you arrive. Or you may go by train. By that time there will be a few fast tracks available in the eastern corridor and possibly on the west coast, high-speed trains traveling up to 200 m.p.h. By 1995 to the year 2000 those trains could be travelling up to 300 m.p.h.

So, what will hotels be doing? Will there be robots serving food? Checking you into the hotel? Making martinis? Some hotels might do that, but most hotels will be a refreshing contrast.

You can well imagine the role that this industry will play by holding on to the few remaining graces of hospitality: the service, the friendliness, the warmth, the entertainment—all of these things will be needed, wanted and desired by people who are otherwise surrounded by the chill of technology.

The word hospitality is going to mean more than it ever has. We simply can't treat customers with impartiality. Well, possibly some can. I can imagine some of the new inventions: you walk up to a front desk, a camera focuses in on your identification card, reads your number, records everything and hands you a room entry card. You enter into an immaculate room with the latest of everything. Suddenly you decide to get out and go to a place where there are people, people who are going to welcome you with the warmness that you are looking for. So, they make a few mistakes, goof up, overcook your steak or spill some soup, you will say "thank you Lord for people, people; I have people around me."

What does this all have to do with marketing? We are going to have to make decisions on how these hotels are going to operate well into the 21st century. Some of us are going to be contributing to those decisions on what this industry is going to look like then. Our business has not changed greatly over the years and there is no need for it to do so in the future, not drastically. Certainly we must keep up with the type of technology that will be in demand and that will improve operations, but we have still got to keep the human element involved. And that is where we all come in.

In one facet of this business, conventions and meetings, there is much discussion today about teleconferencing: creating meetings for people who will be located throughout the country or around the world through the use of telephone lines and cameras. We will be able to conduct large meetings without having to gather the participants all in one location.

I think that is possible. Certainly teleconferencing is going to play a role in the future. But what kind of role is another question. Will large regional, national, international conventions be split up into 14, 25 or 50 locations? A few might, those that do not need anything other than a brief program of basic information that can be disseminated quickly.

However, there will always be a need for people to gather together for the purpose of not only receiving information on behalf of their profession, business, or other associated endeavors, but also to be able to react to that information with their peers, competitors, suppliers and others, all of whom are also vitally interested in that particular profession or business. It is the shoulder-to-shoulder conversation and the side discussions that give you the sounding board, the experience, and the testing of ideas. This is an experience that gives the attendee the confidence of judgment that just cannot be acquired through a television camera. Teleconferencing can be a good service to small corporate meetings, some committee meetings of associations and, in a few cases, even motivational meetings, but there will always be those meetings where it will simply be inadequate to perform the necessary function of bringing people together.

Let us consider for a moment travel agents, tour operators, and airlines and how they are going to be a part of what we are going to do in the future. We will have to work even more closely with them so that all of us, in a joint effort, can sell more travel. Many people will be receiving travel awards as part of the economic package they get from their companies. Students will have travel included as part of their education. People will be able to pick out different types of holiday trips, business trips and other types of travel on their home television screen by simply using a computer attached to the television.

The link with travel companies, airlines, hotels and others is going to be a relatively uncomplicated situation. Travel agents will be a part of the total service. Not only will they be able to confirm everything through one source, but they will also arrange for baggage to be flown ahead of time, they will take care of other arrangements that are not included in the package, and they will make sure that the right wardrobe with your own proper size will be waiting on your arrival at a destination hotel.

I believe in the future that travelers to resorts and some foreign countries will often wear disposable clothing. It will be great clothing—comfortable, light, disposable, and rather inexpensive and it will be available to you at certain destinations. This means that you will not have to own several different types of clothing. If you live in Boston you can leave in February and not worry about having your summer wardrobe ready for your trip to Hawaii, or wherever, for a weekend.

Travel is going to be important. People are going to live a lot longer and travel is going to be a great part of their lives. Look back 25 or 50 years and ask yourself if people during that time ever dreamed of things that we now take for granted. What we are going to do in the next 10 to 15 years will far surpass all of the creativity, the inventions, the services, and many other facets of our lives that came into existence in the last 50 years. The hospitality industry is going to be more important than ever.

We have to prepare for that future. We have to market for it. One job is to prepare the young people who are going to step into the travel industry that will serve the public in an exciting and rewarding way.

It will not all be smooth sailing. There will be times when you will think it's just not working. The main thing is to be realistic and always run a little scared of what your business is going to be like next month or next year. Spend 25% of your time thinking about and actually helping to market your business. If you are in education, emphasize that to your students. It is that kind of an attitude, that marketing approach that will enable them and us to keep moving ahead in the future.

POSITIONING MARKETING

We have learned a great deal just in the last few years about how important it is to be able to market and move people from one part of the world to the other. More Europeans are enjoying trips to North America, more people from North America are going abroad and to different locations. There are so many new marketing opportunities for a restaurant, a hotel, airlines and rent-a-car companies. New languages have to be spoken, new ways of handling credit have to be found, new kinds of communication and other changes in attitudes have to be understood in order to better serve different people from different parts of the world.

As you participate in these endeavors day by day, keep one word uppermost in your mind as often as possible: *marketing*. Whatever the discussion, whether it involves controlling, training, food and beverages, even casino operations, marketing must play a role. If it doesn't you haven't positioned it on a high enough level, or you don't have the right people or the right experience handling that function. It is up to us to help sales people become marketing people. It is up to us to give them that type of experience and capability, and to place them into all of our activities. These are the people who will contribute to the final goal of running a magnificent operation and providing a great service to the public as well as making good profits.

Not too many of us are geniuses and there won't be too many in the future. There will be a lot of people who are willing to work hard, to learn, to participate on the team; all of these need encouragement and leadership. It is these people who will come up with the ideas, the new ways of doing things. These are the type of people who will innovate, provide better service and stir up the public to buy your product more than that of the competition. Someday we will look back and realize how many people have helped in creating the hospitality industry of tomorrow because we positioned marketing in its proper role as the generator of future business.

36

Marketing to the Woman Traveler[1]

Nita Lloyd, CHSE

This paper is about Eve and her place in the current travel patterns all over the world today—and about her importance to the hospitality industry. This woman could be Eve Brown, Eve Smith, or even Eve Doe; but rest assured, there is an Eve who travels and who represents an increasing portion of the industry's growth potential. It has been widely reported that career women are fast becoming as active as men in the world of travel. This has been coming on for several years and yet some of us have not really included Eve in our market plans.

EVE NUMBER ONE

First, there is an Eve who travels for pleasure. She may be traveling with her husband, she may be traveling to meet her husband or she may not even be married. She may be a single, a career-minded woman, looking for relaxation through travel. Eve's horizons are broader than ever before. She's developed specific and particular tastes in vacation destinations. She might be looking for a seaside resort, prefer a shopping spree in a major fashion center or just be visiting friends or relatives. For whatever reasons, her travel needs are important and they must be recognized.

This Eve is an adventurous lady. She vacations with a purpose, she wants to see new and interesting things: big city excitement, quaint restaurants, famous landmarks; and she looks for luxurious accommodations. She enjoys being pampered. She tends to splurge during her leisure travel. She will plan far in advance by pouring over brochures.

---

[1]A version of this paper was previously published in HSMA World.

She's attracted by the extras that make her trip special, something that she can remember.

Eve is turned off by brochures that picture the stereotyped sex symbol in a bikini. She wants to see what the hotel offers and what she can do if she decides to vacation there. She likes activity. Her leisure time is precious and she wants to use it to its fullest advantage. She responds to descriptive brochures, to special amenities and to recognition.

Eve is also becoming an international Eve. She now carries a passport and travelers checks and she is becoming increasingly bilingual. Eve appears to be somewhat more liberal now than perhaps in the past, and this has in some instances caused problems at the front desk.

EVE NUMBER TWO

Let us go on to Eve #2 who is what I call the experienced Eve. She has been traveling for quite some time because her job requires it. She has learned to cope, to some extent, with most of the difficulties and challenges that business travel brings. But that does not mean she likes them. She may suffer in silence but she responds with loyalty to the hotels that treat her the way she wants to be treated.

Eve knows how to make reservations. And she knows how to pack. She can hail a cab, she can carry her own bags and she can even plan a convention. But she has had her share of trials and tribulations too. She has been ignored, insulted and hassled. She is scared because she has been propositioned. And she has prejudged and has the emotional scars to prove it.

Many business women relate to this Eve. She is the one who is ignored by the airline stewardess while she watches the smiles and friendly service come quickly for that nearby male traveler. She is also the one left waiting in the lobby while the bellman tends more quickly to that prosperous looking gentleman with less luggage than she has. This is the Eve that is seated in the almost empty dining room, way back, behind the pillar and next to the kitchen door at a table with no light, facing the wall. Exaggerated, perhaps, but it happens.

This Eve tires quickly of the hoteliers who continue to ignore her. She is critical, but she is also fair. She understands that the bottom line in operations can prevent some of the frills she would like, but certain things will bring her back often.

Eve looks for hotels and restaurants whose employees have good and friendly attitudes, employees who are hospitable—no one likes a grouch at the front desk. Another sore spot for this Eve is the frequent automatic assumption that she is the wife of one of the business men who may be checking in when she is. She cringes at being called "dear" or "sweetie" by the phone operator or by the waitress. She has her own name, and we must train our staff to use it, and to use it correctly. Eve wants to be called Miss Brown, Miss Smith, or Miss Doe. This Eve also looks for security in accommodations. She needs to feel safe as well as comfortable and wants to feel that the security of the hotel she chooses is dependable.

Eve #2 has been traveling on business for quite some time, and there are many times when she would like to relax with a cocktail after a busy day or before dinner, but she usually has difficulty finding a lounge that is comfortable for her as a woman, a lounge that is inviting without being suggestive. She appreciates and enjoys the concept of lobby bars that are well lit and spacious, where she doesn't have to worry about an attempted pickup.

This Eve's responsibilities may also include occasional entertaining, and she dreads the old "menu—wine list—check" merry-go-round. She wonders why restaurateurs do not teach their staff to place the check in the middle of the table rather than automatically assume that the man is host every time.

Our experienced Eve travels frequently and she is probably on a very good expense account. She tends to overtip to get good service. She undoubtedly lives very well. We must keep her as a satisfied client and keep her coming back, again and again. This Eve is a highly desirable customer for us—and can actually act as a referral. If treated properly she will spread the word when she finds the type of accommodations she is looking for, the quality of service she can enjoy, and the welcome, inviting atmosphere that makes her feel comfortable.

This Eve would like to see more business women pictured in television and radio ads, magazines and trade journal advertising geared toward the travel market. She is flattered and responsive to hotel brochures that give her recognition and that make her travel arrangements easier and less time consuming. She's been around for quite awhile and it is time we recognized her.

EVE NUMBER THREE

Now let's look at another Eve, Eve #3. This is the Eve that is part of the new wave of women on the move in their careers. Perhaps she has been on the job for several years and has recently been promoted to a position which requires travel for her company, or she could even be one of the so called "displaced homemakers" now entering the job market in such massive numbers; or she may even be the Eve who recently left the university to take a position which requires travel.

The needs of this Eve are very important. She is making her way in the business world and she needs all the help we can give her. She is somewhat unsure, very cautious, and will respond through loyalty to those of us who will recognize her special needs and help her with them.

This Eve is anxious to learn. She tends to emulate her peers but she still has butterflies in her stomach when making travel plans. Previously she depended on others to handle this for her: her husband, a friend, her parents. She may even now have a secretary or travel agent but she still wants to handle arrangements first hand, by herself.

She is a novice, and knows it, but certainly doesn't need to be reminded by our industry. She looks for all the things Eve #2 looks for and even more. She needs support, relates to well-known hotel names and in many instances will pay a little more to feel safe and secure.

This Eve will be verbally critical of rooms that are not clean, rooms that have poor lighting and not enough electrical outlets. She looks for hotels that offer full-length mirrors, plenty of desk and counter space and extra hangers in her closet. She appreciates 24-hour housekeeping and 24-hour room service. She would like printed material in the room that tells her about shopping locations, hairdressers, and other good restaurants. She would welcome the chance to use health club facilities which, in many cases, have previously been reserved for just her male peers. A map of the city in her room would save her time in getting around.

Eve feels safer in hotels that have well-lit and monitored corridors, rooms that have security locks and peepholes in the door. She craves a feeling of safety and security when she travels—perhaps a little more than her more experienced career sister does.

ALL THREE EVES

All three Eves will be your friends for life if you recognize them not only as business travelers but also as women who may forget a hairdrier, a makeup mirror, or an over-sized shower cap. If you can make these available, either in her room or through the housekeeper, I guarantee she will remember your hotel when she travels. But don't forget to let her know that these extras are available and how she can find them by using tent cards in the room or some other means of communication.

It is extremely interesting to note that in almost every instance our traveling Eve is looking for the very same things that her male counterpart is also seeking: a clean room with good security, friendly service, hospitable atmosphere at a reasonable cost, personnel with good attitudes, and most important, recognition.

The travel trends indicate that Eve is here to stay. However each of us feels about the so called "women's movement," because of our industry and because of the services it offers, we must be aware of the "movement of women," in its truest sense. Only then can we obtain our share of this increasing market through new and repeated business.

This is a growth opportunity for our industry, perhaps more competitive than ever before. Eve is a very important lady to all of us as she carries her portfolio into the challenge of the 1980s. Eve will continue to increase in numbers and she will increase in experience. She's ready to be wooed and she's willing to be won. We'd better be ready for her.

37

Hospitality Marketing: What Business Are We In?[1]

David C. Dorf, CHSE

The start of each new decade seems to be a logical time to do some forecasting, some probability analysis, some future "state of the art" speculations—and I'm certainly not the first person to take advantage of this opportunity, nor will I be the last. And I do so fully recognizing the dangers of prophesy.

PRACTICAL PROPHESY

Prophesy, thought, does have some practical benefits, especially for those of us involved in hospitality industry marketing.

First of all, marketing—by definition—includes the establishment of long-range programs for attracting, developing, maintaining, and extending profitable business. Much of the business you will be getting in 1982, 1983, even 1985 and beyond, has to be worked on and sold today... just as much of the business you enjoy now was initially developed and secured in the 1970s.

To properly accommodate and service tomorrow's business, even though you may book it today, means you will have to "crystal ball" certain considerations of the future. And looking at it from the marketing viewpoint, this very specifically relates to anticipating *future* needs and desires of your customers—and then properly preparing yourselves ahead of time to meet this challenge.

There's a key word involved here, because the images in a crystal ball are not static. They are always changing, since the future is based on a

---

[1] A version of this paper was published in HSMA World, September/October 1980, 11–17.

whole set of variables. That key word is *"flexibility"*: one of the most important concepts in hotel/motor inn marketing.

A second reason for prophesying: one of the main reasons why we would want to look toward the future in the first place and speculate what our industry might be like 3, 4, 5, and 10 years from now is that this allows us to anticipate probable conditions, and thus we can prepare *contingency plans* to cover any changes in forecasted conditions with more "flexibility".

To give some semblance of order to this discussion, here are three different crystal balls:

1. One which will *forecast* what I believe will be taking place over the next 10 years.

2. A second one which will show my personal *hopes* as to what should evolve over this decade...and,

3. A third crystal ball which will offer some insight as to the *outside forces* we may have to contend with which may affect both our industry and the way we do business.

Before we gaze into any of these crystal balls, however, we have to set a proper foundation. We have to establish some basic premises, so that we can more correctly read or interpret the images of things to come.

THE NATURE OF OUR BUSINESS

Let us recognize right at the start that we are NOT in the business of selling hotels. Our products are NOT rooms, food & beverage, or space. In fact, to really be accurate, we are not in the business of selling *anything*. People do not buy things or features...they purchase *benefits*. And each person purchases only those sets of benefits which specifically satisfy his or her own personal and/or professional needs, wants, desires, hopes, aspirations, and dreams. Our marketing challenge is not one of selling better; it's one of *motivating* better. We in marketing are really in the business of motivating people to purchase those benefits which satisfy their very specific (and often very changing) needs and wants.

We must also be aware of the true nature of our business—not just from our viewpoint, but more importantly, from that of the *customer*. If you ask hoteliers what business they are in, they will usually respond that they are in the lodging or accommodations field, the service industry, the people business, the hospitality industry, and so forth. All of these answers are right—but only partly.

Ask customers what business we are in; as far as they are concerned here, we are in the business of satisfying them. To put it just slightly differently, we are actually in the "problem-solving" business. Realizing this and acting upon it will help set us on the right direction as far as profitable marketing in the 1980s.

To understand this problem-solving function, keep in mind the three broad reasons why people travel and thus utilize hotel accommodations:

1. Business.
2. Pleasure (Leisure).
3. Health (or Physical/Mental Fitness).

Since a person can travel either independently—alone (or including the family)—or within an organized group, you come up with six basic categories of hotel users.

Sample "Problem-Solving" Roles

To illustrate the "problem-solving" role of our industry, let's take a look at several of these categories.

Groups organized for business purposes can be divided into two main sections: company or corporate business and the association or congress market. Let's consider the latter, and specifically the problems of the association meeting planner or the congress organizer. What are they most concerned about? Basically, it is to find a site location and facility which can be attractive and at the same time *best* house, feed, and have the space for a group of people who have come together because each individual in the group wants to know more about the current state of the profession he belongs to; wants to have a forum for the exchange of ideas; and wishes to fraternize and extend personal relationships with peers in the same occupation or trade. So you thus have the needs of the individual attendees, which in combination create needs on the part of the organizers who bring them together.

Our responsibility when we host such a gathering is to be able to solve the myriad of problems, needs, wants, and desires of both the people running the meetings and functions and those of the individuals who are in attendance.

Now, let us look at the problems of a market we ourselves have all been part of...that of the *individual leisure traveler*. What are his or her problems? Usually it can be boiled down to a need on the part of the individual to "get away" from familiar business, social, and domestic surroundings ("get out of the rut"); to break away from the mental confines of everyday routine; to extend one's horizons; for some, to "swing away" and seek the new and the different; and for others, to find space, solitude, and silence.

You'll note that in these examples the concept of "satisfying needs" is synonymous with "solving problems", and, in fact, the two phrases are virtually interchangeable.

Since the problem-solving concept will be so essential in our marketing endeavors during this decade, I'd like to offer some key, though basic, pointers on this subject.

Basic Problem Analysis

1. We never will, or should, have the option of saying to any customer, "I'm sorry, but I just don't have time for your problem." We're in a 24-hour, 7-day-a-week business—and most customer problems or needs are *immediate,* ones which cannot be "put off ".

2. We can, however, be *selective* in our problem-solving efforts. We can, and should, become *specialists* by going after those market segments we can *best* satisfy. We can do this by developing a unique product with specific features, which can then be translated into specific benefits which can best solve the specific needs and wants of specified groups of people. In simpler words, we have to find the best markets for our particular property. We have to position ourselves in the marketplace; we can't profitably be all things to all people.

3. We must recognize that the same person can have entirely different problems, totally different sets of both real and perceived needs, depending upon which "role" he or she assumes at a particular time. The needs of a person required to attend a sales training session put on by his company (a command performance "you will attend") will be quite different from the needs and desires of the same person on a leisurely weekend vacation with his family. Also, a person can assume a combination of different roles within the same travel experience. A 62-year-old woman from overseas traveling on business represents at least four different major market segments—with four different sets of needs—which can surface in all sorts of combinations depending on the circumstances.

4. We must also be aware that the same person can have different problems or needs, depending on *where* he is. If at "home", for example, in a property or restaurant where he is well known, he will act confident and active; in a more distant and unfamiliar destination, he may act more passive and less confident. This is also tied into travel experience: the first-time traveler to a new destination acts completely different from the person to whom that same destination is a virtual "second home".

5. People are also looking more and more for the different, the novel,

the ingenious, or the creative solution to common problems...they are not necessarily satisfied with traditional solutions. How many times have you had a good customer come to you and implore, "Do something *different* for me!" I'm sure you face this challenge all the time. The company meeting planner who wants a different room arrangement for his training sessions, the chairlady of the local garden club who wants you to do something "new and daring" for her annual end-of-the-year dinner-dance, the congress meeting planner who wants a new theme for his annual meeting, the luncheon chairman who wants something besides chicken or steak.

6. In solving all of these problems we also have to be cognizant that there is no one way, or best way, or correct way.

    a. What works for one property can be disastrous if tried in a similar style property across the street.

    b. What works for one particular market segment could be costly and non-productive if attempted for another type of market.

    c. What is effective today could, in light of changing conditions, be totally unproductive tomorrow.

OUR "REAL" COMPETITION

The next overall preliminary thought is the awareness of our *real competition*. It's not just other properties, other destinations—or for those of you in resorts, not just campers, recreational vehicles, or suburban "backyard resorts".

It is also the new technology which has sprouted up around us and created new products that compete for the consumer's discretionary income—his or her disposable dollars. The home entertainment center, the video-cassette recorder, the home video-camera and the home computer center each can cost about the same as a vacation but the marketers of these products are doing an effective job of instilling in the minds of the public that these items are "household necessities" and not one-shot frivolous indulgences.

By doing so, they are competing for the monies which very well could have found their way into hotel and restaurant properties.

Customer Sensitivity

The last fundamental aspect of hospitality industry marketing relates to communications: *customer communications.* For too long our industry as a whole has been far too *product-oriented,* rather than being *customer-sensitive.* We talk too much about the wonderful features of our properties, rather than relating them to the *benefits* customers are seeking.

A second language which we must become more proficient in is the language of the consumer. In order to speak this language properly, we must be aware of trends and changing consumer needs. Right now we are in the midst of a whole series of lifestyle changes which will affect our customers' future priorities, needs, buying habits, and buying selection criteria. Let us examine just a few of these, since they reflect the language of the times and also provide a bridge to the rest of this decade.

1. People are more *time-conscious* than ever before, especially since the value of time seems to increase in direct proportion to the amount of discretionary income one has. Both leisure and business travelers are increasingly influenced by time-saving and labor-saving products, services, and procedures and are demanding them in hotels and resorts. Along with this, people are seeking more instant solutions to their needs—the concept of "instant gratification".

2. *Simplification.* People are looking for the simplified procedure, the noncomplicated solution. This is also tied into time-saving. If you do a needs analysis of the individual business travel market, for example, you'll find that high on the list of needs and desires of this important market segment are such features as speedy check-in procedures, instant check-out methods, quick valet and laundry service, fast breakfast service (such as breakfast buffets), centralized billing, etc. All of these, in the customer's language, offer time-saving, inconvenience-eliminating, and procedure-simplifying *benefits*—in other words, real solutions to everyday customer problems.

3. People are exceedingly conscious about improving both their bodies and minds through *physical and mental fitness.* People of all ages have turned from being spectators to participants. There are currently on the world market some 3000 different diet books and some 2000 different volumes on self-improvement. This has already created changes in the services and amenities we offer in many of our properties. And this change has just begun. In addition to extending existing recreational facilities, for example, we now put in saunas, steam baths, whirlpool massage units, hot tubs, massage and sunroom facilities, special diet programs, health clubs, jogging tracks, and gym equipment.

FORECASTS FOR THE NEXT DECADE

1. Customer needs and wants will in most cases change faster than the product. The better we can anticipate, react to and adjust to the

changes which will be affecting our markets, the better our chances of gaining our fair share of the market. It's critical that we remember that we have to adapt to the customer, not he to us. The "take it or leave it" days are gone forever. It's a buyer's market and will be even more so during this decade with the expansion of chains and franchise systems around the world, with new and more sophisticated properties coming on line in all corners of the globe, the ease and speed of transportation to all areas of the world, and the virtually limitless choices a customer has for a tailored vacation package which suits his or her desires and lifestyle.

2. There will be greater market segmentation, even market "splinterization", during the next 10 years. Such specialized markets as women, senior citizens, overseas visitors, youth, ethnic and nationality groups will become increasingly important, especially as each of these groups bands together more tightly for greater purchasing power. Also, these market segments can profoundly influence business because they are the *growth markets*. In the United States, for example, women took 16 million business trips during 1977; in 1979 the number jumped to 28 million business trips. Four or five years ago, to give another illustration, the amount of business from Europe was relatively insignificant for Fort Lauderdale, Florida. Right now, business from Germany alone accounts for about 20% of the total business for many of the major properties there.

3. The continued growth of such specialized markets will in turn create the need for us to devote more attention to providing the special services and amenities most pertinent to the needs of each segment. This is true of even the broader-based markets. What is the basic problem of the business people, for instance? I think it can be stated in one word: *communications*. They want more and better communications facilities available for their use at the hotel they will be staying at. Depending on the nature of their trip, they may have to make the hotel their "branch office". Thus they want cable and telex availability, direct dial phones, facsimile transmitters, photocopy equipment, personal paging devices, and stenographic, secretarial, and translation services. On the other hand, the senior citizens market couldn't care less about any of these services...this particular market segment has an entirely different set of needs and desires. The successful hotel of the '80s will be the one which can identify the best and most profitable market segments for the particular product it has developed, and who can then best provide the specific services and amenities each of the segments demand.

4. The successful operations of this decade will be the ones which more fully understand the forces which *motivate* people to travel. In

cooperation with the other segments of the travel industry, they will best utilize the power of persuasion to motivate people to travel to their particular areas or destinations. This will require a practical, working knowledge of people's human behavior, lifestyle profiling, demographics, and psychographics. This in turn will have to be reflected in our advertising and sales promotion messages. We will have to become more adept and expert in the concepts of target marketing and how to specifically reach and influence the movements of various target market segments.

5. The successful hotel of the '80s will also be the one whose product has kept pace with the ever-changing needs, habits, and lifestyles of the *general public*. We've got to rid ourselves of the old worn-out hotel industry philosophy that a hotel is "Your home away from home". People want a lot more than what they are constantly surrounded by day after day. They are seeking spaciousness and free open space, glamour and allure, esoteric atmosphere and ambience, romance and intrigue—a chance to fulfill their dreams. They are also seeking an abundance of niceties which must be built into our rooms and public space. Even our bathrooms have to be redesigned to reflect this new set of values. People are now seeking illuminated dressing mirrors, in-room steam baths, hydro-massage tub units. The public also seeks specialty and atmosphere dining. They don't want eating facilities; they are looking for *creative settings for culinary adventures*. In many areas we have already seen the demise of the sterile hotel dining room, with its sneering obtrusive waiters and its archaic rules of haughty formality. They are also looking for the *personalized servicing* they usually don't get at home: the experienced concierge, the helpful guest relations manager, and the attentive social or recreational director. And if you look at the popularity of the Club Med concept and its imitators, many of the "fun unlimited" resorts of the Caribbean and the Riviera, you'll readily note that people of all backgrounds and ages are now seeking the *sensual*. I came across a term not too long ago which seems to sum up this yearning and I think we will have to be aware of its application in reaching and communicating with certain segments of our markets, especially the active, self-confident portions. The term is "creative eroticism".

6. In a totally different area, *computerized marketing* can well come into its own during these 10 years. We already utilize computer technology for reservations, accounting, payroll, food & beverage control, housekeeping supply inventory, and utility and power conservation. There's no reason why the computer can't also be used as a marketing tool. I don't necessarily mean in the direct selling process; our customers for the most part are too intelligent to buy from "canned" computer

messages. However, the computer can offer a means of *preparing* us to sell more effectively and professionally by providing quick, finger-tip, and up-to-date data and information relating to the current requirements, habits, peculiarities, patterns, and past history of each of our major prospects and customers. As a sophisticated information storehouse, it can prove invaluable.

7. Finally, *training* will have to become one of the chief components of the marketing discipline. Not necessarily technical training; that's best left to each individual department, but rather *awareness, attitude, and courtesy training*. Also included in this area would be "training for sales-minded servicing"—that is, training guest-contact employees such as room clerks, bellmen, waiters, and bartenders how to up-sell and how to extend the sale. These types of training programs must be directed at the staffs of the operating departments since the sales department has no direct control over them in any way, yet it is these people who do—or do not—fulfill all of the promises and commitments made to the customer by the sales or marketing department on behalf of the hotel. I think in the next few years we will see more organizations recognize the importance of sales-minded training in all areas of the property, and that one of the main responsibilities of the sales/ marketing department will be to ensure, through proper training programs, that the entire hotel becomes the "sales department".

PERSONAL HOPES FOR THE FUTURE

These "predictions" are more personal in nature; they reflect my feelings as to the directions I'd like to see the industry be taking. Again, none of these are particularly new; they are mentioned here for reemphasis and perhaps a little personal impatience in that there still seems to be a lot of the road to be covered.

1. First and perhaps foremost; something we have been saying for a quarter-century: *all* General Managers and Owners have to become *totally* sales and market oriented. In the same light, Sales and Marketing Executives have to become more knowledgeable about operations; particularly about the costs of doing business, the costs of servicing a particular piece of business, and how to determine what constitutes a profitable sale. As I said, this is nothing new, but it's going to be more important than ever during the next few years.

2. I hope to see more *intelligent* customer communications, especially in our media advertising and direct mail advertising efforts. There is still too much material being produced which are total wastes of time, effort, and promotional funds. The types I'm referring to are those

which, for example, refer to a property as a "modern, first-class hotel, located in the heart of the business and social community, central to all transportation facilities, with the finest of food and beverages, the most courteous staff, abundant audio-visual aids, and complete function and meeting facilities". The all-purpose promotional message...just fill in *your* name and address in the blank space provided. Totally meaningless; totally wasted; if it does anything, it alienates the recipient. Hopefully each property will be able to determine its position within the marketplace, and through specific appeals to buyer needs, in the buyers' language, convincingly convey its image and message to those markets most suited to profitably fulfilling the property's purpose, objectives, and goals.

3. I'd like to see better *accounting systems* in our industry. Too many current systems, especially those involving billing procedures, are set up to suit the convenience of the accounting department, without any consideration of the person paying the bill. Many of these systems are cumbersome, inconvenient, and archaic, but more critically, make it difficult for the customer to pay the bill even though he stands there with ready cash. We'll all agree that our biggest operational problem is "cash flow", yet our wonderful accounting procedures at times seem to do everything possible to prevent payment of bills. Systems have to be devised and used which make it easy for the customer to promptly pay the bill, especially the group meeting planner or the conference organizer who must have a proper bill acceptable to *his* auditor or comptroller.

Another aspect of accounting I would like to see are better systems of showing the impact of sales and marketing efforts on the financial statements. Many hotel auditors and comptrollers seem to look at the sales or marketing department as a cost center. Well, it wouldn't be too difficult in about 2 hours time to design a workable accounting system which would show every operating department as a cost center, and only the sales and perhaps catering departments as profit centers, since they are the only departments which specifically create and generate revenue. Daily departmental reports, profit and loss statements, occupancy reports, balance sheets, and other similar data can and should be used by both operations and marketing. But more realistic methods of reporting and recording operating statistics have to be used, especially those which truly reflect the impact of sales and marketing on each department and on the entire operation.

4. The last item in this area relates to the *better preparation* of those who will soon be entering our industry especially from the more than 650 institutions around the world who offer programs in hotel manage-

ment. I would first of all like to see more *"reality"* in the curricula, reflecting the industry and its challenges as it really is today, rather than what it was like (in far too many cases) when the 65-year old instructor was last in the field...which in some cases was his grand-mother's boarding house a half-century ago. Not only will it be essential that every school of hotel administration have at least one *required* course in sales and marketing, but also equally important, the market-ing philosophy must be included within every subject taught—whether it be food, accounting, or engineering. There is no activity which takes place in a hotel, no policy decision which affects the customer, which does not in one way or another relate to the marketing function. This must be related to the student so that he or she will be properly prepared to enter our industry and meet the challenges of modern hotel/motor inn operation in this decade.

OUTSIDE FORCES

Now, just a few comments from crystal ball #3, which offers a look at some of the outside forces which we usually have no control over. Yet these factors can greatly influence and affect the marketing picture, particularly in the way we may or may not conduct business.

We have seen, for instance, the impact of *fuel shortages* on our cus-tomer markets, which in turn impacts on us. Unless unanticipated energy breakthroughs occur, we can expect additional shortages during this decade which, for example, will affect the public's vacationing habits. The effect will be one of *changing patterns,* rather than elimination. People will be looking more for the nearby destination. They may take more frequent vacations to close-by destinations, or if they do travel to an away destination, it will be for a longer period but with less fre-quency.

The future will also be influenced by *inflation,* which means we will have to readjust our pricing structures from time to time, yet still maintain our competitive position within the marketplace. Inflation also has another, rather strange effect in that it can positively generate business into certain areas, as well as reduce it in others. Right now, because of the escalating price situation in Europe, the U.S. has become a prime destination for the European leisure traveler. It's more econom-ical at the moment for many Englishmen to spend two weeks holidays in Florida than in Spain or Portugal, as was formerly the tradition. So we must be alert. Today's destination area could be bypassed tomorrow; today's undiscovered region could become the tourist mecca of the next 5 years and not always because of forces under our control.

Government regulations form another set of influencing factors not necessarily under our control. Originally government concern in our industry centered around liquor laws and serving regulations, fire and safety codes, sanitation and food handling standards and inspections, minimum wage regulations, and sales and occupancy taxes. However, more and more inroads are being made by governments into the hospitality industry. On my side of the ocean we are particularly affected by anti-trust regulations, tax-deduction allowances on "out-of-the-country" meetings, truth in advertising legislation, the future of the United States Travel Service—to name just a few.

Several of our states, to give you an example, recently passed "truth in advertising" bills, which among other things regulate what you can say on menus. We can no longer list "homemade bread" unless the loaves were baked, probably by a sweet little old lady, in a private home. We can no longer paint appetizing word-pictures and say that today's lobster were only last night frolicking in Chesapeake Bay, unless we have a half-dozen witnesses attesting to the love life of those particular crustaceans!

What I am concerned about is how far it could go. Will we ultimately have at the end of this decade a board of censors before whom you would have to perform a "full dress rehearsal" before going out to make a sales call?

All of this has a spin-off effect on the general public, resulting in a negative form of "consumerism". Some degree of consumer protection can be valid; it's the over-reaction by vocal minorities which can cause concern. A recent court case in California is a perfect example. A doctor and a lawyer were awarded $18,000 in a sex discrimination case because a restaurant refused to serve them since they weren't wearing neckties. The point was that the hotel did not require their wives to wear ties. What concerns me is the dangerous legal precedents being established. One of the characteristics of this decade may be a proliferation of such regulations and cases—and I hate to think of our industry being run by politicians and lawyers.

On the other hand, not all is bleak; there may be areas where there will be a relaxing of some of these forces beyond our control. One such area relates to *airline deregulation,* which can "open up" marketing potentials in many areas around the world.

CONCLUSION

We could go on making many more projections, predictions, and forecasts for the next 10 years...but I would like to leave you with several thoughts which in a sense sum up the messages behind the three crystal balls.

1. What happens if you should drop your crystal ball...if what you have predicted or forecasted fails to materialize—or if the exact opposite occurs? The answer, I believe, is in that word singled out in the very beginning of this chapter: *"flexibility"*. When formulating your marketing plans, are you at the same time drawing up contingency plans and programs? If the markets you are developing, for example, are attracted elsewhere because of a local economic or inflationary situation, what other markets could you also be developing which would not necessarily be influenced by the same factors? If the energy shortage curtails the distant vacationing markets, have you been cultivating any local markets to take their place? If the disco craze dies out (as it already has in many areas), what types of alternative offerings are you prepared to install in your entertainment lounges...and how soon?

2. The second thought relates to *professionalism*. That's become the key measurement of success in our part of this industry—and education, experience, knowledge, insight, creative abilities, initiative and the ability to follow-through are going to be even more vital attributes during these next 10 years.

In order not to drop the crystal ball, you will have to be a true professional, ready to adapt to the changing times. This can be one of the most challenging, yet rewarding decades you will ever face if you can fill these requirements.

38

Four Unexplained Dimensions of Hospitality Marketing

John D. Correll and *James M. Graham*

For some time, now, the authors have been perplexed by the absence of a unified theory for both describing and prescribing the marketing process of the hospitality enterprise. Until recently, we assumed the problem was one of application; we assumed that the necessary conceptual base had already been established within the realm of "general" marketing theory, and all that needed to be done was to convert or apply that theory to the hospitality situation.

Finally, we decided to make that conversion and went to work researching how general marketing theory could be adapted to the hospitality situation. After a summer of research, we came to a startling conclusion. While many of the *peripheral* concepts and principles of general marketing could be successfully adapted to the hospitality situation, there was something lacking in way of a basic theory that could be utilized for describing the central activities of the hospitality marketing process.

Why can't we adequately explain the process of hospitality marketing with general marketing theory? The question vexed us. Finally, we made what was for us an eye-opening realization: "General" marketing theory is, in fact, not general, but *specific*. It does not adequately explain or apply to all business situations, rather it explains very well the situation of the *manufacturing* enterprise and only falteringly, and sometimes incorrectly, the situations of other businesses. In short, we realized that the principles, concepts, and theory espoused by marketing writers as being universal in application were, in fact, parochial.

After having made that realization, we felt the need to explain how that situation came to be. Although we can't say for sure, we believe this situation has been caused by the historical focus of marketing thought on the manufacturing enterprise to the relative exclusion of other forms of business, such as the hospitality industry. We surmise that this situation has given rise to a "follow-the-leader" approach in the development of marketing theory. In short, rather than challenge the validity, relevance, and universality of current theory, and then seek to develop better or more comprehensive theories, many marketing writers have contented themselves with accepting the current theoretical constructs and have simply sought to build upon or embellish what already existed.

This approach to marketing thought development would be fine if all prior premises and theories were universally correct and applicable; however, they aren't. Why aren't they? We suspect that at the beginning of marketing theory, around 1900, when the pioneer marketing thinkers surveyed the economic/business scene to observe the marketing process, they perceived two overriding facts:

1) That the economic system was dominated by manufacturing enterprises, to the extent that all other forms of business seemed insignificant by comparison;

2) That the output of these businesses was hard-goods or tangible products, and everything else involved in the marketing process or sales transaction was only for the purpose of expediting the sale of the tangible good.

Naturally, then, the early marketing thinkers designed their terminology, models, and theories with these two conditions as assumed premises, or a priori facts. At that time, of course, they were. Today, however, that is not the case. Manufacturing enterprises do not dominate the economic scene, and there is much more to the marketing transaction than the simple conveyence of hard-goods. What has happened is this. The nature and structure of the economic/business world has changed drastically in 75 years but, in many aspects, marketing theory has not kept pace. Many concepts and theories which were, at their inception, almost universal in application are today parochial. But instead of recognizing the increasingly limited application of these once "general" concepts, and then seeking to develop more correct and comprehensive concepts, most marketing theorists have assumed the original concepts to be universal and have simply proceeded to heap theoretical embellishments on top of a parochial conceptual base.

The result of this process can be seen in any business library. In the marketing section there is stack after stack of books dedicated to the purpose of explaining the terminology, concepts, and systems of marketing—most of which purport to be universal in application. At the end of most of these "general" marketing tomes, usually in the form of a "miscellaneous" chapter, can be found a few pages which quietly and apologetically acknowledge that there are some situations in which "general" marketing concepts are either incorrect or inapplicable. Upon examining these few pages, we gain the eerie realization that the exceptions might be a widespread phenomenon. We discover that businesses classified as service businesses and hospitality businesses are more dominant and widespread than manufacturing businesses. In short, we discover that the "general" is actually specific, the exception is actually the rule, that we have a ponderous amount of theory for explaining "hard-goods marketing," but very little which explains how to market anything else.

In conclusion, we suggest that the body of marketing knowledge centers around a "goods-oriented bias," a situation which has created a lopsided theoretical construct and which has caused the process of marketing theory development to be out of synchronism with the evolving structure and process of the economic/business world.

We feel this one-sided focus of marketing theory on the manufacturing enterprise has stifled the full development of marketing thought in non-manufacturing areas, and has caused some incomplete and distorted conceptual developments in marketing theory. In this paper, we would like to examine four of those incomplete conceptual developments:

1) The incomplete and possibly confusing definition of marketing, which has given rise to a misunderstanding of the relationship of the production function to the marketing function;

2) The incomplete description and development of the marketing mix concept, particularly as it applies to the hospitality industry;

3) An incomplete explanation of the *functions* of marketing management;

4) A lack of explanation of how the human element fits into the marketing program and how the effectiveness of the organization's people and people management process determines the success of the total marketing effort.

Thus, we in the hospitality industry face the exciting challenge of having to formulate marketing theory and concepts that correctly describe the marketing process of the hospitality enterprise. The purpose of this chapter is to point out four conceptual areas (listed above) where general marketing theory is inadequate for the hospitality firm, and to suggest some basic concepts upon which we feel a "theory of hospitality marketing" should be built.

CONCEPTUAL AREA #1

General marketing theory derives from a limiting and, in our opinion, inadequate definition of marketing. The American Marketing Association defines marketing as "the performance of business activities that direct the flow of goods and services from producer to consumer or user." Considering that the AMA presumably represents some of our finest marketing minds, this is a disappointing definition. First, it leads us to believe that services can flow from a producer of services to a consumer. In fact, services are not capable of "flowing" from a producer to consumer because they are an *activity* performed *by* one person *for* another; thus, they are momentary and intangible. This aborted definition of services probably stems from the goods-oriented bias of general marketing thought. The second reason this definition of marketing is inadequate is that, in essence, it says marketing is nothing more than a distribution function.

As a probable response to this inadequate definition, many marketing people have proposed their own definitions of marketing, from very elaborate to very simple. Three that seem to be good ones are:

Marketing consists of those differentiating actions taken by the firm to establish its legitimacy, enhance its power, improve its negotiating ability, and resolve conflicts in its own favor (Anderson, Bentley, and Sharpe 1976).
Marketing consists of the activities involved in the generation of markets and customers and in the development and distribution of customer-satisfying goods and services (Kelley and Lazer 1967).
Marketing is human activity directed at satisfying needs and wants through exchange activity. (Kotler 1980, p. 17).

All three definitions provide a good basis for a full, functional concept of marketing; however, the writers do not follow through in the development of their definition to a full, encompassing concept of marketing. Instead, they tend to formulate a limited concept of a firm's total marketing process and the function of marketing management.

Why do we make that accusation? It's because we take a very broad view of the marketing process, which we feel is necessary for a full understanding of a firm's marketing effort, particularly for a hospitality enterprise. Specifically, we suggest that, in its broadest context:

Marketing consists of the activities involved in the creation of form, time, place, and possession utilities and the exchange of them for the benefits desired by the individual or firm.

Actually, this definition is not radically different, in its implications, from the three above. However, we suggest some different developments than the above authors describe in their books.

We propose outright what some marketing theorists have heretofore hinted at, and circuitously alluded to; we propose that we finally recognize the conclusion of the past 75-year evolution of marketing thought—that is, marketing is *not* an activity separate from production! Rather, *marketing incorporates production.*

At first encounter, this statement may sound illogical, irresponsible, and maybe even demogogical. However, we suggest that instead it is a conclusion that naturally follows from the purpose of the production function, which is to create form utility to be used in the organization's marketing exchanges; therefore, production is an activity involved in the marketing process. Consider how that fits into each of the above four definitions of marketing. By creating form utility for the organization's exchanges, it means the production function:

a) Is a differentiating action taken by the firm to establish its legitimacy, enhance its power, and improve its negotiating ability;

b) Is an activity involved in the development and distribution of customer-satisfying goods and services;

c) Is a human activity directed at satisfying needs and wants through exchange activity;

d) Is an activity involved in the creation of utility.

In other words, the production system is a sub-system of a larger system—namely, the marketing system. In marketing jargon, that means the production function is a component of the marketing mix.

CONCEPTUAL AREA #2

The second inadequate explanation within current marketing theory lies in the definition of the marketing mix concept. Although there are a number of alterations and additions the concept must undergo before it is fully applicable to the situation of the hospitality enterprise, we will focus on probably the most crucial of the missing elements in the traditional definition of the marketing mix concept—namely, *people.*

To begin our argument for the inclusion of people in the marketing mix, we start with a popular definition of the marketing mix, given by Kotler (1980). He defines marketing mix as "the particular blend of controllable marketing variables that the firm uses to achieve its objectives in the target market." On the surface, this seems like a good definition; however, it defines marketing mix as marketing variables. In other words, it provides no explanation, but only raises another question: What are marketing variables? Kotler then proceeds, as other authors do, to assume that those variables roughly correspond with McCarthy's (1971) 4 P's—product, price, place, and promotion. We suggest that Kotler's definition would have much more usefulness if it simply referred to controllable variables rather than controllable *marketing* variables. In other words, the determination of whether something is a *marketing* variable will be made depending upon whether the variable is something "the firm uses to achieve its objectives in the target market."

Thus, we revise Kotler's definition to read: "Marketing mix is the particular blend of controllable variables that the firm uses to achieve its objectives in the target market." When stated that way, we avoid any preconceived arbitrary notion of what is and isn't a component of a marketing mix and, instead, can use this definition as a starting point for ascertaining what the components of any firm's marketing mix are.

Thus, we propose that for almost every business, particularly in a hospitality firm, *people* must be recognized as a component of the marketing mix. Specifically, we are saying the firm's employees are a controllable variable used to achieve the firm's objectives in the target market. That notion is easy to accept when we consider that the firm's employees—through their words actions, appearance, and attitude—affect the following:

1) The quality of the firm's products and services;
2) The customer's overall satisfaction (or lack of satisfaction) with his purchase—specifically, his perception of the value he received for his money;
3) The communication or interaction between the customer and the enterprise;
4) The customer's and community's image of the enterprise;
5) The cost of the marketing effort (referring specifically to the cost of labor).

While it is not our purpose to propose the idea that people are a component of *all* firms' marketing mixes, we feel certain they should be considered part of the hospitality firm's marketing mix. In short, we suggest that (1) the core process of the hospitality marketing effort is the set of activities we call "operations," or the process of creating, delivering, and selling the company's products and services; (2) the successful operation of this system of activities relies heavily on the controllable variable called people (employees); therefore, (3) people are a key component of the hospitality marketing mix.

CONCEPTUAL AREA #3

The third inadequate explanation within current marketing theory lies in the definition of marketing management. Most authors define marketing management by listing what they consider to be the *functions* involved in managing the marketing effort. For instance, one list goes like this:

1) market delineation
2) purchase behavior motivation factors definition
3) product-service adjustment
4) channel selection
5) physical distribution
6) communication/promotion
7) pricing
8) organizing the marketing staff
9) administering marketing operations (Staudt *et al.* 1976).

A four-function breakdown by another marketing thinker goes like this:

1) marketing opportunity assessment
2) marketing planning and programming
3) marketing organization and leadership
4) evaluation and adjustment of marketing effort (Kelley and Lazer 1967).

Still another author (Kotler 1980) gives us a simple definition in sentence form: "Marketing management is the analysis, planning, implementation, and control of programs designed to create, build, and maintain mutually beneficial exchanges and relationships with target markets for the purpose of achieving organizational objectives." This definition alludes to four basic functions—analysis, planning, implementation, and control—which roughly correspond to the functions listed above.

While we have no problem with these definitions (in fact, we like them), we do, however, have a problem with what we feel is a lack of adequate explanation of *how* to manage all these functions. Specifically, most marketing authors devote ample words to describing three of the marketing management functions—namely, the analysis, planning, and control functions—but almost completely disregard the implementation or administration function. In other words, they focus at length on how to manage all components of the marketing process except one: the human component or, in other words, the implementation/administration function.

We certainly do not suggest that any less time or study be given to management of the analysis, planning, and control functions. But we most certainly suggest that much more time need be given to management of the administration function. Although the term "administration" is appropriate, we suggest that a more descriptive term would be "people management." In other words, we are saying, one of the vital functions of marketing management is *managing the people* involved in the marketing effort. In the hospitality enterprise, the majority of people involved in the marketing effort is what is known as the "operations people." Thus, if we are going to effectively manage a firm's marketing effort, we must effectively manage the operations people who sustain that effort.

Unfortunately, current marketing theory hardly recognizes that idea. While most authors' definitions of marketing management allow for it, the content of their books almost ignores it. However, one heartening observation is that when some writers discuss the direct selling function they automatically discuss the *management* of salesmen, or the processes of organization structure design, recruiting and selecting, training, compensating, supervising, and evaluating salesmen. In short, they recognize that one doesn't manage the sales function without managing the sales people. The sales force of a manufacturing/wholesale business is closely analogous to the operations staff of a hospitality enterprise. Thus, the obvious conclusion is: we don't effectively manage the hospitality marketing function without effectively managing the operations people.

Although a few books delve into the people management aspects of marketing management we have found them to be only surface treatments. They do not come close to providing the marketing student with the insight and knowledge necessary for effectively managing the firm's marketing personnel. This oversight is not only sad but most perplexing as ineffective people management can cause the most brilliantly designed marketing plan to fail, while effective people management can make a mediocre plan succeed (maybe not in all industries, but certainly so in the hospitality industry).

In conclusion, people management involves the activities of interviewing and hiring, orientation, training, employee development, supervision, motivation, productivity assessment, appraisals, promotion, compensation, communication, and human relations problem-solving. And, because one function of marketing management is people management, and people management involves all of the above activities, then marketing management must incorporate these activities in the implementation phase of the marketing program.

CONCEPTUAL AREA #4

Current marketing theory fails to emphasize that a marketing effort, primarily and ultimately, is a people effort. The purpose of a marketing program is to achieve a firm's objectives. Thus, we as marketing theorists must concern ourselves with *how* an organization's leaders—through their style, aspirations, attitudes, and values—create and shape a marketing program. Once formulated, a marketing program is implemented through the firm's employees. Thus, once again, we must concern ourselves with *how* employees (managers and nonmanagers) are managed so they achieve optimum performance and results. And marketing theory should point out that there is more to creating optimum performance than simply creating an organization chart and writing a job description. Ultimately, a marketing effort is a team effort; and winning at marketing is *not unlike* winning at any team sport.

The great teams—the winning teams—analyze the competition and evaluate their opponent's and their own strengths and weaknesses (marketing analysis). They plan their strategy in light of their objectives and the other team's competitive position (marketing planning). Then they implement their strategy through practice and, finally, in the game event itself (marketing program implementation). And when it's over, they examine how they did and take corrective action for the next game (control).

While we have just described the four-step process through which a sports team manages its athletic effort, which is much like the process marketing writers describe for how a company manages its marketing effort, we know there is much more to winning than that brief four-step procedure describes. Likewise, there is much more to winning a marketing effort than is explained by most theorists of marketing management. Whether we are dealing with a sports team or a marketing team, there is a bundle of intangible elements that greatly impact upon the effectiveness and ultimate success of the team. We are referring to those intangible but crucial elements which every perceptive leader—coach or executive—and every perceptive player knows he needs in order to maximize his effectiveness and optimize the team's winning percentage. We are referring to those age-old team ingredients which, for some inexplicable reason, have been almost totally ignored in marketing texts. We are talking about such vital elements as:

1) unity of team purpose;
2) a worthy, exciting goal for each team member to pursue;

3) inspiring leaders—ones that create self-respect and inspire the extra effort in team players;

4) esprit d' corps—a burning desire in each team member to win, to excel, to do better than the opposing team.

These are subjective, intangible elements, to be sure. But that is no reason to ignore them in our business schools and marketing texts. They are elements that impact on the final outcome of the firm's marketing effort. Therefore, they should be studied along with all other elements of the marketing process. When understood and properly applied, these elements are simply another category of controllable variables that the firm can use to achieve its objectives in the target market. In short, these elements can be, and should be, part of the marketing mix. And understanding them, including them, and sustaining them is part of the job of the firm's marketing leaders.

CONCLUSION

What are the benefits of a fuller understanding and implementation of these four conceptual areas? We see five broad benefits.

1) The eventual development of a specifically defined and functional marketing mix for the hospitality industry;

2) Better correlation between "general" marketing theory and hospitality marketing theory, which will result in better correlation between the content of general marketing courses and hospitality marketing courses;

3) A conceptual framework for integrating the various components or functions of hospitality management. If the marketing concept utilized by the hospitality firm is accurate and fully-encompassing, then that concept should serve as the vehicle for strategically integrating such diverse functions as site selection, food production, cost control, housekeeping, public relations, advertising, manpower training, evaluation and appraisals, building design and decor, supervision, menu development, sanitation and maintenance, kitchen layout, management information systems, customer and market research, equipment selection, customer service, new product research, and more;

4) A greater emphasis on developing expertise and strength in the most weakly defined of the four marketing management functions— namely, the implementation or administration of the firm's marketing plan—what we call the people management function;

5) The understanding that "in the final analysis, firms market them-

selves" (Anderson, Bentley and Sharpe, 1976). Or, to state it another way, the understanding that a total marketing effort is a total company effort. This implies, that to have an understanding of the total marketing process we must first have an understanding of *how* the firm's people and its people management processes affect the following:

a) the direction and impact of the firm's total marketing plan;

b) the spirit, attitude, and performance of the people who must implement the plan;

c) the impact of the marketing program on the customer, and therefore, the degree of attainment of the firm's marketing objectives.

In conclusion, we look forward to the development of a unifying, fully-functional theory of hospitality marketing; and we believe such a theory must necessarily embody some marketing concepts not yet described in current "general" marketing theory.

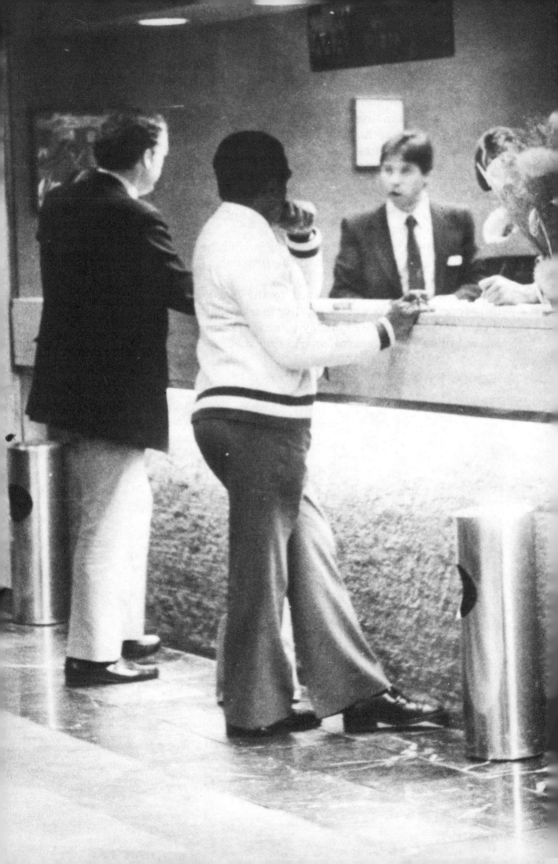

39

The New Marketing Mix:
Marketing Strategy Development for the
Hospitality Industry

Leo M. Renaghan, Ph.D.

This chapter suggests a "new marketing mix" as part of a total marketing strategy for improving the performance of hospitality service firms.

Service possesses many characteristics that substantially differentiate it from physical products; thus service marketing requires strategies different from those manufacturing firms employ. Sasser *et al.* (1978) have noted that the unique aspects of service that give direction to service market strategy formulation include: (1) the *intangible nature* of service that makes a consumer's choice among competitive offerings more difficult than among products, particularly since he usually cannot taste, touch, feel or try the service before deciding on it; (2) the *simultaneity of production and consumption,* which increases the importance of the service's location and tends to decrease the choice of alternatives since only a limited number of service outlets tend to be available in a trading area; (3) the *perishability of service*, which precludes the use of inventory to solve demand problems and increases a firm's financial risks; (4) the *variability in service output* caused by the intangible nature of service, the presence of the consumer at the point of production, and the need for humans to be involved in the delivery of the service; (5) the *ease of duplication* of the service, attributable to the few barriers to market entry which encourage competitors to duplicate services quicker than they duplicate products, and (6) the amount and nature of *perceived risk* (or "pre-purchase anxiety") that accompanies service selection as a result of all these factors.

To prosper in the decades ahead, hospitality firms must develop a competitive marketing strategy that takes all six of these service marketing characteristics into account. This strategy formulation, moreover, ought to address itself to two objectives: (1) identifying target markets and their needs, and (2) developing a marketing mix that satisfies these needs. Fortunately, the process of identifying and determining profit potential in target markets follows the same general principles whether one is dealing with a product or a service. It is in the marketing program formulation or marketing mix of the strategy that important differences appear.

THE MARKETING MIX

Neil Borden (1968) pioneered the concept of the marketing mix in the early 1960s. It is derived from the term "mixer of ingredients" coined by one of Borden's colleagues to describe a business executive attempting to discover the right combination of policies and procedures to elicit the consumer behavior that produced a profit. Borden reasoned that if the executive was a "mixer of ingredients," then what he designed was a "marketing mix." From this basis, Borden proceeded to "the development of a concept that would comprehend not only this variety of mixes, but also the market forces that cause management to produce a variety of mixes. It is the problem raised by these forces that leads marketing managers to exercise their wits in devising mixes or programs they hope will yield a profitable business operation."

The marketing mix concept underwent constant refinement as its acceptance in the business and academic communities increased. Various researchers added or deleted elements in accordance with their perceptions and analyses of the market forces. The most popular refinement currently in use, and the one most frequently applied to the hospitality industry, is the "Four P's" of E. Jerome McCarthy (1975):

(1) *Product*. The product may involve a physical product and/or some combination of services. The crux of the matter in the product area is to develop some thing which will satisfy some customers' needs.

(2) *Place*. Place is concerned with where, when, and by whom the goods and services are to be offered for sale.

(3) *Promotion*. Promotion denotes any method that communicates to the target market information about the "right" product sold in the "right" place at the "right" time.

(4) *Price*. This element focuses on the need to set a price that will make the offering as attractive as possible.

The problem with the use of this and similar product frameworks in the hospitality industry is that none of them accounts for the substantial differences mentioned earlier. Therefore, none has adequately "comprehended" the hospitality market forces Borden thought crucial to designing a mix or a program that would lead to a profit. For example, Coffman (1970) lists twelve "factors" in his marketing mix ranging from "product planning" through "display" to "marketing research." Crissy, Boewadt and Laudadio (1975) list the customer-prospect mix, the service mix and the promotional mix. Eison (1980) lists no marketing mix at all. Thus, a hospitality manager or operator trying to utilize the marketing mix in developing a cohesive and inclusive strategy could easily get confused.

If the marketing mix is supposed to provide the framework upon which to build a strategy, none of these authors provides workable blueprints. What is needed is a marketing mix that accounts for the differences between service and product, i.e., delineates the elements of a service marketing strategy, weighs them correctly, and makes clear their interrelationships.

TOWARDS A NEW MARKETING MIX

A new hospitality marketing mix that is part of a strategy that reflects the differences between products and services by delineating those specific elements that must be addressed must deal with the relative importance of each element that must be addressed, must deal with the relative importance of each element and identify the interrelationships between them. The proposed mix contains three major sub-mixes:

(1) *The Product-Service Mix:* that combination of products and services, whether free or for sale, made available to satisfy the needs of the target market;

(2) *The Presentation Mix:* all those elements under the direction of the firm that are used to increase the tangibility of the product-service mix in the eyes of target market at the right place and time; and

(3) *The Communication Mix:* all communications of any kind between the firm and the target market that increase the tangibility of the product-service mix, sets or monitor consumer's expectations, or persuade consumers to purchase.

I will now discuss each of these sub-mixes in more detail.

The Product-Service Mix

The term "product-service mix" reflects the fact that the hospitality industry normally offers a simultaneous blend of products and services to satisfy its customers' needs. Notwithstanding this knowledge, the tendency among firms in the hospitality industry has been to focus almost exclusively on the product elements because (a) the marketing program mixes available are usually borrowed from product strategy formulations and (b) because operators tend to respond to the familiar tangibility of products. Hospitality managers prefer to deal with something that can be seen, touched, and demonstrated, rather than with a nebulous concept that is difficult to define in terms of the target market, difficult to operationalize as an offering, and even more difficult to control. What is "friendliness" in a fast-food restaurant or a Marriott Hotel? You can test market a product, but it is difficult to test market a service.

Unfortunately for hospitality firms, consumers do not perceive the product and service elements of the mix separately; they perceive them instead as a whole. The *elements* of the marketing mix are not made available to satisfy consumer needs but the *entire mix*.

A change in the elements of the mix changes the entire mix and the perception consumers have of that mix, sometimes dramatically. Thus, in the determination of the product-service mix in the overall development of a marketing strategy, a firm must acknowledge the importance of the service elements, as difficult as they may be to comprehend and develop. The firm must also consciously decide what services to sell. In the case of services, satisfaction for the consumer derives from performance rather than possession. The misunderstanding of this truism among some hospitality firms espousing "elegant," "friendly," "adventurous," "unique," or "exciting" service offerings leads only to trouble. These adjectives echo the outmoded product strategy framework that lures firms into seeing these elements as merchandising or sales promotion ploys, rather than the elements of the product-service mix that they are. In his novel *Mother Night*, Kurt Vonnegut (1972) stated the idea succinctly in another context. "We are," he said, "what we pretend to be and must therefore be careful what we pretend to be."

How a firm decides what to be has been made easier in recent years by the development of sophisticated multivariate statistical techniques which elicit the service elements of the product-service offering important to consumers and which can delineate the consumer's purchase intentions for different combinations and levels of elements in the offering (Myers and Tauber 1977).

The Presentation Mix

The term "presentation mix" serves as an umbrella concept. It signifies the importance of all those elements under the control of the firm that act in concert to increase the tangibility of the total product-service offering in the eyes of the consumer, and to differentiate that offering from those of the competition. The term connotes the notion that a firm "presents" the product-service mix at its best to the target market in the right place at the right time. What differentiates the offering of one firm from that of another is, to a large degree, the presentation of the offering.

The tangible product a restaurant sells is, of course, food, but not all restaurants are alike. What are the differences? A hotel sells the use of a room with a collection of furnishings, but not all hotels are alike. What are the differences? In each instance, the customer perceives the whole offering or the total experience, not just the food, or not just the room. The differences are the elements of the presentation mix.

The major elements of the presentation mix are: (1) physical plant, (2) location, (3) atmospherics (light, sound, space, smell and accoutrements), (4) price, and (5) employees. Some of these elements get routinely included in product strategy formulations, but they have a different significance in a service marketing strategy.

Two parts of the physical plant of a hospitality property make it part of the presentation mix: the exterior and the profit center proximities. The exterior of the physical plant in which the product-service mix is being offered should tell the customer what is happening inside. This projection goes beyond the idea that a restaurant should look like a restaurant and a hotel like a hotel. The physical structure should reflect the intangible service elements that are part of the total offering. Trader Vic's does not look like a restaurant, but a *Polynesian* restaurant. A hotel designed by John Portman is not a hotel, but an *exciting* hotel.

Profit Center Proximities.—The term "profit center proximities" specifies the relationship between the profit centers of a property with a wide product-service mix and its customer traffic flow. Profit center proximities are an important element of a service strategy formulation for at least three reasons. First, the intangible nature of services makes them difficult to describe or illustrate; therefore, it becomes even more difficult to provide customers with the information and enticement necessary to effect purchases. Advertising, especially in the print media, may not sufficiently describe, for example, an "elegant" restaurant.

Second, the fact that the service must be produced close to the point of consumption means that the proximity of the service outlet to the customer is important. Given several competitive offerings (for example, when a hotel guest is making a restaurant choice), it becomes important to intercept the guest's normal movements through the property. A good example of profit center proximity is a hotel where, on a walk from the front desk to the elevator, guests pass (and can see inside) the cocktail lounge, the dining room and a modern game room. They should also be able to glimpse the indoor pool. A bad example is a hotel that has placed its cocktail lounge so that it is invisible from any part of the lobby so that a guest has to pass through the dining room to reach it.

The third reason that profit center proximities are an important element of a service strategy formulation has to do with the risk a consumer perceives in making a wrong decision. All purchase decision-making contains some element of risk. In those instances where the decision is important, consumers will act to reduce these risks. Warranties, guarantees, and testimonials all constitute elements of product marketing strategies intended to help consumers perceive a reduced risk. These tactics are normally unavailable to someone buying services. Where they are available defects are difficult, if not impossible, to prove. Few advertise a money-back guarantee on a hotel room. How does a customer prove a meal is bad or the service unfriendly?

As an element of the presentation mix and as a part of the overall service marketing strategy, location is important for two reasons. The first has to do with consumer purchase behavior and the importance of the purchase decision to an individual. In those instances where they consider their decision important, consumers will go a long way to reduce perceived risk and to ensure that their needs are met. Thus, the product-service offering need not be located near the consumer relative to the competition. If the cost of making the wrong decision is high enough, consumers will locate the right offering.

Where the decision is less important, consumers will pick the offerings most conveniently "presented." For example, all fast food restaurants seem to stretch out along the same street or "fast food row." Fast food does not present an important decision; therefore, consumers will not go far out of their way to find a fast food restaurant. In this case, the location (presentation) of the restaurant becomes crucial. As one anonymous executive stated, "There's no such thing as a good secondary location in fast food."

The second reason location is an important element of the marketing strategy has to do with barriers of entry to the competitors for a particular market. As part of its marketing strategy, every firm must consider how it can build and protect a strong competitive position. Product-oriented companies normally use capital and patents as barriers to the competition. Service businesses, particularly those that are people-based like travel agents and tour brokers, rarely enjoy this luxury. "The service, because it is an abstract, perishable quality, must be produced and delivered by a single company, often by a single unit of equipment or people. The result is a decentralization of the service production process at the local level and a reduction in the opportunity for developing economies of scale. As a result, location decisions are often very important and multiple locations can serve as a barrier to entry" (Thomas 1978).

"Atmospherics," a term coined by Philip Kotler (1973 – 74), are important elements of the presentation mix. They reinforce and make the service offerings more tangible in the mind of the consumer (that is, they act as cues) and they can directly affect purchase behavior. It is one thing to develop a product-service mix; it is quite another to somehow make the intangible elements clear to consumers. When a firm offers "elegance," it is atmospherics, in the form of furnishings, lighting, space utilization, music and decor, that convey elegance to the consumers and reinforce it in their minds. Kotler asserts that atmospherics also directly affect purchase behavior by acting as an attention-creating medium, a message-creating medium (as illustrated above) and as an affective (or emotion-creating) medium.

The next element in the presentation mix is price. In product marketing, price is commonly set against costs. This approach, however, is of little help in respect to services. (What is the cost of "friendliness"?) Price, it is often stated, must be considered in light of value in the eyes of consumers and its psychological effect on their purchase behavior. There is little guidance here for a hospitality firm, except to suggest that a low price may have as much of an adverse effect on purchase intent as a high price. In situations where consumers have little information, as when they must purchase something new or unfamiliar to them, they often use price as an indicator of quality. In effect, they may perceive a low price as indicative of low quality.

The final element of the presentation mix are the firm's employees. Because of the intangibility of services and the consumers' presence at the point of production, a firm may find it difficult to establish service standards and even harder to ensure that the standards are met each time service is delivered. The way to solve this problem for people-based firms is through employee training calculated to make employees an important element of the service marketing strategy. As George (1977) notes, "For services, employees are perceived to be the product; they become the physical representation of the product. . . . The successful service company must first sell the job to employees before it can sell its services to customers." Thus we see McDonald's putting all employees into snappy uniforms, even though it increases costs, and Disneyworld hiring employees with a particular "look" and calling them "actors." Both of these companies have realized that to a consumer the employee is a large part of the product.

The Communications Mix

The third sub-mix of the new marketing mix is the communications mix. This term emphasizes the idea that communication is a two-way process encompassing more than the purchase persuasion normally associated with advertising.

A communications mix in a service marketing strategy serves two major purposes. First, we have seen that service's intangibility makes it difficult and sometimes impossible to illustrate a service form and imply its benefits. (How does one narrate "friendliness" or describe "elegance?") Service promotion depends, therefore, on visual appeals so that the intangible can be seen. How much better to show an elegant restaurant or a friendly waitress, than to describe or assert them. A picture *is* worth a thousand words; accordingly, some hotels now show slides and films of their service offerings on the guest's television rather than describing them in a brochure. The first major purpose of the communications mix, then, is to effect this persuasive visualization and make tangible the services being offered.

The second major purpose of the communications mix is to help set and monitor a consumer's service expectations. The intangibility of service and the variability in output associated with service, challenge a firm to ensure that the meaning of "friendliness" stays the same for both the firm and the consumer and that friendliness is delivered every time that consumer makes a purchase. Visuals help establish consumer expectations by more or less closely reflecting the firm's service capabilities. But the need to develop a system to monitor and change, when necessary, these expectations is often ignored. Few operators understand such a system as an element of the service marketing strategy, or they see it as too difficult to implement. New point-of-purchase computers, like TELLUS, which register attitude and satisfaction levels, will make it easier for firms to develop such useful monitoring programs (Cadotte 1980). Some hotels have already tested such monitoring programs with positive results (Cadotte 1979).

CONCLUSION

As competition increases in the hospitality industry, a general marketing orientation and the successful development of specific service marketing strategies will start to spell the difference between hospitality success and failure. To follow the traditional marketing strategies because "that is the way it has always been done" is to court disaster. Empirical evidence and the ample research literature already accumulating suggest another way. It remains for the hospitality marketing practitioner to adapt this new knowledge to his operation in order to compete sucessfully in the marketplace.

40

Developing a Benefit Matrix for Positioning Hotels[1]

Robert C. Lewis, Ph.D.

The concept of positioning in strategic marketing has become an accepted dictum in recent years but until very recently, it seems to have largely escaped the attention of hotel marketers. Hotel advertising has traditionally featured objective product characteristics such as number of rooms, prices, facilities and amenities. In this situation, it is not uncommon that all or most of the competing properties are very similar in the objective characteristics of the physical product and its functional features. Positioning, however, constitutes creating an image of a property's subjective attributes vis-a-vis the competition where the perceived image of the property is not the product, but rather is the consumers' mental perception which, in some instances, can differ widely from a property's true physical characteristics. This distinction is particularly acute for hotel marketers.

Hotel offerings are a bundle of goods and services along a bipolar construct of tangible dominant and intangible dominant offerings (Shostack 1977). Services represent the intangible end of the continuum. This often makes it difficult to know which attributes are most important to the consumer's purchase decision. The intangible attributes of services make the decision just as difficult for the consumer because: (1) he cannot taste, touch, feel, see or try before deciding; (2) he must consume concomitantly with the productive process; (3) the heterogeneity of a firm's services constitutes a higher level of risk-taking and (4) the ease of duplication of services often prevails against clear distinctions among competitive offerings. Thus the consumer objectively measures and compares values monetarily and actively consumes tangible

---

[1] A version of this paper was published in the Cornell Hotel and Restaurant Administration Q., 1981.

products. But he subjectively measures and compares, has difficulty valuing monetarily and passively consumes (is acted upon and reacts to) intangible services. Further, tangible hotel products tend to have a short term cognitive and affective impact whereas services have a more long term effect.

Those hotel marketers who have come to recognize the place of intangible attributes in the consumers' decision making processes have often reacted by advertising the abstract: the ineffable ("escape to the ultimate"); the euphoric ("surround yourself with luxury"); the euphuistic ("capture the spirit"); the ephemeral ("make any occasion special"); and the antithetic ("get away to it all"). The problem here is that in the selection process the consumer will not buy a service no matter what its intangible attributes unless the tangible ones have reached a minimum threshold. A halo effect, in fact, is possible. That is, the existence of certain tangibles is assumed to signify certain abstract quality levels. Many goods producing companies have recognized this and often advertise by adding abstract qualities to recognized tangible goods. Charles Revson, former head of Revlon Cosmetics, is reported to have said, "In the factory we make cosmetics, in the store we sell hope." Revlon advertising continues to reflect this strategy.

But hotel products have a high degree of sameness and hotel services *are* abstract. To compound the concrete is to fail to differentiate and to compound the abstraction dilutes the reality that the marketer is trying to enhance. Thus hotel marketers should focus on the enhancement and differentiation of abstract realities through the manipulation of tangible clues—the peripheral clues that the consumer can comprehend with the five senses. "The degree to which the marketer will focus on either tangible evidence or intangible abstractions for (positioning an entity to its target market) will be found to be 'inversely related to the entity dominance' " (Shostack 1977). Picture, for example, the intangibility of Merrill Lynch services with the tangibility of their bull strolling through a china shop.

CONSUMER NEEDS AND WANTS

In the final analysis any positioning statement must be directed at the needs and wants of the consumer. Those hotel marketers that have adopted positioning strategies sometimes fail to incorporate this basic marketing concept into what are otherwise fine "positions." In projecting positioning as the first of a three step approach to cultivating an image, Sill (1980) suggests establishing "an explicit statement of the type of restaurant it (management) *wishes to present to patrons*" (author's italics). Tissian (1979), in the same vein, states that after having "identified the property's competitive strengths and weaknesses, the results of this analysis are articulated in the form of a positioning statement. The positioning strategy reflects a conscious decision . . . to communicate to the market a definition of the property as a particular type of hotel . . . this definition must be consistent with the property it describes. . . . " The next step, says Tissian, is to select the target audiences. Sill and Tissian's concepts are essential to effective positioning and may lead them to fine positioning statements following their own dicta. The failing, however, is that they may as easily lead to a position in accordance with the image that management wishes to project or thinks it projects, rather than one that differentiates from the competition along the needs and wants of the target market.

Good positioning entails three essential elements. First, and least important, it creates an image. Why is this least important? Because images are good and bad, persuasive or nonpersuasive, inspiring or uninspiring. Images alone do not incline the consumer to buy. Creating an image, any image, is relatively simplistic—albeit many hotel ads fail to do exactly that.

What does influence buying behavior is the most important of the three elements—the benefits perceived in the environment in which the product or service is used. Positioning a product or service along benefit dimensions in order to reflect positively an attitudinal disposition forms the basis of the development of more effective strategy. Once defined, it is possible to isolate target markets of those consumers who hold similar attitudes about the usage situation for a particular hotel or hotel class.

The third essential element of the positioning statement is that it differentiate the brand from the product class, i.e., one hotel from other hotels that may be different but may, as easily, offer essentially the same products and services.

Most advertising creates an image, albeit a different one to different people. The positioning statement should be designed to create *that* image which reflects the perception of the property that management wishes its target market to hold and on which the property can deliver and make good. That desired perception must be benefit based, first on needs and wants and second on available differences between it and the benefit perception of the competition, if it is to be successful. Consumers don't buy products or services. They buy expectations. Statements that promise the consumer something and give him a reason to believe in the benefit promised are most effective in persuading him as to what he can expect and why he should stay at a particular hotel.

Aristotle's ethos (credibility), pathos (emotional appeal) and logos (logic and reasoning) are still the best foundation for persuasion that we have—but first, said the philosopher, you must know your audience. Development of the positioning statement comes after the development of the strategy which is first based on the target market.

THE DIFFERENTIATION ELEMENT

Differentiating in the positioning statement means demonstrating to the consumer the unique attributes of the property. Success in developing collateral (or advertising) depends more on the positioning decision than any other but "most brochures (and the properties they describe) look alike . . . " (Maas 1980) and few reflect any attempt at unique differentiation or positioning. When products or services are similar, it is the unique benefits that must provide the positioning differentiation.

Yesawich (1980) makes the claim that lodging properties must become competitor-oriented to be successful in the 1980s. Knowing what your guest wants is of little value if five of your competitors are already serving his needs. Finding unique attributes or benefits means not only knowing your own strong points but also locating the weak points in the positions of competitors. Carried to the optimal, one may find an unoccupied position where an entry may generate new customers or lure them away from competitors.

The consumer benefit concept in positioning means developing the proper consumer perception of one property's benefits vs. the competition. Here, perhaps more than anywhere else, the consumer seeks tangible clues to distinguish between competing benefits of intangible services. Good research and self-examination can reveal how one property can be set apart from others, its unique advantages, or what areas can be pre-empted.

Positioning statements that differentiate and do offer unique benefits are:

- "a beautifully orchestrated idea in hotels" (where every room is a suite)
- "soars 46 stories over Central Park" (for panoramic views not usually found in New York City)
- "we think that vacation costs are outrageous" (for a unique, inexpensive vacation experience)
- "there *is* an alternative to high-priced hotels" (for the value conscious professional traveler with all the usual hotel amenities mentioned so he can be sure nothing is left out)

Positioning statements that have failed to differentiate properties or offer unique benefits are:

- "the flair and style of a Hyatt. The efficiency and courtesy of a Marriott" (explicit in differentiating the competition, assuming the consumer has the same perceptions, but leaves this hotel in a confusing betwixt and between position)
- "the golden opportunity for the 80's" (for a chain that competes head-on with other "golden opportunity" chains)
- "we have room" (announcing additional rooms making this hotel the largest in the state)
- "we're the difference" (with no supporting evidence for a hotel that looks like hundreds of others)

THE BENEFIT ELEMENT

The benefits are the real reason the consumer comes to a hotel. They *are* the image and they *are* the elements that differentiate a hotel from its competition. Benefits come in bundles and it is the benefit bundle that positions a hotel to its particular target market. Further, differences exist in the importance of attributes with respect to benefits offered, as perceived by consumers and as applied to different service levels (Lewis 1980). Positioning the benefits means marketing the expectation which, in the final analysis, is what hotels have to sell to the selected target market.

The first problem is to determine the key characteristic of the various benefit segments. Sophisticated market research can employ statistical procedures such as conjoint analysis, multi-dimensional scaling, or discriminant analysis for this purpose.

More easily, it is possible to utilize some older concepts by adapting them to services and hotels with a consumer behavior application. Economists have traditionally tried to explain purchase behavior with a utility model.

Lovelock (1979) proposed a revised conceptual structure of consumer utility for services:

1. Form utility
2. Place utility
3. Time utility
4. Psychic utility
5. Monetary utility

This classification, of course, is no more than a gross taxonomy of benefits from the consumer's viewpoint which, conversely, are costs or disutilities in their negative aspect. Consumer information processing determines the balance between the benefits and such costs as inconvenience, time-wasting, fear of disillusionment and risk. It is the marketer's job to accentuate the positive utilities and diminish the negative ones.

The problem for the marketer is the need to translate the intangible utilities into consensus realities that define the service entity to various target markets. The marketer must rely on tools of the behavioral sciences to create image and on peripheral clues to create tangible evidence that the consumer can comprehend with his five senses.

Renaghan (1980) has proposed a new marketing mix to distinguish the offerings available for the marketing of hospitality services to identified target markets and their needs:

1. *The Product-Service Mix*
   That combination of products and services, whether free or for sale, that are made available to satisfy the needs of the target market.
2. *The Presentation Mix*
   All those components under the direction of the firm that are used to increase the tangibility of the Product-Service Mix in the eyes of the target market at the right place and the right time.
3. *The Communications Mix*
   All communications of any kind between the firm and the target market that increase the tangibility of the Product-Service Mix, set or monitor consumer expectations or persuade consumers to purchase.

THE BENEFIT MATRIX

Lovelock's utilities concept and Renaghan's hospitality mix can be combined in a benefit matrix to use in determining the key characteristics of various benefit segments. The hotel marketer has only to complete the matrix in terms of the property's benefits and management's capabilities, and the market's perception of the property and its offerings. Table 40.1 abstracts some of the elements which such a matrix might contain.

TABLE 40.1.   HOTEL BENEFIT MATRIX

	Product/Service	Presentation	Communications
Form	Food, room, pool, beach, lounge, room service, bed, performance	Physical plant interior and exterior, employees, tangible presentations	Product/service tangible attachments, tangible use and performance
Place	Convenience, ease of use, ease of buying, facilities, reservations	Location; nearby attractions such as business, shopping, arts; availability	Where available, where can be used, use and performance related
Time	Convenient times; when needed, wanted or desired	Pleasant use of time, time saving, service level, seasonal aspects	When available, when can be used, use and performance related
Psychic	Good feeling, social approval, prestige, re-assuring personal service satisfaction, rest and relaxation	Atmospherics: light, sound, space, smell, accoutrements	Tangible attachments to intangibles, dissonance reduction, people who go there, prestige address, satisfied guests
Monetary	Cost, fair, save money, how much	Price-relation in value, easy payment, psychological effect, quality	Value perception, terms, quality connotation, risk reduction

A similar matrix can be prepared for the competition. The marketer is then ready to do an aggregated (nonsegmented) concept positioning analysis. When the target market is identified, a joint space configuration (conjoint analysis) can be utilized to evaluate the properties by benefit segments. Or, for discriminant analysis, the predictor variables are identified that will determine the key discriminating characteristic of the benefit segments. Lacking this sophisticated knowledge of his target markets the marketer is still prepared from his own perception research to develop the positioning statement to include image, competitive differentiation and consumer benefits. This essential exercise utilizes the benefit matrix to identify the tangible clues that make credible the intangible benefits to the desired target market.

THE POSITIONING STATEMENT

Communications should be customized to fit the needs of individual target markets. Each service should be promoted to its own target segment instead of attempting to crowd all information about every service into one campaign. The central theme, however, should be featured as the unifying element or positioning statement. Thus, to make itself competitive, the hotel should implant its main services

FIG. 40.1. THE MARKET IS IDENTIFIED, BUT NOT THE BENEFITS; A FAILURE TO DIFFERENTIATE OR TO CREATE AN IMAGE.

(benefits) in the consumer mind while providing each service with its own individual identity and image, e.g., to the business man, the meeting planner, the travel agent or the pleasure traveler.

The positioning statement, then, is singleminded and all subpositionings are promoted under the one umbrella positioning. This creates an image that personalizes the operation; the customer is buying an abstract service and wants to be reassured. It differentiates from the competition; the customer knows why he is choosing one hotel over another. It promises benefits; the customer is promised that his needs and wants will be fulfilled. Finally, positioning supports these elements with tangible clues that the consumer can grasp with his five senses and which communicate to him that there is substance behind the promises.

Accompanying this article are examples of advertising which incorporate positioning statements. In Fig. 40.1 the positioning statement is very specific: "America's Most Recognized Business Address." This statement clearly identifies the target market but fails to provide an image, or indicate benefits or a promise to provide them, or differentiate from the competition. There are no tangible clues to support the intangible contention.

In the second advertisement (Fig. 40.2), "Capture the Spirit Worldwide" is a positioning statement that is tenuous, nebulous and intangi-

Discover the unique Hyatt experience in downtown Columbus. 660 rooms, 30 suites, Regency Ballroom accommodates 2500. 25 meeting rooms. Adjoining Ohio Center convention, shopping, and entertainment complex.

Capture the spirit in Columbus

HYATT REGENCY COLUMBUS

CAPTURE THE SPIRIT℠ WORLDWIDE

Call Worldwide Group Desk at 800 228 9000 or any Hyatt Worldwide Sales Office.

FIG. 40.2.   MAKES THE INTANGIBLE MORE SO AND FAILS TO DIFFERENTIATE; BENEFITS AND IMAGE ARE NEBULOUS.

The 45 story Chicago Marriott stands just in size where the going is no more in the middle of things

The right hotel is never hard to find

The Marriott Hotel people have built their reputation on doing things right.

And one of the things they do most consistently right is to be, somehow, in just the right location for the business you want to conduct, in any given city.

In New York, for instance, Marriott's Essex House is right on Central Park. In Chicago? Right on Michigan Avenue (photo)—and also at O'Hare International Airport. In Kansas City, Cleveland, Miami, L.A. and Rochester, also conveniently right near the airport. In Philadelphia? Right at the edge of the Main Line.

Some cities already have several Marriotts.

Atlanta, four. Houston, three. Five in Washington, D.C. And new Marriotts are blooming worldwide. Marriott can now do it right for you in Saudi Arabia, Kuwait, Holland. Even right on the beach in resorts like Acapulco, Barbados, Santa Barbara, and Marco Island.

To reserve at a Marriott where you're headed, call a professional, your travel agent. Or dial toll-free 800-228-9290.

WHEN MARRIOTT DOES IT,
THEY DO IT RIGHT. **Marriott Hotels.**

FIG. 40.3.   GIVES TANGIBLE CLUES OF THE PROMISED BENEFIT THAT DIFFERENTI-
ATES THE TARGET MARKET.

You gloat over a
great hotel the
way you do over a
rare antique find.

We designed
The Stanford Court
for you.

Photographed at the Stanford Court

The
STANFORD COURT
Hotel on San Francisco's Nob Hill
For people who understand the subtle differences.

For reservations anywhere in the U.S. except California call toll free (800) 227-4736
In San Francisco call (415) 989-3500 Elsewhere in California call toll free (800) 622-0957
Member of Hotel Representative, Inc. and Preferred Hotels Association

FIG.40.4. EXCELLENT POSITIONING SHOWS STRONG IMAGE, DIFFERENTIATION,
AND PROMISED BENEFITS.

ble and contains no real tangible clues of benefits that differentiate this
hotel from those of the competition. It compounds the abstractions and
provides no consensual realities.

The statement is part of a series of larger advertisements in a campaign that is creative and attention-getting, but lacks the positioning
that commits it to long term memory in consumer information processing especially in a meeting planning medium where it has appeared.

The third and fourth advertisements (Fig. 40.3 and 40.4) are examples of good positioning. Marriott's advertisement targets to the businessman, differentiates the benefits by place and time, provides tangible clues in its presentation and communication (see the Benefit
Matrix), creates an image and supports these elements with a graphic
promise so that the consumer can believe: "The Right Hotel Is Never
Hard to Find."

The Stanford Court advertisement is an outstanding example of good positioning. The image is ultra clear. The differentiation and the utilities (form, place, time and psychic) are clearly presented and communicated with strong, tangible benefit clues. All elements are integrated and the target market is identified in the single positioning statement, "For people who understand the subtle difference."

Smaller, not well-known properties can be positioned just as well as the large ones or chains. Note how the first advertisement for La Quinta Hotel (Fig. 40.5) identifies its target market, creates an image and differentiates in terms of the Benefit Matrix. However, note the second La Quinta advertisement (Fig. 40.6). Both ran in the Wall Street Journal. The first is effective in its positioning. The second loses the advantage and positions the resort as "one of the crowd" of many golf resorts.

In sum, any hotel can create a positioning statement. If it fails to communicate a unique benefit image supported by tangible clues to the target market the statement will fall far short of its potential.

FIG.40.5. PROVIDES BENEFITS AND DIFFERENTIATION WITHIN AN IMAGE OF PLEASANT SECLUSION.

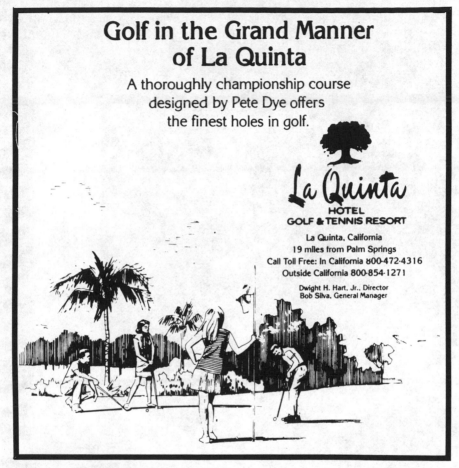

FIG. 40.6.   JUST ANOTHER GOLF RESORT.

41

Competitive Marketing: Challenges and Guidelines

Peter C. Yesawich, Ph.D.

Marketing today is a task unlike any other the hospitality industry has faced in recent years because most operators find themselves between the rock of stagnant growth in both commercial and leisure travel and the hard place of ever-spiraling inflationary costs. To compound the problem, we are forced to deal with these two villains at a time when consumer confidence in the economy is perilously low—with over 40% of American households stating they feel their economic situation is worse in 1981 than it was in 1980.

As we progress through the 1980s, I think many of us feel like the morning after a grand celebration: hoping that as the day wears on we will be able to recharge and renew, hoping we will be able to regain our balance and maintain the momentum we enjoyed through the 1970s. We have all seen the impact of an economic downturn, particularly its effect on the housing and automotive industries. The same downturn has also had its effect on the lodging industry.

Hotel occupancies nationwide have been running at a rate less than they were a year ago. This shortfall would have been greater had we not been the beneficiaries of a tremendous surge in traffic from Latin America, Britain, the rest of Europe and Japan. Domestic gasoline shortages have accounted for a 7% decline in total sales nationwide for all attractions, hotels, resorts and restaurants when discounted for inflation. Approximately 250,000 travel industry employees have been laid off due to decreased travel and inflationary operating costs. Airline traffic has experienced an unprecedented decline.

It would be nice to think that all of this is behind us but it appears that the future holds much of the same. We are likely to continue our bumpy economic ride through the 1980s.

THE ECONOMIC ENVIRONMENT

Today, the average American worker earns more than twice as many dollars as he did in 1970, but his real income after taxes and inflation is 5% less. The biggest attack on family budgets came in the second half of the last decade, and real after tax income has been decreasing at an annualized rate of 4% since 1979.

The Bureau of Labor Statistics has set 3 standards of living for a hypothetical family of 4 in an urban area and tabulated the income levels they must achieve to enjoy these lifestyles. For 1979, the most recent Bureau projection, the low budget line starts just above the $11,000 mark. It was only a few years ago that hoteliers and travel marketers carefully studied this group as a viable source of business, but today, the typical family of 4 at this income level lives in a rented house or apartment, does its own repair work, uses *free* public recreation facilities, and has an annual disposable income of $1016 after settling bills for food, housing, transportation and personal necessities.

The middle income family earns between $17,000 and $19,000 per year. The typical family at this budget level has a 38-year-old husband who is employed full-time, and a wife who stays at home to look after their 13-year-old boy and 8-year-old girl. This segment of the market has filled countless airline seats and hotel beds in the past, yet inflation has dealt them a wicked blow and there is little left in their kitty once this family has met its expenses for basic necessities. This family of 4 has an annual disposable income, after typical living costs, of $1,766. When looking at consumers in this income bracket we have covered a significant percentage of our prospects for business. In fact, we have now covered more than half of the working adult population of the United States, because in 1979, 55% of the adult U.S. population made less than $18,000 annually.

Let's move on to the typical high income family. According to the Bureau of Labor Statistics, the hypothetical high income family of 4 enjoys an annual income of just over $27,000 and has a net annual disposable income of $2,942. That's all that is left over for family vacations, entertaining, gifts, home decorating and all the other things that make working worthwhile.

If you look at the three families together, you see that annual disposable income ranges from $1000 to $3000, and if you examine the figures broken down on a weekly and daily basis they do not come up to very much. This is even more true when you consider that inflation is currently reducing these figures by 13% annually. To put the figures in proper prospective, let us see how long it would take the typical middle and high income families to pay for the services we sell out of their current *disposable* income.

	Cost	Middle	High
Dinner for two	$ 35	7 days	4 days
Day at theme park	$ 75	15 days	9 days
Airline ticket	$300	62 days	37 days
Vacation package	$575	119 days	71 days

- Dinner for two: Including beverages and tip
- Day at theme park: Including admission tickets, food, beverages, film and souvenirs
- Airline ticket: Round trip New York/Orlando/New York
- Vacation package: Including discounted airfare, hotel transfers, 7 nights accommodation, meals and tips (per person)

It is not difficult to see that consumers are rapidly losing their buying power in today's stagnant, inflationary economy. There is not likely to be any reversal of this trend in the short term. As long as inflation outpaces advances in income, there will be no real growth in personal income and traditional middle and high income family markets for the lodging industry will erode.

THE TECHNOLOGICAL ENVIRONMENT

When contemplating how to adjust your marketing efforts to respond to this economic dilemma you must also be sensitive to the imminent changes in our technological environment, and how these changes are likely to affect the manner in which we go about the business of marketing and the channels of distribution through which we work to generate sales. For example, the electronic tentacles of advertising and direct mail will play an increasingly important role in prequalifying the purchase interest of prospects, particularly as the cost of personal selling continues to escalate. The cost of staging a typical sales call today is just under $100 and as this figure rises management will look at less expensive forms of client contact to minimize the cost of prospecting. Accordingly, media exposure will become more intensive at a time when the effective use of media will be confounded by the following developments:

1) We are about to see a dramatic change in the complexion of traditional forms of media, especially electronic media. Broadcasting as we know it today is on the verge of deregulation, and this will lead to a proliferation of stations, satellites and cable networks that will double our media fare by 1990. As these become operational, broadcasting will

in effect become "narrow casting," and what were once national strategies for advertising will have to be written on a regional or even a local basis to deliver the correct prospect audience.

If we add to this the anticipated cable penetration of American households, the television set will become more than a source of entertainment. It will become an interactive communication device that will allow consumers to make purchases, including reservations, directly from a console attached to the television set in their living room. Television will be transformed into a point of purchase display. Now, this may sound a bit Orwellian, but there is one such installation functioning right now. And, I might add, quite successfully.

2) This anticipated change in the complexion of media will amplify an already existing problem known as advertising clutter—the problem of too many advertisements bombarding the same prospects. For example, the average American adult is exposed to just under 450 different commercial messages daily through radio, television, newspapers, magazines, billboards and signage. That means if you are one of the 450 sponsors you had better be pretty good if you are going to implant a lasting, positive impression. With the addition of more cable networks, UHF stations and video discs, this figure is even likely to soar to 650 different exposures per day.

3) The Postal Service 9 digit zip code will provide marketers with one of 2 things:

– A colossal headache because the extra 4 digits will render the Postal Service 4 times more confused than it is at present, thus adding to existing delays and providing justification for more rate increases, or

– A unique opportunity to target direct mail with a degree of precision never before seen.

If it works as planned, the new code will allow you to align direct mail efforts in accord with census tracts to deliver a pre-determined audience by income level and buying power, thus greatly increasing the efficiency of the mail medium.

4) New technology will provide more convenient ways of ticketing and reservation networks will be accessible via hand-held computer printers similar to pocket calculators which may be plugged into any telephone to secure printed confirmations. The era of electronic mail is imminent and this will allow more rapid conversion of inquiries through "conversational" office terminals, without the involvement of the United States Postal Service.

5) There will be a dramatic change in the size and composition of the travel agent market, a distribution channel through which many of us have marketed our services in the past. Today there are approximately

22,000 conference-appointed agents in North America of which probably no more than 10,000 will be around in 1990. Their attrition will be inevitable because of the other direct forms of ticket and reservation access mentioned previously, as well as the advocacy of net rates by airlines and hotels interested in increasing their yield and eliminating what may be perceived as unnecessary commission payments.

Marketing research will gain increasing prominence in future years as inflation continues to weave its insidious web around the buying power of marketing budgets. Media and production costs, for example, have escalated 16% over the past 12 months. Thus you will have to increase your budget by an equivalent amount just to *preserve* your media buying power next year. As this trend continues, management will place greater reliance on research to insure available funds are targeted against the right markets at the right time. Comprehensive guest histories will profile everything from the origins of your business by media market to expenditure patterns and seasonal shifts in market mix by the time of year. Properly controlled qualitative research will reveal guest preferences and enable new product development by far more than just casual examinations of in-room questionnaires which, incidentally, usually provide unreliable data because there is no control exercised over the manner in which the data are obtained.

The customer will remain king in the 1980s, therefore it will be necessary to know as much about him as possible. It will be necessary to anticipate how his changing behavior and media habits will impact the manner in which he conducts his business and how he consumes his leisure time.

GUIDELINES FOR ACTION

How do you market against these problems? How can you build occupancy and increase market share in the midst of all this adversity? The answer to this question depends on 3 considerations:

- Your current mix of business (or room nights by type of guest and geographic origin);
- How many direct competitors you have and how *they* plan to market against the same problems;
- How much you are prepared to budget for marketing.

Business Mix

By mix of business, I mean the room night distribution at your property by type of guest. Supposing your property ran an occupancy of

72% for the year, with 30% of your room nights coming from commercial independent traffic (or business travelers not affiliated with a meeting or convention group); 25% from social independent traffic (or guests traveling primarily for recreational reasons but not affiliated with a tour group); 20% from commercial group traffic (corporate or association members traveling as *part of* a group to attend a meeting, seminar or conference); and 25% from social group traffic (individuals traveling primarily for recreational reasons as *part of* an organized group).

One of the most difficult decisions you have to make is just how much attention you are going to devote to each of these segments in coming years. Do you want more "independent" business, more "group" business, or some combination thereof? To determine which of these segments should receive the greatest emphasis, you need to establish: 1) from which type of guest you make the most money and thus, hopefully, the highest profit, and 2) what current trends indicate is likely to happen to demand from each of these guest segments over the short and long term. The answer to the first question about profitability may be found in your guest history. The answer to the second question is one about which I would like to speculate, because I think the facts are straightforward enough to allow me to prognosticate.

Rooms demand from the commercial independent segment is likely to parallel our gross national product. As the gross national product rises, so will travel by business persons *not affiliated* with meeting or convention groups. If the GNP remains stagnant, demand from this segment will probably go unchanged or even drop slightly.

Rooms demand from the commercial group segment of the travel market is likely to display schizophrenic tendencies in the future— schizophrenic to the extent that I expect to see an increase in the number of corporate meetings and seminars wherein companies foot the bill for employees in attendance, and a decrease in association meetings wherein attendees themselves may have to foot the bill or a major portion thereof.

Rooms demand from the social independent segment is likely to decline in the foreseeable future, even within the 3% of American families that enjoy incomes of $40,000 a year or more. As we saw earlier, most individuals simply will not have adequate disposable income to travel on their own the way they used to, even *if* they could obtain the fuel.

Finally, rooms demand from the social group segment is likely to increase as more consumers can no longer afford to travel on their own, assuming costs don't get so far out of hand that the prices tour operators will have to charge for a vacation will be beyond the reach of middle and high income families.

The bottom line of my prediction is that most of the growth in rooms demand during the 1980s will come from group markets. The reason we are likely to see limited growth among independent business travelers and in the number of independent social travelers is very simple: the prices we will have to charge to cover the construction costs we will pay to house them, the fuel we will use to transport them, the energy we will use to cool and entertain them, and the food and beverages we will serve them will force them to conduct more of their business over the phone or, in the case of social guests, seek other forms of recreation.

Competitive Analysis

Much of what you will have to do to see your way through this period of economic stagnation must be in response to what you anticipate your competitor will do simply because most of you are vying for business from the same pie. Therefore, one of the steps that must be taken is an analysis of your competitors—an analysis that will size up their strengths and weaknesses along every dimension that is meaningful to your guests.

I would encourage you to place yourself in the shoes of your guest and focus a critical eye on both of your establishments. As you conclude your competitive analysis you'll realize that there are some things both you and your competitor do equally well, other things you do equally poorly. But the purpose of the whole exercise is to isolate the things you do *better* than all others. These are the features of your establishment you must highlight in your own marketing efforts to attract a larger share of business.

Take a moment and reflect on what the typical consumer sees as he evaluates you and your competitors. To him, most hotels look the same. They offer accommodation in 300 square feet of space featuring a bed, 2 chairs, a dresser and some pretty uninspiring fixtures that all look like they were shipped from the same warehouse. So to attract his attention away from competitors, three basic guidelines need to be followed:

#1: Don't Be Boring.—Be different from your competitors in a manner that will be meaningful to your customers. If you have some distinctive features now, then reinforce those in your promotional efforts. If you do not, then build them in. And do it in such a way that it will be readily apparent to your customers. Do not base your marketing plan on manufactured differences the consumer cannot see or experience, do what Miller did when it removed calories from beer. Do what Burger King did when it announced you did not have to take the lettuce and the pickle but, instead, you could have it your way. Be different in a meaningful way. Remember, no one ever bored someone into buying something.

#2: Offer Value for Money.—We have already seen what inflation has done to the disposable buying power of the American family, and as this continues to erode, the only travel product that will attract their attention is one that offers good value for its cost. Does this mean you should cut your rates? Absolutely not, and if you ever think about doing it take a moment and calculate what you will have to gain in occupancy to make up the dollar shortfall in rooms revenue just to maintain your current gross.

Offer value by trimming packages of their expensive frills and concentrate on selling your accommodation EP. The price will look much more attractive and value-laden that way. If you find it necessary to add some sweeteners so you won't be boring, then add the things you can get co-oped or subsidized by other local merchants that derive business from the guests that stay at your property. Chances are if you are feeling the squeeze so are they, so offer them an opportunity to participate in your effort to build business and structure it so they'll have to share the cost.

#3: Focus your Marketing Effort.—Many properties have seen a decline in traffic from long-haul drive markets and traffic from scheduled service on long-haul air routes. Business from close-in drive markets and charter carriers (who, incidentally, offer good value for the money) has maintained a relatively stable flow. Therefore, do not spread your marketing effort through areas that do not provide convenient transportation access to your destination. Concentrate on markets that provide non-stop or direct air service, as well as close-in markets within a one-tank drive radius. Transportation costs have escalated faster than any other component cost of commercial and pleasure travel. Fuel now represents 35% of the operating cost of an airline ticket and a substantial chunk of the cost of a drive vacation. And the only place fuel costs are going is up.

When advertising to prospects follow the same guidelines. Trade off reach for frequency. Rather than select media that will expose as many prospects as possible, concentrate on providing fewer, more highly selected individuals with heavier doses. This will bring them to the decision point much faster.

Budgeting

One of the most difficult decisions you will have to face is that of budgeting for these tough times. How much should you spend to talk to your prospects? The intuitive reaction to the question is to reduce marketing expenditures in proportion to the anticipated decrease in total revenue in order to keep the percentage in line. This can be a perilous course, however, because you must continue fueling the marketing machine to insure accelerated performance. If you do not, and your competition does, you generally end up that much farther behind when the economy revives. Let me give you an example.

A representative sample of *Fortune* 500 firms who weathered the economic downturn of 1974 was broken down by those who decreased their marketing expenditures during the period and those who maintained them. The sales growth experienced by each of the two groups through 1977 compared to sales during their fiscal year in 1972 was compared. The firms that decreased their marketing budgets during the economic slump of 1974 experienced a 67% rate of real sales growth. Those that maintained their budgets showed growth of 150%— or better than 2 times the rate of the other companies.

I am not suggesting that you arbitrarily increase your marketing budget to deal with today's adversity. I would suggest that you reevaluate how you establish your budget given all of the considerations I have reviewed. I suspect that, in the past, most of you have used one of two methods to establish your marketing budget: either the percent of gross sales method or the whatever is left over method. The first is self-explanatory, wherein you establish your level of expenditure as a function of a projected level of sales—usually between 4% and 6%. The whatever is left over method is far less sophisticated, oftentimes computed on the back of a stained cocktail napkin and, as the name implies, marketing is given whatever is left over after provisions have been made for direct operating costs and general and administrative costs.

If you are currently using either of these two methods, I suggest that you consider changing your style and adopt a task orientation when deciding how much long green you're prepared to pump into the marketing machine. Calculate the cost to penetrate the markets you have targeted for future growth, to offer value for money, to outflank your competition, and do all of this in a way that *will not be boring*. Then write your budget against these objectives, regardless of what you have done in the past. You might find that you have to dig into your pocket more deeply the first few times around, but this sacrifice will pay off in spades when the economic shakedown is over.

THE CHALLENGERS AND THE CHALLENGED

The marketing environment today is unlike any other the industry has known before. And the irony of the situation is that the potentially turbulent 1980s already have an industry-wide inventory of guest rooms that is 750,000 greater than it was just 10 years ago, with more on the way. Competition can only intensify as a result. Success will no longer be guaranteed by cleanliness, cordiality or reputation. No longer can you afford to be all things to all guests, unless you want to end up as everyone's second choice. The current state of affairs is likely to alter the marketing approaches used in the future.

Operators who anticipated today's environment sought distinct areas of opportunity in the marketplace through the 1970s and launched the era of market segmentation. Borrowing segmentation tactics from consumer goods marketers, perceptive hoteliers began to classify groups of guests by specific combinations of demographic characteristics, interests, and lifestyles, and provided the amenities thought to appeal to these groups in new accommodations. As operators became more conversant with market-segmentation strategies, they borrowed another concept from their counterparts selling toothpastes and automobiles: positioning, the practice of promoting a product or service in such a well-orchestrated, consistent way that it takes on a distinctive "personality" in the mind of the consumer.

One result of hoteliers' burgeoning awareness of the techniques of positioning has been the projection of a more streamlined image of lodging properties in marketing efforts. For example, a resort is no longer just a resort. Today a resort is visually defined as a golf resort, or a tennis resort, or a health resort, or a family resort, or a singles resort. All elements of the product and its promotional efforts are carefully selected to achieve the desired positioning.

Operators who have actively positioned their properties to achieve a specific image have enjoyed a high degree of market penetration and generally a healthy bottom line. Those who have been slow to recognize the growing importance of positioning generally find themselves plagued by the prospect of eroding occupancy and challenged by a variety of well-positioned competitors. Some operators believe the problem can be solved readily through changing the decor in the dining room, the addition of a discotheque, or the replacement of worn bedspreads. Unfortunately, such simple solutions will no longer guarantee a healthy share of the market.

A Competitive Stance

Meeting the needs of the guest will remain the key to success, but customers' needs and preferences will become more specific. Today, the consumer can opt for low-caloric or traditional beer when imbibing, first-class or "supersaver" seats when flying, eating at home, eating out, or taking out when dining, and any of four "life-cycle" formulations when purchasing food for the family dog. And as marketers have become more conversant with the techniques required to stimulate latent needs, consumers have become more eclectic in their choice of the products and services offered to sate those needs.

What impact will the past decade of positioning have on marketing strategies in the 1980s? Ironically, we are rapidly approaching a time in which it will become difficult to develop a successful "positioning strategy" in the lodging industry simply because the strategies already developed by chain-affiliated and strong independent properties have worked so well that the options remaining for new positioning strategies are dwindling. Stated quite simply, it will become increasingly difficult, if not impossible, to dislodge a well-positioned leader who dominates a given market. Any property that does not currently enjoy a dominant posture may face adversity in the years ahead, particularly independent properties that lack the financial resources required to secure a unique market position through promotional efforts and to effect the physical-plant modifications necessary to reinforce this image.

Lodging has always been a service industry and over the years its orientation to guest needs has grown more pronounced through the provisions of various amenities other than the basic of bed and board. As a result, most of today's properties are for the most part "marketing-oriented." But knowing what your guest wants is of little value if five of your competitors are already serving his needs. Thus, in future years, your problem will not be your customers. Your problem will be your competitors.

To be successful in the 1980s, a lodging property must become "competitor-oriented." It must look for weak points in the established positions of competitors and then mobilize its marketing forces to exploit them. Most operators consider their competitors when developing a marketing plan, but they typically do so with equanimity, even as an afterthought. Marketing plans will be developed differently in the 1980s. In fact, they may not even be called marketing plans, but competitive plans. They will begin with a trenchant analysis of competitors, encompassing a realistic evaluation of the strengths and weaknesses exhibited by each. And at the heart of each plan will be a series of strategic steps designed to capitalize on these weaknesses.

Thus, in the coming decade, hoteliers are likely to select one or two courses of action, depending on their current market status. Those that now enjoy a dominant position within a given market will direct their efforts toward penetrating established segments even further, to the exclusion of peripheral sources of business. Those that do not will embrace a new strategy for marketing—competitive repositioning. These operators will develop strategies with reference to the well-established positions of their competitors. And this is likely to result in the advent of new forms of accommodation and service built around emerging life-styles, with the sameness we now see among properties rapidly becoming a thing of the past.

These new strategies will dictate that operators pay more attention to "packaging" their facilities, building cues into their offerings to reinforce a desired image. Furthermore, hoteliers will come to rely on more sophisticated forms of marketing research to discern both competitive and consumer trends, and become more adept in the manipulation of the media vehicles (in particular, radio and television) at their disposal. Marketing programs developed from managerial hunches are likely to become increasingly scarce, if not extinct.

CONCLUSION

The task of hospitality marketing will become increasingly difficult in future years for all of the reasons that I have highlighted. The key to success during the next few years will be innovation: innovation in product development, innovation in management, innovation in marketing and innovation when exploiting the weaknesses of your competitors. I would encourage you to stimulate the exchange of new promotional ideas within your own organization and treat your most productive sales and marketing personnel with the deference they will deserve, as they will become your most valuable asset. Remember, always, nothing will happen until someone makes a sale.

42

The Marketing of Smaller, Independent Properties with Professional Help

Robert G. Averill

The small hotel property, usually with fewer than 50 rooms, often has equally small resources which reduces the ability to capitalize on the marketplace. Many smaller properties have joined group associations or marketing groups. While this is a step in the right direction, the expertise and resources of professional marketing organizations could increase the impact and results of these properties as well as save time and money. Thus, utilizing this expertise and these resources is an important alternative for small, independent properties.

Large marketing organizations often maintain a segregation of specific categories or classes of property. These may include small as well as very large properties. While the successful marketing of a mix of motels and resort hotels, rural inns and motels, or city hotels is not easy because different markets exist for each and many are not compatible with the others, older properties and newer properties of the same category may be compatible. The size, personality and character of each can often be similar.

The smaller property is becoming increasingly important in today's marketplace. The country inn and some beautifully restored smaller hotels are often sought after by the traveling public. Throughout the world and especially in the United States, there are many historic, old, but well-maintained hotels. Today's tourist is more expansive and more sophisticated, more demanding in terms of things to do, to see and to experience and thus increasingly seeks small inns and restored properties at which to stay. The competition of the smaller, independent property is other kinds of travel or holiday. It is not the nearby motel or resort. The use of professional marketing organizations can be an important factor in reaching the market.

PROBLEMS OF MARKETING FOR
THE SMALL PROPERTY

Effective advertising in selected media to reach the market may be beyond the budget of most smaller properties. Advertising can be more effective when repeated and when the proper media are utilized. A $50,000 budget or more for a short duration for this purpose is not beyond the realm of reality.

Direct selling to selected travel agents or corporate accounts is also beyond the scope of most smaller properties as it is a full time project involving considerable travel expense. Developing group sales from corporate accounts, selected group-producing travel agents, selected tour operators and near-by organizations falls into the same expensive category. Many small properties shun travel agents and groups for this reason.

Some objectivity is necessary in marketing a property when first determining what it is that needs to be accomplished in line with objectives. Often this objectivity is lost in small properties. For example, when New England properties in a fall foliage area advertise, promote, or sell the foliage season of September and October, it is time and money wasted because this market already exists. A concentrated effort over the past 15 years, led principally by the state of Vermont, shows what cooperation and a real effort can produce and has already developed this market.

WHAT MARKETING ORGANIZATIONS
CAN ACCOMPLISH

Marketing organizations can combine the efforts of many to develop new markets, e.g., April in southern New England, May in northern New England. Emphasizing the beauty of spring in blossom or maple sugar gathering in March can lead to sizeable group travel at these times. Such groups can be compatible with individual guests if the tour operator and the group are properly chosen and marketed. Often these groups travel from afar, probably by air to a central point which can be called a gateway city. A motor-coach gathers the group and it embarks on a pre-established prepaid itinerary and tour. These tours are leisurely, cover less than 150 miles daily and often include two nights at one lodging. Travelers pay full tariff and have two or three meals daily with full choice of menu. They are escorted and driven by a professional escort and a professional driver who have been trained and are experienced in working with groups.

These are the customers who yesterday arrived independently via automobile. They mix with today's client who has arrived by automobile. They are the same people sharing the same objectives and backgrounds though they come from different areas of the country or the world. Such a group is often stimulating to other guests and shares the same enthusiasm for what they are doing, the area they are visiting and the property in which they are staying.

Groups put together by national or international tour operators can profitably balance quiet seasons with busy or high seasons by directing their marketing and operating effort to areas of opposite seasonal requirements. Properties in certain geographic regions such as New England have seasonal requirements which vary from those of other properties in other geographical regions. They may not be far apart in terms of straight line distance but seasons apart in terms of market such as properties on lakes which have only summer seasons versus properties in the mountains which have summer and winter or summer and foliage seasons. Thus, market associations can tailor requirements to properties so that they meet each seasons' needs.

Other groups are corporate meeting groups. These may come from a much closer radius within two to three hours driving time. Some properties have the advantage by being located in such heavily developed regions. The northeastern United States is again a good example. This market is often off-season or it can exist during the week for properties that tend toward mid-week vacancies, especially in rural and vacation-oriented areas.

This corporate market is a difficult one and is best approached and developed by personal acquaintance and contact through a sales, technical or other department. Companies that have several divisions and locations may plan and maintain one or more group meetings in each category, off premises, a year. Again, profession marketing associations are best at developing this market.

ANALYZING THE PROPERTY

A complete appraisal or inventory of a property is necessary before reaching out to appeal to a group market:

What are the physical facilities?

    number of beds, twin, single, double, etc.;
    size, area, and location of meeting rooms or rooms that can "double"
      as meeting rooms and how they can be set up;
    audio-visual equipment available;

electrical outlets and maximum voltage load and voltages available;

safety factors, such as sprinkler systems, fire alarms, escape routes, sealed or open windows;

exhibit areas . . . indoors, outdoors;

parking availability;

security. This may be the top selling point for a small property for some meetings. No security required, it's isolated!

A layout and plan of the property which is printed or reproduced is a necessary part of the marketing approach. A map of the location with an easy to read and interpret "best way" to reach it, modes of transportation, travel times, and shuttle services available between the properties and public transportation are also essential informative marketing tools.

A property's rate structure must be consistent with the market objective while it also covers the costs of operation and returns the desired profit. Meshing this is the art of innkeeping but, again, professional expertise is helpful when developing business. Travel agents who produce individual as well as corporate meetings and group business naturally expect a commission. The usual commission in North America and many other areas of the world is 10%. Assume, for a minute, an annual gross of $172,000 based on a property of 20 rooms with 60% average occupancy all year, and a room rate of $40. If a 10% commission were paid on 100% of the room nights, the total commission would be $17,200. More realistically, 15% of sales may be from business received from travel agents. This would be $26,000 in annual gross travel agent sales and $2,600 in commissions. An increase in the all-room, all-year rate of only 60¢ will cover this commission cost.

Groups, on the other hand, are quoted "net." Net is the basic rate to be charged per person times the number of persons in the group and no commission is paid. The group rate is usually the regular or "rack" rate less 10% and often more. Tour operator groups, for example, will ask at least 15% because the tour operator pays a 10% commission to selling travel agents filling seats in the group. Yet, groups being sold with small properties, such as country inns, in the itinerary are not always price conscious. One reason, especially in New England, is that small properties are often under-priced in relation to prices in other properties or in other areas. Additionally, group members are frequently sophisticated travelers with much travel experience who will choose an itinerary for its uniqueness and its air of sophistication. These groups tend to come from a far distance requiring air travel from home to gateway point.

USING PROFESSIONAL HELP

There are 18,000 travel agents, perhaps 400–500 tour operators and coach companies, thousands of businesses, schools, colleges and organizations, and hundreds of advertising media opportunities. Which to choose and how to do it?

My urgent suggestion is to rely on professional help. The hospitality and tourist industries are very different from any other in marketing approach and fulfillment. These industries deal in dreams and in personal psychology. The one who can determine the dream, find the means to attract the dreamer and then fulfill the dream has won the market, but only one facet of the market. There are many more out there, all different.

What and who are these markets? If near a major attraction like Disneyworld, then the market is families, honeymooners, school groups. If near a big city, the market becomes many things: families, with or without children; wider age range; senior citizens (the largest single market there is today in terms of numbers and travel dollars); corporate meeting groups; sales and technical personnel of companies; catering to or working with companies located in the area of the lodging property.

If near a historical attraction, or folklore, such as Pennsylvania "Dutch", then the market is all age groups and especially senior citizens, families and school groups. If rural with no principal attraction, the property and its immediate environment is the attraction and must be exploited as such. Such a property can appeal to its surrounding natural beauty, even appeal to its isolation if that is a factor. Turned to advantage, the isolation will sell, emphasizing the privacy, the good meals served, the hiking, walking, summer theatre, concerts, auctions, horse riding or whatever. Company meeting groups may be attracted to isolated properties because many are specific in their desire for privacy and isolation. Tour groups and other short-stay groups, however, may not be attracted. Of course, if the property is unique historically, architecturally, or by virtue of a former occupant, owner personality, celebrity or perhaps the innkeeper who, today, may be such a personality or celebrity, then that too is an attraction. Personalities make small properties.

Pricing must not be forgotten and is carefully analyzed by the professional. Often the room rate structure indicates the basic market that will be attracted. It must be determined, however, that this particular market is of the size and availability to merit the expenditure of time, effort and money to attract it, whatever market we talk about. A price that is low in relation to the real value of the property will attract the low end of the market when the property is otherwise not particularly distinguished. The real low end of the market, however, which is unaffected by values or attractions above those of an almost purely commercial nature, will be attracted by price alone. On the other hand, a price lower than value in a distinguished property will attract a sophisticated, usually older traveler who is habitually value conscious above all else. But don't mistake the senior citizen market as all low price. Much of it is not.

Another consideration of the professional's knowledge and expertise is the physical facilities of the property. The American market usually demands private bath and toilet. There is a segment, however, in the more sophisticated group and often over 35, that will accept a share bath basis in an unusually attractive property of small dimension with a certain air of exclusivity about it.

Another element is the number of beds per room, room type and style. A room with a double-sized bed is limited in sale to singles or the increasingly fewer travelers who will share a bed. As with all statistics or averages, however, there are major exceptions. The double bed—regular, queen or king—is accepted in resort areas, properties near major attractions and distinguished very unusual small properties. Such room arrangements, however, restrict the ability to handle groups, whether tour groups or company meeting groups. A two-bed room can be sold as a single and thus offers the greatest flexibility.

For business meetings the smaller property can be very much in the market by pointing out that a group has the whole inn to itself, the dining room can be converted quickly and easily to a meeting or conference room, and so forth.

For group arrangements, the group market must be carefully chosen to make certain that the facilities are desirable and that the groups will be compatible with individual guests.

Professionals use their knowledge and expertise to analyze all these factors and many others.

THE PROFESSIONAL PRODUCT

The image of a property is reflected by:

the brochure;
the rate structure;
innkeeper personality;
sign board;
interior decoration and exterior appearance.

The brochure image is reflected by:

> the kind and grade of paper;
> graphics;
> content and language.

The professional knows how to deal with these reflections.

A four-color brochure on good quality paper with sharp images illustrating active sports such as tennis, swimming, skiing, and with language indicating that these are "on your own initiative" activities attracts an active younger audience.

A four-color brochure of the same quality but illustrating activities such as golf and fishing with language indicating that these activities are "on your own" will probably attract a more passive audience of no special age group.

The same brochure with language indicating that "we will meet for dinner and a film following dinner" and/or that there are group dancing lessons, bridge games, and other organized activities, and that the property has a social director, will attract the inactive guest and probably an older group.

A budget image must not be confused with a luxury image. They cannot be mixed. Successful marketing requires a single, cohesive pattern. Even the name conveys a market image. "Auberge des Indies" or the "Governor's Inn" may attract an adventurous guest, probably a holiday guest and no particular age group. "Executive House" will attract the business traveler.

A signboard says a lot, too. It should be professionally done. A rustic sign for a historic Victorian property just does not go. Similarly, a beautifully formed and lettered sign that suits a lovely old inn is hardly the sign for a rustic, woodsy resort.

Properties should emphasize what is available to the competitor's disadvantage. If the nearby properties are chain motels or a large hotel, the smaller property cannot and must not mimic either, but establish an independent image of its own that is very different. Indeed, the smaller property is different. If it possesses Colonial or Victorian charm, perhaps historic, with period furnishings, than this is what must be emphasized, and SOLD. The room rate should be as high, if not higher than the nearby other properties. It is in a different market.

The brochure should be descriptive, readable and contain a map. A rate folder should be enclosed and should indicate by graphics or photographs a guest room, dining room and living area and/or exterior. A brochure (and advertising) must include a telephone number, address and mail address. This goes without saying, but amazingly, is sometimes left out.

Mailings should include a stamped, self-addressed envelope or, at least, a self-addressed envelope or post-card to make the response easy.

Aim for the "after-market" if near cities or urban areas. That is, stay longer and enjoy the activities which are available or near-by. Or, "get away for the week-end in rural warmth and charm" and similar inducements. Or, one can offer, for the active and inactive client:

sports clinics (usually a blue collar market);
bridge clinics (usually senior citizen);
dance clinics (usually older, passive clients);
snorkeling, scuba diving, canoeing, hiking, skiing (for the active);
bird-watching, nature walks, etc. (for the passive);
seminars, cultural and historical forums for different group types.

Markets must be analyzed. For example, the blue collar market is both high and low income, senior or youth or family, and often group. It tends to be inactive and likes the confidence and security of a group or group activities. It often takes 4 to 6 weeks of annual vacationtime. The smaller property, however, is seldom for this particular market. A smaller property by its very nature indicates a confident, adventurous guest.

Or, it might be possible, for example, to shift one segment of an existing market into another period of the year, or season, or month, or even week to open up a period of time in which an entirely new market could be attracted. Such a new market might required a specific, non-negotiable period of time, as families with children, school and college faculty and students and other.

Marketing small, independent properties requires knowledge, expertise and resources that the small, independent operator rarely has. Collective effort for smaller properties is the answer to successful marketing with professional marketing and sales organizations providing the expertise.

43

Marketing Strategies of Caribbean Tourist Boards vs. Cruise Ship Lines—Conflict or Compliment?

Ernest P. Boger

FOREWORD

Originally, this chapter arose out of my concern for the current validity of the traditional idea of the cruise passenger as an "island sampler." A central teaching point in my presentation of hospitality marketing courses was sensitizing prospective hotel managers to the opportunity for creatively stimulating the return of cruise passengers as long-stay guests.

In summer of 1978, I noticed a trend toward cruise vacation advertising which suggested that specific island visits were, perhaps, less important than the actual experience of being on board ship. These advertisements spoke glowingly about the ship's cuisine, activities and entertainment while making only cursory mention of island ports-of-call.

The culmination of the informal investigation and data collection on this apparently changing promotional/market thrust was my participation in session 8.1 of the World Hospitality Congress (WHC-81). This session was a panel discussion on the topic:

Conflict or Compliment? Marketing Strategies of Caribbean Tourist Boards vs. Caribbean Cruise Ship Lines.

This chapter is not a transcription of panel discussion 8.1. It is, however, a direct outgrowth of concepts, ideas and approaches that were introduced during that session, plus research and background material utilized in pre-congress preparation.

Special thanks is given to Jeremy Bonnett, Vice President Marketing for Nassau/Paradise Island Promotion Board. Mr. Bonnett provided a wealth of information, insight and inspiration while a co-panelist.

THE PROBLEM

The floating resort hotels of the 1980s, as today's Caribbean cruise ships are now characterized, have become enormously successful competitors of traditional land-based island resort hotels. Competitors in the sense that cruise passengers are no longer (if they ever did) sampling specific islands for the purpose of, perhaps, returning as long stay guests next year.

The ship itself is the destination. The island (any island) simply provides a rounding out of the fantasy: sandy beach, crystal waters, palm trees, etc.

Island hotels constitute the so-called "physical plant" of tourism. In island economies where tourism dollars potentially account for upwards of 75% GNP, and the single largest bloc of civilian jobs:

> empty beds mean empty pockets,
> empty pockets mean empty stomachs,
> and, perhaps most importantly,
> empty stomachs severely exacerbate
> 'coitus interruptus' in political careers

Given this scenario, it seems certain that governments, their mortality necessarily at the will of the electorate, must champion repressive measures to create inefficiencies in cruise line operations thereby enhancing the competitive posture of their hoteliers.

Moreover, a popular anti-cruise ship campaign fueled by the zeal of post-colonial protectionism could, in fact, get out of hand, thereby undermining the atmosphere of industrial harmony and tropical tranquility that must obtain if any Caribbean vacation concept is to thrive.

While industry professionals are, for the most part, confirmed disciples of the profit motive, no one wants to see healthy creative competition stifled by mutually ruinous trade barriers, punitive tariffs, or labyrinthine bureaucracy.

Thus, something of meaning and significance will occur if this chapter highlights potential for conflict and stimulates a few ideas for creative cooperation or complement between the floating hotelier and his land-based counterpart.

MARKET MOMENTUM OF THE CRUISE EXPERIENCE IN THE 1980S

Ship as Destination: An Advertising Sampler

A current full-page color magazine advertisement (Tropic, Sept. 7, 1980) by Carnival Cruise Lines presents a 2¼″ × 1¾″ photo of an airy, tastefully decorated hotel room with king-size bed and wall-to-wall carpet. It carries the identifying ¹⁄₁₆″ caption:

"A hotel room, juice, a roll and coffee."

Along side, a bold ¾″ caption reads:

ON LAST YEAR'S VACATION, ALL WE GOT FOR $65 A DAY WAS THIS

Below this, another bold ¾″ caption reads:

THIS YEAR FOR $85 A DAY, WE GOT A FUN SHIP CRUISE THAT INCLUDES ALL THIS:

The "this" consists of 8 additional 2¼″ × 1¾″ color photos of cruise activities. The 8 photos carry the following ¹⁄₁₆″ identifying captions:

(1) Eight meals and snacks a day
(2) Excellent service
(3) Great live entertainment
(4) A full gambling casino
(5) Gala parties
(6) Dozens of activities
(7) 3 ports-of-call
(8) No covers or minimums

Predictably, the photos dramatically enhance the fantasy suggested by the captions. For example, the eight meals and snacks a day photo depicts a smiling chef presiding over a lavish buffet. The gambling casino photo radiates with the euphoria of a couple who just won at roulette!

Another Carnival Cruise Line full-color magazine ad (Tropic, July 7, 1980) carries across the top of the page the bold ⅝″ caption:

THE THREE MOST POPULAR RESORTS IN THE CARIBBEAN

The remainder of the page simply shows the three flagships of the line photographed in dress formation against a deep blue sea. Result! A simple but powerful message—"not all of the world's great resorts are on land" as the text reads.

Similarly, Royal Caribbean Line presents a full-page magazine ad (Miami Herald, April 9, 1978) featuring its two flagships photographed against the background of various Caribbean ports-of-call. The bold ⅝'' caption reads:

SEE EIGHT ISLANDS IN 14 DAYS AND TAKE YOUR HOTEL WITH YOU

These and similar market outreach activities are solid testimony to the coming of age of the ship as a destination in itself. As pointed out in the February 1980 issue of 50 Plus Magazine:

Self Contained Glamour of Floating Resort—

"Today's luxury cruise ships are floating cities equipped with pools, gyms, movie theaters, sauna baths and activities for the whole family. Your can play shuffleboard, practice tennis and golf, shoot craps, attend lectures, or watch closed circuit TV—while the kids or grandchildren are looked after in a nursery or play school staffed by trained counselors.

"And there's no packing and unpacking at each port-of-call, no traffic jams to and from the airport, and no last minute searches for accommodations. Indeed, on today's cruise ships, getting there can be *all* the fun."

The Saturday Review, Aug. 4, 1979, issue goes further to suggest that "Almost everyone will have booked an organized tour, but inevitably as the cruise progresses, more and more people will prefer the ship to the shore."

The largest ship afloat, Norwegian Caribbean Line Norway, insures that its 2000 passengers prefer the ship by unabashedly marketing itself as "a destination," reports Ric Widmer, Marketing Director. Accordingly, the ship stops only twice during the seven-day cruise as the New York Times magazine (1980) puts it:

> "The ship will stop only twice. Mondays
> at a private island called little San Sal-
> vador for languor and Thursdays at St.
> Thomas for loot."

While on the high seas, however, passengers can select from outdoor and indoor olympic pools, several night clubs, a theater, closed-circuit TV, 2 deluxe restaurants, a library, and a disco. Moreover, sports facilities include squash and racquet ball courts, exergym, plus sauna and whirlpool. Additionally the ship features a chapel and a playground for children.

The promenade or international deck is filled with boutiques, cafes and lounges as well as strolling musicians, mimes, and magicians. Slot machines and a Las Vegas style musical review round out the package.

Market Capacity and Demand

Not quite so elaborate but highly similar and competitive facilities are offered on more than 20 ships sailing out of port of Miami's Dodge Island, the world's busiest cruise port. More than 12 ships call at nearby Port Everglades.

Port of Miami director Carmen Lunetta expected a record 1.5 million passengers to move through the port in 1980. Moreover, a 250-million-dollar master plan is now underway and will result in the port's ability to handle the four million cruise ship passengers expected by the year 2000.

While another 6 ships continue to cruise Caribbean waters out of New York, the Miami ports dominate the market, by far. So you say, "Great, but isn't it going to cost a fortune to reach New York or Miami?"

Fly/Cruise Concept and Convenience

In the last five years, all cruise line companies have developed subsidized fly/cruise plans of some type. The subsidy takes many forms. One popular approach is the "One way free" plan. Another is the fixed allowance for airfare. Norwegian America Lines sets one price of $75 for roundtrip air to Florida from anywhere in the United States east of the Rockies and a second price of $125 from west of the Rockies and Canada. In most cases, passengers make same-day connections at the seaport and go directly aboard ship. Thus, smooth air-sea connections have brought previously landlocked vacationers into the Caribbean cruise market. Favorable air fares have drastically reduced the costs.

Fly/cruise has helped in the last two years to establish San Juan, Puerto Rico as a potential rival to the port of Miami.

"We can call at more ports from San Juan", said Alice Marshall of Cunard Line, which in 1979 shifted its Cunard Princes from Port Everglades to San Juan. This permits seven ports-of-call in seven days. Ships sailing from south Florida do not call at more than four ports, and some only two because of the time and distance between islands.

Marketing

Two major factors have acted to keep cruise ship load factor well above 80%, even in the face of expanding capacity. These are the Love Boat p.r. bonanza and the agents' commissions.

Love Boat P.R. Bonanza.—The Love Boat, ABC-TV's weekly sea-soap opera has single-handedly dispelled the image of cruising as "just for the newly-wed and nearly dead," to quote Newsweek magazine (Jan. 2nd, 1979). Moreover, Newsweek points out that although the boy-meets-girl-on-every-cruise premise rarely proves out on real-life cruises, the sitcom's shenanigans of cafes, gambling, disco dancing, entertainment, exotic ports, and over-eating are drawing passengers of every age and expectation. A lucky few even manage to book passage on Princess Cruises the two or three times a year when new episodes of the shows are filmed.

Now into its fourth successful season, the weekly one-hour series draws from 30 million to 40 million viewers in the United States alone. The biggest names in show business, from James Cagney to Jimmy Walker to the Dallas Cowboy cheerleaders, revolve in central roles as three separate story lines unfold.

Its ratings usually range from 28 to 33 as compared to 9 to 11 for CBS and NBC offerings in the same time slot. Already re-runs are aired daily during prime-time morning hours, adding tens of millions of viewers. Saturday Review (Aug. 1979) suggests that the real pay-off may be during the coming decade. After its prime-time days are over, the Love Boat, in syndication and in re-runs, is expected to be on TV screens for the next 10 years. The cruise ship Love is bound to embrace new converts every winter when people who will have to shovel snow from their walks see other people just like themselves sunning on the deck as the Love Boat leaves a wake on an azure sea.

Agents' Commissions.—Jeremy Bonnett, Marketing Manager of the Nassau/Paradise Island Promotion Board, pointed out during the World Hospitality Congress in Boston that "travel agents love this business because it allows them a commission on the total package of air, room, food and entertainment. A non-cruise passenger often wants only an air fare booking." The world's largest cruise company's head, Piergiorgio Costa, Director of Costa Cruises, estimates that agent commissions by the end "of 1981 in the North American market may top the $12 million mark." Moreover, this author estimates that cruise industry revenues will exceed $20 billion, in the same period.

Innovative Capacity Expansion

This fortuitous combination of quality product and powerful promotion is not lost on cruise line moguls who are frantically scrambling to expand capacity. While contracts are routinely being signed for construction of new ships, the lead time and costs are spurring reclamation and stretching projects that will permit faster participation in the booming inertia of the marketplace.

The purchase of the *France* for $18 million in 1979 and its $52 million refurbishing as the spectacular *Norway* still stands as the most ambitious reclamation project. In one fell swoop it increased the capacity of the line by 2000 passengers or 70%. Royal Caribbean Lines captured the imagination of the industry in 1978 by actually sawing its Song of Norway in half and inserting a new mid-section, thereby increasing the liner's double occupancy capacity to 1040 passengers from 724. Since then, the process has become a standard first option to be considered when expansion is desired.

False Alarm? Psychographic Profile Difference?

While no hard evidence yet exists, a few Caribbean resort hoteliers are beginning to grumble that the cruise ships are stealing their customers. Jeremy Bonnett responded to this concern during WHC-81 session 8.1 by pointing out that both cruise ship and hotel visitor arrivals for the Bahamas grew by some 30% in 1980. Thus, the numbers do not immediately suggest crossovers. Moreover, Bonnett suggests that the psychographic profiles of the cruise passenger and the hotel visitor may be quite different. The cruise passenger in his opinion is a conservative or "cautious homebody." The hotel guest is viewed as a more active "adventure seeker."

In view of the fact that the travel and tourism product addresses a human need/want that is increased rather than reduced by its consumption, this author suggested at the same conference that these profiles might be changing or changeable.

In any case, it is evident from the advertisements at the beginning of this section that the cruise lines are aggressively focusing on the same customer market as the resort hotels and are making clear cut efforts to influence a choice of "floating resort" over "land-based resort."

ISLAND GOVERNMENT COUNTERMEASURES

Tourism's Economic Impact

Before presenting measures which regional island governments might be driven to institute, in the face of highly successful cruise ship competition, it is useful to note the impact of hotel-based tourism on a typical island economy.

According to J. Bonnett, approximately two million visitors selected the Bahamas for vacations in 1980. The population of the entire country is 210,000. Most guests visited Nassau/Paradise Island which has a population of 135,000. Thirty percent of these visitors arrived by cruise ship. Yet, cruise visitors contributed only 5% of total revenue. Total visitor revenue for 1980 was $641 million. Since the cruise visitor is a lower level revenue producer, a shift of visitors from hotel beds to cruise ship berths would appreciably reduce the overall visitor economic impact. Moreover, each hotel room supports the existence of approximately one employee. Cruise visitors only require, apart from assorted souvenir merchants, services of a few taxi and ground tour car operators. As Bonnett puts it, "even these activities (tours) have a high impact content (cars, petrol), so the economic impact is further reduced."

Perhaps there is no connection. However, total Bahamas guest arrivals were up for 1980. In the last quarter, however, revenues were down from $130.8 million in 1979 to $54.3 million in 1980. Could visitors be deserting hotel rooms for cruise ship berths? At least one regional hotelier, Joan Mason, General Manager of Nassau's Cable Beach Manor, suspects this to be the case. Are other islands having similar experiences? Both questions certainly deserve further investigation.

Perceptions and Protectionism

Even if investigation does not confirm this hypothesis, island governments can be moved to institute repressive measures if enough hoteliers *perceive* cruise ship visitors to be a threat with which they can only effectively compete via direct government assistance. Anti- or repressive cruise business measures are highlighted because they are likely to create more problems than they cure. This is largely because the Caribbean visitor market still views the region as one essentially undifferentiated bloc. Thus, unrest or disruptions of any kind, anywhere in the region, produce negative customer reactions. Incredibly, civil misconduct in Bermuda causes great concern among travelers packing to visit Bonaire, 3000 miles and another ocean away!

Given the euphoria of protectionism that has accompanied the independence of most Caribbean countries only in the last decade or so (Jamaica in 1962, Bahamas in 1973), what anti-cruise ship measures might governments take to facilitate the ability of land-based hoteliers to compete with their glamourous floating counterparts? Five possibilities were debated during the WHC-81 session 8.1. They are:

1) Employment of local nationals
2) Regional flags of convenience

3) Compensating ports of call
4) Complete facilities shutdown while in port
5) Formal passenger orientation to destination

Employment of Local Nationals

Amazingly, cruise lines that earn millions of dollars from Caribbean tourism only hire local nationals as "window dressing" in special positions; say, a native bartender to prepare special island rum concoctions.

If cruise ship berths are perceived to be occupied by guests who might have selected hotel beds, then governments might require cruise lines to hire a fixed percentage of "displaced" nationals. Failure to meet a required quota could result in a denial of docking privileges, or payment of penalty tariffs. This requirement would add to ship's operating costs by reducing or eliminating the cheap labor force available from under-developed country nationals outside of the region. A positive spinoff of this action as emphasized by Bonnett would be the training bonus of nationals being prepared in all categories of operating positions. Eventually, these individuals might return to upgrade the quality of land-based operations.

Regional Flags of Convenience

Currently, many cruise ships are registered in countries like Panama and Liberia which permit far more flexibility with respect to health, fire and labor standards than the more restrictive countries like Great Britain, the United States and Norway. Through regional cooperation, governments might amend their sea powers legislation and require or at least make it advantageous for ships to fly flags of either regional countries or of the more restrictive ship registration nations. Naturally, regional nations would collect fees for registration and thereby permission to fly the flag would be obtained.

Again, higher costs would face cruise operators due to the expense of upgrading facilities and staff for stricter health and fire/safety standards. Also, wage and benefit schedules might require approval before registration is accepted. Hoteliers might be appeased if registration fees are utilized to subsidize property operations, especially where these are government-owned hotels.

Compensating Ports of Call

Norwegian Caribbean Lines originated and perfected the idea of calling on a deserted island, importing food, drink and entertainment from the ship, for a day-long beach party. The result, a sort of "sandy mixer", that gets the cruise off on the right foot, first day out, with great fun for all. The immediate advantages for cruise line profits are:

1) No need for high-fuel-consumption docking in major ports
2) No competition from land-based shops, restaurants, clubs, etc.
3) No chance for future revenue loss due to cruise guests returning as long stay guests, for neither hotels nor regular transportation to the island exists.

If this trend gathers momentum among other lines, island governments might consider requiring a major port city call for each deserted island call or some other formula which would not permit the liners to totally avoid the major ports at will.

Complete Facilities Shutdown While in Port

Already ships calling at Nassau/Paradise Island are allowed to keep only one live band on board while in port. Also, all gaming facilities must be shut down. This ban could be extended to shops, theaters, discos and virtually all facilities except rooms and food. This would be an extremely unpopular action but is certainly not an impossibility. Since precedent is already established, the question is simply a matter of degree or scale.

Formal Passenger Orientation to Destination

Cruise lines could be required to conduct a formal passenger orientation, preferably with slides or films, prior to arrival at the port-of-call. A national might be permanently retained for this task at the line's expense.

It must be emphasized and clearly understood that the writer is in no way recommending that island governments institute these measures. The objective here is to create a realistically negative scenario that could occur if governments are pressed by their hoteliers to "do something to help us fight the cruise ships." It is hoped that consideration of the scenarios will suggest that no long-term gains can result for land-based or floating resorts, if this atmosphere prevails. Certainly, cruise lines could be expected to take their own retaliatory measures. In short order, the entire region would suffer in the wake of controversy or unrest as earlier pointed out.

CREATIVE, MUTUALLY ENRICHING PROJECTS AND PROCEDURES

Certainly an excellent starting point is the reversal or adaptation of some of the measures suggested in the previous section. For example, visitor orientation programs could be developed as joint ventures. Tourist or promotion boards could conduct several pre-arrival sessions in the ship's theater. Or, ships might consider increasing the number and level of positions available to qualified regional nationals. Additional projects are proposed below.

People to People at Sea

This program would place regional national families or individuals aboard ships for every sailing. These individuals would be of similar demographic and psychographic profiles as regular passengers. Their role would center around interacting informally with regular passengers for the purpose of familiarizing them with their island home. Some more structured activities could be organized to highlight their presence aboard ship. For example, slide or film shows, cocktail parties, lectures on island, music, art, history, etc.

The Bahamas and Jamaica have enjoyed success with this concept and will probably expand to other ships this season.

Sandwich Cruises

Travel Weekly (1979) carried a 2-page double spread advertisement from Norwegian Caribbean Liner (NCL).

THE NEWEST ADDITION TO OUR FLEET IS NOT A SHIP

The advertisement goes on to explain that NCL had recently purchased a plush private resort on Jamaica's lush tropical northeast coast. Passengers would book the *Starward* and begin the regular 7-day cruise. However, upon reaching Port Antonio, Jamaica, on or about the third day, desiring passengers could disembark for 7 days ashore at the Jamaica Hill Hotel (formerly Goblin Hill). The following week passengers would reboard the *Starward* for the continuation of the cruise as another group disembarks for 7 days in Port Antonio. Cruise lines need not actually buy hotels to create this type of adventure. Most hoteliers would welcome the idea with open arms.

Market Research

Fodor's (1981) highly respected Guide to the Caribbean—1981 opens its discussion of cruising with this statement:

> The main reason to cruise the Caribbean is to visit a multiplicity of islands and sample the flavor of each with minimal effort.

The Caribbean Tourism Association publishes a pamphlet entitled: How to Convert Cruise Ship Passengers into Long-Stay Visitors. On page 5, readers are reminded in bold print:

> Remember each cruise ship passenger is on a "Fam Trip" and is a prime prospect for conversion to a long-stay visitor, if you do it right.

In spite of these bold pronouncements from two highly credible sources, there is some concern in the industry that the psychographic profile of the cruise passenger and the hotel guest may be different. As Jeremy Bonnett puts it, "their media habits and demographics are similar but their psychographics are those of the cautious homebody (ship) vs the adventure seeker (shore)." Anthony Hall, University of the West Indies, Nassau, Lecturer in Tourism, suggests that "while this may be so, the profiles are not immutable for the more a person travels, the more he is stimulated to travel again."

Obviously this is a natural project for market segmentation research cooperation between the two camps. If cruise passengers are on fam tours then cruise lines and destinations alike should be delighted to facilitate their quest. If they are of different psychographic profiles and not likely to be interested in resort hotel vacations anyway, then solid data could reduce tension between land-based hoteliers, their governments and cruise lines. Currently, the growing general perception is that they are competing outright for the same customer markets.

Inclusive Shore Excursions

As the shore excursion is an area of major tension between the two resorts, it is an area of major opportunity. Several factors contribute to the problem. It is the only significant activity *not included* in the cruise package price. Thus, the line has no entrepreneurial interest in its success. This is *not* to say that cruise line executives do not wish their passengers to have positive experiences ashore. However, passengers may quickly discover the "relative rarity of a first-class shore excursion" (Saturday Review 1979) as contrasted with the relative rarity of poor food service or entertainment aboard ship. Local tour or tour car operators must sell potential customers on their particular service under less than ideal negotiating conditions. If one can picture several hundred (or several thousand) passengers pouring off four ships and being simultaneously rushed by scores of tour car/taxi operators while trying to figure out which cars are for tours, what tours are available and which cars are strictly for taxi service, the potential for chaos is evident. The crush of passengers often strains local facilities as everyone tries to "do the island" in a few short hours. Tour car operators necessarily keep a steady pace in hopes of conducting several tours during the prescribed period.

Certainly some destinations are more professional in their handling of shore excursion than others. However, the critical issue is to eliminate the us/them syndrome that exists between the cruise ship environment and the shore experience. By including tours in the package price, responsibility is shared for the experience, just as dual responsibility is shared for the smoothness of fly/cruise arrangements. The additional revenue to the line might also prove not insignificant.

Precedent currently exists for these kinds of joint ventures. One line for example offers a golf cruise to the Caribbean. Passengers get to call on three or four islands and play some of the finest links in the world. Tennis tours, museum tours, art or music tours could be promulgated in similar fashion. A good starting point might be to test market these concepts with 10 to 20% of guests on regular cruises. Naturally, their cruise fares and perhaps state room accommodations would be set at a higher level to reflect the special inclusive tour or tours.

SUMMARY AND CONCLUSION

Section one outlined the importance of the tourism dollar in Island destinations and proposed the scenario of disruption that could occur if island governments are pressed to erect barriers to floating resort competition with their land-based resorts.

Section two described the glamor, magnetism and mass market appeal of today's Caribbean cruise ship vacation. While further research is required, evidence is presented which strongly suggests that cruise lines are seeking to convert prospective vacationers who traditionally have selected hotel beds.

The third section presented repressive anti-cruise ship measures that island governments might be forced to take if their resort hoteliers perceive cruise ship competition to be successful, at their expense. The measures discussed were not recommendations but only a devil's advocate type of scenario forecasting.

Finally section four recommended cooperative ventures that, if instituted, will facilitate land- and sea-based resort positive interaction.

Conflict or Complement?

Further evidence is needed and research indeed encouraged. However, the battle lines of ruinous conflict with region-wide negative implications are clearly drawn. It remains to be seen just how long island resort hoteliers will ignore the potentially negative impact of cruise package success on their rooms business. Also, it remains to be seen just how long island tourist boards will ignore the potentially negative economic impact of an increase in the cruise passenger component of the customer mix.

Ultimately, the most prudent course of action seems to be open communication and mutually enriching projects. Hopefully this paper will stimulate the growth and expansion of such ventures, thereby preserving the harmony and tranquility that will always be central to a thriving Caribbean tourism with economic prosperity for all.

44

Paratourism and Its Contribution to the Hospitality Industry

Jafar Jafari

People who patronize various tourism establishments while away from home are considered travelers or tourists. But it is not clear how to consider them when they consume the same tourism goods and services in their own community. Restaurants, for example, serve both tourists and residents under the same roof. At one table, tourists are having "touristic" fun; and at the next table, some residents are having "residential" fun. This idea, however, cannot be extended to hotels. People in every guest room are having touristic consumptions. Unlike restaurants, hotels do not draw from the local community, but depend almost entirely on the external market.

This article discusses why restaurants and not hotels have this double capacity and why residents "eat out" but do not "sleep out." It suggests that the hotel industry could explore and promote the idea of "sleeping out," along the same line as "eating out." This concept should serve the hotel industry in particular and the tourism industry in general.

At the outset, we could ask some basic tourism questions: Why do people travel? Why do they select given destinations for their trips? Is the act of going or being away (from home) a definite purpose and function of tourism? Is tourism a change of place or state of mind, or both? Can one be a "tourist" in one's home town?

The subject of travel and tourism is still in the process of being defined and refined and its boundaries are being marked and remarked (Jafari 1977, 1979; Leiper 1979). There is not even a consensus of what the study of tourism encompasses, let alone excludes (Jafari and Ritchie 1981).

The urge or motivation for travel ranges from psychic needs to unknown motives. The purpose of the trip ranges from business and obligation to pure pleasure and fun. Distance traveled (depending on which definition is used) ranges from a few miles to 100 miles or more. And time spent away from home ranges from one night minimum to 24 hours or more.

In short, tourism's definition, typology, and units of measurement are uncertain and thus any expression of the concept of tourism is admittedly incomplete. These uncertainties in our theoretical and practical thinking imply that we still have much to learn about tourism. The most optimistic view is that tourism is on its way to becoming a well defined and researched field of study.

PARATOURISM

Research in various aspects of tourism cannot be postponed just because we do not have a clear understanding of its scope and definition. While we are exerting efforts to deal with these fundamental concerns in tourism, research on various aspects of tourism must go on. In the long run, exploration in old and new research concerns should enable us to better understand the tourism parameter and identify its frame of reference.

The purpose of this chapter is to discuss whether the scope of tourism, the way we understand it today, can be expanded to also include the *locally* generated and *locally* accommodated tourism demand: People becoming "tourists" in their own towns. To distinguish this type from the traditional tourism, we refer to it as *paratourism* and the people who practice it as *paratourists* (PTs).

The prefix "para" from Latin means "among other things," "along side of," "closely related to or resembling" and "associated in a subsidiary and accessory capacity." In this broad sense, from a resident's point of view, paratourism means a *subsidiary vacation spent at home.* From the travel industry's point of view, paratourism means a *subsidiary business generated from, and accommodated within, the local community.*

In other words, paratourism means people having touristic fun in their own home town, by going to a typical tourist oriented place, enjoying the hospitality resources of the city, attending local theme parks, wining and dining out and even staying in hotels.[1] This type of "tourism," not quite defined and never studied before, requires some serious consideration, especially now that we are experiencing serious energy price increases and now that the influx of tourists to some tourism destinations may consequently be down.[2]

To make the task manageable, this chapter focuses only on one segment of paratourism: the idea of accommodating residents in local hotels. Other aspects of the paratourism business need to be studied separately and then brought together for a fuller grasp of paratourism in its own and in relation to the broader parameters of tourism.

RECENT CHANGES IN DISTANCE TRAVELED

Prior to the energy shortage, during the days of abundance, going away, to those "far away places with strange-sounding names," was a way of life. The further away the destinations were, the more appealing they appeared. People could clearly hear the "calls" of these destinations: "Tahiti calls you." Even people in Oshkosh, Wisconsin could hear the call. Americans thought (and some still do) that they were "born under a wandering star," "wanderlusting" to all directions during their vacation, zig-zagging the highways of America and criss-crossing the skies, here and abroad. They would drive or fly as far as their time and budget would allow (Fig. 44.1).

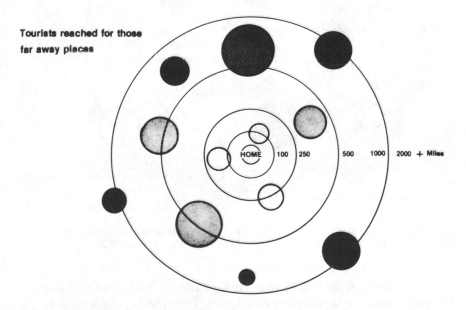

Tourists reached for those
far away places

Darker shades represent stronger pull

FIG 44.1.   SPATIAL (AND PSYCHOLOGICAL) DISTANCE BETWEEN HOME AND DESTINATION PRIOR TO THE ENERGY SHORTAGE

However, during recent years, in response to energy price increases, the distance between home and destination has had to be reduced. We could still hear the "calls" but we quickly learned to ignore them. Some nearby destinations were gradually accepted instead of those far away places, substituting the near-to-home destinations for the far-away ones (Fig. 44.2). Jafari (1980) noted this transition by examining some industry reports published in trade journals and daily newspapers. At this early stage it is difficult to suggest to what extent this inward movement might continue, whether it represents a temporary transition or whether it is gradually evolving towards a permanent shift.

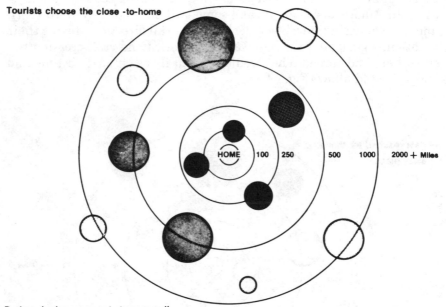

Tourists choose the close -to-home

HOME | 100 | 250 | 500 | 1000 | 2000 + Miles

Darker shades represent stronger pull

FIG. 44.2.   REDUCTION IN THE PSYCHOLOGICAL AND SPATIAL DISTANCE BETWEEN HOME AND DESTINATION DURING AND AFTER ENERGY AWARENESS

Now, some new questions may surface which would further confuse our conceptual understanding in tourism. *How far* do people have to go away from home to have a touristic leisure? To what extent can the distance between home and destination be reduced and still provide touristic feelings or attitudes? Where does tourism end and nontourism status start? Is it conceivable that home and destination can be eventually superimposed, witnessing the emergence of the paratourism market in fuller capacity (Fig. 44.3)? Do people have to *go away* from home to have the touristic sensation?

These are all important questions which require the close attention of tourism researchers. Not all these questions can be addressed here. But we can at least move towards that direction, by looking at some of these issues from a conceptual perspective and offer some examples for clarification.

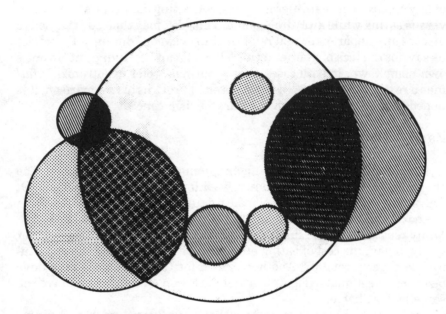

FIG. 44.3.   HOME AND DESTINATION PARTIALLY SUPERIMPOSED

OUTINGS IN ONE'S OWN COMMUNITY

What are some of the tourism oriented experiences that one can have both at home and away from home? Eating out is one of these experiences. When people go out for dinner in their own home town, they do not consider themselves tourists. They may even be residents of a multi-million population city and have to drive a couple of hours to reach the restaurant; nevertheless they still consider themselves *residents*, not *tourists*. Even when they go to a new or exotic restaurant, order food from an unfamiliar menu, consume exotic foods and drinks, in an atmosphere representing a different culture, etc., they still do not consider themselves tourists.

While away on a trip, the same individuals may go to a typical chain restaurant with familiar and standardized decor and service, and order typical items from a familiar menu. In this instance, they do consider themselves tourists. Therefore, the determining factor here seems to be a *spatial* or even a *psychological* distance (or combination of both) from home.

An examination of this aspect may lead us to a broader understanding of any apparent or real difference between eating out in one's home town versus eating while away from home. This idea may then be extended to discuss any apparent or real relationship between "dining out" and, let us say, for the lack of a better term, "sleeping out" or "living out" in one's own home town. In both cases, these "outings" refer to patronizing *full* menu restaurants and *full* service hotels. Through this comparison, it is hoped to shed more light on the paratourism concept.

Early Restaurants

Eating out, simply stated, means doing without the kitchen, the shopping, the cooking, the serving, washing dishes and cleaning up. Of course, there is that "special" pleasure or urge of eating out. However, in the earlier days (centuries ago), people were quite reluctant to eat out. Many reasons could be suggested, one being of course the expense. For many, today, the cost of eating out is less of a concern and the opportunity is eagerly sought.[3] Another reason for this reluctance may have been the questionable logic of eating out when a family could have the same food at home.

It is believed that original restaurants actually evolved from the inns, i.e., restaurants evolved from the necessity to provide for travelers. Thus in those early days, only tourists would patronize them. When it was later learned that these "inn-restaurants" were also popular with the people in the community, the "free standing" (without hotel) restaurants began.[4]

Mini-Vacation in Local Restaurants

Whatever the historical background might be, restaurants are now in both resident and tourist business. Residents somehow have found ways to justify "dining out" and frequenting restaurants, with or without any special occasions. Actually, today, dining out is an important part of the American culture (Institution 1980). Besides satisfying the biological needs, dining out is an eagerly sought leisure activity. Could we then consider "dining out" as a kind of "mini-vacation?" The question does not seem to be a far-fetched one. People are in need of some relaxation and change and eating out provides them with an excursion opportunity to both familiar and exotic restaurants. Like traveling, which means leaving all the day-to-day headaches and worries behind, and getting away from it all (thus being on a vacation), going to a restaurant also means not worrying about food preparation and other work associated with it. In this context, dining out is also "getting away from it all" (and thus being on a "mini-vacation").

In restaurants the choices on the menu are many times larger than what the kitchen at home can offer. The food is supposedly better. Waiters and waitresses are expected to serve customers in a most cordial and pleasant manner. In such a setting, people enjoy their meals and are having fun, too. They are experiencing a "mini-vacation."

Thus, eating out means taking fun "trips" or "vacations" into the world of restaurants. These customers of restaurants do not consider themselves tourists, but residents. Keeping everything the same, but putting some distance between their home and the restaurant, will make these people consider themselves tourists.

Therefore, it is quite apparent that people can and do sort out the two experiences coming from the very same settings: dining out "touristically" or "residentially." Whether at home or away from home, they look forward to such opportunities.

Mini-Vacation in Local Hotels

Why don't people stay in hotels in their own home towns? The question may sound odd or may seem as if the concept of "dining out" is stretched too far. But, after some considerable thought may seem not so different than the logic of eating out.

Sure, people have beds and bedrooms at home and, sure, they feel at *home* in their very own bedrooms (including all other good reasons that one can offer along this line). But then people have kitchens and dining rooms too. Nevertheless, they have already found some reasons (psychologically or otherwise) for "dining out." Can the same reasons operate for "living out" in a hotel? Tables 44.1 and 44.2 represent some attempts to further analyze this question/comparison.

Lessons from Restaurants

It appears that the same logic which causes people to treat themselves to dinner in a restaurant could also cause them to treat themselves to an overnight or weekend stay in a local hotel. Then, why have people accepted and acknowledged the need for one sort of outing and not for the other?

TABLE 1.   REASONS TO EAT AND LIVE AT ONE'S OWN HOME

Eating In	Living In
Have their own kitchen	Have their own bedroom
Have selected their own favorite dining room furniture	Have selected their favorite beds
Have selected their favorite tablewares and table clothes (which is an expression of their own way	Have selected their favorite bed sheets mattress and pillows (with the right touch and pleasing way
Can make their favorite dishes (food) anynight (time) they want to	Can play their favorite serenade to put them to sleep
And more	And more
All factors suggest that theys should eat (dine) at home	All factors suggest that theys should sleep (live) at home
But, they do not really follow this logic and do wine and dine out	And, they find this logic acceptable and sleep at home
Can we explain this phenomenon?	Can we explain this phenomenon?

TABLE 2.   REASONS TO EAT AND LIVE OUT

Eating Out	Living Out
Need change of pace	The same could be said here
The kitchen dining becomes a bore	The bedroom can become a bore too
Need variety	Staying in hotels also creates variety
Want to have fun	Staying in hotels can be fun
No bother with food preparation, pots and pans, serving, and then clean up all the mess	No beds to make and rooms to keep tidy no bath tub to wash
Food will be served as soon as one arrives	The room is ready as soon as one arrives
Restaurant can respond to (almost) every whim of simple or gastronomic expectations gourmet foods, best service, delightful atmosphere, pleasant waiters, waitresses	Hotels can respond to (almost) every wish of the guest choice of room, X-rated movies, private bar, 24 hour room service, breakfast in bed (with champagne)
It is chic to "eat out"	It can be even more chic to "sleep out"
Ad infinitum personal reasons to "eat out"	Ad infinitum reasons to "sleep out"
All these factors suggest that people need a break and should "eat out" at least every now and then	All these factors suggest that people need a break and should "live out" at least every now and then
And they comply with this urge occassionally for some and frequently for others	But they do not "sleep out" neither occasionally nor frequently
Can we explain this phenomenon?	Can we explain this phenomenon?

It may be that the restaurant industry, through the ages, presented itself in a way which fostered the development of its dualistic potential. Another factor may be that people have always been in need of vacations, short and long. Realizing this, the restaurant business readily responded to this need by providing them with "mini-vacations" (para-touristic opportunities) without leaving town—a market that the hotel industry has until very recently overlooked. In contrast the hotel industry responded only to the need of travelers away from home—a market that restaurant business did not overlook (see Figures 44.4 and 44.5).

A. Tourism

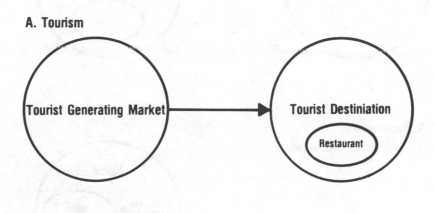

B. Paratourism

FIG. 44.4. RESTAURANTS IN RELATION TO TOURISM AND PARATOURISM

In other words, the restaurant industry maintained its association with the travel industry, but also moved into the resident market. But the hotel industry did not follow suit. People continue to perceive hotels within the "touristic" rather than the "residential" realm. If this is the case, it appears that the hotel industry has failed where the restaurant industry has succeeded.

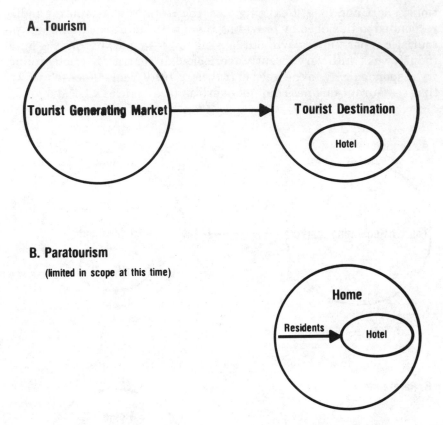

A. Tourism

Tourist Generating Market

Tourist Destination

Hotel

B. Paratourism

(limited in scope at this time)

Home

Residents

Hotel

FIG 44.5.   HOTELS IN RELATION TO TOURISM AND PARATOURISM

One may argue that the restaurant industry appeals to both resident and tourist markets because it responds to a basic biological need while the hotel and travel industry does not. The weakness of this argument becomes apparent when we note that it is not only the food and drink that people are seeking. They actually want a full service restaurant and more. The substantial extra that they pay beyond the cost of food is in relation to the restaurant's appeal, what makes the meal and experience a delight, a "mini-vacation." Dining in such a restaurant is consuming a luxury item.

Future research may even show that since the energy crisis, the business volume of local restaurants has increased. This implies that the money that people are not spending on their trips, they are spending at local restaurants, and other local recreational and entertainment activities. They are taking several "mini-vacations" in restaurants, in place of a vacation away from home. In the case of restaurants, eating out is taking a "vacation." In short, people are having paratouristic vacations at home.

The Logic of It All

"Living out" in a hotel provides the residents with more than the basics. A full service hotel, with its swimming pool, tennis courts, sauna, restaurants, bars and entertainment, is also a luxury item, a mini-city in itself. It offers a delightful experience, a special overnight treat, a "mini-vacation."

But, one may also argue about the poor appeal of paratouring in one's hometown or checking into a hotel for the weekend as a form of vacation. The argument may be that paratourism does not provide, for example, any cultural encounters or enrichments, worldwide views, linkage with the outside world, and the like.[5] But, as yet, it has not been documented that tourism by nature and automatically provides tourists with these opportunities. It is certainly up to the tourists—or for that matter to paratourists—to look for and take advantage of various valuable experiences. The transfer of "knowledge" to the tourist via traveling is not automatic. Paratourism's claim is not on any cultural enrichment opportunities that it provides, although indeed it has the potential to provide experiences along this line. Its claim is on readily providing "mini-vacations" and relaxation for the residents, and at the same time additional income for the businesses normally patronized by tourists.

If people have accepted visiting look-alike cities, amusement parks, attractions, etc., including staying in look-alike hotels, popularized two to three decades ago by several large chain hotels, while away from home, we could really argue that not all people are always looking for novelty during their trips and that they do not like to encounter familiar scenes.[6] Paratourism can offer, to some extent, many of the "familiar" experiences as well as the "home-away-from-home" ideology without requiring people to leave town. It certainly can offer total relaxation.

SUMMARY AND RECOMMENDATIONS

The time has arrived for the hotel industry to evolve to the dualistic functional capacity of the restaurant industry. The hotel industry can be involved in both paratourism and tourism, serving residents who want "mini-vacations" and tourists who are on a prolonged vacation. To move the hotel industry to think along this line, it should be sufficient to remind the industry that while every night they have a proportionally large number of rooms going unoccupied, there are hundreds and hundreds of people only a few blocks away from the hotel—sleeping in their own beds.

It is not the intent of this chapter to discuss the marketing of paratourism, how other segments of the travel industry may benefit from the development and popularization of paratouristic services or how to market paratouristic packages to residents. Since this chapter represents a pioneering effort in the study of paratourism, it seemed more realistic to simply identify and introduce the topic and deal only with one component of paratourism at the same time—how hotels fit into the paratourism picture. But some guiding thoughts on marketing paratourism may be offered.

In order to reach into the paratourism market fully, the hotel industry needs to better understand the psychology involved in serving the residents. It has to find ways to initially put some "distance" between the hotel rooms and the bedrooms of people so that the idea of "sleeping out" or "living out" does not sound "ridiculous." The idea of "living out" should become appealing and desirable.

Initially, for example, the idea of "living out" for the weekend in larger cities and its satellite towns may be promoted. During the last few years, some large cities have indeed tapped into this market but have not worked on fully developing it. Full service hotels and resorts certainly have more potential to attract residents at the earlier stages of the market development. When people experience "living out," it should then become easier to promote paratourism to a fuller capacity, including developing weekend packages which offer various experiences in town.

It is not suggested that this transition can be easily made, but it is important to recognize the immense magnitude and potential of paratourism to the hotel industry which cannot afford to ignore it any longer. The time for exploring this market has certainly arrived, especially now that it has become more and more difficult for people to go away for a vacation, due to the still rising cost of transportation.

In the final analysis, the hotel industry will do itself a service by selling rooms and other amenities not only to travelers but also to residents, increasing its own volume of business and the overall income generated in the community. Equally important, this can help in conserving our limited sources of energy.

For the hotel industry, paratourism provides an excellent opportunity to become more responsive to the needs of the local population. It performs a valuable service to the community by providing its members with "mini-vacation" opportunities. Involvement in paratourism allows hotels to be more truly a part of the local community, in the same way that restaurants are regarded by residents, versus its usual image of serving the needs of the outsiders. This may be particularly important to the communities which have experienced tourism oriented conflicts or are conflict prone.

At still a more societal level, paratourism creates a sense of community awareness and community belonging, a sense that America lost during its years of rapid technological development but is now eagerly seeking to restore. Paratourism can be a definite tool toward this goal. Paratourism can indeed become an industry in the service of the community, an opportunity that the hospitality and travel industry has not fully addressed in the past.

ACKNOWLEDGMENT

The author wishes to thank his colleagues in the Department of Habitational Resources, Univ. of Wisconsin-Stout, for the reading of the first draft of this chapter and for their many valuable suggestions.

FOOTNOTES

1. Though several relationships between paratourism and use of local recreation and entertainment resources can be named, what distinguishes paratourism is that it emphasizes those local goods and services typically consumed by tourists.

2. This paper must be regarded as being preliminary and exploratory in nature and scope.

3. We are dealing not with the entire population, but only that segment of population which can afford and actually patronize local restaurants.

4. It is then important to note that this latter form of "tourism" business (restaurants) evolved into that of serving both tourists and residents while its former self (hotel) remained exclusively in the sphere of travel.

5. The issue of tourist attractions, "things to do and to see at the destination," is purposefully left out in this article. It should be clear that we are discussing not the whole spectrum of tourism but rather a segmentized paratouristic experience—why "eating out" and not "sleeping out." For the importance of attractions in tourism, see Jafari 1979.

6. But one could argue that the act of traveling to these monotonous places makes the stay in them delightful and thus the novelty emerges. If this is true, we should see how this spatial obstacle can be handled. By creating a psychological mood of receptiveness and leisure/tourism-like feeling in one's own home town, many residents can be sent to local hotels for overnight accommodation. This is a task for a marketing specialist, not a purpose of this paper.

45

Research Applications to Hospitality Marketing

Joseph Varga

In the first year of this decade, the lodging industry has experienced a number of old and new problems which suggest the need for more comprehensive and diverse marketing planning in the future. It is no surprise that the problems surrounding energy, inflation, high interest rates, tight money and the on-again/off-again recession seem to be recurring with such regularity as to suggest that these are now normal business conditions under which we all must operate. What makes these conditions a source of concern and frustration to all in business is that being external to the property, they cannot be influenced or controlled. Yet business must go on as usual! About the only options available under such conditions are to adapt, to adjust, to arrange, to avoid or to anguish.

From a marketing standpoint, avoiding the problem may work in the short run, but unless problems are addressed and solved, they simply do not go away. The fifth option, anguishing over a problem—let us face it—is for losers. The first three—adapt, adjust and arrange—fit into the marketing concept because they are action oriented. To my way of thinking, correct actions revolve around sound planning. And planning requires information. Information is derived through systematic research. What will be discussed in this chapter is a research and planning approach that we at Robinsons feel fits into the overall development of sound marketing programs. First, though, let me outline some recent industry trends which I have found alarming. These trends suggest that the marketing approach used in the past may have to change dramatically if we are to prosper and survive in the coming decade.

SIGNALS IN THE INDUSTRY

There is no question that the economic conditions are having a negative impact on lodging demand. The latest reported occupancy figures for the twelve months ended 1980 show the country as a whole experiencing a 3% to 4% decline in occupancy from the previous year. The occupancy rate by December was pegged right around 68%. This occupancy certainly is not the worst level that has been reported during the past five to ten years. That figure happened in 1971 and was reported at around 54%.

What does signal alarm to industry trend watchers is this: Occupancy declines are being reported in nearly every segment of the hotel industry. Chain operations are down over 3% from a year ago, independents off by 7%. Larger hotels seem to have lost 1.2% of occupancy, but even smaller properties are off by 3.2%. In each region of the country, northeast, south Atlantic, north central, southwest and even the west, and in nearly every metropolitan area from coast to coast, occupancy rates during this past year fell behind the previous year's levels by 1% to 8%. There appears to be no relief in sight for 1981 as occupancy projections for the next 3 to 6 months show 3% to 5% additional declines. These, by the way, are not Robinsons Inc.'s figures. My statistical references here are the accounting/consulting authorities who regularly report such data. But, we service over 2000 clients worldwide and the reports we are receiving from our North American clients substantiate these trends.

THE MARKETING CHALLENGE

These statistics suggest that the future for the lodging industry *may not* be filled with the cornucopian market opportunities that were present in the 1960s and 1970s. In that era, the industry was growing physically and financially at an unprecedented rate to satisfy a burgeoning population base that was traveling more. That population was literally feeding off an ever increasing economy and with increased affluence, they were spending more on travel. The consumer had a wide range of choices among many types of lifestyles, and greater choices for a widening range of vacation experiences were being offered to those various lifestyles.

The last decade was an era in which market segmentation was the key marketing strategy which worked for nearly every business sector and it certainly seemed to work for many successful hotel properties. Perceptive hoteliers planned their success formula around filling the needs of specified groups of guests who could be conveniently classified by combinations of demographic characteristics, interests and lifestyles, such as the upscale, business executive earning over $40,000 per year vacationing with his family in exclusive mountain or ocean resorts. The property needed to have only the right amenities, services and that little something extra that was unique to their operations. With a distinctive image, the property's market share could be secured. There was a feeling that you didn't need to know who your market was. They would find you if you just filled the need.

That response to the market environment, as it was in the past decade, was so successful that a number of chain-affiliated and strong independent properties have survived and are now well-positioned leaders dominating their respective markets. But, for every one successful operation that found its nitch, four other properties have floundered literally accepting whatever business crossed their doorstep. Those did not really understand or even care to know for whom and what markets their operations had the greatest appeal.

Under this situation, the marketing challenge which has emerged for the 1980s revolves around two distinct industry positions. The first position, which applies to only a small portion of the industry (20%), centers around those properties enjoying a dominance in their market. They experience higher occupancy, greater repeat patronage of loyal guests, and the ambience of their property seems to be in harmony with the type of clientele they attract. To minimize the threat of the possible erosion of their customer base, such properties must direct their marketing efforts toward penetrating established market segments even further, possibly to the exclusion of peripheral sources of business.

The second position, which applies to the remaining 80% of the industry, has to do with those hotel properties that are less fortunate in the market. These are properties with marginal occupancy levels which have little or no identity among select market segments. There appears to be no homogeneity in their base of guests and very little is really known about their guests. The hotelier in this circumstance is not content with the type of clientele that walks through the door. At best, they may reference the well-established positions of their more successful competitors, search out the weak points of the successful adversaries and try to mobilize all of the marketing forces at their disposal, to exploit their more fortunate counterparts. A property that stands still in either of those positions is soon passed by. So the marketing challenge in either position is to take action and move forward. At Robinsons, we view client situations as being in one of these two positions. To help plot the proper marketing course for them, we have devised a four step formula.

THE FORMULA FOR EFFECTIVE MARKET RESEARCH AND PLANNING

Step 1—Research

The formula begins with research and includes:

− *A profile of the client's property* to identify attributes, services and amenities which are offered to the guest at that particular establishment.

− *A profile of the competition* to identify what attributes, services and amenities competing properties may also offer to the same base of guests.

− *A profile of the guest prospect for the area and the property* defined in terms of type, origin and stay characteristics.

− *An examination of previous marketing efforts* to determine what exposure the property has been given to the market, the dollars they have spent in the past and most importantly, how and where those dollars have been spent and what results have they produced.

Step 2—Planning

Planning involves the actual setting of marketing objectives based on research results and the means for achieving those objectives which is the strategy.

Step 3—Execution

Execution is the actual implementation of the plan involving the appropriate action with all of the various marketing vehicles to be used in the program.

Step 4—Measurement

Measurement provides the means to accurately determine how effective the plan has been in the execution and delivery of the desired goals and objectives.

The first and second, research and planning, will be discussed in detail in this paper. The last two, execution and measurement, will only be touched upon lightly although these are critical parts of any marketing program. Those steps involve putting actions into the plans and modifying the actions on a day-to-day basis to assure maximum results.

RESEARCH

As mentioned before, the first component of the formula is research. This generally begins with a property profile which provides a clear definition of the hotel's amenities and services to be marketed. Through the use of a checklist, tangible and intangible features of the property are noted and evaluated. Tangible factors include the property's location (downtown, surburban, beach), type of facility (resort, commercial hotel, convention hotel) and its operating status as an independent, chain operated or chain franchised property. These characteristics tell us what type of customer base we should expect to find in such operations and therefore, what markets we should be looking at.

In addition, a complete description and evaluation of the physical facilities should be included in the property profile, itemizing the number and mix of available rooms; size, number and diversity of meeting space; food and beverage outlets; and listing the various recreational amenities offered such as golf, tennis, diving, health club and the like.

An important element of any lodging marketing program is the price that is charged. Rates need to be examined by season, range of rates among the various room classifications, the room rates charged by stay-plans such as EP or MAP and special room rate discounts offered to specific guest type categories such as corporate rates and special IT package plans.

Among the intangible factors of a property profile are: perceived quality of services, general condition of the property, the hotel's image and reputation in the community and the popularity of the property or the destination as perceived by guests, management, employees and the community. Since nearly every operating department in the hotel in some sense is involved in marketing the property in one way or another, the checklist is completed with input from the entire management team consisting of the general manager, sales manager, marketing director, food and beverage manager and the controller.

For competing hotels, the same type of information that is developed on the individual property should be assembled on each competitive property. However, specific data on the nature and type of guests attracted to competing hotels is generally proprietary and therefore often impossible to access. Through the use of secondary sources of data, that is, previous research that has been done on the area, information on the markets served by area hotels may be fairly well defined.

One such source might include the area Chamber of Commerce. Chambers often maintain origin statistics on inquiries of cultural events, lodging facilties or area attractions. These can provide some rough estimates of where area visitors come from. There may also be a local convention and visitors bureau which regularly conducts special surveys on tourist or group meeting attendees giving origin characteristics and lodging preferences.

Major air feeder markets can be tracked in over 600 cities across the country through the CAB's (Civil Aeronautics Board) quarterly origin and destination survey tables. Similar data is available on U.S. travel to international destinations from the U.S. Department of Transportation.

The advantages of using secondary information for research are obvious. When accessible, existing sources of statistical data represent a good starting point for any research exercise. The cost of the data source is minimal and often free, although someone must take the time to locate and sift out just the data that are needed. The organizations responsible for compiling the data mentioned are fairly reputable and therefore, the data are usually reliable.

The limitations to secondary information are that the data are often too general to have any direct application to the marketing program of a specific property. In addition, the information is sometimes dated. In a marketing environment where the passage of six months can produce significant changes in travel trends, this can be a major problem. Rarely are such data categorized by identifiable market segments such as recreational, commercial, group meeting or group social travelers. So the exact information that is required may not be available and a great deal of interpretation may be needed.

Therefore, the major research effort should be directed at developing primary research data, that is, developing information which was not previously assembled or known. In many properties, the primary research vehicle to solicit guest data and their reactions about the facilities has been the in-room guest comment card. Personally I do not believe in the value of guest comment cards. For the most part, these surveys are little more than a "gripe" sheet for the extremely irate guest. Seldom are these cards completed by registrants who are fully pleased with the range of services and amenities offered by the hotel. One final point on guest comment cards is that, because they are left in the room or on the dining room table to be completed at the option of the guest, they simply are not statistically valid. Basing key marketing decisions on that kind of information could result in the serious misdirection of any marketing program.

Short of administering expensive special research surveys, every property has primary source documents of current data available to it which are invaluable for marketing purposes. These include the reservation form, registration card and guest folio. From any one or all three of these documents, a minimum of 15 pieces of marketing data is generally captured on every guest registrant including the following:

1. Reservation date
2. Reservation method
3. Reservation source (travel agent's name and address)
4. Guest type
5. Special package requested
6. Guest name
7. Guest address
8. Zip code
9. Date of arrival
10. Number in party
11. Mix of party (children and adults)
12. Room rate
13. Length of stay
14. Total folio charges
15. Payment method

Most properties do not consolidate this information on a single document (such as transcribing all the information onto one registration card). As part of an ongoing guest history research program, we advise our clients on the best way of doing that. Additional marketing information could be obtained if available. For example, in heavy commercial houses, special company codes may be used to identify the volume of business booked by major corporate accounts. In a condominium resort complex that provides a wide range of accommodations, it may be desirable to track the rental patterns of such accommodations by type of guest and season of the year. This could help determine the ideal mix of accommodations to be constructed in future expansion. Purpose of trip, previous stays in the area and at the hotel, and mode of travel to the city are other questions that can be included on the registration card and are usually completed by the guests with little or no inconvenience to them.

All of the data described can be routinely captured and is available at no cost to the property. However, the property must have some means of retrieving and analyzing that data.

Unless the property is quite small, say under 100 rooms, the maintenance and retrieval of guest registrant data for analysis purposes can be a major undertaking. This is almost always the case when guest names and addresses are captured for direct mail purposes. Thus, for any sizable property, the use of a computer to compile and process the large volumes of computations is almost mandatory. Although some in-house computing systems used by the industry today have the means of capturing and storing guest history data, most still lack the capacity and necessary software to generate anything more than simple totals and percentages. To get at good marketing information, a lot of additional clerical effort and interpretation is required.

For our clients and our own marketing needs, we have developed a wide range of computer programs to analyze hotel data in a variety of ways. For statistical analysis, we use frequency distributions, crosstabulations and breakdowns. Simple frequency distributions provide the common percentage to total calculations. For example, we can look at the percentage of different types of guests (social, commercial, convention) compared to all registrants. We use frequency distributions to see what percentage of guests come from each market area, percentages and totals of guest arrivals by month, number of registrants using different packages, percentage of one, two, three and four person parties and so forth. The more diversified crosstabulations allow examination of two or more variables which are related such as areas of residence by guest type by season of the year. Breakdown analysis provides the rudimentary components of higher level statistical comparisons such as correlation and multiple regression and for marketers who are into marketing models can provide data in decision tree format. For example, through breakdown analysis, a report can be displayed on a single page which might show the average room rate paid by type of guest, month of the year, room type taken and number in party. Or, you could examine length of stay by distance of residence by purpose of trip. Breakdown gives a great deal of flexibility in analyzing the characteristics of various market segments. Needless to say that when there are thousands of registration records to be analyzed, a large capacity computer with programming flexibility is a must.

Obviously, the data on a registration card must be tabulated or entered onto a computer. Several points need to be made on data entry. To be certain that the guest history information is complete, procedures for adequately recording all guest data should be implemented at the time reservations are taken or when a guest checks in and completes the registration card. On check-out, all other data must appear on the card as well. For the most part, editing must be performed visually. The data can then be transferred to some machine readable form such as punched cards, magnetic tape, magnetic diskettes or the new laser optical scanning forms which require only a typewriter that has the machine-recognizable font. With this type of system, if you have the typewriter, you need only invest $32 in the typing head and you are in the data entry business. Of course, the scanner is $100,000. In one of these forms, the data can then be read into the computer.

Once the data has been entered onto the computer, the actual analysis process can begin. For hotel marketing purposes, the unit of analysis that is most meaningful is the count of guest registrants rather than the count of room nights. It is the guest registrant to whom a hotelier must market his property. It is that registrant in turn who generates the room nights and other revenue activities at the property rather than the other way around. So, when researching your market, be sure it is defined in terms of registrants.

The first level of analysis addresses the market composition of guest registrants. Specific types of guests would fall under the traditional categories of social commercial or group. But this can be supplemented with other data, such as the purpose of trip, booking source or booking method. This analysis will provide the basis to differentiate the origin, stay and purchasing patterns of the key market segments that comprise the base of guest occupancy.

The next level of analysis examines geographical origin of the various guest categories. By using the 5 digit zip code, it is possible to group guest registrants according to pre-defined geographical markets. Although origin can be broken down into states or cities, for marketing purposes, these area designation are often too broad to be of practical use. Where various advertising media such as radio, newspapers, magazines and even television are used in the marketing program, a more specific definition of geographical markets is required.

In our market planning, we use market delineations called Areas of Dominant Influence or ADI's. The United States is divided into 214 distinct ADI's. These are ranked according to market potential from the highest which include New York, Los Angeles and Chicago, which include 10% of the country's population, to the lowest which is Miles City, Montana, population 10,000. When buying print or broadcast media of any description, advertising rates are directly influenced by the size and ranking of the ADI's in which they are present. The higher the ranking, the higher the cost. Therefore, it makes good dollars and cents to place marketing efforts in those ADI's which are strongest producers. Research on guest origin helps determine what ADI markets are important to every individual.

We determine guest origin through the 5 digit zip code. By the end of next year, we will have nine digits in our zip codes. To the marketer, the 9 digit zip is a two edged sword. Those additional digits mean a lot more computer storage space and processing headaches. But, with expanded codes, for those willing to expend the extra effort, it will be possible to pin-point markets down to census tract accuracy. That means more directed target marketing by using more cost effective vehicles such as direct mail, suburban newspapers, and even community access cable television. That could mean big marketing dollar savings in the future, while at the same time, reaching precisely the market segments one wishes.

The third level of analysis examines guest arrival patterns by month, season and days of the week. Knowing precisely when to expect the bulk of your guests to arrive by time of year helps in scheduling media advertising and saving many dollars. The arrival date, coupled with the reservation booking date, provides an indicator of booking lead time.

By knowing how far in advance a guest prospect is thinking of booking a room, the placement of major newspaper advertisements or the advanced distribution of direct mail pieces can be scheduled at precisely the time when that potential customer is ready to make a travel decision. The proper coordination of your promotional pieces could result in a new booking at the property rather than a booking at a competitor.

The fourth level of analysis covers all the related characteristics associated with each market segment. These include stay pattern and purchasing information such as:

- Length of stay
- Reservation vs walk-in
- Percentage of reservations through "800" number
- Percentage of reservations made by guest
- Percentage of reservations made by travel agent
- Percentage of guests using various stay plan
- Average room rate paid by segment
- Average total folio charge by segment
- Percentage settling accounts by different credit cards
- Estimated total revenue contributions by market segment

Obviously, if only statistical data are desired, capturing information on each and every guest registrant is a waste. Unless the need exists for maintaining guest names and addresses to be used in future direct mail campaigns or promotional news letters and the like, there is no need to examine every registration document. A cost effective approach for such research would be to take a sample of the source documents. Our experience shows that a sample size of around 10% of the registration cards selected on a systematic stratified basis yields reliable and valid results at a reasonable cost. So, the use of sampling should always be considered for this type of research. If you are considering a direct mail guest history file, you should capture all statistical profile data as well, to enable you to perform target market selection on your mailing lists.

When the research and analysis are completed and detailed market profiles can be developed by major market segment, the actual work on developing the marketing plan can begin.

MARKETING PLAN—OBJECTIVES AND STRATEGY

The marketing plan is comprised of two activities: (1) the setting of marketing objectives and (2) the development of an appropriate strategy in light of the market situation of the property.

The marketing objectives are set by two significant measures:

1. Guest room occupancy
2. Market mix of room nights

These objectives are set with a specific time period in mind such as 6 months, 12 months or 24 months into the future. A desired goal might be to move average annual occupancy from the current level of 62% to a new higher level of 74% over the coming 12 months. Suppose the present market mix of business represents 55% social, 20% commercial, 20% corporate group and 5% special package. As a goal, the new mix of business would be influenced by the desire to stabilize peak demand periods and introduce special promotional campaigns during the lower shoulder season periods which might attract more package plan business and a more directed effort at the corporate segment. With the 12-point rise in occupancy, the desired market mix of business may change to the following:

50% social	Down 5%	How well one is moving to
15% commercial	Down 5%	these goals would be deter-
23% corporate	Up 3%	mined by on-going research.
12% special package	Up 7%	

One might ask, what about room rate goals? Average room rate would not be established as a specific goal since prices are determined to a large degree by the amount and intensity of competition. However, from information provided through the research, it is possible to carefully select those market segments which characteristically spend more on rooms and other amenities. Through careful selection of target markets by guest category and geographic origin, not only can room revenues be maximized, but other revenue sources such as food and beverage, recreational amenities or property boutique sales can be increased as well.

The third element of objective setting in a marketing plan is setting how many dollars are to be spent on the marketing effort. In many properties, particularly under present economic conditions, that decision option may not be available since some arbitrary upper limit may have been established. Under such circumstances, the goal of the marketing program would be to get maximum mileage from the fewest dollars spent.

However, certain guidelines on the total marketing expenditure do exist. For the following sizes of properties, we can get some idea of the dollar range that might be considered.

– For the medium-sized property of 200 rooms with average annual occupancy of 75% and a room rate running $30.00, the guideline

would be up to 5% of room sales for a total budget of $82,125, or $411 per available room.
- For the large property of 750 rooms in a metropolitan area averaging 80% annual occupancy and $90 average room rate, the guideline would be up to 4% of room sales for a total budget of $788,400, or $1,051 per available room.

As illustrated, there is a considerable range and, of course, properties spend far greater and much smaller amounts on marketing than indicated here.

Where marketing dollars are distributed more liberally, such as properties building a customer base, it is suggested that a zero-base budget approach be used. At the zero-base level, one starts with the question "How many dollars of sales can my property generate without any marketing expenditure?" Then, against that minimum sales volume, one begins building the marketing program, component by component, matching costs against the incremental revenues generated. One should rigorously examine the return on investment generated by each additional marketing dollar. This approach will assure that marketing dollars are always spent for the intended purpose—that being to generate new and more profitable sales.

The final element of this stage of market planning is the development of a specific strategy to carry out the program. The prior research should show where the property stands in its business development cycle. Is it at the bottom of the cycle where occupancy is low and growth is minimal but on the upswing? Or is the property in its growth phase where room demand is increasing rapidly? Has the property reached the maturity stage where demand has plateaued and growth has stopped or has begun declining? These conditions will influence the shape of the marketing strategy by placing the emphasis on one of the following approaches:

- Developing new sources of business
- Stabilizing existing sources
- Selectively discriminating among the most lucrative sources

CONCLUSION

With thorough market research and planning of a hotel property's existing guests, sufficient information on the nature and pattern of business source should be developed to generate a sound marketing program. A successful plan must begin with the preparation of property, competition and prime guest prospect profiles. Once the hotel marketer knows which of the property's amenities and services are to be marketed and to whom, plans can proceed with setting realistic and achievable marketing objectives of the strategy by which to accomplish those objectives.

The stage then is set for the execution of the marketing program. Getting the program underway requires the initiation of a creative approach, a theme, logo, concept, slogan, the marketing message to be conveyed to the potential guest prospects (like newness, traditional, friendly, exciting, secure, adventure, sex and so forth), the actual budget commitments to the various marketing vehicles to be used such as print, broadcast, outdoor advertising, direct mail, audiovisual, public relations, special promotions and personal selling. Once the program has been documented in writing, implementation can begin.

The final component in the marketing program is some form of follow-up measurement to evaluate the effectiveness and performance of the marketing plan to determine if it is achieving the desired goals. This we would see as an ongoing guest history research program. Having done the research, developed plans, objectives and strategies, executed the program and measured the results, the marketing process begins once again, but hopefully, at a higher and more prosperous plateau.

ACKNOWLEDGMENT

ADI is a term developed and used by Arbitron Inc., New York, who are engaged in measuring media effectiveness.

46

Factors Affecting Consumer Food Preferences and Their Utilization in Hospitality Management

Mahmood A. Khan, Ph.D., R.D.

Consumer food preferences have often been ignored as a tool in the management of the hospitality industry. Emphasis is more often given to efficient service, perfect atmosphere, rich decorations, shiny silverware, attractive chinaware, but little attention is paid to matching food with consumer preferences.

Yet no matter how sophisticated a food preparation method, how attractively served, how economical a menu, it is of no value if it is not accepted by the consumer. The principal reasons food preferences are not commonly used as effective management tools are:

1. Food preferences are intricately related to several factors and are very complex.
2. There is a considerable lack of data pertaining to food preferences.
3. There is a lack of simple methodology for evaluating food preferences.
4. Study of food preferences involves several disciplines such as behavioral sciences, medical sciences, etc.
5. The potential uses of food preferences need to be researched, developed and outlined.

In order to comprehend fully the intricacies involved in food service preferences it is necessary to analyze all the aspects with which they are associated. When a person is presented a menu or a food display, there are a variety of factors acting simultaneously before the menu item is selected and/or the food is consumed.

"A person prefers to eat what he/she likes and likes to prefer what he/she eats" summarizes the complex nature of food preferences. Managers in the hospitality industry should recognize that all consumers have previous knowledge and experience of food (no matter how limited that may be), which makes them highly critical compared to other services or products.

Food preferences are simply defined as the selection of food items from choices available among acceptable foods. Patterns of food selection may emerge as a consequence of temporary or permanent food preferences. Food habits have been defined (Committee on Food Habits 1964) as the way in which individuals, in response to social and cultural pressures, select, consume and utilize portions of the available food supply. Food acceptance is defined (Schuh *et al.* 1967) as a complex reaction determined by the physiological, psychological, biochemical, social, educational, and sensory reactions of individuals who move within a framework of race, religion, tradition, economic status, and environmental conditions. Other investigators have emphasized the importance of sensory, social, psychological, emotional, cultural, health, economic, preparatory and related factors as determinants of food acceptance. Finally, food habits, and food acceptances are learned, acquired and finally become a part of oneself. They become a form of individual self-expression that constitutes food preference.

FACTORS AFFECTING FOOD PREFERENCES

Several influences start acting on one's food preferences from birth and continue to have impact throughout life. Although an attempt is made here to outline some of the factors, particularly those having an indirect impact on management, they are by no means exhaustive. In order to emphasize the most pertinent aspects, the factors affecting food preferences are better grouped into categories and discussed individually.

Intrinsic Factors

Intrinsic factors include certain influences directly associated with food such as appearance, color, odor, texture, temperature, flavor and quality. The manner in which food is presented with desirable or undesirable attributes, the way food is arranged on the plate, the temperature at which it is served, etc., all have an impact on food preferences. It has also been suggested that when choices are available (Maller *et al.* 1980) consumer quality ratings may be higher regardless of the choices available. Standardized large quantity food production may lead to a different food preference ranking than if similar foods are prepared at home. Variability in these intrinsic factors affects food preferences.

Extrinsic Factors

Extrinsic factors include the direct external influences on food preference. There can be numerous external influences. The most common ones are these.

Environment.—Food preferences are affected by the environment prevalent in homes, restaurants, clubs, etc. Hospital studies provide a good example of the effects of environment. The effect that a candlelight environment in a restaurant would have on food preferences compared to a fast food restaurant can be imagined.

Situational expectation.—The quality of food one expects is a function of the situation in which it is to be consumed. Food is expected to be especially good when it is associated with social, ritual, or religious occasions. Meals served at a banquet or wedding party carry a presumption of a certain expectation.

Advertising.—The influence of advertising of food selection patterns and preferences has been studied (e.g., Moore 1957) and it has been shown that advertising can potentially influence people's attitudes toward foods.

Time and seasonal variations.—Food selections appear to be somewhat immune to the influence of certain naturalistic events such as seasonal variations, outdoor temperatures, and the day of the week (Zifferblat et al. 1980). However, availability of seasonal foods, particularly fruits and vegetables, affects selection. For example, hot chocolate is not generally a summer favorite while watermelon is generally preferred during the hot summer months. Other factors such as the hours of meal service, the length of the meal times, and the selection of food as close as possible to the meal times may also have an effect on food preferences.

Biological, Physiological and Psychological Factors

These factors are each broad in scope but are grouped together here since they are closely interrelated. Physiological disorders can have profound effect on food preferences by changing appreciation, perception or appetite toward food. These changes are often associated with psychological influences commonly related to physical well-being.

Age and sex are major demographic factors influencing food preferences. A common example of age and food preference relates to the higher acceptance and preference of "fast foods" by the younger generation.

Personal Factors

Individuality and personal attributes are classified under this category under the following subheadings:

Level of expectation.—The level of expectation that one has for a food or foodservice has been shown to have an effect on food preferences and selection. Patients in hospitals have a low expectation regarding foods. When these patients find the food better than they expected, the preference ratings are favorably affected. On the other hand, the level of expectation is much higher when entering a restaurant. If the food is of lower quality than expected, the ratings can be adversely affected. This phenomenon coincides with socio-psychological theory that the lower the level of expectation, the more easily satisfied the person; and that people perceive things as they expect them to be, rather than as they are.

Priority.—is indirectly related to the level of expectations. Airline foodservices or hospital foodservices are good examples where consumer priority is to reach their destination or recovery and well-being, rather than food. Thus, other aspects are more likely to be critically evaluated than food.

Familiarity.—The conditions (both environmental and social) under which a person initially experiences food has an impact on acceptance behavior (Peryam 1963). Familiar terms on menus produce controversial results. Some research has shown that menu acceptance is enhanced by the use of familiar terms (Kincaid 1975). Others have indicated that interesting or descriptive menus may increase food appeal (Rucker 1978).

Influence of other persons.—Influence of friends, relatives, and family members affects food preferences. Even those being served on a cafeteria line can influence the food selection of a person behind them in the line. Individuals have been found to accept food advice best from those they consider as friends or professionals. As can be expected, parents are most influential in the introduction and acceptance of foods by children.

Appetites, moods and emotions.—These represent a complex intermingling of preference factors. A careless waiter/waitress may be

spared for serving cold food when one is in a good mood. Preferences for similar foods vary based on moods. Moods are unpredictable and are constantly changing, which causes problems in the interpretation of research data. Moods and appetites are also influenced by physiological disorders, as well as by factors such as satisfaction with work and salary. Food is also used as a means of demonstration of one's personality, mood, and emotions or is an expression of gratitude, emotions and feelings.

The family unit.—A mother's educational achievements and her employment status are one item associated with this influence. A young family is more concerned with economizing than a couple between 45 and 60 years of age who are primarily concerned with cutting calories and cholesterol.

Educational status.—Educational status affects food preferences and selections. Nutrition education also influences food preferences, but nutritional knowledge or education alone does not insure an adequate diet.

Socio-economic Factors

Socio-economic factors dictate if one can follow set food patterns or must alter them temporarily or permanently to meet economic limitations. Abundant evidence exists in both developed and developing countries to demonstrate that the food choices are related to income. During short-term crises, such as illness or unemployment, people tend to cut back on expenditures associated with food and drink.

Food is also used as an aid to one's security or retaining past habits and resisting any change in them. Food preferences can be a means of demonstrating group acceptance, conformity and prestige.

Cultural and Religious Factors

Cultural and religious motivations for food preferences are transmitted from one generation to another. Various religious restrictions have resulted in stable and rigid food preferences. For example, Jewish and Muslim populations restrict the use of pork and pork products. Religious beliefs affect food preferences, which become rigid food habits and influence vast segments of populations. In foodservice marketing, realizing these population segments and their food preferences is crucial. Differences in food preferences are obvious among cultures in different parts of the world.

Evidently, food preferences are influenced by a complex inter-mingling of multifaceted factors. Figure 46.1 is an attempt to represent these factors and their relationship.

After reviewing these factors, it it imperative to explore the applicable methodologies for evaluating food preferences.

METHODOLOGY

Most of the methodologies used in studying food preferences are based on surveys focused on the measurement of attitudes such as those which are commonly used in socio-psychological studies. A list and description of these studies are given below.

Food-attitude Questionnaires

Questionnaires are the most commonly used instruments in which data are collected either through interviews, recalls, food diaries and records, and/or diet histories. They are either completed by those respondents under study or by a trained interviewer. They are commonly used because they are economical, easy to administer and yield useful data on food preferences. There are certain drawbacks in questionnaires which should be considered: Questionnaires require very careful de-signing, assessment and pretesting. Number of food items to be evaluated has to be restricted, based on a particular situation. Respondents may not be enthusiastic or may get discouraged by multipage question-naires. Food measures or serving sizes are often omitted and/or not properly reported. Age and education of the respondent affect the answers received in response to these questionnaires. It is always easy to evaluate single food items. However, foods are seldom consumed singly. Complexities occur when more than one food is combined, as in casse-roles. For example, a person may like carrots and raisins, but may not like carrot-raisin salad. Respondents may not be familiar with the type of the food or terminology associated with its name or method of prepa-ration. The time-lag between food consumption and food recording may have an influence. Respondents may be biased in reporting due to time, occasion, or personal beliefs.

Food preference questionnaires, if properly used, can provide useful data. Open-ended questions, multiple choices or preference ratings can be included in the questionnaire. Questionnaires can be completed by the consumer or trained interviewers. Some of the common methods of evaluation include: food like and dislike ratings; visual observations;

recalls—24-hour, 3-day or 7-day records; assessment of plate waste; longitudinal studies; clinical tests; and anthropometric measurements.

POTENTIAL UTILIZATION OF FOOD PREFERENCES IN MANAGEMENT

Since there is a considerable lack of research data pertaining to consumer food preferences, their potential utilization as a management tool can only be predicted. More research is needed to develop effective means of their utilization. Some of the areas in which food preferences can prove to be valuable are:

Forecasting

Forecasting is one of the most important and often ignored function of management. Food preferences can be used to evaluate the menu and use in forecasting production.

Sales-Mix

Many segments of the hospitality service industries have to base the pricing decisions on sales in more than one department. Variances result in revenues, since a menu-analysis to determine the sales-mix is not normally maintained. The unpredictability of food and beverage sales adds an additional variance in the analysis of food sales. Differences in the actual to expected sales-mix can be reduced by utilizing food preferences.

Menu Development and Improvements

Food preferences are valuable in improving old menus and developing new ones. Items scoring low on preference scales can be replaced or improved. This would definitely be an asset in improving food quality.

Choice Selection

When more than one item is to be provided on a menu, choices can be based on preference ratings. If an item is ranked higher, it can be grouped with similar items based on preference. This would facilitate provision of equally acceptable choices.

FIG. 46.1.   FACTORS AFFECTING FOOD HABITS, ACCEPTANCE AND PREFERENCES

Combination and Complementation

Combinations and complementation can be presented by providing foods and beverages which complement each other. This can also be used in providing special sauces and seasonings. It will definitely be helpful in serving wines that match with food items.

Attracting Target Populations

Since a group of the population may have specific food preferences, they can be used as an integral part of market analysis. Menus can be devised based on the target population preferences.

Providing Special Meals

Food preferences may vary by age, sex and physiological conditions. Special meals can be included in the menu by realizing food preferences, e.g., kosher meals, meals for senior citizens, etc.

Product Development and Analysis

New products can be developed based on most preferable items. Also, some of the products can be improved. It provides management an opportunity to analyze the highly preferred and least preferred items.

Market Analysis

Food preferences can prove to be important in conducting market analysis and future growth of an industry.

Management Tool

Finally, food preferences can be used as an effective management tool, utilizing them in combinations of one or more of the above described means.

Consumer food preferences should, therefore, be carefully evaluated and profitably utilized in the management of any hospitality industry.

Part VII

The Hospitality
Industry Tomorrow

47

Growth and Change Challenges of the Hospitality Industry

Paul C. Sheeline

It is no news to anyone reading this that there have been tremendous changes in the hospitality business through the years. And it seems as though the changes are occuring faster than ever now. Changes in our markets. Changes in technology. Changes in the services we offer. Changes in the way we finance our expansion. Changes in our relationships with governments. And so on. It's a long list.

In many ways, this period of accelerating change we find ourselves in is a difficult one. It is also a challenge. Alfred North Whitehead, the British philosopher who was also a professor at Harvard, once said that "the art of progress is to preserve order amid change."

And that is what we in the hospitality business must do. We must preserve order—and our profitability—by learning not only how to cope with change but how to *manage* it. Our future success and growth—indeed, our survival—will depend on how well we manage change, on how well we anticipate and understand and respond to the volatile forces of our time.

Let us first take a look at where we are and then look at some of the challenges we face in the rapidly changing environment of the 1980s.

GROWTH CHALLENGES

Tourism, on which our businesses depend, is one of the world's great growth industries. It is second largest item in world trade, surpassed only by petroleum. All indications are that this growth will continue right up to the end of the century.

In 1970, worldwide arrivals were estimated at 169 million. In 1980, arrivals had increased to 270 million. Dollars spent by travelers worldwide reached a record $638 billion in 1980, a figure that exceeds all global military spending. Tourism is now widely recognized as a major contributor to the economies of many nations and a significant factor in the development of international commerce. In the United States, tourism is the largest single source of foreign exchange and employs about six million people. The hospitality components of the travel and tourism industry have experienced the same kind of growth.

The steady growth of travel and tourism in recent years suggests that while the industry is not immune to economic downswings—there were, for example, declines in some parts of the world in 1980—nevertheless, it is less vulnerable than many consumer goods and services. People may change their travel habits, but they don't stop traveling. They travel in good times and bad, often deferring other purchases to do so. More and more, travel is becoming an integral part of our way of life.

At the same time, however, our industry is facing some problems we've never had to confront before—as well as some opportunities—and they will affect our future in many ways.

The first problem plaguing all of us who have international operations is the unstable, unpredictable, often capricious political systems that now prevail in many parts of the world.

Inter-Continental is starting to expand in the United States after more than 35 years as a primarily overseas hotel group. One reason, of course, is that the United States is where the greatest opportunity for growth now appears to lie. It is the world's biggest and fastest growing international travel destination—and as businessmen, we naturally go where the potential is.

Another major reason is that changing conditions have made many foreign investment and operating programs economically less feasible, if not impossible—and one of the ways to respond to this new reality is to expand in our own country.

In the last two years Inter-Continental has terminated operations in Teheran and Kabul because of political upheavals, and in Istanbul because of intolerable operating conditions. In some countries where there are profitable operations we can't get our money out, or only after long delays. In a few countries, an extreme form of nationalism is encountered that is overtly aimed at getting rid of foreign operators as quickly as possible—after they've built the facility, trained the personnel and demonstrated that the hotel is a viable enterprise.

It is not hard to understand why there is some disillusionment with some foreign operations or why diversifying business, so to speak, by expanding within the United States is a prudent and viable strategy.

Let me hasten to add that problem areas overseas are very few in number. In most of the 46 countries in which Inter-Continental operates there are good, long-standing, mutually beneficial relationships with the local and national governments, with the citizens and with local businesses. Inter-Continental has a long record of service, cooperation and profitability in countries throughout all six continents and not only plans to stay in these countries but also to continue to expand there.

Nor should the new emphasis on U.S. expansion be construed as a form of isolationism. The truth is it is impossible today, either as individuals or companies, to isolate ourselves from world events. More and more we find ourselves sharing the same small world, inter-related with other countries whether we want to be or not. A good example of this interdependence is the reliance of most countries on the OPEC nations for a large percentage of their oil requirements, resulting in a sharp rise in prices.

This is the second challenge I would like to discuss—the escalating cost of energy. Expensive energy affects our business in two ways: it impacts on travel decisions and it increases operating costs.

Most people are familiar with the current agonies of the world's airlines. In 1980, they suffered the worst decline in traffic and earnings in their history. Member airlines of the International Air Transport Association, comprising about three-quarters of the world's scheduled airline service, lost a staggering $2.5 *billion* in 1980. A substantial part of that loss is traceable, directly or indirectly, to the higher price of aviation fuel.

Needless to say, when the airline industry has problems the hospitality industry has problems, because what happens to the airlines immediately affects us. When their passenger loads decrease, our business drops off—which was the case in many markets last year.

As chairman of Inter-Continental Hotels, a subsidiary of Pan American World Airways, and a member of the Board of Directors of Pan Am, I have been in a position to see at first hand what a devastating impact the fuel crisis has had on airline operations and earnings. Pan Am was hit especially hard. As an international airline, it has had to buy almost half of its fuel overseas, where prices have been substantially higher than in the United States. In 1970, Pan Am was paying an average of 10¢ a gallon for its fuel. At the end of 1980 it was paying $1.06—a more than tenfold increase in just ten years! Fuel now accounts for almost a third of Pan Am's total operating expenses. The company's airline operating loss of almost $127 million in 1980 is attributable in large part to high fuel prices. Each penny increase per gallon adds another $11. million to Pan Am's annual fuel bill.

The steep rise in fuel prices led inevitably to fare increases. In 1980, U.S. air fares soared nearly 30%. This in turn affected traffic. Demand for much air travel is elastic—as prices go up, demand in certain market segments tends to go down, although not proportionately because travel is not as vulnerable to economic factors as some products and services are. Nevertheless, this elasticity was evident in the slump in air traffic reported by U.S. airlines. In the first decline in more than 20 years, travel on the domestic and international routes of the major U.S. carriers fell 4.7% in 1980.

The airlines have not been passive in this situation. Pan Am, for example, has responded aggressively to the fuel crisis, and has taken many steps to conserve energy and improve its operating efficiency.

These efforts are paying off. Pan Am's fuel consumption last year was 6.9% less than the previous year—a saving of more than 87 million gallons. Similar savings are being reported by the rest of the industry.

But in spite of what the airlines are doing, the problem is still with us. Expectations are that the price of fuel will continue to rise, and this will propel air fares still higher. How these increases will affect travel depends on other factors, primarily the state of the world's economies, but they are certain to have some effect.

The hospitality industry is not, fortunately, nearly as fuel-intensive as the airline industry. Energy costs represent about 4% of the total operating expenses of hotels. Despite this relatively small percentage, the sharply rising price of fuel should be a matter of concern for all of us.

The industry is passing much of this increase along to its customers in the form of higher prices. Nevertheless, to protect our profit margins we must also improve our operating efficiency and develop new ways to conserve fuel, both as an industry and as individual companies.

Conservation, let me remind you, is not just doing without. Conservation is using less to do more and that's just what we and others in our business are trying to do.

A leading industry facility is the American Hotel and Motel Association's Energy Technical Center in San Antonio, Texas. Started in 1977, the Center acts as a clearinghouse for all energy-related information and data applicable to the lodging industry. The Center has monitored and critiqued the development of Building Energy Performance Standards by the Department of Energy and, interestingly, has concluded that many of the proposed standards, because of their complexity and high costs, do not appear to be economically feasible.

Inter-Continental has a number of ongoing programs dealing with energy, some of which were started back in the early 1960s. Inter-Continental was the first hotel group to hold energy workshops for engineers and department heads, in which various procedures and systems related to energy use are presented and discussed.

As a result of industry and individual company programs, substantial energy savings are being achieved. A study of 300 transient hotels in New England conducted by the Energy Technical Center shows a 20% drop in energy consumption since 1977. And at Inter-Continental, we estimate conservatively that our energy program is saving us more than $4 million a year.

Another major challenge facing our industry is the changing economic environment. In some areas, such as the United States and the United Kingdom, recessionary pressures last year combined with fuel-related fare increases to depress travel. These declines, however, were offset by a continuing high volume of travel from continental Europe and Japan where business conditions were better. So while room occupancy in this country dropped 1.2% in 1979, worldwide occupancy rates were up 3%.

Economists have cautiously predicted a continuing recovery in the U.S. economy in 1981 and a stronger upturn in 1982. Consumer sentiment, an important factor in our business, is expected to show a slow improvement in 1981 and then a definite upswing next year as public optimism returns. The reverse may occur in other parts of the world. For example, there appears to be a recession in Germany. This is bad news for the hospitality business because Germans now constitute the largest group of nationals traveling internationally, surpassing in numbers even the Americans.

Whether business conditions improve or not, two economic problems show no signs of going away: inflation and the high cost of money.

The inflation rate in this country peaked, we hope, in 1980 at about 13.5%. It was expected to drop in 1981 to about 11% and in 1982 to around 9.5%, still high by our standards but better than in many countries.

Our goal in the face of constantly rising costs must be to maintain our profit margins. One way to do this is to pass on our cost increases to our customers in the form of higher prices.

What will raising our prices do to our volume? We have found that higher prices do not hurt us significantly if—and it's an important "if"—we continue to offer a product that the customer perceives as having the extra value that makes it worth the higher price.

The advent of consumerism has made this more important than ever. People today, especially in this country, are far more concerned than they used to be about getting what they pay for. So our job is to make sure the customer feels he is really getting good value for his money, that the something extra he demands is visible and meaningful. He must receive the personal attention and recognition that he is entitled to.

Consumer studies show that this relative insensitivity to price holds true for most luxury items. During a period of inflation, business may be slow at Woolworth's but they're still standing in line at Gucci's.

CHANGING CHALLENGES

However, we cannot use this as a justification to raise prices across the board. It is preferable to make selective price increases based on the increases in costs for each item. At the same time, we must endeavor to keep costs down by increasing the efficiency of our operations and by service innovations. The most successful innovations are those that both save us money, usually in terms of lower labor costs, and are attractive to our customers. Two good examples are the mini-bars in guest rooms and the salad bars in restaurants.

We are also getting more sophisticated in the usage of space. Vast unproductive areas cannot be built in hotels without risking economic failure. For instance, in some of the hotels being designed now there are fewer restaurants and they must be more flexible in their use during the various meal periods. With proper planning, hotels can become more attractive, as well as more practical, living environments by eliminating waste areas.

The high cost of money is another troublesome aspect of today's economic environment. It raises the question of whether we will be able to finance our growth in the future with external funds. This is a problem shared by every other capital-intensive business. If the highest return we can expect on our capital investment in a new project is 15 to 16% before taxes—and we have to pay 20% or more to borrow money— we must naturally think long and hard before committing to new construction today.

Naturally, high interest rates are discouraging projects with only a marginal potential. This means that fewer plans are going to be implemented. At Inter-Continental we are now going ahead only with the most viable projects. When we have unusual confidence in a site we will use our own money to finance construction and then later, if rates are more favorable, we will re-finance it. Borrowing money for expansion is expensive, but the money seems to be there for businesses that can demonstrate a good operating performance and can prove to prospective lenders that they know how to spend money efficiently.

Efficient spending depends to a large extent on intelligent marketing strategies. Academics and professional marketing people say that marketing is one of the weakest areas of the travel industry. It is instructive, they say, that some of the most aggressive marketing comes from newcomers to the business rather than from the older competitors. Be that as it may, marketing is a vital part of our business.

Essentially, marketing is getting to know your customers better, giving them what they want and letting them know you are giving it to them. The first thing we must recognize is that our customers are changing and so are their wants.

The United States will see significant demographic changes between now and 1990 and most of the developed countries around the world will experience trends similar to ours. Our population will expand nearly 9% to 245 million. There will be important shifts: the 15 to 24-year-old group will decrease by 16%; the 25 to 34-year-old group will increase 13.5%; the 35 to 44-year-old category will show a 42% increase; and the over 65 group will go up 19%. This means there will be above-average growth in the age groups that have traditionally been the prime market segments for travel and tourism.

There will be about 20% more households in this country by 1990 with an increase in childless and post-child-rearing households. The decreased emphasis on child-rearing, together with more liberal attitudes toward women in the work force, will make the two-income family considerably more prevalent. Other things being equal these trends presage a growth in travel.

Of course, travel is not only a function of numbers of people but also a function of their ability to afford travel. Here again, the outlook is favorable. The United States median family income is expected to rise to about $45,000 a year in 1990, a 15% real increase over 1980 in inflation-adjusted terms. Disposable personal income is expected to rise by about 30% in real terms. Using 1978 constant dollars as a base, households with income over $25,000, traditionally the prime target for travel, not only show above average growth in numbers of households, but will also be the principal beneficiaries of the growth in disposable income.

There will be more women traveling, particularly in the United States. One indication of that is that the ratio of women enrollees in professional schools—law, medicine, advanced business administration and so on—varies between 25 and 40%. These are tomorrow's travelers, tomorrow's hotel guests, and we had better be ready for them. This means we must analyze their needs and wants now and start providing for them.

An interesting recent trend in the travel market is the growth in travel to the United States. In 1980, foreign visitors from overseas countries surpassed the number of U.S. citizens traveling abroad for the first time since 1945.

The appeal of the United States as a travel destination is not new, of course. What *is* new is that today many more people can afford to come here than ever before—the result of higher personal incomes and savings in many countries and relative depreciation of the U.S. dollar.

They have come in impressive numbers. In 1980, almost 22 million foreign tourists crossed United States borders, 38% more than just 5 years ago. The impact on the U.S. economy was significant. These visitors to this country spent an estimated $12 billion, a 118% increase over 1975. Foreign tourism is now the fourth-largest U.S. export industry. While the rate of growth of travel to the United States is expected to slow this year because of weakening economic activity in many countries and higher international air fares, the U.S. Travel Service is still predicting a healthy 7% rise in inbound tourism.

There has been a shift in values and attitudes regarding travel that can be traced to changing demographics and increased education, along with more leisure time and the rise in stress and anxieties in today's world. For growing numbers of people, a trip is a form of self-fulfillment, a reward that they're entitled to. "Getting away from it all" has become a staple of today's living. "Experiences" are replacing material items on lists of family priorities.

Tastes are changing. This is showing up in a number of ways. Restaurants are selling less beef but more seafood, fewer desserts but more salads and fresh vegetables, less hard liquor and more wine. These changes point up the need for our continuously monitoring consumer preferences. If we can anticipate tomorrow's desires, we will be more successful.

The business travel market, on a worldwide basis, has changed very little in recent years. The percentage of people traveling on business has remained about the same since 1977. In the United States in 1980, however, the volume of business travel dropped 17%.

A significant new trend in business travel is that a growing number of companies are considering the establishment of in-house travel agencies to replace their travel departments or outside agency contacts. That means we may have one more group of people to sell to and may have to pay commissions on business that used to come to us in the form of direct sales.

The final challenge of the 1980s is the new technology which is already improving our efficiency and levels of service and making life easier for hotel staffs.

The trend is to total computer package installations which will soon become commonplace. They will provide myriad services, starting with computerized reservations systems and check-in procedures. Instead of a key a guest will be issued a card prepared by a computer console fitted out with a security printer. The first time a guest inserts the card in a door lock he cancels the previous key and from then on the door will open only to his card. The same card will activate and charge for his mini-bar purchases and, with touch-tone type in-room keyboard, arrange for his wake-up call and change channels on his TV set.

Electric sensors will turn off the lights when a guest leaves the room and will even reveal an unauthorized presence in the room and thereby improve hotel security. Electronic devices will monitor energy use by switching off lights and air-conditioning in unused areas.

Charges incurred by a guest in various parts of a hotel—the bar, pool, dining room, the telephone in his room—will all filter into a central computer. Currency exchange, room occupancy status, inventory control and a host of other functions will all be handled by computer systems. For large hotel groups with worldwide operations, individual hotel profit and loss statements and other information will be transmitted to the headquarters offices by satellites.

Not all applications of the new technology, however, are beneficial to our business. Computer-linked communications systems which connect offices in different cities with both sound and visual images are already affecting business travel. New York executives, for example, instead of flying thousands of miles for a one or two-day meeting, can now take a taxi to the New York Telephone Company's Picturephone Meeting Service on 42nd Street. There, for a fee of $600, they can set up a 90-minute coast-to-coast conference. The savings to a company are obvious: no air fare, no hotel rooms, no entertainment, just business. Half a dozen other firms including AT&T and IBM are jumping into the telecommuting business. Arco has set up its own in-house video conferencing system, believing that the high cost of installation will eventually be offset by savings in travel expenditures and time. Predictions are that within a decade or so the requisite equipment will be standard in the headquarters of all large corporations.

Another application of computerized long-distance communications—one that can help us—is the projected hook-up between travel agents and hotels. Travel agents will soon be able to communicate directly with a hotel via a computer and see instantly on a screen what rooms are available and at what rates, and then make the reservation, using their agency's own charge code number.

We all know that change makes some people apprehensive. But change is perhaps the one acknowledged constant in the world. Change is inevitable and essential. Rather than fighting it, we must learn how to turn it to our advantage.

Tourism is the number one growth industry, and that is one thing that is not going to change, and the hospitality business will be the chief beneficiary. According to the American Society of Travel Agents, if the world gross product rises a modest 3% a year during the 1980s, international tourist arrivals should, in turn, increase by about 6% a year. At that rate, international arrivals would increase from 270 million in 1980 to 483 million by 1990—and spending by tourists worldwide should reach the magic figure of one trillion dollars.

But something else will increase, too. Competition. We're all going to have to work harder and think smarter to get our share of this growing business. Competition, however, has a way of bringing out the best in those people who see it as a challenge and not as an excuse for failure.

What we must do is continue to improve our product and make sure that it is always meeting the needs of our customers. There is a saying in our business that the customer may not always be right but still his needs and interests always come first. In the competitive environment of the 1980s, the companies that survive and prosper will be those that put customer needs foremost in their planning.

The management of Tremont House here in Boston back in 1829 did. That's why they decided to give every guest a key to his room and a free bar of soap. And Tremont House did very well for a long time.

We are in a changing world. Welcome the changes. Accept the challenges. If you do, the 1980s will be a stimulating and rewarding decade.

48

The Hospitality Industry 1985–2000: New Concepts and a New Market

Richard W. Brown

A few years ago the services of the Roper Organization were retained to conduct a broad-based study never before undertaken in the hospitality field. It took about a month to complete and involved free-wheeling, in-depth interviews with a battery of specialists in architecture, design, site location, marketing, entertainment and food and beverage services. The purpose of the study was to identify likely developments in the hospitality industry that would occur by the year 2000.

In the three years since the study was conducted a number of the predictions made have already come to pass. Let us take an imaginary trip through time and space.

The year is 2000.

The city: Big City, U.S.A.

The Site: Big City's newest—and most unusual—hotel

The Occasion: Your firm's annual meeting or perhaps a trade convention.

You will have been attracted by a package plan—a grab bag of inducements, unlike any offered by conventions today, resulting from the intense competition among a handful of hotel chains that will monopolize the industry. Independently owned hotels in major cities will be somewhat of a rarity.

The hotel itself will be a high-rise—a super high-rise—and just part of a huge complex of living, meeting, dining, recreational and entertainment facilities, but the staff will be smaller. Conceivably a woman will be running the place. Most hotel services will be computer-operated. Like instant reservations, there will be instant registrations. No long lines at the desk! For diversion, you will not have to put a foot out the door. Life at this hotel will be one experience after another. When you arrive at your room you do not have to fumble for a key. There is no door.

477

An electronic shield will respond to an electromagnetic card assigned to you. You enter a maze, which offers you privacy from prying eyes, and at the end of the maze you find a room that is homey.

You sit down to collect your thoughts and accidentally push a button on a small instrument panel adjacent to the arm of the chair. It is labeled "Atmosphere Involvement". The next thing you know the room plunges into darkness and curtains swish into place forming a 360-degree movie screen on which is projected a roaring ocean in three dimensions with appropriate sound effects. You gain the impression, mentally and physically, that you are riding the surf at Malibu. Another push of the button and the room returns to normalcy. You head downstairs for the bar to soothe your frazzled nerves.

The bar is different, too: no bar stools, no bartender, but a comfortable atmosphere with big, comfortable chairs. You are hardly seated when up drives a young person in a golfcart-like contraption with a built-in bar. The selection of beverages is wide. They include many of today's favorites and others unknown today. You settle for something traditional and down it. Then you screw up your courage to attend the first session of the convention.

You find that the bulk of the crowd has settled in the main convention hall with the overflow assigned to satellite rooms serviced by closed-circuit, 3-D television. The speakers' voices are projected through the hall via quadraphonic sound.

I suspect many of you would welcome these ideas. Some of us might question future tastes and lifestyles just as our ancestors might have questioned ours had they had an opportunity to preview them. As one political analyst has observed, however: "The future will like the future."

If you think I have been conjuring up an Orwellian specter, you are wrong. What I have done, with a bit of poetic license, is cite some of the predictions found in the Roper study. Everyone Roper interviewed did not suggest everything I have described, but each prediction was made by one or more of them.

The purpose of the study, as noted earlier, was an attempt to foretell the shape of the hospitality business up until the year 2000, concentrating particularly on trends affecting hotels and restaurants. We know that the hospitality industry of tomorrow is being shaped by forces in motion today: be it the energy crisis, rising costs, inflation, consumerism, changing lifestyles, changing mores or whatever.

NEW CONCEPTS

First, and most dramatic, the experts Roper interviewed see a revival of the inner cities. More than half of them agreed that economic trends and energy shortages are going to force more and more people to live together. Hotelmen and restaurateurs obviously will locate their businesses where the people are

As a corollary observation, one expert feels that "neighborhood meeting places" will achieve greater importance. This offers promise to the inner city restaurateur or tavern owner. In fact, he specifically predicted the resurgence of the tavern on a large scale.

A copy of the Roper report was given to a noted Chicago designer, A. Peter Florio, whose specialty is restaurant design. He was asked to study the Roper findings and then to fantasize on paper what restaurants might look like 5, 10, 15, even 25 years from now.

Florio concurred with Roper on the revival of the inner city. He also sees more and more money being invested in the restoration of old buildings rather than the construction of new ones. Bankers favor the idea, he says, and are making money easier to borrow for that purpose. They want to see their communities stabilized. Land costs are another reason for the revival of the inner city. As prices in the suburbs skyrocket, locations in town take on greater appeal.

Another interesting Florio concept is an old brownstone or greystone converted into a combined restaurant bar and library. Because of rising costs, Florio sees sharp reductions in city services, including libraries and especially branch libraries. There will simply be fewer of them. The neighborhood restaurant could step into the breech and thereby expand its civic role in the community.

I recognize that an architectural rendering is not the easiest thing in the world to decipher. Let me do it for you.

The building's main function, of course, would be that of a dining and entertainment center. On the first floor there is the traditional bar with both table and bar setting. The library and reading room, plus dining facilities or a game room, are located on the balcony. Across the yard is another dining room or game room and service bar. The rooftop serves as the dance floor, weather permitting.

One of the big problems facing any restaurant located in the inner city today is parking. Tomorrow it could be a bigger problem. Mr. Florio's answer is converted gas stations. Even a city-located gas station is surrounded by a certain amount of open space. His idea is to turn abandoned service stations into sports-oriented bars or restaurants with very heavy emphasis on television entertainment.

For example, a bar with individual booths facing small TV screens permits customers to tune in a wide variety of sports events carried by cable TV. There may be 100 different channels. At one end of the room is a large screen on which would be projected hometown sports events previously filmed by the restaurant operator himself. At the other end is a game room which is strictly electronic. More TV screens on which customers may play full-length films rented from the bar's film library are located in another area, and bar service will be available in all areas of this stool-less, barless, bartenderless bar which will offer not only drinks of all types but freshly made crepe-suzettes and other ready foods.

Another concept is a bar or restaurant offering all of the gambling conveniences of Las Vegas or Atlantic City. The gambling will be state-operated.

Finally, there will be the mobile bar. An enterprising restaurateur or bar owner who wants to host a night at the local ballgame, or conduct a sightseeing tour, or a ride into the country, will do it this way, on a bus. Which means that everyone can ride while "under the influence", so to speak, without jeopardizing life or limb.

Already today there is a bus shuttling between New York and the gambling casinos of Atlantic City, equippped with a well-stocked bar, television, telephones, comfortable lounge chairs, even a powder room.

Here are a few more highlights of the Roper study:

Hotels of tomorrow will feature family oriented sports, self-improvement courses, even a "sensual recreation room"—and I refuse to speculate on that!

The big-name single entertainer will be out and smaller contemporary groups will be in.

Dining rooms and restaurants will feature limited menus. Some will specialize exclusively in fish of which some are totally strange to the American palate today because they inhabit the ocean floor. They will be spotted by satellites and brought up from the bottom by artificial dwellings and processed in submersible plants.

Vegetarianism will be in because it takes 10 times less land to cultivate vegetables than it does to grow plant food for animal consumption. Some vegetables will be ocean-grown or hydroponically-cultivated including square tomatoes. These have become a reality and their raison d'etre is that they pack more easily.

Ethnic restaurants will grow markedly in number. Some will be instant-ethnic. Curtains will be drawn around the diners and a 3-D movie and quadraphonic music will transport the guests to France or Italy or Japan or China, depending upon the cuisine.

As the experts see hospitality trade swinging with the times, so too do they see the alcohol beverage industry swinging with it. The American palate will be more sophisticated and more demanding. Naturally we will be expected to cater to that demand just as we have always been expected to do.

Of special interest are the answers to a question posed to each respondent to the Roper interview. The question was to name possible liquor outlets in the year 2000 where the product isn't commonly sold today. Here are their responses in order of selection:

Sporting Events
Department Stores
Trailer Parks and Camping Grounds
College Dining Rooms
Movie Theatres
Homes for the Aged
Public Parks and Beaches
Interstate and Commuter Busses
Hospitals
Fast-Food Outlets
Beauty Parlors
Space Ships
The Moon

. . . and Churches. That is right, the "Little Church Around the Corner". The percentage ranged from 51% for sporting events to 5% for churches.

A NEW MARKET

In 1980, for the first time in United States history, women outnumbered young men in our colleges and universities. From that one fact we can make a very important abstraction: Higher education eventually will project more and more women into the upper echelons of the nation's businesses. This realization prompted a second bit of research: the women market of the future for hotels and restaurants. For this study the services of Feminine Forecast, Inc. were retained to probe the attitudes of women between 20 and 50 years of age toward hotels, motels and restaurants.

It is no secret that there are more working women today in the United States than there are housewives, that they are hosting mixed groups more often, and that they are traveling alone:

What turns them on?
What turns them off ?

The study was conducted in three major markets, Dallas, Detroit and New York, among college students, careerists and housewives. Many of these hold dual roles. Some were single, others married or divorced. I shall high point the findings.

Some of the things women find in better-run hotels and motels that turn them on:

Personal and helpful telephone operators and reception clerks (on the phone). They make the difference in first impressions and the hotel's image.
Pleasant exteriors, particularly good landscaping.
Special attractions for children; they're important to families.
Economy packages.
Hotels were favored over motels, citing their character, charm, niceties and, above all, security and privacy.

While motels seem somewhat anonymous to most of the women interviewed, they welcomed the trend of having everything under one roof: good shops, restaurants, theatre activities for the children, pools, tennis courts.

Here is what turns these women off:

Advertising brochures that fail to describe the hotel's character so that prospective guests can determine whether they fit in.
Slow check-ins and check-outs.
Uninformed hotel personnel.
Managers "conspicuous by their absence."
Prices quoted over the telephone that are unexpectedly jacked up when guests arrive.
Lack of cleanliness and upkeep, particularly in chain hotels and motels.

When it came to directing their fire at restaurants, the women were no more sparing: They feel discriminated against. They receive much better treatment, they say, in the company of a man or men than they do alone or with other women.

Since it is relatively a new experience for women to pick up the tab, they resent waiters or waitresses who keep deferring to the men at table. Bland menus of hotel/motel chains bother them, and so do their prices.

Even the most sophisticated women rarely feel comfortable going into a cocktail lounge or bar alone. But these days they are more relaxed about going in with other women and some (the very young and the very married) are not too uptight about sitting at the bar.

Women in groups enjoy having a before-dinner drink in the lounge while waiting for a table, but they resent having to do this when they see empty tables. They will consult a wine list, if it is handy on the table and tells something about the wines. They are drinking less and enjoying it more; not less in quantity but less in strength and heaviness. To put it another way, they are drinking less more often.

These are just a smattering of the study's findings but, after probing beneath the obvious, what conclusions can we draw?

Super cleanliness and friendly personnel are obvious demands. If a place is clean, women tend to look more tolerantly at other failures; if not, no other compilation of attractions will compensate.

Women respond very personally to their surroundings, perhaps more so than men. They examine their experiences more closely, look more deeply into the subtleties. Is there a genuine concern for her well-being? There is a clear distinction in a woman's mind between offering assistance because she is a woman and assistance that makes her feel conspicuous as a woman.

Too many hotels and restaurants are "adequate" but not "inspired". They "run together" in her mind. Women see management as making the difference. For the women surveyed, management has been largely invisible. It has to come forward and be "involved".

Bernice Conor Kennedy, President of Feminine Forecasts, sums it up this way: "Regardless of liberation, women are still different from men—and that's the key to approaching them as a market. Since I am a woman, what man is going to stand up and tell me my opinions are wrong? The world of women is changing rapidly, no doubt about it, but there are still the eternal verities. The wise marketer will keep both in mind."

The future of any business is shaped by the power of its long-range thinking. A business that addresses itself only to the problems of the moment has no future. The hospitality trade is a dynamic, imaginative industry and one that we know will be an increasingly powerful force in the U.S. economy as it faces the challenges and changes that will come between now and the year 2000.

49

The Mandate for Growth in the Hotel Industry

James E. Durbin

This industry literally has been home to me since I grew up in a hotel family. The Durbin Hotel in Rushville, Indiana, which dates back to 1840, has been operated by my family for 56 years and is a registered historic landmark in the state of Indiana. So I speak from a special personal perspective when I say that this is a great time to be in the hotel business.

I have not always been so high on a hotel career for my family. It has not been all that long since I used to wonder out loud if my own children would continue in the Durbin Family hotel tradition. I was not persuaded that this industry could be competitive and could attract and retain young people. Or that it made any sense for those young people to consider a hotel career.

Progress was a word long missing from the lexicon of this business. If we went back only to the end of World War II we would see an industry that functioned without development plans for orderly growth, or strategic planning, even things as basic as job descriptions. Budgeting was a still-to-be-learned art. We were badly behind on compensation and benefit programs for our employees. There was no such thing as a training manual.

Then along came the 1970s. I looked around and said to myself, this industry has made real progress. We are learning to be professional managers. We are starting to give the IBM's and Xeroxes a run for their money with our systems, training, budgeting, competitive compensation and marketing.

So you can spell PROGRESS with capital letters in describing the odyssey of this industry toward professionalism in the past 30 years. I believe the hotel business is much more of a profession today and holds more opportunities and rewards for those who work in it than ever before.

The experience of surviving the 1971 recession, the 1973 and 1974 energy crisis, the 1975 depression in our industry and the 1980 recession has made us tougher-minded managers and has forced us to become professional across our operational spectrum. The result has been better productivity. We've learned to be more flexible and to move quickly to keep up with concept changes as our customers change their preferences.

We have learned to harness the computer for our front desks, our backoffice accounting and reservation systems, and our national sales offices. We're doing a much better job of planning and developing. We are doing a much better job of marketing our products. We have learned market segmentation and tier pricing to maximize our sales and fluctuating business cycles. We've put science to work on the state of our art which has produced an ability to perform on a par with the best-managed companies you might care to name, in any industry.

Perhaps the most important area of improvement is people management. Over the years we have developed systems and procedures which permit effective planning and utilization of manpower resources, boost productivity, enhance our training efforts and motivate our people to carve out rewarding careers in this exciting industry. We are light years ahead of where this industry was languishing not very long ago.

FUTURE DEMANDS

Past progress augurs well for the future of this industry and at the same time points to where we must go if we are to continue sound, successful growth as we charge toward the 21st century.

As we look down the road I think it is fair to say that companies which hope to prosper in the hotly competitive business of being hospitable will have to become fully integrated. At this time, only Marriott among the major hotel companies can point to full vertical integration of its organizational structure across the spectrum of development, architecture, interior and food facilities design, construction, operations and marketing.

Technology will—and must— play an increasingly major role in hotel management. For all the progress we've made, our people management systems will have to become even more sophisticated to deal with ever-more-informed employees whose loyalty and confidence will be crucial elements of successful hospitality management.

We will have to make better use of market research to better understand what our customers want and how to give it to them. Computers will give us guest-history information on our repeat customers and enable us to serve them better on a more personal basis, even permitting us to pre-plan a stay.

Looking ahead, instant video displays will be available to show what proposed business and vacation destinations look like. Sitting in our homes or offices we can get a tour of a hotel and its facilities. That same TV screen will display rates, space availability and maybe even make a reservation.

Better weather forecasting will permit us to pick just the right time and place for a getaway. By the end of this decade we will be traveling faster and major cities of the world will be linked closer than ever in terms of time.

Such exciting developments bring with them potential for more business. They also put a higher premium on our professionalism and the quality of our product, indispensable elements in successful hospitality management of the future.

We have done a lot of research and have picked the brains of some of the brightest economists in the business to help us plan for the future, and I can tell you it is easier to project where our industry will be in the year 2000 than it is to predict precisely what will happen this year and next.

The long-range future looks great. The travel industry will grow dramatically in the years ahead. The United Nation's World Tourism organization tells us that by the year 2000 there will be more than two billion tourists, one-third of the projected world population, on the move annually. Futurist Herman Kahn predicts travel will be the world's largest industry by the end of the century. His predictions are predicated on some very positive developments:

1. Increased leisure time for people.
2. Expansion of the new middle class throughout the world.
3. More and better air transportation that will offer more competitive rates because of further reduction of governement regulation. There will be 4600 new, larger, quieter, more fuel-efficient aircraft by 1993.
4. Improvement in communications technology.
5. Better marketing techniques.
6. Better education.
7. The very nature of our modern work, which is highly specialized, repetitious and routine—all these will contribute to a growing need and desire to travel.

We have heard a lot about supply-side and demand-side economics in recent months with the advent of a new administration in Washington. I believe the hospitality industry will grow significantly during the balance of this century because of positive factors flowing from both the supply and demand sides of the economic fence.

On the supply side, hotels are increasingly considered to be attractive investment vehicles to the cash-laden institutions seeking to multiply their money. As a vice president of Prudential Insurance said recently, "The hotel business is a good business to be in. Your tenants leave every day and you can renegotiate the rent much more often . . . you do not have to wait for the lease to expire." Possible depreciation aspects of President Reagan's tax law change proposals could make hotels even more attractive investments.

Hotels are attractive investments precisely because there are companies which can manage them very profitably.

There is an increasing number of people wanting to manage in this industry due to the tremendous advances in the prestige *of* doing so and in the compensation *for* doing so. A hotel general manager for example, has a tremendous amount of personal and professional satisfaction. After all, he or she is running an operation which produces massive cash flows and a manager is recognized in the community as a very important person.

On the demand side, a host of factors fuel our optimism:

● Business travel will increase. Projections vary, but they all agree on a boost in this segment of our business.

● Group business will keep growing, and tapping that market successfully has long been one of the industry's greatest strengths.

● On the pleasure side of the revenue coin, the babies of the post-World War II boom have come of age. They grew up with extensive and wide-ranging travel and want more of it for themselves and their families. The value systems of our young adults tend to favor experiences, such as travel, over money and other tangible possessions.

● The number of people earning $25 thousand or more (in today's dollars) will increase 10 million by 1990. The key here is the additional discretionary spending such a statistic portends.

● A decreasing work week overall, combined with a growing number of two-income households and the new cadre of permanent part-time workers in this country, will mean more money to spend on more leisure time activities and provide even more opportunities to sell weekend space, i.e., more long weekends.

• The aging of the pre-retirement population will free up more and more of those "empty nesters" whose children are grown and who will have the time and money to spend on travel.

• The important 35 to 44-year old segment of the population will increase by 42% in the 1980s, while the population as a whole will grow by only 10%. This group has historically taken nearly half again as many trips per year and accounts for 15 more nights away from home annually than Americans in other age categories.

• The growth of the upscale business travel market with an attendant demand for better accommodations, more and better leisure-time facilities and the like pushes up our sales projections. Last year, total expenditure in the United States for lodging, airline tickets and in food and beverage establishments exceeded the amount spent on national defense.

INTERNATIONAL TRAVEL PROSPECTS

• On the international side, the United States Travel Service tells that there are now some 86 million people throughout the world with the financial resources to consider the United States as a travel destination. The total grows each year. During the next decade the number of international travelers will grow from 270 million to 483 million. That increase almost equals the population of the United States. Total world spending for domestic and international travel reached an estimated 683 billion dollars for 1980, a 10% increase over 1979. International visitors spent an estimated 12 billion dollars in this country last year, the 21 million international visitors to the U.S. in 1980 increased 23% over 1979, which increased 25% over 1978, which was 28% above 1977. Last year was a watershed, for it marked the first time the number of foreign visitors to the United States topped the number of Americans traveling abroad.

Parlez vous Francais? Sprechen sie Deutsch? Comprende Espanol? Well, you better, if you want to get your share of this lucrative market. Good hospitality management dictates that we be prepared to properly serve these very welcome guests.

At Marriott, we enjoyed a 60% increase in the number of international travelers staying at our hotels last year. It is a market we work at, believe me. We have had for a number of years advertising and public relations programs and international sales offices operating in Japan, Germany, the United Kingdom, Mexico and Canada. You can appreciate our reaction when we read recently in *Futurist* magazine that 85% of the international travel to the United States in the 1980s will come from Japan, Germany, the United Kingdom, Mexico, Canada and France.

If we take a good look at our industry we know that travel and leisure pursuits have become a basic human drive. Travel is built into the human animal. People *need* to get away. Given the chance to travel, they will do so. We see this need more than ever in our research about serving the traveling and leisure public. Getting away for business has always been imperative. Nowadays, pleasure travel has also become imperative. People feel they *must* escape.

Not only do people *want* to go, increasingly they *can* go. All over the world there is a growing number of families moving into an income bracket high enough to permit spending for travel. Rising incomes, more working wives, smaller families—all these factors provide the disposable income and freedom to travel that are so important to this industry.

If we add to these forces the industry's growing capacity to meet demand, we can be even more positive. We have reached a new peak in our global system of air transportation, hotels, tourist attractions, cruise ships, rental cars, travel agencies. We have a new level of support for travel and tourism from governments around the world. There's a strong superstructure in place today that has been building for 30 years and it will be even stronger tomorrow with advances in aircraft design, new tourist destinations, more outstanding hotels, more travel agents. All these factors drive the desire for travel.

Further, the improvements in hospitality management brought about by technology will produce hassle-free lodging experiences which will encourage people to get away from home that much more often.

GROWTH AND MANAGERIAL CHALLENGES

All is not roses, of course. Those intending to be managers in the hospitality industry of the future must be sharper, better and more professional to meet the many challenges of the years ahead.

Travel costs are rising at a rate faster than inflation. They were up over 25% last year compared to a 14% boost in the consumer price index.

Considerable new competition will be created as the world continues to shrink and international hotel companies, developers and airlines increasingly encroach upon each other.

Certainly, we must be concerned about such problems as energy and security, the difficulty in getting and training good people to sustain our growth, the need to manage costs effectively. But we are handling these problems. We are more concerned about expansion and being able to accommodate the growing travel market predicted for the years ahead.

At Marriott we are upbeat about the future. We believe we have a mandate from our customers and our industry to grow. And grow we will—dramatically, at a rate of 20 to 25% a year. We will open 22 hotels in 1981 alone in the United States and abroad. Fifty-one Marriott Hotel projects are in the development pipeline for the 1981–1983 period. We are talking about tripling out hotel revenues in the next four years. With plans like that, saying we are optimistic about the future could be considered an understatement.

In 1969 Marriott Corporation's annual sales were $200 million. This year we will reach the $2 billion mark, a tenfold increase in just over a decade. Over the last five years, our sales have grown at an annual rate of 17% and our earnings per share at 30%, an exceptional record. We intend to sustain that rare combination of profit growth and capital productivity. And we're going to do it largely with our hotels. That is where our ambitious corporate growth plans are focused, with good reason.

We project that room supply will lag behind demand during the coming decade. That fact will help us keep our occupancy rates high— the ultimate element of hotel performance and the one in which we have historically been one of the leaders in the industry.

We are going to hold our leadership position by offering our customers even greater value in all parts of our hotels. We will update and upgrade our rooms. We will provide special-priced dining opportunities. We will introduce new restaurant and lounge concepts. And we'll have more deluxe resorts and prestigious properties.

The years ahead promise to be exciting. For those elements of the hospitality industry which are properly prepared to accomodate the growth which will come, introduce new concepts to meet changing customer tastes and develop the people who can perform professionally on a sustained basis, the future indeed shines brightly.

Consistency and quality are going to be necessary ingredients in everybody's formula for success in the years ahead. Growing demand for better services will be accompanied by growing demands for better services. Rather than fret about that, we should welcome it. Such a change in customer approach means even bigger rewards for the winning performers in our industry.

Because people will be more particular, they will also be more selective. I look for what the consumer product people call brand loyalty to intensify. Hospitality management must develop new dimensions of service magnetism to attract and keep customers. The consumerist movement which has swept our society in recent history has shown that being today's best doesn't guarantee you'll lead the parade tomorrow. You must deliver your product consistently well. You must deliver the *right* product.

Ultimately, it all boils down to the proper care and feeding of the individual guest. There isn't anything mysterious about how to succeed in the hotel business. We must develop further the *science* of hospitality management and the *art* of being hospitable. They go hand in hand.

The market forces at work during the balance of this century will push the best hotel managers to new peaks of prosperity. It will be without doubt a great time to be in the hospitality industry.

50

The Traveler: 1981 and Beyond

Hershel B. Sarbin

In its economic forecast issue, Travel Weekly (1981) published the views of major industry executives on the hard challenges of 1981—views supported by the hard data published in the 1981 Travel Market Yearbook, by the Conference Board, the University of Michigan and the latest TRAVEL PULSE Consumer Travel Intention Study. Most economic forecasts offer no hope for an expanded travel market in the current economic climate. The evidence suggests that the number of U.S. travelers will not exceed the levels of 1978.

How urgent and wise it is, then, to look at *travelers*, as distinguished from *travel*; to seek and find more acute insights into *traveler* behavior; to know figuratively where the *traveler* is headed, not only for 1981, but considerably beyond.

Fortunately, the news is not saturated with gloom. Our TRAVEL PULSE data indicate that approximately 80 million Americans did travel in 1979. They took 120 million pleasure trips, an estimated 145 million business trips, and we estimated that 14 million Americans traveled internationally. The ranks of travelers were swelled by 8.2 million overseas visitors and an overall 21.6 million foreign arrivals. At least for purposes of the hospitality industry in the United States, their presence is making up for otherwise lost revenue. But the heart of our market, and our fundamental concern, must be the 80 million U.S. adults who did travel, and another 20–30 million Americans who represent potential growth.

In 1979, 93% of domestic pleasure travelers said they would recommend the same trip to someone who had similar interests. And 77% of travelers said there was no such thing as a bad vacation. But in 1981 there was some disquieting news beyond inflation and economic adversity. In 1978 and 1979, 62% of the population had said that they "love travel and do so whenever they can", but in two measures of that sentiment taken in 1980, the proportion fell to under 50%.

In the 1978 and 1979 TRAVEL PULSE studies, the proportion of people who said they "like traveling, but end up doing other things because of the hassle of traveling" was just one in eight (13%). By October of 1980 that proportion had risen to one in four (24%).

So here we are, in a non-expanding market for the moment, a market under assault from inflation and economic dislocation, with a fairly hard-core group of 80 million adult travelers, and faced with real danger signs in the consumer's perception of the pleasures and rewards of travel.

Where do we go from here? How do we hold the market we have? How do we make it grow and thrive in these difficult times, particularly when there is less money available to advertise, to promote, to lure discretionary dollars into the wonderful world of travel?

I would like to focus on just one aspect of travel marketing which is vital to holding and expanding our market. It is an area in which we are serious under-achievers, an area of lost opportunity, wasted resources, and often a failure to comprehand the most elementary aspects of consumer psychology.

I have referred to it in the past as the "communication gap" in travel—a basic inability, or unwillingness, to talk to the traveler in a thousand different ways that have very little to do with big national ad campaigns—a thousand different ways in which to build customer loyalty, repeat business, more frequent trips by the same customer, and new business through word-of-mouth influence.

No other business has as many of its customers captive—often for many hours in airplanes, buses and trains; for days customers are in hotels or destinations and travel personnel spend so little time talking to them.

What could have a higher priority, at a time when the market is flat, when the economy is against us, and our promotion budgets eroded, than communicating effectively with the travelers who are already with us?

What could have a higher priority—as part of providing the very service and hospitality we have promised—than telling consumers how much we care, keeping them informed, persuading them to come back, persuading the business traveler to return for pleasure—not just business—to the same hotel, the same city, the same state, the same country?

Just imagine the impact of having a satisfied customer tell his travel agent about his experience with you—about your service and your sense of hospitality. That travel agent serves thousands of other customers with the same views about value and satisfaction. Last year 28 million Americans used the services of a travel agent in arranging trips. That means enormous word-of-mouth power, if you know how to capture it.

Take this logic one step further. If the travel agent, or one of his sales employees, were a guest at my hotel, I would make certain that I knew it, and that I took time to say a special hello. I would take the trouble, if the agency's dollar volume and number of employees were unknown to me, to look it up in the *World Travel Directory* (just as the doorman would look at the luggage tag) to establish a more personal touch. How about telling the Smiths, booked into my hotel by the Jones Agency, to say hello to Mr. and Mrs. Jones when they see them?

The opportunities for using the most elementary devices to cement relationships with present customers and of generating new business are literally endless. How could we overlook them so consistently?

Most of us regard travel as very special, and rightfully so. After all, travel is the stuff that dreams are made of. It is, as Dr. Joseph Smith of Oxtoby-Smith says, "Sprinkled with stardust and rooted in inherent psychological needs—the need to escape, to restore, to self-discover, to make connections with others."

Hopefully, we are learning that travel, like most other consumer behavior, can be deferred or postponed, restricted or substituted. And the trip not taken, like the seat or room not filled, is lost forever. Distasteful or not, the recognition that travel is like other consumer behavior is simply unavoidable. People can survive without travel if they have to. And they will. That is why I have focused in this chapter on our failure to achieve our potential in both creating and communicating effectively a sense of hospitality—of making people feel wanted—of making them feel that you care they're here; of sending them away with the confidence that they received full value, and that it will be comfortable and rewarding to return again to the same place.

We have seen dramatic changes in consumer expectations in recent years. Travel is not the same business it was a decade or even five years ago.

The people interviewed in our TRAVEL PULSE research are shouting their messages to us loud and clear. Let us believe them. For if we do, if we act upon what they tell us, not only will we hold the market we have, but they will go back home and tell their friends and travel agents, and they will talk about us in a way that will make our business and our profits grow—in 1981 and the decades beyond.

The data we are seeing on today's traveler are sharp and clear.

(1) People are looking for value—not price, but value—more than ever before.

(2) People increasingly want service, comfort, and all the trappings of hospitality. How clearly this is related to the consumer's perception of value!

(3) People want information. They want to know what to expect and they don't want surprises.

(4) Finally, people increasingly tell us they seek excitement, adventure, the new and the different. For the vast majority, travel is not peace and quiet.

What amazes me is how we can take these unchallengeable expressions of consumer demands, nod our heads in ready agreement, and then do so little to exploit our opportunities.

When we advertise our services—on television, in magazines or the trade press, we are very conscious of cost per thousand, or the cost per inquiry from a particular ad or direct mail piece.

Has anyone ever tried to figure a cost per thousand to reach a customer already in the house? Already in the hotel? Already in the airplane? Already on the bus? Who has placed a proper dollar value on communicating effectively to that captive audience of travelers, at the very moment they are with us? A few, just a few, truly understand and act upon this knowledge.

Suppose we take several examples from the area of hospitality communications. Let us begin at the front door of the hotel. How many doormen say "Welcome to the Sheraton"? "Welcome to the Marriott"? "Welcome to our place"? It is an opportunity lost forever to communicate in the most basic way that "We care. . . . We want you". Some years ago at the Washington Plaza Hotel in Seattle an enterprising doorman, as he took my bag, casually examined the name tag and said, "Welcome to the Washington Plaza, Mr. Sarbin". What an impression that simple gesture makes on even the most hardened traveler.

At the Tower Place Hotel in Atlanta—just 220 rooms—the guest is handed an envelope at the check-in desk containing several pages of what executive Herbert Wasserman calls "down-to-earth, we're-glad-you're-here" information. The guest is told a little history about the Buckhead area in which the hotel is located; told about nearby shopping; told which TV channels get clear reception in the area; told why the hotel's diningroom serves à la carte rather than table d'hôte (diet-conscious business travelers prefer it); told why it costs a few dollars more to take a cab from the hotel to the airport than it did from the airport to hotel, and so on. This is not a fancy brochure, but a plain, offset job that can be changed as needed. And what is more, you will find an extra copy in your hotel room, just to be sure the message gets through.

These communication concepts—saying welcome, good morning, providing useful information, responding to complaints with interest and a desire to please—all go to the heart of customer satisfaction, to that sense of feeling wanted and to the traveler's perception of value.

Too often we forget how broad a concept hospitality communication is. It is not just brochures, or an in-room magazine, or closed circuit TV announcements. A smile is communication. The ambiance of a breakfast room or bar is communication. Just as clearly, a sharp word from a desk clerk, or waitress, or stewardess is communication. An unsmiling face, a glum expression, even a slightly contemptuous look in response to a complaint is communication.

We are all aware, of course, that it is not possible to sustain among employees, or guests, the kind of mood that causes us to be always warm and cheerful with one another. There is indeed some hypocrisy in the kind of hospitality communications I urge. But I suggest there is real value to this form of hypocrisy, not unlike Russell Baker's story about two Englishmen who bump into one another rounding a corner. "So sorry," each says, not really meaning it, and then moving along. How much better than squaring off, ready for a fight. So we must train our people, and ourselves, that a little hypocrisy has merit in our business.

The examples and the opportunities are endless. Take the business traveler whom we see from Monday to Thursday. When we have that customer with us, and in the right mood, think of the climate we have created for selling—at that very moment—the idea of bringing the family back for a long weekend. What an opportunity to sell the entire destination and all its pleaure travel attractions. Over half (56%) of all business travelers said they would like to return on a purely pleasure trip. If only we will exercise our imaginations! If only we understood the incredible dollar value of the traveler already in the house!

That value has so many dimensions. A satisfied guest, a satisfied traveler, will not only be a repeat visitor. That traveler is a walking advertisement for a carrier, a destination, a car rental company, a hotel, a tour operator. And what is wrong with suggesting to guests that they should tell their friends, and their travel agents, about you?

The travel agent dimension needs and deserves much greater attention than it has traditionally been given. When we think of our captive traveler, we must not forget that 53% of all business air travelers, and 51% of all domestic air travelers, are being booked by agents. Today's travel agent is exerting a profound influence on the customer's choice of

hotel, carrier, package and even specific destination. Because growing influence the travel agent must be considered, in p goods terms, as a "heavy user," and treated as such in all prom efforts.

51

The Future Impact of Inflation on the Hotel Industry—A Survey[1]

Thomas J. Beggs, MBA and *Robert C. Lewis, Ph.D.*

One of the most pervasive influences on the hotel industry during the past decade, as on everything else, has been inflation. On the demand side, the industry is generally considered to be greatly affected by the level of disposable income and consumers' increasing resistance to higher prices. Yet, until 1980 (Table 51.1) the overall industry response has been to raise room rates even faster than the steep increases in the Consumer Price Index. Average room rates at the end of 1980 were 58.3% higher than they were in 1975. During the same period the CPI increased 47% and disposable income increased about 50%.

This reality has certainly induced, for one thing, the advent of the budget motel. Yet, in some cities such as New York, Boston, Los Angeles and San Francisco the climb in room rates has been even steeper and the inflationary effect on hotel patronage appears to be non-existent. Single rates of over $100 per night in first class hotels are now a common expectation in these cities. One major hotel chain is known to raise its menu prices 10% every three months as an automatic procedure. Informal reports from at least three major chains are that prices will continue to be increased to "whatever the traffic will bear, and as long as people have to do business [in New York] on expense accounts we haven't reached that limit yet. The more we raise rates, the more occupancy seems to go up." One source, however, attributes it to new construction: "When new hotels [like the Helmsley Palace and Grand Hyatt in New York] charge the rates they have to to achieve return on

[1]A version of this paper was published in the Cornell Hotel and Restaurant Admin. Q., May, 1981.

TABLE 51.1.   THE RISE IN ROOM RATES VS. CONSUMER PRICE INDEX*

	Hotel Room Rates	Consumer Price Index
All 1975	10.1	9.1
All 1976	8.1	5.8
All 1977	8.4	6.7
All 1978	16.4	8.8
I	24.8	7.1
II	12.2	9.5
III	12.6	9.2
IV	15.7	9.5
All 1979	15.8	13.3
I	19.7	11.2
II	12.0	12.8
III	13.8	13.4
IV	17.6	15.6
All 1980	9.6	12.4
I	23.3	18.1
II	7.9	11.6
III	7.9	7.0
IV	−.6	12.9

Source: CPI Detailed Report, Bur. Labor Statistics, U.S. Dept. of Labor
*Seasonally adjusted annual and quarterly percentage increases in lodging room rates and consumer prices for all goods and services over previous year.

investment, then we're not going to be far behind." And new hotel construction, as this survey shows, remains unbounded.

On the supply side, of course, the figures are well known. Increases in labor costs, food and beverage costs, energy costs and other variable expenses as well as fixed costs of insurance, taxes, rent and interest provide a constant upward pressure on food and beverage prices and room rates. Most major expense categories have increased recently at a 10% to 15% annual rate. Table 51.2, however, shows that increased revenues have enabled hotels to keep expenses as a ratio of sales at a better than even level. One senses that while hotel operators are publicly decrying the constant increases in their expenses, their major response, by and large, is to simply increase their prices. In fact, one industry consultant, C. DeWitt Coffman (1981), has publicly stated: "Never in history has the public been so acclimated to rate increases as they are today. Unless you realize this and raise your prices, you can't be a winner in the hotel industry."

Coffman notwithstanding, with these historic precedents in mind and more of the same on the horizon, many of today's "winners" operators are wondering where it will end and what they should be doing to plan for and to cope with the future. To find out how some of the industry's

TABLE 51.2.   HOTEL EXPENSE RATIOS TO REVENUES

	Net Income After Property Taxes and Insurance (%)	Property Taxes and Insurance (%)	Payroll and Related Costs (%)	Food and Beverage Costs (%)
1975	19.5	4.5	35.8	31.1
1976	21.1	4.3	35.3	30.3
1977	22.0	4.2	35.0	30.1
1978	23.8	3.7	34.1	30.8
1979	25.1	3.1	33.6	31.0

SOURCE: Trends in the Hotel Industry, 1980 Edition, New York: Pannel Kerr Forster

leaders are approaching these issues a survey was designed to ask them the following broad questions:

1. What do you perceive the inflationary impacts to be from 1981 to 1985?
2. How will this affect the lodging industry?
3. How will this affect your operations?
4. What are you planning to do about it?
5. What will the lodging industry look like in 1985?

The reality is that forecasting the future is essential for business survival. Strategic planning needs to be based upon logical, objective and systematic attempts at this effort. This is especially cogent for hotels—an industry somewhat noted for basing its future largely on its past, a practice that led to problems in the past and could lead to even more problems in the future.

No one has a crystal ball but a powerful influence on what will happen in the future are those assumptions and consequent decisions made by the industry leaders. Plans now being laid by chief executives will have major impact on how the industry looks in 1985 and how it will get there.

We have surveyed and analyzed the opinions of the chief executives of both independent and corporate hotel organizations in the United States. Our belief is that the results of this study can provide basic inputs into the planning decisions of the industry's organizations. A summary of the major findings is presented in the following sections.

Overall, the survey shows that anticipated higher prices, higher occupancies, lower costs and new properties lead the industry to be somewhat sanguine about the future—at least in regard to their own operations. Very few see a business turndown or a decrease in their profits, and three-fourths plan to build new properties. Eighty-nine percent expect to increase their market share in present trading areas. There is no sense of pushing the panic button. At the same time, however, Jay Schmiedeskamp, Director of the Gallup Economic Service, has cautioned, "business executives' expectations aren't necessarily a good leading indicator. History suggests that, if anything, they are a lagging indicator. So there's a chance that more alarm may develop as time goes on"(Anon. 1980A).

METHODOLOGY AND SAMPLE

Extensive mail questionnaires were sent in October 1980 to 200 chief executives of multi-unit United States hotel organizations listed in the American Hotel & Motel Association 1980 directory, plus 60 chief executives of leading individual hotels and resorts across the United States. A response rate of 68 or 26% was obtained. The organizations which these executives head account for 1645 properties and 358,506 rooms in the United States or over half of the total hotel and motel rooms in the United States that are members of AHMA, not counting referral companies. A summary of these organizations is as follows:

● 85% are multi-unit operators and 15% are individual properties.

● Multi-unit operators control an average of 28 properties (median = 10) and 6143 rooms (median = 1950). A single company this size would rank in the top 25 among U.S. hotel companies.

● 57% of multi-unit operators operate 2 to 10 properties, 29% operate 11 to 40 properties and 14% operate in excess of 50 properties.

● 19% operate under 500 rooms, 22% operate between 500 and 1000 rooms, 47% operate between 1000 and 10,000 rooms, 6% operate between 10,000 and 25,000 rooms and 6% operate over 25,000 rooms.

● 41% own their properties, 27% have franchised properties and 32% have both.

● 19% are publically held and 81% are privately held.

● 16% have properties located primarily in the east, 16% in the midwest, 35% in the west, 19% in the south and 14% are nation wide chains.

● 12% are large companies with annual sales exceeding $100 million, 21% are medium-size companies with annual sales in the $25–100 million range and 67% are smaller companies with annual sales of less than $25 million.

● Total sales for all respondents exceeded $4.6 billion in 1979. Average sales per organization were $67.75 million (median = $14.63 million), per property $2.8 million and per room $12,850.

• Of those persons who completed the questionnaire, 16% are Chairman of the Board, 43% are President, 12% are Vice President, 8% are General Managers, 5% are Marketing Directors and 16% hold other titles.

SUMMARY OF FINDINGS

The overall conclusion from the analysis of the respondents' returns is that the industry will realize little real sales growth between now and 1985. Growth and financial performance improvement will come about to a large extent as a result of building new properties.

Most executives believe that the 1985 outlook for their own company is brighter than that for the industry as a whole. They expect inflation to be a little milder than 1980s was, the prime rate to be lower, and sales and costs to be correlationally higher.

Respondents gave opinions in four major areas of interest: 1) general economic conditions; 2) financial operations; 3) property operations; and 4) marketing.

General Economic Conditions

Executives expect some improvement in the fight against inflation. Overall, they expect the average annual inflation rate between now and 1985 to be 10.05%, somewhat below 1980's annualized rate of 12.4%. Executives in large and medium size companies expect the rate to average 10.6% while those in smaller size companies expect 10%.

The prime interest rate is expected to be 12.6% in mid 1985 compared to its range of 15% to 21% during the survey. Large company executives and those in medium size companies predict 13% and those in small companies predict 12.7%. The range of predictions extends from 1.5% to 23%.

Not quite two-thirds of the executives (66%) expect the United States to experience another major economic recession between now and 1985. Regionally, there were some differences, however, as shown in Table 51.3.

TABLE 51.3.   PERCENT OF RESPONDENTS EXPECTING ECONOMIC RECESSION BETWEEN 1981 and 1985, BY REGION

East	80%
South	62%
Midwest	73%
Far West	65%
National	56%

Financial Operations

The chief executives were polled concerning their expectations of the expected financial strategies and performances of their organizations in the 1981–1985 period. Their expectations concerning sales growth, the costs of doing business, profit margins, return on investment, capital structures and capital investment priorities were determined.

Sales.—The average annual increase in sales (unadjusted for inflation) that is expected between 1981 and 1985 is 12.3%. This forecast is based on organizations having the same properties as they did in 1980. Growth in real sales levels, therefore, is estimated at 2.25%. Overall, only 33% of the executives expect sales growth rates to exceed inflation.

Those executives expecting to add new properties by 1985 (76%) expect these additions to increase their average annual sales by 31%. Adjusted for inflation this signifies a real growth rate of 21%. Thus, real growth in the industry is expected to come primarily from expansion in the number of properties.

Costs.—Total variable costs are expected to increase annually by 10.4% or just above the expected inflation rate and below the sales increase rate. Food and beverage costs are expected to exceed the inflation rate at 11.9%. Payroll costs and energy costs are the major categories expected to exceed it (14.6% and 16.2% annual increase rates). Fixed costs, however, are anticipated to increase annually at 6.8%, substantially below inflation. Through tighter controls, automation and some real sales growth hotel executives expect to keep total variable costs close to the 58% of sales they were in 1979. Table 51.4 summarizes sales and costs predictions.

TABLE 51.4.   AVERAGE ANNUAL SALES AND COSTS INCREASE PREDICTIONS

	Unadjusted	Adjusted
Sales (with same rooms)	12.3%	2.3%
Sales (with new rooms)	31.0%	21.0%
Variable costs	10.4%	.4%
Food & beverage	11.9%	1.9%
Payroll	14.6%	4.6%
Energy	16.2%	6.2%
Fixed costs	6.8%	-3.2%
Room rates	14.0%	4.0%
F & B prices	12.0%	2.0%

Revenues.—The increase in sales and profits expected by executives will not come only through the addition of properties and decreases in costs. Overall, executives expect occupancy rates to climb to 74.2% by 1985 compared to an industry rate of 72% in 1979. At the same time, room rates are expected to increase annually at an average rate of 14%, 4% higher than inflation. Thus room rates will continue to outpace the CPI or, to put it another way, the 1980 $100 room will cost $192.50 in 1985 (still below Hong Kong's New World Center Hotel with present rates of $200–$400!)

Food and beverage prices are expected to increase at an annual 12% rate, two percentage points ahead of inflation. Room sales as a percentage of total sales are expected to fall slightly to 58.2% as opposed to 1979's 58.5% and food and beverage sales share is also expected to decrease (33.1% vs. 1979's 34.8%). At this ratio, then, the decreased share of sales of these two categories (91.3% of gross sales) will be down three percentage points from 1979, forecasting an increase in other income sources.

Hotel executives surveyed also expect improved balance sheets by 1985. The debt/equity ratio is expected to decrease to 0.57 from the industry's 0.64 of 1979. Over 70% plan to finance future expansion with a combination of equity, debt and internal sources. Along with the decrease in debt/equity ratio, return on equity in 1985 is anticipated to be 18.6% vs. 1979's 14.5% for the industry.

Overall, industry gross margin is envisioned to be 24% in 1985, the same as 1979, but the executives responding expect their own gross margin to be 27.8%. On the other hand, the executives foresee an increase in net profits for the industry to 7.5% from 1979's 6% but for their own properties they expect an even more optimistic 12.5% net profit.

Property Operations

Eighty-eight percent of the hotel executives responding to the survey expect to increase market share in their major trading areas while 76% will expand into new trading areas by building or buying. At the same time, 45% are planning to dispose of present properties. Regionally, the midwest at 73% expectation, is the only area where market share increase is not expected by at least 90% of the respondents. In the east and west only 36 and 29%, respectively, expect to sell properties. In the other major areas the range is from 55 to 62% for those who expect to sell.

The net anticipated increase in lodging rooms and properties by 1985 is 75%. It is estimated that there were a "legitimate" 1.8 million hotel/motel rooms in the United States in 1980. This would mean an increase by 1985 to 3.15 million rooms!

Priorities given to capital investment will impact on the hotel industry between now and 1985. Forty-three percent of the organizations will give high priority to construction of new properties but even more (76%) will give high priority to remodeling and upgrading existing properties. Forty-one percent plan to change restaurant and/or lounge concepts.

In the area of capital equipment 44% plan to increase automation to reduce payroll costs, 60% plan to add or expand computer facilities and 79% will concentrate on improving energy use productivity in existing facilities.

The average planned increase in properties per organization is 18 (median = 5) with an average of 219 rooms per property, about the same as 1980's rooms, at an average cost of $79,000 per room excluding land. The upper range of cost per room, however, was $200,000. Executives were asked if they thought the inflation impact would increase the share of lodging sales by budget-type operations. Forty percent felt that budget-types market share would increase, 49% felt it would remain the same and 11% felt it would decrease.

Finally, the hotel executives were asked what use they presently made of computer facilities and what plans they had to increase computer usage by 1985. As would be expected, the greatest use today is in payroll accounting (82%). This is expected to be 94% by 1985. The lowest use of computers today, however, is in marketing operations. This usage is expected to increase 213% by 1985—no wonder 88% expect to increase market share in present trading areas! Food and beverage control and front office systems are also due for very sizeable increased computerization. Table 51.5 shows how executives plan to increase their computer facilities.

TABLE 51.5.   COMPUTER FACILITIES

	Have Now		Plan in '85		Increase in Mean
	Mean	Median	Mean	Median	
Reservation	54%	53%	80%	99%	48%
Payroll	82	99	93	100	13
Finance/Accounting	68	92	92	99	35
Front office	28	10	67	75	139
F & B control	19	5	59	51	211
Marketing	15	1	47	49	213

Marketing

Executives were questioned concerning their marketing activities. Marketing has emerged in the recent past as the tour de force of the major chains in the competitive arena. The results of this survey presented so far indicate that hotel executives are counting on marketing to maintain their companies' growth rates during the next five years. Yet, results of the survey also indicate that marketing in the hotel industry has a long climb ahead before it reaches the level of sophistication and professionalism that it holds in manufacturing firms.

Seventy-five percent of the executives responded that they have separate marketing departments in their organizations that handle all marketing functions such as sales, advertising, promotion, publicity, public relations and market research. Of those who do not have marketing departments, 88% have sales departments and about half of these expect to establish a full service marketing department by 1985.

Forty-six percent of the marketing departments are located in headquarters only, 12% in the individual properties and 42% in both. When asked what functions marketing departments in individual properties performed, however, the responses indicated that these departments have only partial autonomy in marketing activities. Table 51.6 shows the percentage of autonomy that individual property marketing departments have in planning various marketing activities.

TABLE 51.6.   INDIVIDUAL PROPERTY MARKETING AUTONOMY

Mean	Function	Median
65%	Plan strategy	70%
63	Plan advertising & promotion	73
60	Plan budgets	50
57	Plan research	51
67	Plan publicity & public relations	75
69	Plan selling strategies	76
57	Plan pricing strategies	50
56	Plan Product strategies	50

Respondents indicated that an average 6.5% of sales revenues (median = 4.2%, mode = 3%) was presently spent on all marketing activities and that this ratio would remain the same in 1985 (median = 4.4%, mode = 4%). Eighty-three percent of these expenditures are allocated to media advertising (or 5.4% of sales, median = 2%).

Sixty-four percent of the respondents indicated they did not intend to increase or decrease the percentage of their advertising budget spent on media between now and 1985. Twenty-five percent said they would increase the percentage and 11% said they would decrease it. Increases in specific media usage are planned mostly in television, collateral and magazines. Sixty percent use an advertising agency regularly, 30% sometimes and 10% never use one.

Particularly interesting from a marketing viewpoint and reflecting what has already been mentioned about increased room rates is the expected change in the market mix by 1985. A 4% change in individual business patronage is forecast but a 10% increase is anticipated in convention/conference business. Similarly, a 15% increase in tour pleasure business is foreseen accompanied by an 18% decrease in individual pleasure patronage. Thus, both the pleasure and the business markets point toward an increase in group business and a decrease in individual travel. Table 51.7 shows the patronage ratios for now and 1985.

TABLE 51.7.   MARKET MIX RATIOS

Market	1980		1985	
	Mean	Median	Mean	Median
Convention	21%	11%	23%	15%
Business	40	37	41	40
Tour Group	11	8	13	10
Pleasure	33	28	27	25

Executives responded that 58% of their food and beverage business now comes from in-house and they foresee almost no change in this ratio by 1985.

The hotel executives were asked if they had a *formal* strategic marketing plan for the period from now until 1985, a sine qua non for truly marketing oriented firms. Thirty-one percent responded yes, while 69% said no. Fifteen percent of the respondents indicated they conduct formal market research on a constant basis, 32% do it regularly, 20% sometimes, 26% seldom and 7% never. Of those who do formal research, 34% is done by a consultant or market research firm, 24% by an advertising agency, 15% by a public relations agency and 55% of it is done in-house.

In-house guest surveys seem to be fairly common in the industry so executives were asked how many times a year they were conducted. Forty percent said continually, 3% said once a month, 49% said one to 4 times a year, 8% never use them.

Ninety-two percent of the respondents indicated that they segment to some extent their marketing activities by specific target markets. Segments used are demographics of age (33%), income (42%), sex (20%) or geographic area (97%). Only 40% use life style variables and 32% segment by benefit variables. A large 83%, however, segment by usage such as convention, business or pleasure. Fifty-four percent of the executives report they use product differentiation strategies and 59% use positioning strategies.

Although it may not be greatly affected by inflation or future planning, no-shows and overbooking are a major issue in the hotel industry. Executives were asked what their policies were on these issues and what affect they had in their operations. The average property, these executives reported, experiences a 7.1% ratio of no-shows to reservations with a median and mode of 5. One property reported a 25% ratio of no-shows! In anticipation of this the average property overbooks 5.1%. The net result reported is an average of 2 rooms empty 2.8 nights a week due to no-shows or an average of 0.8 rooms per night. On the other side of the coin, the average property "walks" .75 reservations 1.1 nights a week or an average of .12 rooms per night. The overall ratio of walks to no-shows of 15% indicates that the industry continues to bear the brunt of this problem.

CONCLUSION

The impact of inflation appears to be here to stay. Seven hundred eight two executives of large, medium and small companies in American industry interviewed by the Gallup Organization in November and December 1980 see little change for 1981 and only a slight easing by 1984 (Anon. 1980B). The hotel executives that we questioned concur. The focus in this study has been to attempt to forecast some of the most likely changes that would occur in the U.S. hotel industry in the 5 year period between 1980 and 1985.

Alvin Toffler, in *The Third Wave* (1980), has predicted a forthcoming corporate identity crisis and a re-emergence of the prosumer. Translated, this breaks down into the need for smarter executives paying attention to multiple interconnected bottom lines—social, environmental, informational, political, and ethical—in order to relate to the change in the marketplace caused by the consumer who can produce for himself. The results of this study contain important implications for the hotel industry in this future scenario.

The top executive of one leading hotel chain has stated the feelings which have been echoed by many of his counterparts and supported by the responses to this survey. These feelings are that hotel chains have a consumer mandate to grow and to expand rapidly. The challenge, he says, is to have the best people, the best training and the highest standards of service. These challenges, of course, are the same challenges of the past which many lodging operations have failed to meet. Surely, the future will offer even greater challenges that an industry built on the past will have difficulty surviving.

Clearly, this study indicates that the industry is in for significant change and that the pace of that change will be rapid. No longer can the industry plan its future by basing it on the past. To do so may lead it to where the U.S. automobile industry is today. Continued reliance on evolutionary change may well fail to provide the adaptability necessary to manage the environmental change.

The industry must have managers and organizations which cannot only predict and prepare for change, but creatively manage change as well. Traditional managers must learn to be change responsive as they adapt to an environment of ambiguity and conflict. Increasingly, the individualistic problem solving style will give way to more modern interdisciplinary team approaches to both analyzing and managing the future.

For many organizations strategic planning is becoming the critical test for managing the future. Yet, only 37% of the respondents indicated that they had a strategic plan for the next 3 to 5 years that was shared by all management. And only 7% have one shared by all employees. The results of the study define scenarios for the industry in 1985 and indicate the most important factors that must be considered in planning for the next 5 years. The challenges are to create integrative organizations that can respond to these changes with the timeliness necessary to take advantage of the opportunities they present. The implications for strategic planning are tremendous and will be presented in future papers.

Bibliography

ABBOT, W. 1978. Work in the year 2001. *In* 1999: The World of Tomorrow: Selections from The Futurist, edited by E. Cornish. World Future Society, Washington, D.C., pp. 99–104.

ACKOFF, R.L. 1976. Towards a system of systems concepts. *In* Systems Behavior, 2nd Edition, edited by Beishon, J. and Peters, G. Published for the Open University Press by Harper and Row, London and New York, p. 106.

AMERICAN COUNCIL ON LIFE INSURANCE. 1978. Life Insurance Fact Book 1978. Washington, D.C., pp. 29–30.

AMERICAN HOTEL & MOTEL ASSOCIATION DIRECTORY. 1980.

AMERICAN HOTEL AND MOTEL ASSOCIATION. 1979. American Hotel and Motel Association Hotel Red Book.

ANG, J. and CHUA, J.H. 1979. Long Range Planning in Large U.S. Corporations—A Survey. Long Range Planning 12(2):99–102.

ANDERSON, W.T., JR., BENTLEY, C., and SHARPE, L.K., IV. 1976. Multidimensional Marketing. Lone Star Publishers, Austin.

ANON. 1975. Traditional craftsmanship: politic and profitable. Service World International 9(1):35.

ANON. 1977. Travel During 1977. Census of Transportation, U.S. Dept. Commerce, Washington, D.C.

ANON. 1978. Industrial engineering comes to Holiday Inns. Hotel and Motel Management, January.

ANON. 1979. Cruising 79. Newsweek 93:50–52.

ANON. 1979. Dunfey Hotels enjoy gains of productivity increases. Hotel and Resort Industry, September, pp. 12–14.

ANON. 1979. Profile of the Profitable Guest. Time Marketing Services, RR2141, Time, Inc.

ANON. 1979. Restaurant Industry Operations Report '79 for the U.S. National Restaurant Association, Chicago.

ANON. 1980. Add to your knowledge about cruises. Fifty Plus, February, pp. 56–60.

ANON. 1980. Tastes of America. Institution 87(12):49–102.

ANON. 1980. Warming up for the winter—best cruise ideas for 80–81. House and Garden 152:84–90.

ANON. 1980A. Bosses expect business gains in '81. Wall Street Journal, December 19, pp. 27–28.

ANON. 1980A. Goal setting for hotels. Lodging, March, p. 43.

ANON. 1980B. Bosses forecast improved economy in 1981. Wall Street Journal, December 22, pp. 21–22.

ANON. 1980B. How three companies increased their productivity. Fortune, March 10.

ANON. 1980C. Managing for productivity. New England Business, January 16, p. 15.

ANON. 1981. Fortune, March 9, p. 82.

ANSOFF, H.I. 1977. The state of practice in planning systems. Sloan Management Review 8:2–7.

ANZOLA-BETTANCOURT, R. 1972. An architectural approach to tourism in the Caribbean. Paper read at conference, Towards a Lasting Tourism. Hosted by Puerto Rico Tourism Development Co. and the Caribbean Travel Association.

BALINTFY, J. et al. 1967. Computerized Dietary Information System. Vols. 1, 2, 3. Grad. School Bus. Admin., Tulane University, New Orleans.

BARBARAN, R. 1980. Recycling the past. Restaurant Design 3:60–64.

BIALICK, S. 1979. Cruising along. Essence 9:66–67.

BLANK, U. 1971. Tourism in the Lake of the Woods–Rainy Lake Area. Minnesota Agriculture Economist, No. 543, November 1.

BLANK, U. and OLSON, R. 1981. Minnesota's Food Service Industry. University of Minnesota, St. Paul.

BLANK, U. and PETKOVICH, M. 1979. Minneapolis–St. Paul's Travel Tourism. University of Minnesota, St. Paul.

BLOOM, B., ed. 1956. Taxonomy of Educational Objectives: The Cognitive Domain. Donald McKay, New York.

BORDEN, N.H. 1968. The concept of the marketing mix. In Managerial Marketing: Perspectives and Viewpoints, 3rd Edition, edited by E.J. Kelly and W. Lazar. Richard D. Irwin, Inc., Homewood, Ill.

BOSSELMAN, F. 1978. In the Wake of the Tourist: Managing Special Places in Eight Countries. The Conservation Foundation, Washington, D.C.

BOZZELL, R.D. 1966. Competitive behavior and product life cycles. In New Ideas for Successful Marketing, edited by J. Wright and J. Goldstucker. American Marketing Association, Chicago.

BRODNER, J., CARLSON, H.M., and MARSCHAL, H.T. 1951. Profitable Food and Beverage Operation. Ahrens Publishing Co., New York.

BRODSKY-PORGES, E. 1978. Welcoming the handicapped traveler. Cornell Hotel Restaurant Association Quarterly 21(1):6–7.

BROWN, F.A. 1980. Rehabilitating Historic Hotels: Preservation Case Studies, Peabody Hotel, Memphis, Tennessee. Heritage Conservation and Recreation Service, U.S. Department of the Interior, Washington, D.C.

BUREAU OF NATIONAL AFFAIRS. 1975. Compensation. Washington, D.C., pp. 343–344.

BUREAU OF NATIONAL AFFAIRS. 1975. Employee Performance: Evaluation and Control. Personal Policies Forum Survey No. 108. Washington, D.C., pp. 1 3.

CADOTTE, E.R. 1979. The push-button questionnaire: a new tool for measuring customer satisfaction. Cornell Hotel and Restaurant Administration Quarterly 19(4):70–79.

CADOTTE, E.R. 1980. TELLUS computer lets retailers conduct in-store marketing research. Marketing News 14(12):17.

CARIBBEAN TOURISM ASSOCIATION. 1978. How to Convert Cruise Passengers into Long-stay Visitors. Caribbean Tourism Association, New York.

CHAMBER OF COMMERCE OF THE USA. 1978. Employee Benefits 1977. Washington, D.C., pp. 5–6.

COFFMAN, C.D. 1970. Marketing for a Full House. School of Hotel Administration, Cornell University, Ithaca, N.Y.

COFFMAN C.D. 1981. Coffman on management. Lodging Hospitality, January, pp. 20–22.

COMMITTEE ON DEFINITIONS. 1960. Marketing Definitions: A Glossary of Marketing Terms. American Marketing Association, Chicago.

CRISSY, W.J.E., BOEWADT, R.J., and LAUDADIO, D.M. 1975. Marketing of Hospitality Services: Food, Travel, Lodging. Educational Institute of the American Hotel and Motel Association, East Lansing, Michigan.

DALLAS TIMES HERALD. 1979. Travel Section, November 25.

EISON, I.I. 1980. Strategic Marketing in Food Service: Planning for Change. Chain Store Publishing Corp., New York.

EMERSON, R.L. 1979. Fast Food: The Endless Shakeout. Lebhar-Friedman Books, New York.

FINLAYSON, G. 1980. Sonesta's Dutch treat. Fortune 102(8):70–76.

FLAIM, P.O. and FULLERTON, H.N., JR. 1978. Labor force projections to 1990: three possible paths. Monthly Labor Review.

FODOR, E. 1981. Guide to the Caribbean and the Bahamas.

FREMGREN, J.A. 1973. Captial budgeting practices: a survey. Management Accounting, pp. 19–25.

FULLERTON, H.N., JR. 1980. The 1955 labor force. Monthly Labor Review.

GALT, G. 1979. Is tourism good for heritage? Heritage Canada 5(3):19–22.

GEORGE, W.R. 1977. The retailing of services—a challenging future. J. Retailing 53(3):85–98.

GEORGE, W.R. and BARKSDALE, H.C.   Marketing activities in the service industries.   J. Marketing 38(4):65–70.

GO, F.M.   1980.   Socio-cultural values: implications for travel marketers. Unpublished paper.

GRAHAM, J.   1980.   New life for a liner.   New York Times Magazine, May 11, pp. 34–36.

GREGOOE, P.   1980.   On board the floating palace.   MacLeans 93:20–21.

HAMILTON, J.L.   1972.   Tourism: private benefits versus public cost.   Cornell Quarterly 13(3):61–64.

HOFER, C. and SCHENDEL, D.   1978.   Strategy Formulation: Analytical Concepts.   West Publishing Co., St. Paul, Minn.

HOPEMAN, R.J.   1969.   Systems Analysis and Operations Management. Charles E. Merrill, Columbus, p. 64.

JAFARI, J.   1977.   Editor's page.   Ann. Tourism Res. 5:7–8.

JAFARI, J.   1979.   The tourism market basket of goods and services: the components and nature of tourism.   Tourism Recreation Research 4(2):1–8.

JAFARI, J.   1980.   The function and significance of travel and tourism: challenges and opportunities in the face of energy shortage.   Unpublished paper, Dept. Habitational Resources, University of Wisconsin-Stout.

JAFARI, J. and RITCHIE, J.R.B.   Developing a framework for tourimsm education: problems and prospects.   Ann. Tourism Res. 8(1).

JENKINS, G.M.   1976.   The systems approach.   In Systems Behavior, 2nd Edition, edited by Beishon, J. and Peters, G.   Published for the Open University Press by Harper and Row, London and New York.

KASAVANA, M.L.   1978.   Hotel Information Systems.   CBI Publishing Co., Boston.

KELLEY, E.J. and LAZER, W.   1967.   Managerial Marketing: Perspectives and Viewpoints.   Richard D. Irwin, Inc., Homewood, Ill.

KINCAID, J.W.   1975.   Patients evaluate cycle menu entrees.   Hospitals 49:71.

KLAMMER, T.   1972.   Empirical evidence of the adoption of sophisticated capital budgeting techniques.   pp. 387–397.

KOTLER, P.   1973–1974.   Atmospherics as a marketing tool.   J. Retailing 49(4):48–64.

KOTLER, P.   1980.   Marketing Management: Analysis, Planning and Control, 4th Edition.   Prentice-Hall, Englewood Cliffs.

KRECK, L.A.   1969.   Personnel planning for foreign hotels.   Cornell Quarterly 9(4):82–86.

KRECK, L.A.   1978.   Operational Problem Solving for the Hotel and Restaurant Industry: The PULLMAN METHOD.   CBI Publishing Company, Boston.

KRUM, J.R.   B for Marketing Research Departments.   J. Marketing 42(4):8–12.

LAIRD, D.   1978.   Approaches to Training and Development.   Addison-Wesley, Reading, Mass., p. 110.

LAWSON, F.   1976.   Hotels, Motels, and Condominiums: Design, Planning and Maintenance.   Cahners Books International, Boston.

LEBELL, D. and KRASNER, O.J.   1977.   Selecting Environmental Forecasting Techniques from Business Planning Requirements.   Academy of Management Review 2(3):373−397.

LEIPER, N.   1979.   The framework of tourism: towards a definition of tourism, tourist, and the tourist industry.   Ann. Tourism Res. 6(4):390−407.

LEVINE, J.B. and VAN WIJK, A.   1980.   Counting on Computers.   Lebhar/Friedman, New York.

LEVINE, J.B. and VAN WIJK, A.   1980.   How to select a computer system: parts I and II.   Cornell Hotel and Restaurant Administration Quarterly 21(1):8−18 and (2):60−71.

LEVITT, T.   1960.   Marketing myopia.   Harvard Business Review 38(4):24−47.

LEVITT, T.   1971.   Production line approach to service.   Harvard Business Review, October, p. 41.

LEVITT, T. Exploit the product life cycle.   Harvard Business Review 43(5):81−94.

LEWIS, R.C.   1980.   Benefit segmentation for restaurant advertising that works.   Cornell Hotel and Restaurant Administration Quarterly 21(3):6−12.

LOVELOCK, C.H.   1979.   Theoretical contributions from service and non-business marketing.   In Conceptual and Theoretical Developments in Marketing, edited by O.C. Ferrell et al., American Marketing Association, Chicago.

LOVELOCK, C. and YOUNG, R.   1979.   Look to consumers to increase productivity.   Harvard Business Review, May−June, pp. 168−178.

MAAS, J.   1980.   Better brochures for the money.   Cornell Hotel and Restaurant Administration Quarterly 20(4):21−34.

MacGREGOR, M.   1980.   Cruising: lure of the love boats.   MacLeans 93:18−21.

MAGER, R.F.   1962.   Preparing Instructional Objectives.   Fearon, Palo Alto.

MAKI, W.   Minnesota Regional Economic Impact Forecasting and Simulation.   Dept. of Agricultural and Applied Economics, University of Minnesota, St. Paul.

MALLER, O., DUBOSE, C.N. and CARDELLO, A.V.   1980.   Consumer opinions of hospital food and food service.   J. Am. Dietetic Assoc. 76:236.

MARKO, J.A. and MOORE, R.G.   1980.   How to select a computer system: parts I and II.   Cornell Hotel and Restaurant Administration Quarterly 21(1):8−18 and (2):60−71.

MASMICK, G. and BANE, M.   1980.   The Nation's Families: 1960–1990. Auburn House Publishing Co., Boston.

McCARTHY, E.J.   1971.   Basic Marketing: A Managerial Approach, 4th Edition.   Richard D. Irwin, Inc., Homewood, Ill.

McCARTHY, E.J.   1975.   Basic Marketing: A Managerial Approach, 5th Edition.   Richard D. Irwin, Inc., Homewood, Ill.

McCARTHY, E.J., MINICHIELLO, R.J., and CURRAN, J.R.   1979.   Business Policy and Strategy: Concepts and Readings.   Richard D. Irwin, Inc., Homewood, Ill.

McFARLAND, D.E.   1974.   Management: Principles and Practices, 4th Edition.   Macmillan, New York.

MIAMI HERALD.   1979.   Caribbean Springtime.   Special Advertising Section, April 9.

MIAMI HERALD.   1979.   Cruising 1979.   Travel Journal, February 4.

MIAMI HERALD.   1979.   Special Cruise Issue.   Travel Journal, September 9.

MOORE, H.B.   1957.   The meaning of food.   Am. J. Clin. Nutr. 5:77.

MYERS, J.H. and TAUBER, E.   1977.   Market Structure Analysis.   American Marketing Association, Chicago.

NATIONAL CENTER FOR PRODUCTIVITY.   1975.   Quality of working life, improve productivity.   Series I.   National Center for Productivity, Washington, D.C.

NATIONAL RESEARCH COUNCIL.   1964.   Manual for the Study of Food Habits, No. 11.   Committee on Food Habits, Natl. Research Council, Washington, D.C.

NATIONAL RESTAURANT ASSOC.   1973.   How to Invest in People: A Handbook on Career Ladders.   Natl. Restaurant Assoc., Chicago.

NATIONAL RESTAURANT ASSOC.   1976.   1976 Foodservice Industry Employment.   Natl. Restaurant Assoc., Washington, D.C.

NATIONAL RESTAURANT ASSOC.   1981.   Foodservice Industry Pocket Factbook.   Natl. Restaurant Assoc., Washington, D.C.

NEW YORK TIMES.   1981.   Travel Section, March 29.

ODIORNE, G.S.   1970.   Training by Objectives.   Macmillan, London, p. 81.

ODIORNE, G.S.   1979.   MBO II: A System of Managerial Leadership for the 80's.   Fearon Pitman Publishers, Inc., Belmont, Calif.

OLSEN, M.D. and DE NOBLE, A.F.   1981.   Strategic planning in dynamic times.   Cornell Hotel and Restaurant Administration Quarterly 21:75–80.

PATTERSON, W.D.   1976.   The Big Picture: Annual Report World Travel Trends and Markets.   ASYA Travel Communications, Inc., New York.

PERYAM, D.R.   1963.   The acceptance of novel foods.   Food Technology 17: 711.

PETER, L.J. and HULL, R.   1969.   The Peter Principle.   William Morrow, New York.

PIZAM, A. and REICHEL, A.   1979.   Big spenders and little spenders in U.S. tourism.   Travel Res. 18(1):42−43.

RENAGHAN, L.M.   1980.   A new marketing mix for the hospitality industry. Paper presented at the National Conference of the Council of Hotel, Restaurant and Institutional Education, Dearborn, Mich.

RIFKIND, C.   1979.   Cultural Tourism.   Tourism International Air Letter, pp. 2−4.

ROSENBLATT, S.R., BONNINGTON, R.L. and NEEDLES, B.E., JR.   1973. Modern Business: A Systems Approach.   Houghton-Mifflin, Boston, pp. 43−44.

ROTHCHILD, W.E.   1980.   How to ensure the continued growth of strategic planning.   J. Bus. Strat. 1(1):11−18.

RUCKER, M., ARMSTRONG, L., WU, C. and WU, A.   1978.   Descriptive menus enhance food acceptance.   Hospitals 47:67.

SAN FRANCISCO EXAMINER.   1980.   Travel Section, August 10.

SASSER, W.E., OLSEN, R.P. and WYCKOFF, D.   1978.   Management of Service Operations.   Allyn and Bacon, Boston.

SATURDAY REVIEW.   1979.   Romance of ships symposium.   Saturday Review 2:22−24.

SCHMITT, S.   1981.   Courtesy Needs of the Disabled.   Stout Vocational Rehabilitation Institute, University of Wisconsin-Stout, Menomonie, Wis.

SCHUH, D.D, MOORE, A.N., and TUTHILL, B.H.   1967.   Measuring food acceptability by frequency ratings.   J. Am. Dietetic Assoc. 41:340.

SERRIN, W.   1981.   No Cuts Here: The Life on the Tab.   New York Times, March 29.

SHOSTACK, G.L.   1977.   Breaking free from product marketing.   J. Marketing 41:73−80.

SILL, B.T.   1980.   Restaurant merchandising for the independent operator. Cornell Hotel and Restaurant Administration Quarterly 21(1):27−30.

SOMMERS, A.T.   1978.   Productivity: Annual rates of change vs. productivity—not a disaster but certainly a dilemma.   Across the Board, October, p. 57.

STASCH, S.F. and LANKTREE, P.   Can your marketing planning procedures be improved?   J. Marketing 44(4):79−90.

STAUDT, T.A., TAYLOR, D.A. and BOWERSOX, D.J.   1976.   A Managerial Introduction to Marketing.   Prentice-Hall, Englewood Cliffs.

STEARNS, G.K. and NINEMEIER, J.   1980.   Beverage control systems: Assessing bottle sales values.   National Conference of the Council of Hotel, Restaurant and Institutional Education, Dearborn, Michigan, August 13−16.

STEINER, G.A.   1979.   Strategic Planning: What Every Manager Must Know.   Free Press, New York.

STEINER, G.A. and MINER, J.B.   1977.   Management Policy and Strategy: Text, Readings, and Cases.   Macmillan, New York.

TAMPA TRIBUNE.   1979.   Part IV, Travel, January 21.

TARRANT, M.   1980.   Finding the right winter cruise.   Money 9:94–96.

THOMAS, D.R.E.   1978.   Strategy is different in service businesses.   Harvard Business Review 56(4):158–165.

TISSIAN, N.   1979.   Quoted in Advertising that sells hotels.   Cornell Hotel and Restaurant Administration Quarterly 20(4):17–23.

TOFFLER, A.   1980.   The Third Wave.   William Morrow, New York.

TRAVEL WEEKLY.   1979.   Cruise Guide, July 2.

U.S. DEPT. COMMERCE, BUREAU OF ECONOMIC ANALYSIS.   1980.   Regional and state projections of income, employment and population to the year 2000. *In* Survey of Current Business, November.   U.S. Govt. Printing Office, Washington, D.C.

U.S. DEPT. COMMERCE, BUREAU OF THE CENSUS.   1977.   1977 Census of Retail Trade.   U.S. Govt. Printing Office, Washington, D.C.

U.S. DEPT. LABOR, BUREAU OF LABOR STATISTICS.   1978.   Hotels, Motels, and Tourist Courts.   U.S. Dept. Labor, Washington, D.C.

U.S. DEPT. LABOR, BUREAU OF LABOR STATISTICS.   1980.   Occupational Outlook Handbook.   U.S. Govt. Printing Office, Washington, D.C.

VANCIL, R.F. and LORANGE, P.   1975.   Strategic Planning in Diversified Companies.   Harvard Bus. Rev. 53(1):81–90.

VONNEGUT, K., JR.   1972.   Mother Night.   Avon Books, New York.

VRISKO, J.A.   1975.   Productivity in hotels and motels 1958–1973. Monthly Labor Review, May, pp. 24–28.

WILSON, I.H.   1974.   Socio Political Forecasting: A New Dimension to Strategic Planning.   Mich. Bus. Rev. 26(4):15–25.

WINCHESTER, J.   1979.   Cruiseship turnaround behind the scenes.   Travel/Holiday 151:30–32.

WRISLEY, A.L.   1978.   An Information System for the Planning and Control of a Food Service Operation.   Ph.D. dissertation, University of Massachusetts, Amherst.

YESAWICH, P.   1980.   Marketing in the 1980s.   Cornell Hotel and Restaurant Administration Quarterly 20(4):35–38.

ZIFFERBLATT, S.M., WILBUR, C.S., and PINSKY, J.L.   1980.   Understanding food habits.   J. Am. Dietetic Assoc. 76:9.

Index